Selfhood and Sacrifice

Selfhood and Sacrifice

René Girard and Charles Taylor on the Crisis of Modernity

Andrew O'Shea

continuum

NEW YORK • LONDON

Continuum International Publishing Group
80 Maiden Lane, Suite 704 New York NY 10038
The Tower Building, 11 York Road, London SE1 7NX

www.continuumbooks.com

First published 2010
Paperback edition first published 2012

Library of Congress Cataloging-in-Publication Data
A catalog record for this book is available from the Library of Congress.

ISBN: 978-1-4411-1882-0 (hardback)
ISBN: 978-1-4411-1793-9 (paperback)

Typeset by Newgen Imaging Systems Pvt Ltd, Chennai, India
Printed and bound in Great Britain

To my parents . . .

CONTENTS

PART II

FROM SACRIFICE TO SELF: TAYLOR'S PHILOSOPHICAL ACCOUNT

ACKNOWLEDGEMENTS

There are many people who have helped me to undertake and complete this work. Those to be acknowledged without too much fan fare but with deep appreciation are as follows: John and Frank, for reading and commenting on an early draft; Jack, for the use of his cottage in Donegal at a critical time when I needed a 'space to write'; the other members of my 'Taylor group' whose conversation helped me to understand Taylor's 'Dilemmas' (and my own); Padraig, Dara, Brendan, Sarah, and Hilary for being there at different points along the way, with one kind or another of assistance or inspiration. I owe you all a sincere thanks. My colleagues in Human Development, Maeve O'Brien and Jones Irwin have shown immense generosity to me throughout the course of this work, especially toward the end with the editing when I was under considerable pressure to finish. I am humbled by their care and grateful beyond words. A special thanks is reserved for my mentor and friend Joe Dunne whose continued belief in the work is the true heroism of this story. His thoroughness and commitment to good practice were exemplary, and his patience, encouragement and good humour were appreciated beyond measure.

INTRODUCTION

I

Why write a book on the work of René Girard and Charles Taylor? The reason for placing these contemporary thinkers in conversation is not immediately evident since both occupy quite distinct realms of discourse. Girard is a literary critic and cultural anthropologist, while Taylor is much more firmly rooted in academic philosophy. Indeed the question arises as to whether such different figures share enough of a common language to have a fruitful dialogue. It is not easy to see how a preoccupation with scapegoating and sacrifice through the critical lens of literary and cultural theory (Girard), and a practical approach to philosophy and articulating the sources of the modern identity (Taylor), can be brought together in a coherent and purposeful engagement. Surely there is just too much clarification needed before either side can address any substantive content?

Yet while Girard nowhere refers to Taylor's work in any direct way, Taylor on more than one occasion refers to Girard's work with admiration and genuine sympathy that appears increasingly receptive to his central preoccupations. Moreover, both thinkers share an interest in, and concern for, the continued relevance of religion and transcendence in exploring some of the most pressing issues of our time – issues that might well make a sober observer of the contemporary world fear for the future. And, importantly, they both take seriously the significance of the Christian revelation in helping us to understand our predicament as historical subjects existing in community, and more broadly in a web of social and cultural relations. But, before we can properly grasp the connections that may make them an exciting, if not urgent, match it is perhaps worth saying something about each of their varied careers and then explaining how I first came to find them so appealing – each in himself *and* as a potential dialogue partner with the other.[1]

Girard's early historical work seems remote from his later concerns, which involve a pursuit of what might be called a 'grand unified theory'.[2] The beginning

---

1. In a private conversation in St Paul's University, Ottawa, June 2006, Girard acknowledged the plausibility of his and Taylor's similarity in describing certain aspects of the modern period, and, when pressed further on this similarity, encouraged me to explore it.
2. Girard was born in Avignon in the south of France in 1923. He received his baccalaureate at the Lycée of Avignon in 1941 and attended the Ecole des Chartes in Paris from 1943 to 1947, graduating with a degree in medieval studies. He travelled to the United States of America the same year where he enrolled as a Ph.D. student

of Girard's interest in broader social and cultural questions is often identified with his time preparing for and teaching a course on French Literature at The University of Indiana. This was the first of several posts that he held after completing his doctoral work: others were at Johns Hopkins University (where he Chaired the Department of Romance Languages 1965–1968), The State University of New York at Buffalo, where he was appointed in 1971, and where he stayed until he accepted his final post as Andrew B. Hammond Professor of French Languages, Literature, and Civilization at Stanford University in 1981.

In 1966, while still at Johns Hopkins University, Girard helped organize a conference which was to have significant impact on the emergence of critical theory in the United States of America. Entitled *The Languages of Criticism and the Sciences of Man*, this conference included papers by Jacques Derrida, Jacques Lacan and Roland Barthes, among other (mainly French) Continental thinkers, whose attacks on prevailing theories of structure and consciousness formed the driving force of a new post-structuralist criticism. In was also during his time at Johns Hopkins that Girard wrote his first two books: *Mensonge romantique et vérité romanesque* (1961), and *Dostoïevski: du double à l'unité* (1963). In these works of criticism he first began to develop his key idea of imitation and to articulate a theory of desire through a detailed reading of literary texts.[3]

In 1972, while at SUNYB, he wrote *Violence and the Sacred*, which represents the first substantial stage of his exploration of the ramifications of his theory of mimetic desire in relation to anthropological thought. Developing the theory that imitation leads to rivalry and conflict, Girard posited that the origins of cultural order and stability reside in repeated acts of violence against a victim, who in effect becomes a scapegoat for the community, and thereby a vessel for its own destructive energies and hence, in a peculiar way, 'salvific'. This hypothesis was further expounded in his subsequent publications, *Things Hidden Since the Foundation of the World* (1978), *The Scapegoat* (1982), and *A Theatre of Envy* (1991), among other books and articles.[4] These works elaborate Girard's sustained reflections not only on the role of violence in cultural formation but on the central

---

of history at Indiana University, graduating in 1950, with a dissertation entitled *American Opinion of France, 1940–1943*. He has remained living and working in the United States of America ever since.

3. The main authors that Girard examines when he first posits a theory of imitative desire, are: Cervantes, Stendhal, Flaubert, Proust and Dostoyevsky. Although he has lived for over thirty years in the United States of America, Girard continues to write in French. Nonetheless almost all of his works have been translated and are available in English.

4. In addition to the works already mentioned, and not including his many articles, interviews and reviews, Girard's other books are: *Critique dans un souterrain* (Lausanne: L'Age d'Homme, 1976); *To Double Business Bound: Essays on Literature, Mimesis, and Anthropology* (Baltimore: The Johns Hopkins University Press, 1978); *Job: The Victim of His People*, trans., Y. Freccero (Stanford: Stanford University

place of the Judeo-Christian scriptures in unveiling, critiquing and repudiating this violence. Human beings can overcome violence only by confronting their mimetic desires, and renouncing all claims to originality – 'the dearest of all their illusions'.

The 'Colloquium on Violence and Religion' was set up in 1990 to promote Girard's central ideas concerning the role of violence in culture and society and to encourage dialogue and scholarship in the budding field of 'mimetic theory'. Since then the conference has met bi-annually. The journal *Contagion*, subtitled *Journal of Violence, Culture and Religion,* was also launched in 1990 with the inauguration of the new Colloquium helping Girard's theory to reach a wider audience. Girard is considered by many to be one of the most original and influential cultural theorists on the contemporary scene.[5] Yet, however much my own analysis of his work may attempt to 'make him more philosophical', he is not strictly speaking a philosopher. And so it should be stressed that his literary and cultural theory cannot be properly understood simply through an elucidation of central concepts.[6]

When we consider the course of his long career two phases stand out as significant. The first comprises his work in literary criticism and the second his work in cultural anthropology. The former phase provides an analysis of the intra- and intersubjective dynamics at work in and between the characters in the various novels that he treats. Essentially it is a theory of how the novel emerges as a powerful existential force in the modern period, the profound insights of which subvert all idealist philosophies. The latter phase sets out in a more scientific vein to make the case that human culture has evolved from its origins in

---

Press, 1987a); *Quand ces choses commenceront . . .* Entretiens avec Michel Treguer (Paris: arléa, 1994); *The Girard Reader,* ed. James G. Williams. (New York: The Crossroad Publishing Company, 1996); *I See Satan Fall Like Lightning,* trans., J. G. Williams. (Maryknoll, NY: Orbis Books, 2001); *Celui par qui le scandale arrive* (Paris: Desclée de Brouwer, 2001); *La voix méconnue* du réel. *Une théorie des mythes archaïques et modernes.* Traduit de l'anglais par B. Formentelli (Paris: Bernard Grasset, 2002); *Oedipus Unbound: Selected Writings on Rivalry and Desire,* ed. Mark R. Anspach (Stanford: Stanford University Press, 2004); *Achever Clausewitz* (Paris: Carnets Nord, 2007a).

5. He has been the recipient of a number of honorary doctorates and been awarded the Prix de l'Académie Française for *Violence and the Sacred,* and more recently has had the French Academy's Grand Prix du Philosophie bestowed upon him 'in recognition of his position as one of the outstanding philosophical anthropologists of his generation. Chris Fleming, *René Girard: Violence and Mimesis,* (Cambridge: Polity Press, 2004). In 2008 he won the MLA Lifetime Award.

6. As Fleming asserts in relation to his own work on Girardian theory: 'The abstract movement of his thought cannot be appreciated in the absence of the extremely dense evidence he enlists to bear out his claims; Girard does not present, in other words, a theoretical framework that somehow stands by itself.' Fleming, *René Girard: Violence and Mimesis,* p. 3.

collective violence, and that the order and stability of cultural forms depend on a continuous re-enactment that attempts to harness the efficacy of an original murder – an event that is always shrouded in misapprehension. The first phase of Girard's career then is characterized by a preoccupation with 'self and other', while the second phase is characterized by a preoccupation with the role of the collective in generating order; this second preoccupation leads to the articulation of a generative anthropology, which Girard then applies in explaining historical development and in particular the abiding concerns of the modern world. What these two phases have in common, as we shall see, is a method of structural analysis that Girard appropriates from Claude Lévi-Strauss.[7]

Taylor's career is just as distinguished as Girard's. Born in Montreal in 1931 to a French-speaking mother and an English-speaking father, he first studied history (like Girard) at McGill University from 1952 to 1955, before going on to read philosophy, politics and economics at Oxford University, where he remained until he completed his doctorate in 1961. His personal narrative is in some respects the reverse to that of Girard, who travelled from Europe to North America; but unlike his European counterpart, Taylor travelled from a relatively 'new world' to a much older world where he was not to make a permanent home. His training in analytic philosophy provided him with a plain unembellished style of clear and sequenced argumentation. But against the Oxford grain Taylor familiarized himself with the phenomenological and hermeneutical traditions of Continental Europe, and especially with the works of Hegel, Heidegger and Merleau-Ponty. He resisted the notion of philosophy as a specialized discipline separate from the human sciences, a notion that interfered with the pursuit of his broad interests and investigations. In this pursuit he sought to present a critique of the so-called human sciences, arguing that much in their dominant methodologies systematically excluded what is most specific about human beings. His first book, *The Explanation of Behaviour* (1964) is as much a work of psychology as philosophy especially as manifested in the then dominant behaviourist paradigm whose reductionist view of 'human nature' it strongly contests. His second book, *Hegel* (1975), considerably broadened the scope of his enquiry to combine philosophical

---

7. Although Girard himself is highly critical of structuralism (see *The Scapegoat*, 1986) his approach to texts has inherited a prejudice against the conscious intentional subject that aligns him with this tradition. Both Richard Macksey and Chris Fleming maintain that Girard is not a 'structuralist': see Macksey's introduction to *The Structuralist Controversy: The Languages of Criticism and the Sciences of Man* (Johns Hopkins University Press, 2007), p. xiii, and the introduction to Fleming's work entitled: *René Girard: Violence and Mimesis* p. 3. Granted, if the main criteria of 'structuralism' disavow 'extra textual claims', then it must be admitted Girard is not a structuralist. However, as I will argue, if the principle criteria involve a disavowal of all philosophies of consciousness then Girard maintains the same basic starting point as Lévi-Strauss and therefore his work can be considered, at least in the first instance, as 'structuralist'.

interpretation with historical and sociological reflections on the nature of modern society. His later *magnum opus, Sources of the Self: The Making of the Modern Identity* (1989), continues his Hegel-inspired attempt to understand the modern epoch through a profoundly historical mode of philosophical reflection; in it he provides an analytic framework for thinking about the self – a philosophical anthropology – before proceeding to explore ideas of selfhood drawn from modern literature, art and theology, as well as conventional history of philosophy.[8]

While its eclectic nature makes it difficult to classify, Taylor's work can be characterized in light of its practical goal: '[t]he realisation of vital human goods in accordance with the best available interpretation'.[9] His practical concern for human flourishing and the struggles that this sometimes entails led him to become actively involved in politics (on the left) both in Oxford and when he returned to his native Canada in 1961. He has been a singularly dialogical thinker, entering wholeheartedly into several philosophical and cultural debates. For example, he was a key protagonist in the debate between 'liberals' and 'communitarians' that dominated political theory throughout the 1970s and 80s. And his essay *'Multiculturalism and the "Politics of Recognition"'* (1992) has become a key text in debates about multiculturalism, citizenship and identity. Like Girard, he has received numerous awards for his contribution to scholarship. These including the

---

8. Not including his many articles, interviews and reviews, Taylor's other books are: *The Pattern of Politics* (Toronto: McClelland and Stewart, 1970); *Hegel and Modern Society* (Cambridge: Cambridge University Press, 1979); *Social Theory as Practice* (Delhi: Oxford University Press, 1983); *Human Agency and Language: Philosophical Papers 1* (Cambridge: Cambridge University Press, 1985a); *Philosophy and the Human Sciences: Philosophical Papers 2* (Cambridge: Cambridge University Press, 1985b); *The Ethics of Authenticity* (Cambridge, MA: Harvard University Press, 1992a); *Multiculturalism and 'The Politics of Recognition'*, ed. Amy Gutmann, (Princeton: Princeton University Press, 1992b); *Multiculturalism: Examining the Politics of Recognition*, ed. Amy Gutmann, (Princeton: Princeton University Press, 1994); *Reconciling the Solitudes: Essays in Canadian Federalism and Nationalism*, ed. Guy Laforest, (Montreal and Kingston: McGill-Queen's University Press, 1993); *Philosophical Arguments* (Cambridge, MA: Harvard University Press, 1995); *A Catholic Modernity? Charles Taylor's Marianist Award Lecture, with responses by William M. Shea, Rosemary Luling Haughton, George Marsden, and Jean Bethke Elshtain*, ed. James L. Heft (Oxford: Oxford University Press, 1999); *Varieties of Religion Today: William James Revisited* (Cambridge, MA: Harvard University Press, 2002); *Modern Social Imaginaries*, Dilip Gaonkar, Jane Kramer, Benjamin Lee and Michael Warner, eds (Durham, NC: Duke University Press, 2004); *A Secular Age* (Cambridge, MA and London: Belknap Press of Harvard University Press, 2007). This last work, while covering much of the ground that Taylor covers in *Sources of the Self*, will be brought within the compass of my overall argument at the end of the book (apart from one significant footnote in chapter four).
9. Nicholas H. Smith, *Charles Taylor: Meaning, Morals, and Modernity* (Polity Press, 2002), p. 11.

'Marianist Award' for his work in helping to understand the impact of Christianity on modern culture – a theme to which his more recent work has been increasingly addressed. The paper that he delivered on accepting this award, 'A Catholic Modernity?', has been read widely and with great interest. In 2007 he won the prestigious Templeton Prize for his contribution to the area of religion and humanities. In 2008 he won the Kyoto prize for a lifetime achievement in the arts and humanities. For my purposes in this book, it is noteworthy that, in his acceptance speech for this award, Girard was among the very few contemporary thinkers whom he singled out, and whose work he acknowledged as important for his own interest in the often-marginalized field of religious studies.

Both Taylor's 'philosophical anthropology' and 'philosophical history' have constructive and therapeutic aspects that differ from Girard's analysis in at least one important respect. Taylor's persistent concern is not only to unmask the 'universalist *mis*representation of contingent modes of self-understanding'[10] – what Girard characterizes in terms of 'myth' – but also and crucially to identify and release the moral sources of human potential that, as he discerns, lie buried deep within the modern aspiration toward freedom. One of Taylor's main contentions – developed at length in *Sources of the Self* and more accessibly in *The Ethics of Authenticity* – is that if we are to overcome the malaises that threaten our high standards of human worth and fulfilment today we need to retrieve neglected sources of meaning and value, and in doing so to understand the present within a horizon of new possibilities. This contention, emphasizing the importance of self-realization through an ideal of authentic or original selfhood, is precisely what Girard's mimetic theory fundamentally contests.

Having looked briefly at their intellectual biographies, we can perhaps see why, taken separately, Girard and Taylor provide ample material for a rich and engaging enquiry – focused on one or the other's work *per se* or on its contribution to wider cultural and philosophical debates. But as to how they might both be brought together within the purview of a single enquiry – this is still not in relief. My own encounter with both of them may help here, and begin to explain why the prospect of a meaningful dialogue between two apparently divergent protagonists came to seem both possible and desirable.

What first drew me to Girard's theory was not the work itself, but the person. While doing my graduate studies in Berkeley at the Graduate Theological Union in 1998, I had the opportunity to hear him speak in a small, quite intimate setting. What immediately impressed me was his thoroughly unconventional style of presentation, one that was wholly unapologetic about his non-liberal and apparently non-egalitarian credentials. His stance appeared all the more out of step in a place like Berkeley that took pride in the radical nature of its politics. He came across as someone who was not afraid to speak his mind against a tide of 'political correctness' that saw no problem in saying one thing as long as it was the 'right' thing, while perhaps feeling and thinking something altogether different.

---

10. Smith, *Charles Taylor: Meaning, Morals, and Modernity*, p. 8.

When, towards the end of his talk, he replied to an obviously disgruntled member of the audience who challenged his dismissive approach to a liberal position on 'identity and equality', his words were bracingly uncompromising: 'You liberals are all the same . . .' The shock wave from this blatant 'transgression' was felt around the room, if not beyond. Girard, as far as I could gather, was challenging the presumption that a sense of 'fairness' and an appeal to universal respect did not in fact conceal a deep resentment – what he described as 'weakened vengeance'. Given the right circumstance, such weakened vengeance could become contagious, leading to violence and bloodshed. And if anyone thought that being a neo-Nietzschean was a more honest calling, as many in the audience clearly did, such an 'aestheticizing' of violence, Girard wanted to insist, gravely underestimated its propensity to envelop all in its path, or, failing outward contagion, to plunge the individual into psychosis.

Admittedly I had not read anything by Girard when I heard him speak, so I had not formed an opinion as to whether his 'boat could sail'. But I did vow that evening, based on what I witnessed, to become acquainted with his work. What was so 'wrong' with the dominant modern story as to compel him to such combative speech? Something in the manner of this elderly French intellectual who 'didn't take prisoners', and was obviously not intimidated either by advocates of 'pluralism' and 'relativism', or by traditional religious adherents, had stirred me, perhaps from my own rather eclectic slumber.

My initial contact with Taylor's ideas was a very different experience. Where Girard had made a lasting first impression, Taylor whom I never actually heard speak, captured my imagination gradually. It was some four years before my trip to Berkeley, during my second year of undergraduate study that I was introduced to Taylor's philosophy while studying Descartes' *Meditations*. Sections of *Sources of the Self* provided the secondary material that was to help students come to terms with the revolutionary consequences of the *Cogito*. In my final year we studied the *Ethics of Authenticity* and my research project that year involved an analysis of what Taylor describes as the 'boosters and knockers' of the contemporary culture and the need for greater 'articulacy' about the moral sources motivating its most admirable projects. His diagnosis of modern culture, and his ability to engage with the full range of perspectives concerning modern freedom, was impressive and relevant, and his analysis seemed at least to this novice to ring true. Here was a thinker whom my tutor had referred to as a 'philosopher's philosopher', who seemed to have his finger on the pulse of our age. What was more, the way he explained the notion of 'uniqueness' (the singular and particular in human experience), while at the same time situating it in a historical context, allowed a reader to feel connected to others and the world in a personally meaningful way. This feeling of connection on my part, often combined with a contrary impulse to stand apart, was the beginning of what became a sustained interest in philosophy and provided the conditions for what was to become a more mature engagement with Taylor's work. If Girard later arrested my naïveté, Taylor earlier cultivated my sense of the possible. A tension was becoming evident that required further consideration. Could I take resentment and the cultural tendency toward violence seriously, as Girard clearly expected his readers to do, and still believe in the moral ideal of authenticity that Taylor seemed so ably to defend? This tension took on greater significance the more I continued to delve into these thinkers, and for good reason.

II

Being very much at home in the liberal philosophical tradition, Taylor places a premium on the self as the locus of a genuinely moral inspiration that he sees as having come about through the various religious, cultural and political revolutions that ushered in the modern period. Girard by contrast sees the freedoms gained through these revolutions as an attempt to replace one form of 'divinization' involving the community, with another that now centres on the individual. Whereas the traditional form of divinization could at least maintain order and peace (more or less), the modern form of 'self-divinization' has lost the vital religious ingredient that can channel our resentments, restore order when required, and thus keep everything from slipping into chaos. For Girard modern individualism is not only naïve, it is *dangerously* naïve.

The apparent conflict between Girard and Taylor concerning the self and the modern identity is made all the more intriguing because, as I mentioned above, both are Christian thinkers who grant a large role to religion in helping to bring about the modern age. For Girard, Christianity has made modern individualism untenable. The question of having a personally derived identity is not open to the individual in the way modern liberal philosophy claims due to the fact that human beings come to know themselves only in and through their relationship to a religiously ordered world. Hence their so-called 'identities' come from the community that forges for them a place in that ordered world, without which there can be nothing coherent or unified in their self-understandings. Trying to 'be oneself', a mode of self-determination popular in contemporary culture, simply flies in the face of the prescriptive role of language and culture. It is precisely the loss of religion, as the binding force that guarantees a sense of belonging, which makes everything today seem unclear and in danger of falling apart. Whether identity is social or personal, without religion as a means of keeping order and peace, Yeats' apocalyptic vision seems prophetic for most Girardians: 'Things fall apart; the centre cannot hold; / mere anarchy is loosed upon the world, / The blood-dimmed tide is loosed, and everywhere / the ceremony of innocence is drowned . . .'[11]

However, for Taylor contemporary culture is morally meliorist[12] *precisely because of its individualism*, which is largely owing to the emphasis on personal commitment so essential to the Christian teaching that has itself so substantially

---

11. Quoted in Gil Bailie *Violence Unveiled: Humanity at the Crossroads* (New York: Crossroads Publishing, 1997), p. 42.

influenced this culture. Like Girard, he believes that individualism as pure subjectivism or 'centring on the self' is wrong-headed because it does not take into account how human beings generate meaning, only as always already participating in and partly shaped by a tradition or community.[13] But he nonetheless argues that reducing modern individualism to a form of 'egoism' is a simplistic explanation of a complex phenomenon.[14] When set within a historical context this individualism can be understood to contain a genuinely moral inspiration.

Both Girard's and Taylor's concepts of the modern self appear profoundly at odds despite their shared belief in Christianity. Can the problem here be explained with reference to their different disciplinary approaches to a similar phenomenon? Indeed, Girard's concept of the 'identity of the self' can appear misleading. When we unpack his claims we learn that it is not simply that individuals fail to achieve an identity today where once they succeeded in doing so. To have an 'identity' in a premodern society was to have the question 'who am I?' answered for me and therefore to be assigned a place, as it were, 'by nature'. As Girard uses it in the context of the modern age, 'identity' is associated with an *inability to distinguish* one thing from another.[15] It thus becomes a form of 'sameness' that generates confusion and conflict. In other words, it has to do with the threat of a crisis that

---

12. By 'morally meliorist' here (and in any subsequent use of this expression), I mean to connote the possibility of gradual, albeit painfully won, improvement in the human lot. In *The Malaise of Modernity*, Taylor describes something close to what I mean by the phrase: 'I suggest that . . . in this matter we look not for the trend, what is up or down, but that we break with our temptation to discern irreversible trends, and see that there is a struggle here, whose outcome is continually up for grabs' (Ontario: Anansi Press, 1991c), p. 79.

13. Smith, *Charles Taylor: Meaning, Morals, and Modernity*, p. 3.

14. 'Individualism has in fact been used in two quite different senses. In one it is a moral ideal, one facet of which I have been discussing, in another it is an amoral phenomenon, something like what we mean by egoism. The rise of individualism in this sense is usually a phenomenon of breakdown, where the loss of tradition leaves mere anomie in its wake . . . It is, of course catastrophic to confuse these two kinds of individualism, which have utterly different causes and consequence. Which is why Tocqueville carefully distinguishes "individualism" from "egoism."' Taylor, *The Ethics of Authenticity*, p. 125–126.

15. Kierkegaard also saw the modern period as losing significance: 'In *The Present Age*, he describes his own culture as having lost an agreed-upon sense of qualitative distinctions accepted within society as a whole. People no longer make a clear distinction, for example, between fine art and schlock art, or between great writers and hacks. As a result, there is no longer a basis for experiencing things as genuinely worthwhile or significant in life. As such distinctions are levelled down, Kierkegaard claims, the possibility of finding meaning and fulfilment in our lives is diminished. We would then lose any generally accepted bases for making the kinds of commitments that would give our lives a point and a sense of direction.' Guigon, Charles and D. Pereboom, eds, *Existentialism: Basic Writings* (2nd Edition), pp. 1–2.

can easily escalate, the prospect of which, Girard believes, traditional religious communities were well equipped to protect themselves against. For Girard, to try and have an identity in the modern sense is to ignore the fact that identity is first and foremost about difference that can only be conferred by the cultural order and the generative processes that fully belong to the sacred. And his emphasis on the role of imitation in these generative processes tends to reinforce his distrust of any existential appeal to 'uniqueness' on the part of the modern subject.

Taylor does not ignore the potential difficulties that can arise in the transition from a religious to a secular world view. Indeed, I want to argue, his profound sense of the difficulties here is one of the key factors that brings him close enough to Girard to provide the basis of a worthwhile conversation. However misunderstood their respective projects appear from the other's viewpoint, both thinkers are in fact attempting to tell a similar story, one in which the modern age still owes a lot to the traditional view of transcendence – *whether or not* it can actually live up to this view of transcendence once the debt is acknowledged.

For Taylor, the term 'identity' only takes on significance in the modern period *because it can no longer be taken for granted*. In the premodern world, he believes, 'identities' were too unproblematic to be considered as such. The very thing that makes a personally derived identity both challenging and worthwhile today is that it cannot be taken for granted, it must be won, and it can fail. Taylor reminds us that the toppling of hierarchies provides precisely the conditions in which it can fail. Therefore it is not simply the case that the proponents of modern freedom are unaware of the risks here, as Girard's thesis seems to suggest (though certainly for Girard the risks are incomparably greater). With his grasp of the dangers, Taylor sees the modern age in a less deterministic way than Girard: having an identity need not be a euphemism for 'sameness', and hence crisis. On the contrary, it can involve genuine difference. Taylor's confidence in the notion of particularity, as the moral force behind the 'ideal of authenticity', challenges one of Girard's central arguments; that the modern emphasis on freedom and identity tends irrevocably toward sameness and therefore toward crisis and decline. And surprisingly from a Girardian point of view, Taylor can articulate this confidence while at the same time taking seriously the religious impulse and how it can continue to organize our most deeply felt aspirations.

So, Girard and Taylor share an interest in the meaning of religion in a secular age, in which religion is more than a set of beliefs and practices, and constitutes something of the preconditions of human community. But both draw very different conclusions from their analysis of the role of religion and the sacred in the transition to the modern world, conclusions that we can now see have to do with the nature of 'identity', and whether individualism is producing 'sameness' or 'difference'. Girard's hypothesis concerning the role of collective violence and scapegoating implies that there is no way for the modern subject, in its attempt to realize or fulfil itself, to produce anything but crisis. And this leads him into a curious *cul de sac* when attempting to meet the ethical challenges of our age. He offers a powerful critique of the moral bankruptcy of liberal culture. The attempts by individuals today not only to 'keep up with the joneses', but continuously to 'surpass their own highest achievements' are ultimately, in his view, self-defeating.[16] While brilliantly diagnosing the desperation and futility of the modern subject in a world emptied of transcendence in the traditional sense, and the increasing urgency that prevails when religion no longer functions to 'hold things together', his bleak view of the modern age leaves the individual devoid of religion and powerless when confronted with the forces that lead to violence. Hence, not only do we run the risk of failing to live up to an exacting standard regarding the realization of the goal of universal respect (something that Taylor admits is a danger that contemporary culture must face), but the whole liberal project is fated to run aground because it is predicated on an unsustainable concept of the self-sufficient individual. In the process of equalizing individuals and levelling a hierarchically ordered world that discriminated in terms of 'rank and station', between what goods were available and to whom etc., Girard believes, we have fatally weakened a system that channelled our envious and rivalrous desires in constructive ways, and thus unwittingly unleashed the violence of *homo religiosus*.

Herein lies what I take to be the central *aporia* in Girardian theory. According to this theory a modern individual has no capacity to act in an ethical, or indeed constructive way, since, outside a religious context that could once guarantee order and stability, the 'ethical agent' can now 'act' only in ways that sooner or later break down meaningful categories of difference. Without an ethical subject who can compensate for the loss of hierarchy a serious question arises for the proponents of this theory. By undermining the conditions of the ethical, whereby an individual can take a stand in relation to a community and the cultural forces that prevail there, a stand that is potentially creative and transformative, is Girardian theory not contributing to the very problem of 'escalating crisis' that it is so keen to warn us about? And this in turn highlights a deep tension in Girard's own theory. This theory leads him to annul any individual selfhood and thus deny any human agency. Given such a thorough undermining of the personal, does Girard not undercut his own professed faith in an idea of transcendence that can empower the individual to act despite if not because of his or her capacity to lose anchorage in the world? Does not the faith he professes empower persons – individually as well as collectively?

---

16. Girard provides a nice metaphor for thinking about an individual's desires and how they culminate in self-defeating projects in the absence of externally conferred clearly marked differences: 'Rather like an insect that falls into the crumbling trap its rival has dug for it, with the grains of sand that it tries to grasp giving way as it tries to move its feet – desire counts on differences to get up the slope. But the differences are *obliterated precisely because of its efforts . . .*' René Girard, *Things Hidden Since the Foundation of the World: Research Undertaken in Collaboration with J.-M. Oughourlian and G. Lefort*, trans. S. Bann and M. Metteer (Stanford: Stanford University Press, 1987b), p. 303.

To restate the problem, both Girard and Taylor place considerable emphasis on the role of a religious world view in maintaining order and purpose in a pre-modern context, and on the corresponding problem that occurs for the individual with the decline of such a world view. But both thinkers, their shared Christian commitments notwithstanding, differ considerably with respect to how, or even whether, the modern subject can productively engage with his or her desires and purposes in a post-religious age. Our values and beliefs, that mediate our relationship to the world and provide a source of meaning, appear deeply fraught. Central concerns of the book, then, are whether Girard's thorough undermining of the subject is sustainable within the terms of his own discourse *and* whether Taylor's confidence that modern individualism has a genuinely moral inspiration can be vindicated when tested against Girard's analysis of crisis and unity.

Without too much qualification, we can say that the proposed conversation between Girard and Taylor is broadly located on the axis between structuralism and hermeneutics, or between those theories that see the subject existing only within a web of language, viewed as a totality, and those theories that see the subject as always already existing within a horizon of experience and historically mediated understanding.[17] My own analysis is not neutral on the question of whether Girard's or Taylor's approach to structure is more suitable for under-standing the human reality with which each grapples. But while I am more critical of Girard's work, I am in no way unappreciative of the immense efforts made by mimetic theory to come to terms with the issue of 'transcendence' – efforts, moreover, that can be related constructively to the practical concerns of Taylor's philosophy.

One of Girard's main contributions to cultural theory is his analysis of desire. It is an analysis that fundamentally undermines any autonomy individuals might

---

17. Girard is interested not only in the operation of human signifying systems, but also their origins. See *Things Hidden*, pp. 6–7.14. His own theory of myth, which attempts to explain language as a development of an original scapegoating or murder, is 'worked out in close proximity with the work of Claude Lévi-Strauss, the most influential structuralist anthropologist of the twentieth century'. Fleming, *René Girard: Violence and Mimesis*, p. 77. The latter's work helps to bridge the disciplines of structural anthropology and linguistics. See 'Structural Analysis in Linguistics and in Anthropology', in Claude Lévi-Strauss, *Structural Anthropology*, trans. Claire Jacobson and Brooke Grundfest Schoepf (Allen Lane, London: The Penguin Press, 1969), pp. 34–51. Taylor, in contrast to Girard, aligns himself with the 'the post-Heideggerian' hermeneutics of Gadamer, the central thesis of which claims that human beings are (in Taylor's phrase) 'self-interpreting animals'. Here the layers of meanings that the individual encounters, in addition to extend-ing outwards, also extend inwards, claiming the interpreting individual in the act of knowing. The 'self-interpreting act' in turn presupposes a more fundamental thesis, which properly belongs to 'post-Heideggerian existential phenomenology': 'that human existence is expressive of and constituted by meanings shaped by self-interpretations.' Smith, *Charles Taylor: Meaning, Morals, and Modernity*, p. 34.

claim to have, since it presents them as imitating the desires of others for the sake of their own sense of worth, and hence as having no essential capacity for a self-generated identity. Consequently, the self who wants to be 'individual' must deceive itself with greater degrees of subtlety and a correspondingly greater potential for frustration. The 'Other' does not simply call for a meaningful relationship if the self is willing, rather it poses a serious problem for the self, whether willing or not. Girard's central thesis concerns the universality of mimetic desire, with individuals denied any capacity for effective change or any way of positively transforming their negative imitations.[18] According to the mimetic hypothesis, beyond the claim to 'having an identity', which moderns assume as a right, is the spectre of the other's desire that always threatens to remind me that the game is up: that I am not in fact myself but rather a pale reflection of another, whose desires I imitate – an imitation hidden behind the mistaken belief that I am unique. The insight of the 'great' novels, Girard claims, exposes this 'uniqueness' as illusory. 'If the lovers are never in accord it is not because they are too "different", as common sense and sentimental novels assert, but because they are too alike, because each is a copy of the other. But the more they grow alike the more different they imagine themselves. The *sameness* by which they are obsessed appears to them as an absolute *otherness*.'[19] Trying to be different reminds everyone just how alike he or she is, 'and the effort to leave the beaten paths forces everyone into the same ditch.'[20] Thus, attempting to be an individual in the modern period actually stifles the process of having an identity, by destroying all independent marks of difference. A theory of mimesis (or more precisely of desire as mimetic), then, helps explain how striving to have one's own identity makes distinctions already marked within a community identity insignificant, thereby generating crisis within the individual as well as the community.

The first part of the book examines the elements of Girard's literary criticism that inform his analysis of crisis, leading him to an uncompromisingly hostile view of selfhood and identity that continues to be articulated in his theory of culture. While not contesting the theory of crisis developed in his later work, I argue that

---

18. In his later work Girard acknowledges the existence of positive mimesis, as the basis of a fundamentally loving relationship, to counter his early explicitly negative view of mimesis. See Rebecca Adams, 'Loving Mimesis and Girard's "Scapegoat of the Text": A Creative Reassessment of Mimetic Desire', in *Violence Renounced: René Girard, Biblical Studies, and Peacemaking*, ed. W. Swartely (Telford, PA: Pandora Press, 2000), p. 281. However, accounts of more positive forms of imitation, that Girard later wants to claim are also fundamental to the human condition, have been only persuasively argued from a strictly theological perspective. For example, see, Petra Steinmair-Pösel. 'Original Sin, Grace, and Positive Mimesis', *Contagion: Journal of Violence, Mimesis and Culture* (Volume 14, 1007).

19. René Girard, *Deceit, Desire, and the Novel: Self and Other in Literary Structure*, trans. Yvonne Freccero (Baltimore: Johns Hopkins University Press, 1965), p. 106.

20. Ibid., p. 100.

Girard's hostility here is based on a deep division between two radically different 'selves' that he 'postulates' – a division that is then overcome in a finally achieved 'unity'. This division and unity (involving a former self that has been renounced and a latter self generated through this renunciation) are formulated in terms of 'death and rebirth'. The individual must die to a false self and be born to a true self, a 'death and rebirth' that brings (as well as a new peace with the other) unity for the hero of the novel – and, Girard claims, for the author who through his art achieves a depth of insight that unites him with other 'great' novelists (and indeed for readers who adequately inhabit the literary space produced in the great novels). However, it is this very structure of death and rebirth that his later anthropology exposes as false, or rather as a transition that can establish unity only through violence, that is by the community's meeting an immanent crisis only by excluding and scapegoating one of its members and so in truth – though a truth that remains unacknowledged – by *dividing* itself. My argumentative move is to take this later theory of cultural crisis seriously and to apply it retrospectively, so to speak, to Girard's early theory: the final 'unity' of literary space, I suggest, is achieved only at the cost of scapegoating the 'self' who must 'die' – a scapegoating that is itself concealed in *Deceit, Desire, and the Novel*.

Girard, however, does not see the division at the heart of culture as having any relation to the unacknowledged division that, as I claim, is inscribed in his early work.[21] Hence (if my intuition here is correct) the conclusion of his early work continues to be employed to explain his later theory of the scapegoat. The crisis in literary space that ends in the unity of the literary community, when the author stops trying to be 'individual', becomes the crisis in cultural space that ends in the unity of the anthropological community. However, on one hand, the literary community's renunciation of part of itself, through the author, is the source of a *true* unity based on death and rebirth, while, on the other hand, the anthropological community's renunciation of part of itself is the source of a *false* unity based on death and rebirth. What constitutes the former unity as 'true' is the actual guilt of the one set apart (the Romantic hero), but what constitutes the later unity as 'false' is the actual guilt of the community, and the innocence of the one set apart (the scapegoat). Both early and later works evince the same pattern of unity from crisis, but two different agents in each instance are seen as bearing responsibility. This is the *aporia* examined in the first part of the book, in which I attempt to answer the following question: Can both spaces (literary and cultural), which are

---

21. Speaking of sacrifice in the context of King Solomon's solution when two women claimed the same child as their own, Girard argues that the king 'decided to divide the child in two'. Girard claims, '[t]he Latin word *decidere* means etymologically to divide by the sacrificial knife, to cut the throat of a victim'. Girard, *Things Hidden*, p. 238. If myth and ritual form a 'cover-up' of original division (or violence), as Girard claims, then a concealed division in his own theory must be a serious charge for the proponents of his theory.

constitutionally the same in terms of the generative nature of crisis, unproblematically maintain two different explanations of unity?

Taylor's philosophical preoccupations speak to Girard's hypothesis in a number of ways, though not directly. Taylor does not concentrate on the dynamics of desire (mediating relations between self, object and other), as Girard's mimetic theory does. He is concerned more with the meanings and values that individuals find in their desires and purposes – meanings and values that may not be readily available to them but can nonetheless be seen as significant when explored, clarified and tested through practical reason. For Taylor, the questions are not whether desire is mimetic or whether it is more in control of us than we are of 'it', but rather whether individuals, as subjects, can make sense of their lives (since for him all human understandings and meanings are subject-related). The individual subject, however great the delusions to which he or she may be prone, and however deep and extensive the cultural webs within which he or she is inserted, is the central and undisplaceable locus of human understanding. Contra Girard's literary self, Taylor makes the case that there are some basic ontological conditions whereby the self, while always already constituted in large part through relations with others, can negotiate its commitments, more or less, in a meaningful way. It is this possibility that allows him to claim that having an identity can be something truly 'different', and not a form of sameness that leaves everyone in 'the ditch'. Thus, Taylor, like Girard, is concerned with crisis and the need for identity and unity, but unlike Girard, he develops a morally meliorist account of subjectivity and history. And he does so by articulating a concept of selfhood that can grapple constructively with cultural tendencies toward fragmentation in the modern period, while at the same time maintaining some nourishing continuity with the past.

Why should these competing interpretations of selfhood within a religious-philosophical horizon concern us today, preoccupied as we are, for the most part, with getting away from grand narratives? In other words, why should the problematic that emerges between Girard and Taylor interest a reader who has perhaps decided long ago that concepts like 'self', 'history', 'identity', 'transcendence', 'origins' etc. are so fraught with complexity (even 'violence') and that theorizing that gives them any real play ought to be deconstructed, rendering them 'undecidable' and silent. Perhaps we are well advised here, but I believe there is much at stake in not taking these value-laden terms seriously – that is, in not attempting to give them (or ascribe to them) any real content. More and more within discourse today the undermining of these categories is the default position, even as the same cultural theorists acknowledge the dangers that lurk in the shadows of such antirealism.[22] This is not a risk that either Girard or Taylor appears willing to take.

---

22. I am thinking here of two recent works whose analysis of 'the sacred' are influenced by post-structuralist thought, hence rendering impossible the content of the categories mentioned above, or indeed religious revelation. See: Slavoj Žižek,

One question I tease out in the first part of the book concerns whether Girard's literary criticism locks him into a mode of thinking about the subject that obstructs his later anthropological work and forces him into a position in the human sciences not dissimilar to the one adopted by Lévi-Strauss.[23] I try to rally Taylor's hermeneutical philosophy (and in particular its account of self and history) in order to respond to the problems in Girard's work that radically undermine selfhood; and thereby I open the possibility of what I claim can be a more genial exchange between both thinkers concerning religious violence and sacrifice. The following outline of each chapter presents an overview of the main developments of the book. It briefly charts the way I first expose what I see as the major theoretical problem in Girard's work and the difficulties this problem creates for his theory of religion, and then, moving into Taylor's work, it further charts the way a perhaps chastened Girard might see his own theory working out at the level of a philosophical hermeneutics – in other words, as a theory of sacrifice *within* the context of selfhood.

III

Part I of the book, entitled 'From Self to Sacrifice: Girardian Theory', explores Girard's overall work – his literary criticism and his anthropology. In Chapter 1 'Division and Unity in Literary Space: The Romantic Fallacy' I consider the context of the literary world within which Girard was writing during the 1960s. His early debunking of subjectivity takes the form of an attack on the Romantic individual (the personification of all philosophies of consciousness) for the mistaken belief that his desires are his own. Girard's first major work *Deceit, Desire and the Novel*, makes the case that this individual's belief in his originality – especially in the sense that he is at the origins of his own desires – is fundamentally mistaken (constituting what is called the 'Romantic fallacy'). His own deconstruction of this 'fallacy' ensures that no conscious, intentional subject appears in literary space as he analyses it in a series of great novels. His criticism charts the journeys of the heroes of these novels from lofty preoccupations with their own self-sufficiency

---

The Fragile Absolute: Or why the Christian Legacy is Worth Fighting for? (London: Verso, 2001); and Gergio Agamben, *Homo Sacer: Sovereign Power and Bare Life.* Trans. by Daniel Heller-Roazen (Stanford: Stanford University Press, 1998).

23. Of the linguistic revolution in France in the 1960s, and the influence of Saussure's insistence on the arbitrariness of the sign on Lacan among others, Seán Burke writes: 'Lévi-Strauss could thus declare: "the goal of the human sciences is not to constitute man, but to dissolve him"'. *The Death and Return of the Author: Criticism and Subjectivity in Barthes, Foucault and Derrida* (Edinburgh: Edinburgh University Press, 1998), p. 13.

(an illusory originality) to a descent into the underground of obsessive emotions as they struggle, with ultimate futility, to maintain their own separateness from a model whom they are in fact imitating. Finally each heroes' struggle ends when he reaches the apotheosis of self-deception – the illusion that he can have the 'Being' of 'the Other' as his own.[24] At this point he renounces his desire to be original and acknowledges his dependence on models. At the end of *Deceit, Desire, and the Novel*, the real hero of the 'great' novel is revealed as the author who overcomes his false desires in the process of writing. The subject who dies in and through his work is born anew. The unity achieved is a unity shared in by all great novelists and the literary community more broadly.

When Girard writes his second major work, *Violence and the Sacred*, the structure of 'death and rebirth', that was part of the author's 'sublime lucidity' at the end of the earlier critical work, is re-examined in the context of cultural space with surprisingly different conclusions. The crisis that had earlier been detected in literary space *is now also detected in myth, and other historical texts*, thus highlighting its wider anthropological significance. According to Girard, the evidence of 'death and rebirth', found in the structural similarities detectable in primitive and traditional cultures, suggests that the motif of eternal recurrence must be rooted in an original act of violence by the community against a victim, who, in death, takes on the aura of divinity. His hypothesis of the scapegoat sets out to explain this cultural phenomenon. The majority of Chapter 2 'Division and Unity in Cultural Space: The Scapegoat Mechanism' is concerned with an explication of the main thrust of Girard's argument in *Violence and the Sacred* in the context of the preceding argument of *Deceit, Desire and the Novel*. In this chapter I try to bring out the structural similarities between literary space and cultural space. These similarities centre on *loss of difference* as the basis of the intra- and inter-subjective crisis in literary space and of the sacrificial crisis in cultural space.

According to Girard's anthropological theory this crisis is brought about by the symmetrical patterning evident among partners in conflict, a conflict which can escalate to the point of threatening the very foundations of a community. Sacrifice is understood therefore, as a way of protecting the community from the mimetic contagion of violence. But if we accept this, Girard argues, then we must also acknowledge that ritual sacrifice itself must imitate an earlier more spontaneous process of containment, since, he claims, the original violence must first stop before the ritual re-enactment can be efficacious in a restorative and protective way.

---

24. Girard uses the masculine pronoun when discussing his conception of 'triangular desire' even though he intends to include female desire within this conception. This creates awkwardness for commentators on his work committed to the use of non-sexist language. Although I have sometimes found no way of avoiding this awkwardness when dealing at close quarters with Girard's texts, I have otherwise sought to avoid such usage in this thesis. I refer the reader to note 82 in Chapter 1 where the issue of gender in Girardian theory is given some further treatment.

Hence there must be some initial 'mechanism' within culture that is triggered so as to stop the escalating violence and restore order before the crisis destroys the community. To explain this earlier form of containment Girard posits the scapegoat mechanism. The overall aim of Chapter 2 is to set out Girard's anthropology of the scapegoat in the context of division and unity in cultural space, and to argue that the early literary work informs the anthropological work at all times, *except* in relation to how the resolution of the crisis, and the restored unity, is now understood. I shall claim that Girard's own early literary criticism evinces the same structure that his later work reserves for myths that *conceal acts of scapegoating*, leading to the conclusion that the 'unity of literary space' is achieved *at the expense of* the Romantic hero – the true anthropological significance of whose early 'death' remains hidden. Is Girard's anti-subjectivism thus itself a form of scapegoating that permits him to pass two unrelated subjects – one who dies and the one who is born again – off as one and the same subject?

In Chapter 3 'Negating Subjectivity and History: Problems within Girardian Theory' I argue that Girard's theory of catastrophically undermines the possibility of ethical agency on the part of a responsible subject. When he introduces his theory of religious violence the need for such a responsible subject is all the more pressing, due to the potentially runaway nature of mimetic violence. However, instead of a theory of a human subject capable of understanding its own relationship to this violence we find a peculiar fidelity to his earlier theory of desire and the structure postulated in his earlier literary criticism. Taking account of his analyses of literary and cultural space, I argue that Girard attempts to maintain two apparently incompatible theories: 'the Romantic lie' and the 'scapegoat mechanism'. In this chapter I make the case that Girard extends the early work into the later work making them appear continuous when, as argued at the end of Chapter 2, there is a structural difference that does not get taken into account: the community is now responsible for separating out (or expelling) the individual, whereas in the early theory the individual is responsible for this separation. If this structural difference is taken into account, as I argue it must, all continuity between the early work and the later work is entirely inconsistent with the spirit of Girard's cultural anthropology and his theory of the scapegoat. Furthermore, in this chapter we learn that the problems for the Girardian subject are also reflected in his account of historical change. For, once again, without tempering his hostility towards the modern subject in light of his new insistence on the guilt of the community, Girard's later historical account of the loss of religion as cultural degeneration is made to appear compatible with the dynamic of the novel and the degeneration of the self in literary space.

Thus, it is made to appear that Girard's theory of mimesis *depends* on the absolute instability of an ontological subject. This, as I try to show, places his work – ironically – within the family of modern ideas that flow from Schopenhauerian Will. He ends up reifying desire by giving it more status in his discourse than a thinking feeling agent. As I want to argue, however, it is his continued antipathy towards the subject for the sake of a mistaken compatibility between his early and later works that leaves him with little alternative but to exclude a responsible agent from his theory of the scapegoat. By making 'Desire' entitive (after Schopenhauerian Will) he undermines any prospect of a more meliorist (or less dystopian) account of historical change when faced with the limits of human experience. And, in the process, he suggests a close relationship between mimetic desire and the darker side of the modern story touched on below. As part of my attempt to explicate this anti-subjectivism and the tension it generates in Girard's overall theory, I make the case that his overly psychological reading of the novel plays down the voices of the authors whom he discusses to the detriment of their own social analyses. This is a conclusion that, in the final analysis, results from his strict allegiance to the structuralist method of ruling out any subjective influence on the process of writing. This last point reminds us once again of the problem of propounding a theory of mimetic desire and sacred violence without an ethical subject who can stand in relationship to his or her world. What I attempt to highlight at the end of this chapter as something that ought to concern Girardian theorists is that, once we lose an identifiable subject, we cannot really speak of a genuine quest for the supreme good, or of Christian conversion.

Chapter 4 'The Early Modern Period: Transposing the Old Cosmic Order' opens my engagement with Taylor's work in Part II of the book ('From Sacrifice to Self: Taylor's Philosophical Account'), and covers Taylor's philosophical account, which he details in his major work *Sources of the Self*. While Taylor provides us with a subject that can locate itself in moral space and discern some concept of the good, despite if not because of the uncertain nature of desire, the question remains as to whether historical developments in the west allow us to posit a self that can compensate for the loss of the social order that Girard argues once channelled violence in protective ways. This part of the book thus responds to what have been identified in Part I as the two problem areas in Girard's overall theory: subjectivity and historical change. And it does so through the two distinct but complementary lenses of his work, namely his philosophical anthropology and his philosophical history. While there is no way of entirely separating out these two aspects of Taylor's work, by discussing his analysis of the transition to the modern period my aim will be to first consider his analysis of the *historical* issues that also arise for Girard in the context of crisis. In Chapter 4 (the beginning of Part II) I argue that, while Girard sees the toppling of hierarchies as the source of a sacrificial crisis in the modern period, Taylor understands this toppling as occurring within the context of a re-appropriation of order in the Deist picture and the emerging individualism that places priority on rational control. Hence, order is not undermined, as Girard believes, but transformed.

In this chapter I set out how Taylor's philosophical history can address some of the main concerns of Girard's later theory without forfeiting a meliorist conception of human development. I consider a number of specific problems already outlined with respect to Girard's theory of subjectivity and the transition to the modern age, including his problematic analysis of Augustinian 'love' in *Deceit, Desire, and the Novel*, and his equally problematic comparison in *Resurrection from the Underground* of Descartes and Corneille as harbingers of egoistic individualism, and what he characterizes as the whole modern movement toward self-divinization. However, the main problem in Girard's theory that this chapter tackles is his analysis of the modern world as being in a state of 'sacrificial crisis'. When speaking about order, both Girard and Taylor analyse the concept of 'Degree' in ways that provide a stark contrast for my analysis of them. In this context both thinkers understand the Renaissance notion of a 'great chain of being' very differently, allowing me to contrast sharply their core ideas concerning 'identity and difference'. For Girard the notion of 'Degree' that is found expressed in 'the great chain' is essentially an anthropological principle that he uses to explain how order is maintained; the loss of degree in the modern period, then, precipitates disorder and leads irrevocably to crisis. For Taylor, on the other hand, it is not so much 'degree', or the gap between grades of difference, that is significant, as Chapter 4 attempts to make clear, but rather how the overall order in nature is conceived. In *Sources of the Self* he explains how the older cosmic order that had reigned in Europe since Plato, is transformed in the early modern period, with the advent of Deism, into a mechanistic order. With this transition, the significance of 'Degree' is displaced by 'efficient causality' and the rationalist belief that all things in nature share 'interlocking purposes'.[25] By comparing Girard and Taylor with respect to the role of 'Degree', I will contest Girard's analysis of the modern world as a form of disintegration, by highlighting, with Taylor's help, how order is effectively reconstituted, and internalized, by a new mode of subjectivity. By placing 'degree' in light of Taylor's analysis of the transition to the modern period, I hope to show how it is reinvigorated by a new order that provides the individual with more control.

Even if Taylor's consideration of the early modern period managed to convince Girardians that order was indeed transformed rather than dissolved, they might still argue that these historical developments only plug the dam against a swelling flood of violence. Even if we do grant that a new order prevails for a period within a more rationalized Christianity, this 'reordering', they might claim, need not continue to be efficacious into late modernity and postmodernity. Does even a mechanistic order not 'fall apart', they might ask, once we realize the full import of modern disenchantment?[26] In Chapter 5 'Rethinking Division and

---

25. Taylor, *Sources of the Self*, p. 279.
26. In his essay 'Nietzsche versus the Crucified', in Williams, James G., ed. *The Girard Reader* (New York: Crossroads Publishing, 2003b) Girard argues that the true significance of Nietzsche's aphorism 125 (*Gay Science*), as a statement of modern atheism and disenchantment, is its account of the collective murder of god, which substantiates his own theory of the recurrence of original violence through myth and religion. However, Girard believes that Nietzsche failed to recognize the radical nature of Jesus' life and death in exposing the cult of violence once and for all by his innocence.

Unity: Subjectivity, Religion and the Current of Life' I argue, once again with Taylor's help, that the Romantic voice of nature continues the process of internalization already well underway by the eighteenth century and invigorates it with a new confidence in possibilities of integral expression and an affirmative impulse towards unity and wholeness. In contrast to Girard's reading of Romanticism, Taylor helps us to see how, from Rousseau onwards, the distancing by the individual from the potentially corrupting influences of society should be seen as a form not of separation but rather of authentic connection.

Taylor's work on Hegel provides a way of thinking about significant developments in the modern period as a gradual subjectivizing of the religious need to unify around a victim. By examining the eighteenth-century expressivist movement and its preoccupations with 'division and unity' (what Taylor calls 'radical freedom' and, 'integral expression') I draw a parallel with Girard's theory of scapegoating and sacrifice, and the way he understands how cultural unity is generated through division or separation – what he calls 'unanimity minus one'. I try to show how some of Girard's insights about the sacred (in particular the idea of unity through division) have parallels in modern philosophical accounts of subjectivity. The philosophical problematizing of selfhood during this period confronts the basic problem of 'division' without forsaking the possibility of nonviolent unity. The self can be seen to attempt to meet the challenge of generating difference in a subjective mode, by remaining in touch with our 'inner nature'. However, by the nineteenth century, as Taylor points out, almost all confidence in our inner nature as a source of good has been eroded by the prevalence of technological control. The power of the creative imagination to benevolently transform the world dwindles, while the darker side of the modern story begins to loom large. Other, more primordial sources of the self begin to make their presence felt, which, Taylor believes, now must also be confronted. His own philosophical project attempts to diagnose the modern malaise and, unlike Girard, present an account of selfhood that can stand up to its challenges.

Chapter 6 'Crisis and Unity in Moral Space: Identity and the Good' explores Taylor's philosophical anthropology in the context of his already examined philosophical history. Specifically, it targets what I have identified as some of the problem areas in Girard's theory of subjectivity, and begins to make the case that human agents, in the absence of traditional forms of religion, can still orientate themselves in relation to their desires and purposes. While Taylor's philosophical history can respond to a crisis of Degree in cultural space by interpreting order as being transposed and internalized in the modern period through the affirmation of ordinary life, in this chapter I try to show how, similarly, his philosophical anthropology can respond to the crisis of subjectivity in literary space. It does this by articulating the transcendental conditions of an experiencing agent. Taylor's hermeneutics give us a way of understanding some of Girard's central concerns without in turn doing violence to the subject by eliminating it from the space of positive reflection. The early modern preoccupation with rational control, Taylor believes, can be seen to place the subject at the centre of the ordering process whereas previously such ordering was secured by a metaphysical view of nature and cosmos stretching back to Plato. The Romantic reaction to 'rationalism', far from fragmenting us further, as Girard claims, allows us, for a period, to conceive of our inner nature as good, and to bring forward the expression of 'something new' as a way of compensating for the loss of a purely rational world. What I attempt to argue is that Taylor's philosophical history closely parallels Girard's analysis of the source of modern disenchantment. Both acknowledge the role of Christianity in helping to shape our modern age. However, Taylor's account, unlike Girard's, does not see any radical discontinuity in the modern age with the moral sources that sustained human life in a premodern world.

Taylor's depiction of the self as always already orienting itself in moral space, I argue, provides a more realistic and convincing account than Girard's depiction of selfhood in literary and cultural space. For this self can find its bearings, in however halting or piecemeal a fashion, in relation to the good and, crucially, it can make qualitative distinctions by reflecting strongly on its desires. Moral frameworks are inescapable, especially when we can no longer take them for granted. Our language communities ensure that we are always interlocutors who participate in a broader conversation that reflects the vagaries and fragile continuities of tradition. Taylor also explores how our life has temporal depth and is narratively configured in a way that challenges Girard's notion of rebirth as something completely new. Gaining orientation in moral space and within a temporal horizon is not simply a case of 'deviated transcendence', as Girard claims; rather, through a series of maturations and regressions, we project a future that can somehow redeem the past, as part of our lived experience and not just our literary work. In this way, Taylor believes, our life story can have narrative unity (so that 'death' and 'rebirth' are never absolute and so never entirely discontinuous), spanning a whole life, in which something of the past is *always* left unfinished and hence part of our future projects. Within the narrative picture that Taylor elaborates, the gathering of our life is only ever more or less accomplished.

Once the temporal space is opened up in this way we can see how, what Taylor calls 'making qualitative distinctions' in the context of some higher standard of the good that offers itself as a correct interpretation of the world, becomes an active way of re-marking difference in relation to our identity. He recognizes that our highest standards may in fact be incommensurable, but he argues that we should not accept this possibility as an in-principle limit. From within our western 'universalist' perspective we can only offer the 'best account available' at any given time, if we are to adequately make sense of our lives, including the actions and feelings of others. For Taylor, 'reasoning in transitions' is the best if not only way to ensure that we take seriously our moral intuitions and what we actually do when we try to make sense of our lives on a whole range of issues concerning our identity and the good. Making transitions through the practical process of articulating our best account may indeed involve sacrifice – a sacrifice that he believes, like Girard, once played a ritual function. But notwithstanding the historical depth to which the subject now has access, without the recognition of frameworks, Taylor suggests, we can never know what to keep or what to let go – in short, what to decide. The Epilogue that follows this chapter, concluding the book, gathers together the argument up to then, and points to some important connections between Taylor and Girard, regarding their often complimentary insights into the problem of 'transcendence by violence'. It makes the case that Taylor's recent work *A Secular Age*, provides a way of taking up Girard's central anthropological concerns (voiced again in his recent work, *Evolution and Culture*) by giving us a plausible account of the deep historical resonances of violence within a modern imaginary. It also looks at the debates about religion within contemporary culture in the context of the main argument of this book, hence boldly asserting that selfhood and sacrifice can begin to be understood from a more hermeneutical perspective, one that can take cognizance of the generative religious experience that is part of our earliest human story and is arguably shared by all cultures.

In summary, then, the first part of the book attempts to analyse and expose what is, I claim, a highly problematic discontinuity in selfhood at the heart of Girardian theory. It considers how Girard's work develops from a critical account of the self and its relationship to others in the context of literary space to an account of sacrifice as a basic structure of cultural space – that is, from 'self to sacrifice.' It includes a critique of Girard's early work, a critique that draws on his own later theory of the scapegoat (which I do not put in question); and it sets out some of the problems that arise when his early and later work are seen as continuous. The false division within the self, as I try to show, is itself based on a form of scapegoating, the unacknowledged nature of which continues to play an active role in Girard's anti-subjectivism. I make the case that Girard's hypostatizing of desire, which arises from his hostility toward subjectivity, has ominous similarities with Schopenhauerian Will and is difficult if not impossible to relate to Christian *agapē*. The second part of the book, dealing with Taylor's philosophical history and his philosophical anthropology, reverses the order of analysis and considers developments 'from sacrifice to self'. Taylor's philosophy offers us an analysis of the self, as it develops *within* western religious and philosophical traditions, that attempts to take seriously in a self-conscious manner the religious violence that is, from the beginning, partly constitutive of human reality. In contrast to Girard, Taylor attempts to explain the historical 'toppling of hierarchies' and articulate a 'plausible interpretation of human history', in a way which suggests that an individual need not be understood as terminally fragmented and hence prone to violence in the absence of a religiously ordered world, but can rather confront the problem of sacrifice, and the modern spiritual crisis, creatively. Through expression and articulation, the self can recover the background meanings that are frequently left implicit because of the prevailing antipathy towards transcendence in cultural and political debates today.

By examining Taylor's account of the transitions to modern culture in the context of Girard's hypothesis of the scapegoat, it becomes conceivable that the latter's theory of sacred violence, which details the need for a careful prescribing of difference in terms of an externally arranged order, is internalized by the emerging individualism of the modern period – a transition that, following from Descartes, owes much to Deism and the Protestant affirmation of ordinary life. Arising from this, we can begin to see how modern selfhood becomes a development of the traditional need for sacrifice, and thereby takes on the defining characteristics of the sacred as a way of overcoming the undifferentiation, or 'divisions', that could, given the right circumstances, escalate into collective crisis and scapegoating. Crucially, in the context of what was earlier established in the book as the alignment of mimetic desire with blind will, and so the further enfeeblement of any effective response to the violence of *homo religiosus*, I argue that Taylor's work enables us to recover a conception of selfhood, that cannot only withstand Girard's mimetic hypothesis but also help to bring Girard's theory of the scapegoat firmly within the discourse of a philosophical hermeneutics. When cast in such a manner our narrative quests from sacrifice to self are in no less urgent need of expression and understanding. Indeed, they are more than descriptive and explanatory; they can be seen as transformative of those very forces that once atavistically determined our human horizons.

PART I

FROM SELF TO SACRIFICE: GIRARDIAN THEORY

CHAPTER 1

DIVISION AND UNITY IN LITERARY SPACE: THE ROMANTIC FALLACY

The ultimate meaning of desire is death, but death is not the novel's ultimate meaning . . . Out of supreme disorder is born supernatural order.[1]

René Girard

If the seed does not die after it has been sown, it will remain alone, but if it dies it will bear much fruit . . . *[This] verse from St. John serves as an epigraph for* The Brothers Karamazov *and it could serve as an epigraph for all novelistic conclusions.*[2]

René Girard

1. Introduction

Since the publication of *Violence and the Sacred* in 1972, Girard has earned an impressive reputation as a cultural anthropologist. What strikes a reader, when attempting to become aquainted with this late phase of Girard's work, are claims that revolve around his understanding of myth and ritual, and how the religious structure of death and rebirth owes its efficacy to a 'real' event which is the basis of his scapegoat theory. The gods of the old pagan cults of nature and eternal recurrence were once real human beings whose immolation restored life and peace to the community. What is less widely appreciated perhaps is that this 'structure' of death and rebirth is also employed in Girard's *early* work, specifically *Deceit, Desire, and the Novel*, although with quite different conclusions to those drawn in his later anthropology. When he published this first major work of criticism the theme of death and rebirth is applied not to the community and the origins of the sacred, but rather to the author as subject of his work. While a theory of how myth functions to conceal the true nature of this structure – the *guilt* of the community, and the *innocence* of the victim – is not yet developed, the focus in *Deceit, Desire, and the Novel* is nonetheless on the significance of this transformation in bringing about a genuine transcendence that becomes the achievement of the 'great' novelists. How are we to understand this 'transformation' that begins for Girard as something individual (intra- and intersubjective) and evolves in time into something collective (cultural and communal)?

---

1. René Girard, *Deceit, Desire, and the Novel: Self and Other in Literary Structure*, trans. Yvonne Freccero (Baltimore: Johns Hopkins University Press, 1965), p. 290.
2. Girard, *Deceit, Desire, and the Novel*, pp. 311–312, (his italics).

If we take the early work on its own terms we discover a subject that struggles in vain to orchestrate a kind of unity for itself, a self-sufficiency that will be impervious to others and can hence withstand the 'slings and arrows' that appear always set to de-throne it, from without and within. Despite its attempts to stay within itself like a 'spider in its web' – intact and complete – the subject is constantly drawn outside by the opinions of others and in his attempts to recover, ends up increasingly more divided. However, the author, Girard claims, only to the extent that he pushes this dynamic to its limits in and through his work can achieve a *true* unity. Only to the extent that, in and through his work, he dies to the false self that deceptively seeks approval from others, can he be born again – freed once and for all from the negative dynamics that 'shrink' his horizon?[3] This self gives up the illusion of its separateness and embraces its dependence on the other for its true identity – a conversion that is the result of a 'sublime lucidity'.[4] What I hope to explore in this chapter is the nature and status of this 'new' subject in Girard's early work. Does any thread of identity connect it with the subject that first constitutes 'the self' and culminates in 'supreme disorder'?

I will begin by considering Girard's literary criticism and its relationship to French structuralism, whose priority is to debunk the conscious intentional subject. By outlining the literary climate in which his early criticism took shape, I make the case that this work incorporates structuralist influences, in particular in its reaction against traditional philosophies of consciousness. While I offer a detailed analysis of Girard's theory of the novel, the main aim of this chapter is to focus on the central thesis of his literary criticism. Therefore, in addition to a nuanced exposition of how individuals subject themselves and others to hatred and deception by pursuing illusory desires, I will focus on the basic argument at the heart of *Deceit, Desire, and the Novel*. This argument claims that the author, in his work, renounces his 'false desire' and is restored to life, a unity that is ultimately the basis of the literary community. The question that each section of Chapter 1 responds to thus concerns the basic structure of 'death and rebirth' played out at different stages in Girard's criticism; how it is that the self becomes so divided within itself that nothing short of a conversion experience can bring an authentic unity. Having examined how some of the main themes of his critical work function to explain the disintegration of the self within literary space, I explore how (what he describes as) this 'ontological illness'[5] culminates in the desire for the very 'Being' of the other, and how, for the author, this stage is the last rung on the ladder before spiritual death and rebirth. The shared experience

---

3. René Girard, *Resurrection from the Underground: Feodor Dostoevsky*, trans., James G. Williams (New York: Crossroads Publishing Company, 1997), p. 31. The spelling of 'Dostoevsky' in this translation of *Resurrection from the Underground* differs from its spelling in *Deceit, Desire, and the Novel*.
4. Girard, *Deceit, Desire, and the Novel*, p. 314.
5. Ibid., p. 279.

with other great novelists of this 'conversion', according to Girard, forms the basis of what he calls 'the unity of novelistic conclusions'. In the end it appears that not only is the subject given new life, but also the literary community – the canon of great authors, with properly enlightened critics and readers – is, once again, established.

2. *Debunking the Modern Subject*

In his study of French criticism, *The Death and Return of the Author*, Sean Burke traces the 'serpentine history of influences' that culminated in the attempt to debunk the modern subject.[6] The main thrust of this debunking, according to Burke, is a form of 'textual dispossession' from the scene of writing, what he describes as 'the power of language to organise and orchestrate itself without any subjective intervention whatsoever'.[7] Outlining the consequences of this movement that was not content simply to 'bracket' the concept of the subject, but was determined rather to 'annihilate' it altogether, Burke argues:

> For Barthes, Foucault and Derrida, the expulsion of the subject from the space of language is . . . seen to extend right across the field of human sciences, and to call into question the idea that man can properly possess any degree of knowledge or consciousness. For should it be that all thought should proceed necessarily by way and by virtue of language, then the absence of the subject from language translates into the absence of the subject or consciousness from knowledge. If knowledge itself, or what we take to be knowledge, is entirely intradiscursive, and if, as it is claimed, the subject has no anchorage within discourse, then man as the subject of knowledge is thoroughly displaced and dislodged.[8]

With the advent of 'deconstruction', the new 'postmodern mode of criticism', puts paid to phenomenological hermeneutics and all expressivist theories: 'man can no longer be conceived as the subject of his works, for to be the subject of a text, or of knowledge, is to assume a post ideally exterior to language'.[9] The 'textual dispossession' of 'subject' and 'author' connects with the undermining of the epistemological subject, already well underway in the 1960s, whereby 'knowledge and the subject are seen to be fictive emanations of a language which endlessly subverts all attempts by the human agent to assert any degree of mastery or control.'[10] The original claims of phenomenology and hermeneutics to disclose

---

6. Sean Burke, *The Death and Return of the Author: Criticism and Subjectivity in Barthes, Foucault and Derrida* (Edinburgh: Edinburgh University Press, 1998), p. 10.
7. Ibid., p. 9.
8. Ibid., pp. 14–15.
9. Ibid., p. 15.
10. Ibid.

'deep' or 'hidden' meanings behind the play of language are made increasingly problematic by the new French criticism.[11] But what is lost and, perhaps more importantly from a theoretical point of view, what is gained by such a total rejection of subject and author?

In his much cited essay, 'The Death of the Author', Barthes makes the case that literature should not be understood as an 'expression', but as an impersonal 'play', of linguistic signs. Writing is privileged over any particular stance of the author who relinquishes his status as an experiencing agent with a point of view, and allows his imagination free rein through the process of his art so that nothing of any importance can be attributed to his intention. The result, according to Richard Kearney, is that the 'life of the text presupposes the death of the author.'[12] Furthermore, our understanding of texts must be 'de-psychologized', which 'effectively means *de-humanised* in the sense of dispensing with the claims of romantic idealism and existentialism'.[13] The absence of authorial presence, as the determining characteristic of poststructuralist theories, is the result of the 'textual dispossession' of the subject from the scene of writing.

For Barthes, the author's voice – his or her biography, intention, sensibility etc. – should have no bearing on how we read a text.[14] Language itself works against any potential carry-over of meaning from author to text:

> Structuralist linguistics, Barthes claims, furnishes us with a valuable analytic weapon in the destruction of the author. The discovery of language as a total system of enunciation which functions independently of the *persons* of the interlocutors, shows that the author is never more than the 'instance writing, just as *I* is nothing other than the instance saying "*I*"'.[15]

---

11. The loss of the creative subject associated with humanism and existentialism is characteristic of what Richard Kearney calls the 'parodic' imagination. However, drawing on the mythic language of death and rebirth he queries whether there might be an ethical summons at the heart of postmodernity to help counteract the ceaseless play of difference wrought by parody. 'Even when it can't go on, the postmodern imagination goes on. A child making traces at the edge of the sea. Imagining otherwise. Imagination's wake. Dying? Awaking?' *The Wake of Imagination: Toward a Postmodern Culture* (London: Routledge, 1994), p. 397.
12. Kearney, *The Wake of Imagination*, p. 274. For discussion on Girard as a 'typical' postmodern author who distances himself from a philosophy of subjectivity, see Guy Vanheeswikck, 'René Girard in Contemporary Philosophy', in *Contagion*, vol. 10 (Spring 2003), p. 99.
13. Ibid.
14. The 'tyranny' of centring on the author is based on the following misconception, according to Barthes: 'The explanation of a work is always sought in the man or woman who produced it, as if it were always in the end, through the more or less transparent allegory of the fiction, the voice of a single person, the author "confiding in us."' Quoted in Kearney, *The Wake of Imagination*, p. 275.
15. Ibid.

As a consequence of this linguistic turn, 'patriarchal consciousness' loses it authority since the status of the author can no longer announce itself through the pen and miraculously confer significance on the text.[16] Moreover, words cease to belong to the person of the author who is now accused of taking over the role of god from traditional metaphysics, and of occupying a privileged place as the new 'transcendent reality' to whom all meaning must refer. In this context, Burke argues that the death of the author can be seen to 'fulfil the same function in our day as did the death of God for late nineteenth century thought'.[17] Or as Kearney argues, Barthes's death of the author thus 'follows from the death of God and announces the death of Man'.[18]

It is the author as divinized presence that becomes such a problem for many of the literary theorists of this period (1960s), and this reaction to 'metaphysics' in its now veiled form as 'humanism' is part of the intellectual atmosphere in which Girard becomes a living critic. The identity of the writer and divinity is a definite motif in Barthes's ground-breaking meditation on the question of authorship, one that 'enlivens' his essay.[19] If the author is, in Derrida's words, the 'transcendental signified', all that criticism can do is to accept the role of passive exegete to the author's intentions. The homology between the critic and the medieval cleric is formulated in such a way as to leave no doubt as to who the new servant is. Burke explains it in this way: 'The text is read as natural theologians read nature for marks of design, signs of purpose. Where there is design there must be intention . . . the old law is enshrined as the universal law of literary causality.'[20] The subservient role of the critic that enshrines the author as the glorified 'object' of criticism is for Barthes the groundless perpetuation of a much older form of deception and enslavement – one that makes the 'Author-God' the univocal, absolute author of his work, 'one who precedes, directs and exceeds the writing that bears his name.'[21] To liberate the text from its oppressive author, as Barthes and others of this period hoped to do, is to reiterate the Nietzschean liberation of the world from God, it is to release 'the ceaseless play of differences that the death of God opens in its wake.'[22]

---

16. Kearney describes these developments as follows: 'Language comes to substitute itself for the productive subject who previously had been considered its owner and master . . . and is thereby revealed as a self-referential process with nothing before it or after it . . . as such it is never original – for there is no "origin" outside of itself, i.e. no transcendental reality or transcendental imagination to which it could refer.' *The Wake of Imagination*, pp. 275–276.
17. Burke, *The Death and Return of the Author*, p. 22.
18. Kearney, *The Wake of Imagination*, p. 276.
19. Burke, *The Death and Return of the Author*, p. 23.
20. Ibid.
21. Burke, *The Death and Return of the Author*, p. 24.
22. Ibid., pp. 24–25.

Burke's argument against the undermining of traditional notions of subjectivity centres on the extreme lengths to which Barthes's '*theo-auteurist* criticism' is pushed. The manner in which the latter represents the 'Author-God' leads Burke to contend that it involves more 'construction' than 'destruction'. 'How much, we should ask, of the joyous work of destruction consists in badly constructing the house?'[23] Barthes, he claims, 'must create a king worthy of killing'.[24] This last comment will be instructive for our analysis of *Deceit, Desire, and the Novel*, which details the fall and rise of the author through a deceived quest that eventually yields a lucidity, one that the critic believes is the '*true*' *raison d'être* of the great novels. As we shall see, this quest (a quest for originality) is what Girard calls the 'Romantic illusion' – a lie that the conscious subject (so beloved of humanist theory) must perpetuate at all costs.

A telling sign of Girard's early structuralist sympathies is the manner in which the author/subject 'dies' at the hands of the critic in *Deceit, Desire, and the Novel*. When Girard thus debunks what he calls the 'Romantic subject' he is no longer in the orbit of the humanistic and existentialist projects that maintain a dimension of depth and rational agency within the conscious subject, but is already traversing a literary space that displaces the centrality of a first-person perspective; he is, like Lévi-Strauss, content to 'dissolve man as part of the goal of the new human sciences'.[25] In his contribution to the conference at Johns Hopkins in 1966, attended by many of the new French theorists, he refers to the influence of Lévi-Strauss's work on his own, by then, well-known theory of the novel.[26]

Burke attempts to make explicit what seems to be implicit in the new French theory: that the author is brought back to life to serve the purposes of this theory – so that in Barthes's criticism, for example, we have what he describes as a new form of 'autobiography' characterized by a movement from 'work to life'.[27]

---

23. Ibid., p. 26.
24. 'What is happening in this procedure is that Barthes himself, in seeking to dethrone the author, is led to an apotheosis of authorship that vastly out-paces anything to be found in the critical history he takes arms against.' Ibid.
25. Burke, *The Death and Return of the Author*, p. 13.
26. 'Claude Lévi-Strauss tells us that the real structure of a cultural phenomenon cannot coincide with the spontaneous account given by the subjects themselves. Thus, the application of structural linguistics to phenomena which are extra-linguistic, at least in the narrow sense, necessarily empties these of their original value, destroying the grip on being itself they appear to have within their original context.' René Girard, 'Tiresias and the Critic', in *The Structuralist Controversy: The Languages of Criticism and the Sciences of Man*, eds, R. Maskey, and E. Donbato (Baltimore: Johns Hopkins University Press, 2007c), p. 19.
27. Burke, *The Death and Return of the Author*, p. 27. About Barthes's criticism Burke claims: 'Two balls must be kept constantly in the air: the author will return but the death of the author must stand. The ingenious way in which Barthes

Girard, as we shall see, *does not hide* the reintroduction of the author. He announces the death of the author only in the context of literary space and the religious symbolism that brings new life. There is no evidence that he follows structuralism to the limits that Barthes explores. Indeed from the proceedings of the conference at Johns Hopkins he appears closer to the idea of a 'transcendental intentionality' at work in the creative process as articulated by George Poulet,[28] than to Barthes's purely linguistic subject – since at least the subject is *clearly* 'returned' at the end of *Deceit, Desire, and the Novel*, which is not the case with Barthes's 'Death of the Author'. However, the somewhat different conclusions of Girard and Barthes appear secondary once their common starting point is established: from the beginning the subject is not given any credibility. Whether the author's subjectivity is killed off *a la* Barthes's criticism, or must simply die, *a la* Girard's criticism, is really not the significant feature of his 'death'. What both thinkers have in common, arguably, is that *originality* in Girard's criticism and *expression* in Barthes's criticism are denied any determining say in the creative process. For both, then, the author/subject can be *constituted* only through the act of writing. I shall argue, however, that an unforeseen result for Girard of his alignment here with French structuralism is that the one who 'dies' in the work bears *no relation* to the one 'who is literally born of the death.'[29]

---

negotiates this problem is through recasting the relationship between author and critic in such a way that authorial return does not impinge upon the idea of the birth of the reader. Thus the author will reappear as a desire of the reader's, a spectre spirited back into existence by the critic himself.' *The Death and Return of the Author*, p. 30.

28. Describing how his work differs from someone like Sartre, Poulet says of the author: 'There is no possibility of re-establishing himself in a true, authentic relationship with his own work as soon as the work is finished. That is the position of Sartre . . . I would say that the only possible way for an author to establish himself in an authentic relationship with his work is precisely when that work is finished, and at the same time the intentional concentration with which the author has continuously gone at his work, trying to realise it, has stopped, then it is possible for the author to look at his work in a purely detached way . . . but at the same time it may be with an extreme lucidity, in such a way that it may be only at this exact moment that he can attain the complete knowledge of what he has done.' *The Structuralist Controversy*, pp. 85–86. Although Poulet's criticism exhibits similarities to Girard there are differences as to how much consciousness the author may be said to have from the outset of the work. For the former some original presence is recognized at the end, for the latter authenticity comes through renouncing any claim to originality – desire fundamentally complicates all original presence. See the discussion on Poulet's conference paper, 'Criticism and the experience of Interiority', in *The Structuralist Controversy*, pp. 73–88.

29. Girard, *Deceit, Desire, and the Novel*, p. 312.

3. Self and Other in Literary Structure

Unlike Barthes, perhaps, Girard *explicitly* reintroduces a subject at the end of his major work of criticism – the death of the author is the condition for the life of the author. This spiritual transformation, he believes, occurs in the author's own life. And, it is the author's relationship to the other that plays a pivotal part in his conversion – by providing the basic intersubjective dynamic that gets played out in literary space. From analysing the characters in the novels, what makes Girard believe that the author's spiritual life is in question? Indeed, what allows him to posit a completely new subject *as the fruit* of literary space? To try to answer these questions we need first to turn to Girard's central claim concerning the inter-subjective relation. It is the *dynamic between* individuals that is key to under-standing the author's spiritual journey, and this dynamic is generated by desire. In *Deceit, Desire, and the Novel*, Girard attempts to show that 'desire' is never immediately directed at an object, but is rather always mediated by the other who thus becomes one's model and eventually (in the modern period) one's rival. This process of mediation releases our baser human emotions – in a concentrated and controlled way in the novel. 'The inevitable consequences of desire copied from another desire are "envy, jealousy, and impotent hatred".'[30] These 'vices' are hence the 'stuff' of literary space. Girard spells out the role of the critic in bringing to light the true course of desire or what he calls the 'mysterious' triangular struc-ture of all human relationships. Thus the novelist through his art explores the most charged relationships (emotionally and spiritually). The result is a painful, obliquely gained, knowledge of the emptiness of one's own desires, gained by the author at the end of his 'great' work. 'Working through'[31] the structures within which she is first imprisoned brings a greater degree of lucidity regarding human reality – a lucidity apprehended and articulated by the critic.

Girard eschews the traditional understanding of desire as 'spontaneous' and directed to its object, as it were in a straight line.

> The straight line is present in the desire of Don Quixote, but it is not essential. The mediator is there, above that line, radiating toward both the subject and the object. The spatial metaphor which expresses this triple relationship is obviously the triangle. The object changes with each adventure but the triangle remains. The barber's basin or Master Peter's puppets replace the windmills; but Amadis is always present . . . [Hence] the triangle is no *Gestalt*. The real structures are intersubjective. They cannot be localised anywhere . . .[32]

---

30. Ibid., p. 41.
31. I use 'working through' in Freud's sense discussed in his essay 'Mourning and Melancholia', in *The Freud Reader*, ed. Peter Gay (London: Vintage, 1995).
32. Girard, *Deceit, Desire, and the Novel*, p. 2.

The triangular structure – the substance of the novel – has been gradually brought to light by the 'great' novelists. According to Girard, structural thinking assumes 'that human reality is intelligible: it is a *logos* and as such, it is an incipient *logic*, or it degrades itself into a logic'.[33] With the novelist's experience in mind he tells us that human reality 'can thus be systematised, at least up to a point, however unsystematic, irrational, and chaotic it may appear even to those, or rather especially to those who operate the system'.[34] Arising from this, Girard's thesis is 'that the great writers apprehend concretely and intuitively through the medium of their art, if not formally, the system in which they were first imprisoned together with their contemporaries'.[35] In and through his own struggles the author 'systematizes' his often-chaotic experience of human reality, thus making it intelligible. Speaking of the critic's role in recovering this logic, Girard writes, '[l]iterary interpretation must be systematic because it is the continuation of literature. It should formalise implicit or already half explicit systems.'[36] Thus the value of criticism depends on 'how much literary substance it really embraces, comprehends and *makes articulate*'.[37] From the linguistic model of subjectivity that Girard outlines here, we can say: *language* speaks louder than individuals. For the critic, human reality is ascertainable as literary substance; his or her role then is like that of the analyst (though from a historical distance) who brings to light through a peculiar therapeutics the true image of the subject and his or her world.

The triangular structure allows Girard to detect the true course of desire as it appears to flow from the various protagonists in the novels that he treats, and structure the relationships between them. He argues that we can only really understand what constitutes these relationships when we see that, despite, or perhaps because of the individual's belief to the contrary, desire does not originate in the subject and rest on objects by virtue of their intrinsic value. Rather it is aroused and finds its object by virtue of a model that holds some prestige or fascination for the subject.

The role of the model in directing the individual to objects forces her to greater degrees of misapprehension in her struggle for a self-possessed consciousness. Girard finds no shortage of cases of mediated desire in the wide array of works by 'great' novelists – for example, in Stendhal's *De l'Amour*, Proust's *Remembrance of Things Past*, Molierè's *Don Juan*. Here I shall advert to two widely divergent novelists (in time as well as in style), Cervantes and Dostoevsky. In Dostoevsky's *The Eternal Husband* Pavel Povlovitch Troussotzkie (the 'husband'), through

---

33. Ibid., p. 3.
34. Ibid.
35. Ibid.
36. Ibid.
37. Ibid, (my italics).

a peculiar fascination, seeks out his deceased wife's ex-lover, to help him become attracted once again to a new wife.

> The Eternal Husband . . . [throws a light] on the novelistic triangle so brilliant it dazzles us . . . The hero is always trying to convince us that his relationship to the object of desire is independent of the rival. Here we see quite clearly the hero is deceiving us. The mediator is immobile and the hero turns around him like a sun . . . Pavel Pavlovitch can desire only through the mediation of Veltchaninov . . . [He] drags Veltchaninov along to the house of the lady he has chosen, so that he might desire her and thus guarantee her erotic value.[38]

Girard also discusses Cervantes' 'The Curious Impertinent' which, he claims, portrays a 'triangular desire exactly like that of Pavel Pavovitch'.[39] In a similar way to the example just given, the protagonist Anselmo pushes his wife into the arms of his good friend Lothario (who had introduced the couple) in an attempt to excite an ultimately morbid desire.

> Anselmo has just married the pretty young Camilla. The marriage was arranged with the help of Lothario, a very dear friend of the happy husband. Some time after the wedding Anselmo makes a curious request to Lothario. He begs him to pay court to Camilla, claiming that he wishes 'to test' her faithfulness.[40]

Taking the triangular structure of desire into account in Cervantes and Dostoevsky, the critic concludes: 'No literary influence can explain the points of contact between "The Curious Impertinent" and *The Eternal Husband*. The differences are all differences of form, while the resemblances are resemblances of essence.'[41]

All the protagonists in the novels reveal a similar insistence that their desires are theirs and *not* in fact mediated – an insistence that is essentially deceived. Each one of them believes in his uniqueness, his self-sufficiency and 'totality' – as a unity attributable to his own special essence – that the other's apparent happiness or fullness disrupts and disperses. Inner division thus prompts him to generate greater degrees of illusion in an effort to excite an unconquerable desire, and to prove once and for all that he is original. This belief in the uniqueness and separateness of the hero, however, is exactly what the structure of the novel will expose as false in the very process of revealing the mediated nature of desire.

According to Girard, the *aporia* that traditional philosophies and psychologies encounter in attempting to understand the 'self/other' relation stems from the same static understanding of desire as having its source in the subject and attaching to objects due to their inherent worth. One of Girard's main contributions to

---

38. Girard, *Deceit, Desire, and the Novel*, pp. 46–47.
39. Ibid., p. 49.
40. Ibid.
41. Ibid., p. 51.

French psychology comes from his radical thesis concerning desire as a dynamic that 'gives rise to the self and by its movement animates it'.[42] The self is thus always brought into being in the search for a model whose desires it seeks to imitate and take as its own.

Girard characterizes the intimate belief that our desires are really our own as a self-deception which he claims is 'the dearest of all our illusions'.[43] The 'great' novelists have explored the *aporia* of desire and how it can lead to deception and hatred.

> We believe that 'novelistic' genius is won by a great struggle against these attitudes we have lumped together under the name 'romantic' because they all appear to us to maintain the illusion of spontaneous desire and of a subjectivity almost divine in its autonomy. Only slowly and with difficulty does the novelist go beyond the romantic he was at first and who refuses to die. He finally achieves this in the 'novelistic' work and in that work alone.[44]

Only truly 'great' novels apprehend the triangular 'essence' that literary space yields. 'As Girard conceives it there are novelists and novels that live up to the potential for the elucidation of human reality, and there are others that fail to do so.'[45] Great literature is thus a source of genuine knowledge, and those who read the great works, Girard claims, and follow in the footsteps of the novelist, 'relive the spiritual experience whose form is the novel itself'.[46] To do so is to discover what the novelist discovers, which is, that our desires are not our own, but rather belong to the models we either consciously or unconsciously admire and imitate (and of course these models have in turn other models for their desires). As Eugene Webb explains: 'Girard terms such models "mediators" because they function as go-betweens linking us to our objects of desire as well as our aspirations for personal being.'[47] Webb goes on to suggest that: 'In Girard's analysis there are two basic possibilities in mediation: (1) that which leads almost inevitably to conflict, because the self and its model are both competitors *within the same field of action*, and (2) that which does not, because the self and its model cannot be competitors, since their fields of action do not overlap. He calls the first one "internal mediation" and the second "external mediation".'[48] Hence in the novel mediation can take a largely benign external form, as in the case of Cervantes' *Don Quixote*, or a largely malign internal form, as in the case of Dostoevsky's *Notes from*

---

42. Eugene Webb, *The Self Between: From Freud to the New Social Psychology of France* (Washington: University of Washington Press, 1993), p. 7.
43. Ibid., p. 9.
44. Girard, *Deceit, Desire, and the Novel*, pp. 28–29.
45. Webb, *The Self Between*, p. 96.
46. Girard, *Deceit, Desire, and the Novel*, pp. 221–222.
47. Webb, *The Self Between*, p. 92.
48. Ibid., p. 93.

the Underground. However, the latter form of internal mediation, or negative mimesis, is the predominant concern of Girard's first two works of criticism because, as we shall see, it is the form that leads to 'inner division' and the dissolution of consciousness that nothing short of spiritual conversion can overcome. In order to fully comprehend the author's achievement we must first fully comprehend the depths to which he must travel in and through his work.

4. *Fusion and Separation: The Futility of the Romantic Spirit*

How does the self become divided to the point that it requires a radical transformation that fashions a unity for the author as well as providing the grounds for a literary community? According to Girard, the mistake that all the heroes of the novels make is that they convince themselves that their own desires are unique, and therefore attributable to their own special being.[49] What they desire has to be desirable because each in his or her singularity desires it. The hero's desire thus flows from him as an expression of his 'Being'. What these protagonists struggle to realize is that the object they each desire is only a means of reaching the other, usually their rival, whose prestige they have exalted. Behind the façade of objects, Girard tells us, 'desire is aimed at the mediator's being'.[50] Despite their attempts to convince themselves otherwise through their various encounters and exploits, the heroes get closer and closer to the awful truth of their dependence on a mediator for their sense of sufficiency; and this 'knowledge' divides them inwardly against themselves.[51]

The inner division that the Romantic hero experiences is exacerbated by the proximity of a model or mediator who, because he is the model, unwittingly reminds the hero – who cannot abide the thought that he is imitating anyone – of how utterly devoid of real substance he is. Since the model holds the key to how

---

49. Traditional philosophical concepts of desire were considered either 'rationalist' or 'voluntarist'. Taking our lead from Socrates' dialogue with Euthyphro, we might say that the rationalist desires something because it is desirable (substance), while the voluntarist might see the value of the object arising from the fact that they desire it (accident). Girard rejects both these concepts for what we might call a mediationalist view of desire, whereby a subject desires the object because others confer it with value. See, B. Jowett, trans., *The Dialogues of Plato*, Volume I (London: Sphere Books, 1970).

50. Girard, *Deceit, Desire, and the Novel*, p. 53.

51. Inner division is a form of alienation that is primarily psychological: 'All heroes of novels hate themselves . . . It is exactly as the narrator says at the beginning of Swann's Way: "Everything which was not myself, the earth and the creatures upon it, seemed to me more precious and more important, endowed with a more real existence". The curse with which the hero is burdened is indistinguishable from his subjectivity.' Girard, *Deceit, Desire, and the Novel*, p. 55.

I see myself, my failure to acknowledge the model *as model* and my insistence on my own originality leads the divisions within myself to generate two opposing images, one of 'self *and* other', and one of 'self *as* other', that constantly threaten to merge. When the Romantic hero manages to keep these images apart through always excessive exploits he experiences a sense (albeit illusory) of 'Being', self-sufficiency and integration. When he fails – as we shall see later in the case of Dostoevsky – he experiences 'Nothingness', self-loathing and disintegration. As long as imitation takes the form of external mediation, the rivalry between self and other and the likelihood of inter-subjective crisis are held in check. However, the problems that beset Dostoevsky's characters occur when the model gets too close, that is when external mediation turns to internal mediation and 'benign' imitation turns to rivalry. As the distance between the mediator and the subject decreases, differences diminish, and . . .

> . . . the comprehension becomes more acute and the hatred more intense. It is always his own desire that the subject condemns in the Other without knowing it. Hatred is individualistic. It nourishes fiercely the illusion of an absolute difference between Self and Other from which nothing separates it. Indignant comprehension is therefore an imperfect comprehension – not non-existent as some moralists claim, but imperfect, for the subject does not recognise in the Other the void gnawing at himself. He makes of him a monstrous divinity.[52]

To understand the imitative nature of desire is to understand how this division structures the lives and desires of the characters in the novels that Girard treats. The key to this structure is the Romantic figure who functions as a kind of archetype for autonomous being, standing apart and believing in his own separation, independence and, as Girard ordinarily understands it, his own selfhood. 'The romantic *vaniteux* does not want to be anyone's disciple. He convinces himself that he is thoroughly original.'[53]

However, the lens of the critic affords a view of literary space that is altogether different from that of the protagonist. The critical lens shows that '[i]mitative desire is always a desire to be Another.'[54] The problem for the Romantic figure, according to Girard, is that he does not see his desires as imitative, but rather as singularly his own. Therefore, he remains unaware that, in all his vain pursuits, he is attempting to appropriate the 'Being' of the other, or the other's desires, which he seeks to maintain *as his own*.[55] However, when the triangular structure of

---

52. Ibid., p. 73.
53. Ibid., p. 15.
54. Ibid., p. 83.
55. According to Girard, it is neither the movement toward the self, nor the movement toward the other that is primary, the dynamic of desire itself is the principle structure. This is one of the claims of Girardian theory that I will challenge: He places the emphasis on desire without any capacity for the subject as agent to take control and determine his or her desire in one direction or another.

the novel is revealed, the 'originality and spontaneity' is exposed as false, as is the much-prised 'separation' between self and other. The 'subject' as he appears in the novels (as protagonist) is simply a negative datum, whose self-deceptions and mistaken desires colour all his intersubjective relationships.[56]

The hero's misapprehension concerning the real source of his desires thus has to do with the object that is valued, and how he sees himself (his very 'Being'), reflected in this object – nothing short of the possession of which will fulfil. 'The romantic *vaniteux* always wants to convince himself that his desire is written into the nature of things, or, what amounts to the same thing, that it is the emanation of a serene subjectivity, the creation *ex nihilo* of a divine ego.'[57] The more the *vaniteux* seeks independence the more he inevitably fuses with the desires of his model who, no doubt, by proving himself to be in every way superior to his disciple and by barring access to the quasi-sacred object, has become an obstacle to the *vaniteux's* 'divine self-sufficiency'. Girard tells us that the felt need to see our desires as our own grows in proportion to our proximity to the model that we are in fact imitating. 'The closer the mediator gets to the desiring subject, the more the possibilities of the two rivals *merge* and the more insuperable becomes the obstacle they set in each other's way.'[58] This merger or fusion with the other is brought about by an attempt to secure its opposite – separation. And so it is also the terrifying reminder of the subject's dependence and his utter lack of 'divine' self-sufficiency – indeed of 'Being' itself.

Because of the danger that the 'Other' poses to the Romantic hero's ideal spiritual quest, his intra-psychic world – although darkened with uncertainty – becomes the space of constant retreat. This movement inward, as the model approaches, is, for Girard, always at the heart of internal mediation and the dynamics that lead deeper into 'the underground' of human reality, where the negative emotions of fear and hatred dominate. Withdrawal is thus a feature of the concealment of desire and therefore constitutes what Girard calls the Romantic hero's spiritual *askesis*.[59] The analogy between the literary quest and the spiritual quest is developed in *Deceit, Desire, and the Novel* when the critic compares the Romantic hero's search for divine self-sufficiency with St Augustine's quest for God, the eternal essence. Describing the paradoxical dynamics of the hero's pride, Girard writes: 'The impulse of the soul toward God is inseparable

---

56. Girard, *Deceit, Desire, and the Novel*, pp. 2–3.
57. Ibid., p. 15.
58. Ibid., p. 26. The notion of the 'mode/obstacle' is later described in Girard's anthro-pological work as the 'stumbling block' or 'scandalon' (from the Greek verb 'to stumble'), into which the obsessive individual continually runs in his or her vain attempts to be original. René Girard, *Things Hidden since the Foundation of the World: Research Undertaken in Collaboration with J.-M. Oughourlian and G. Lefort*, trans., S. Bann and M. Metteer (Stanford: Stanford University Press, 1987b).
59. Girard, *Deceit, Desire, and the Novel*, p. 153.

from a retreat into the Self. Inversely the turning in on itself of pride is inseparable from a movement of panic toward the Other. To refashion St. Augustine's formula, pride is more exterior to us than the external world. This externality of pride . . . makes us live a life turned away from ourselves . . .'[60] With the analogy between the lover of the eternal essence and the lover of the world – between the Saint and the Romantic – we have in effect not *two different loves* (as, for example, we find in Augustine's theory of the will), but rather two entirely different kinds of subject, one with genuine interiority and the other without this because always caught up in illusory pursuits that pull him outward.[61] Speaking about the 'religious world' of the novel in relation to Stendhal's *The Red and the Black*, Girard writes:

> Just as the mystic turns from the world in order that God may turn toward him and give him the gift of His grace, Julien turns away from Mathilde in order that Mathilde may turn toward him and make him the object of her own desire. *Askesis* for the sake of desire is just as legitimate and productive, in the triangular context, as 'vertical' *askesis* is in the framework of religious vision. The analogy between deviated transcendency and vertical transcendency is even closer than we first suspected.[62]

For Girard, such an analogy is very much in keeping with the privileged place he gives to literary space. However, by introducing a dichotomy between 'literary self' and 'spiritual self' he arguably downplays the significance of Augustine's concept of the divided will, a concept that manages to explain the fractured nature of the self by understanding the conflict here as arising from two tendencies of the one will rather that two subjects. This is an argument to which I will return in Part II of my book.

---

60. Ibid., pp. 58–59.
61. Terry Eagleton presents us with a poststructuralist assessment of desire that is remarkably close to Girard's account of the Romantic hero's spiritual vocation – reminding us of Girard's early affinity with the new French theory. Eagleton writes: 'Desire, in Jacques Lacan's famous slogan is the desire of the Other. To desire another is to desire what that other desires, since this desire is of the other's "essence", and only by identifying with it can we therefore become one with the other. This is a paradoxical claim, however, since desire, which splits and disperses the subject, is no kind of essence at all; so that to desire the other's desire is to be as extrinsic to them as they are to themselves, caught up in the process of their own decentrement.' *The Ideology of the Aesthetic* (Cambridge: Basil Blackwell/ Cambridge University Press, 1990), p. 277, my italics. As with triangular desire that is mediated primarily by our external relationships, the Lacanian 'desire for the Other' is more 'external to us than the external world.' Thus, the interior Augustinian quest for the 'God of the human heart' is denied tout court.
62. Girard, *Deceit, Desire, and the Novel*, pp. 155–156.

5. *Underground Psychology: Dostoevsky's 'The Double'*

Having considered how the Romantic belief in spontaneous desire leads to internal mediation and hence division, Girard explains how this condition becomes exacerbated to the point of crisis. Referring to Dostoevsky's *Notes from the Underground*, Girard argues that the narrator's most intense suffering proceeds from the fact that he does not manage to distinguish himself concretely from the persons around him (even though he thinks that he does). It is only slowly that he becomes aware of this failure. 'All underground individuals believe they are all the more "unique" to the extent that they are, in fact, alike.'[63] The rivalry between Dostoevsky's characters is based on a futile attempt to make differences, that are in fact illusory, appear real. The more the rivalry escalates the more the characters begin to resemble each other. The theme of 'the double' recurs throughout Girard's work as a way of describing the symmetry and reciprocity that lead to a loss of differentiation and to conflict. Referring to the depersonalization of Czarist bureaucracy explored in Dostoevsky's *The Double*, Girard writes, 'the individuals constantly opposed to one another cannot understand that their actual personalities are in the process of dissolving'[64] into one indistinct identity.

The structure of the novel allows us to glimpse how the interior world of the characters and the external world they inhabit begin to mirror each other.[65] In *The Double* we find that the madness in the former world continually meets the madness in the latter – the internal and external worlds, the subjective and objective experiences merge. Girard adds to Otto Rank's study of the theme of 'the double' in Dostoevsky's work the observation that, in the novel, the social world and the private world are indistinguishable.[66] He argues that it is not enough to conclude, as Rank does, that the 'milieu favours madness', when this milieu (the intensely bureaucratic nature of nineteenth-century St. Petersburg) is only the external face of a structure whose internal face is the 'hallucination' of the double. 'The phenomenon itself is double in that it bears with it a subjective dimension and an objective dimension that converge in the same result.'[67] This convergence is depicted in the novel by the two Golyadkins, one the intensely self-conscious protagonist and the other the concrete manifestation of the collective persona of all the little petty bureaucrats. Where psychiatry fails, it comes

---

63. Girard, *Resurrection from the Underground*, p. 58.
64. Girard, *Resurrection from the Underground*, p. 59.
65. As with the depiction of the 'enemy twins' common to mythology, or the caricature of 'Punch and Judy' in popular culture, opposing sides become mirror images of each other in and through the escalating violence. We will explore how Girard applies this loss of differentiation to culture as a whole in the following chapter.
66. See Otto Rank, *The Double: A Psychoanalytic Study* (London: Karnac Books, 1989).
67. Girard, *Resurrection from the Underground*, p. 59.

down to the novelist to pose the problem of the double, for it seems only he can place the social structures in question, which he does, profoundly, through his art.

Girard tells us that *The Double* and *Notes from the Underground* are two efforts at the same truth. It is pride in each case that leads to disintegration. In the case of Golyadkin it takes the form of a powerful hallucination. 'This proud man believes he is *one* in his solitary dream, but in his failure he divides in two and becomes a contemptible person and a contemptuous observer of the human scene. He becomes Other to himself.'[68] To the extent that the external model and rival gets close to the protagonist, by in turn imitating him perhaps, he reinforces the contemptuous internal other that results from the protagonist's failure to maintain his own 'originality' – a failure that (as we shall see) appears inevitable in the modern period. The division that pertains to this failure, when it becomes acute in the scene of the individuals' interpersonal existence, gives rise to the hallucination of 'the double'. After giving a startling example of Golyadkin's 'love/hate' relationship with his peers, Girard discusses the double movement that leads to the convergence of the inner and the outer worlds:

> The scornful observer, the Other who is in the Self, unceasingly approaches the Other who is outside of the Self, the triumphant rival. We have seen, moreover, that this triumphant rival, this Other outside of the Self whose desire I imitate and who imitates mine, constantly comes closer to the Self. To the extent that the interior rupture of consciousness is reinforced, the distinction between Self and Other weakens. The two movements converge to produce the 'hallucination' of the double. The hallucinatory phenomenon constitutes the outcome and synthesis of all the intersubjective and objective doublings that define underground existence.[69]

This 'ontological illness' is not curable by traditional science. While psychiatry seeks to heal patients by leading them back to a sense of 'objectivity', Girard suggests that the 'objectivity' of Golyadkin is, in some ways, *superior* to that of the 'normal' persons surrounding him. What makes the great works 'great' is their ability to 'work through' the failed unity and division: it is, in other words, their constant attempts to 'up the ante' on the previous works that fail to achieve unity (and thereby the status of a 'great' novel) and to find the perfect unity that stands independently. But this search for perfection forces Dostoevsky's characters further underground to where the divisions multiply in direct proportion to the desire for unity.

We can infer from Girard's analysis that Romantic desire in its 'weaker form' does not leave the individual 'divided' in himself to the same degree that we find in the more extreme examples of underground existence. There are, it seems,

---

68. Ibid., p. 60.
69. Ibid., p. 61.

degrees of obsession at work here that only the great novelists manage fully to explore.[70] The obsessive dynamism at work in the great novels is thus played out on a broader socio-historical plane, as we shall see in the following section. For the Romantic who, through favourable circumstances and perhaps 'luck', manages his existence well, the social world, although at times dubious, is still a convincing whole. But the 'unlucky' Romantic who clings to the illusion of a self-generating 'unitary identity', while one dream after another collapses, will persist with his desire to the point of madness – or indeed genius. Romantic desire as Girard describes it is no mere 'romanticism'.

> Romantics never recognise their own doublings, and thus they only make them worse. Romantics want to believe they are perfectly one. They choose one of the two halves of themselves – in the romantic era properly named, this is generally the ideal and sublime half, while in our day it is the rather sordid half. But whichever half the romantic tries to pass it off as the totality. Pride seeks to prove that it can gather and unify every thing around itself.[71]

But this is exactly what pride can *not* do. For it is not a power of uniting but rather 'a power of dividing and dispersing'.[72] Dostoevsky's works of genius bring the two halves of underground consciousness together. 'It is not their impossible synthesis that the writer presents, but their painful juxtaposition at the heart of the same individual.'[73] The author's creative genius, accessible through his art, reveals this ineradicable division, and, for this reason, Girard believes, it is a work that truly 'gathers'.[74]

6. The Romantic Lie, and the Historical Struggle for Consciousness

The scale of the disintegration wrought by the unwitting imitation of the other's desires is not confined to an analysis of the self/other relation. In Girard's theory,

---

70. In an essay Girard wrote for the English translation of 'Resurrection from the Underground', he tells us: 'We can formulate the law of the underground in terms of mimetic desire as a fairly benign illness, no doubt, unless it is pushed to what Dostoevsky calls its logical extremes, and then it turns into what I called the obstacle addiction . . . underground people are irresistibly attracted to those who spurn them and they irresistibly spurn those who are attracted to them, or even those who do no more than treat them kindly.' Girard, *Resurrection from the Underground*, p. 152.
71. Ibid., p. 63.
72. Ibid., p. 54.
73. Ibid., p. 64.
74. Sadly perhaps, Dostoevsky's own personal biography, according to Girard, attests to the painful 'divisions' that characterizes underground existence. Girard, *Resurrection from the Underground*. pp. 64–70.

the novel as a historical force reflects the quintessential drama of humanity. Part of the reason he privileges the 'literary space' that renders the triangle 'substantive', as a basic structure of human relations, is the role he sees the novelist play in history. He believes the struggle for consciousness is not purely a philosophical task. Contra the objective struggles for consciousness that form part of the logical movement of history in the Hegelian scheme, Girard argues that the novel is the home of true existential insight:

> The Hegelian dialectic is situated in a violent past. It exhausts its last force with the appearance of the nineteenth century and of democracy. The novelistic dialectic on the contrary appears in the post-Napoleonic universe . . . (The) novelist mistrusts logical deductions. He looks around him and within him. He finds nothing to indicate that the famous reconciliation is just around the corner. Stendhalian vanity, Proustian snobbism, and the Dostoyevskian underground are the new forms assumed by the struggle of consciousness in a universe of physical non-violence.[75]

In their work the great novelists confront the 'image we all have of our own desires';[76] they explore human conflict at its most intense and its most intimate.

> It is the 'underground' forms of the struggle of consciousness which are studied by the modern novelists. If the novel is the source of the greatest existential and social truth in the nineteenth century, it is because only the novel has turned its attention to the regions of existence where spiritual existence has taken refuge . . . Only the novelist, precisely to the extent to which he is capable of recognising his own servitude, gropes toward the concrete – toward that hostile dialogue between self and other which parodies the Hegelian struggle for recognition.[77]

Underground psychology, as the site of a peculiar division within the self, parodies the Hegelian struggle for recognition. Through its entanglements with 'the Other' in which 'Being' is always at stake, the self, for Girard, is not a vehicle of *Geist* (as in the Hegelian dialectic), but rather must come to the humble realization that its historical becoming is also an illusion based on its belief in 'originality'.

Any foundation or ground that the individual occupies is in fact less solid as a result of his struggles, forcing him further and further under as the divisions within the self multiply.[78] History thus constitutes a descent (a terminal case of

---

75. Girard, *Deceit, Desire, and the Novel*, p. 110.
76. 'The objective and subjective fallacies are the same; both originate in the image we have of our own desires.' Girard, *Deceit, Desire, and the Novel*, p. 16.
77. Ibid., p. 111.
78. Much of how Girard describes this existential 'working through' of the author in the novel can be compared quite fruitfully, to Kierkegaard's aesthetic stage whereby the youth who attempts to hold onto the 'perfect self', and embody the

what Girard calls 'deviated transcendence').[79] In this world every statement designed to justify human's existence as noble and worthy rings so hollow that they must dig even deeper into the *illusory substance* of their being to try, in vain of course, to compensate for the profound sense of being out of joint. Nothing of Renaissance and Enlightenment humanism is preserved, as the individual's inner life becomes the shadowy realm brought about through self-deception. For Girard, the individual soul, in the modern period, cannot be reborn out of itself and its own achievements, since without external hierarchy to guarantee positive imitation, its attempt to take over the role of God increasingly divides it, precisely to the extent that it believes it is separate (or individual). For example, in Pico's *Oration* on human dignity we find a concept of the individual diametrically opposed to Girard's: 'Thou shalt have the power to degenerate into the lower forms of life, which are brutish. Thou shalt have the power, out of thy own soul's judgement, to be reborn with the higher forms, which are divine.'[80] In contrast to Renaissance humanism, in Girard's literary criticism there is no faith in the individual's power to raise itself up spiritually since there is nothing left of itself to trust in. Rather the individual's power is only realized in its capacity to pull itself down. Salvation, it seems, must come entirely from outside the self.

Girard views this 'literary existentialism' as a dynamic stage of historical development. It is part of the transition from the premodern religious world of theology where things held their meaning through nature and theologians looked to nature for marks of design.[81] He describes the transition to the modern world as a period when 'men become gods in each others eyes,'[82] since they reflect the

---

figure of the God-Man, will according to Kearney, desperately contrive to negate those divisions which constitute his 'out of joint existence'. *The Wake of Imagination*, p. 206. However, the 'textual revolution', that Girard is arguably a part of, cannot be considered existential in the same way as Kierkegaard's work is existential, since we cannot view the latter's 'silencing' of the author as an absolute nullifying of selfhood without considerable difficulties when thinking of him as a religious figure.

79. Girard, *Deceit, Desire, and the Novel*, p. 289. 'Deviated transcendence' is a term that Girard contrasts negatively with premodern 'vertical transcendence'.

80. Quoted from 'On the Dignity of Man' in E. Cassirer, P. O. Kristeller and J. H. Randall, Jr., *The Renaissance Philosophy of Man* (Chicago: University of Chicago Press, 1948), pp. 224–225.

81. See Burkes' criticism of 'the death and return of the author' discussed above.

82. Girard, *Deceit, Desire, and the Novel*, p. 53. There is an extensive body of literature critiquing Girard for his sexist use of language, his positing of male desire as normative, and his gender neutrality (especially in his early work); all of which, it is maintained, perpetuate male power at the expense of women. See, Nancy B. Jay, *Throughout Your Generation Forever: Sacrifice, Religion and Paternity* (Chicago: University of Chicago Press, 1992); Toril Moi, 'The Missing Mother: The Oedipal Rivalries of René Girard', in *Diacritics*, Vol. 12, No. 2 (Summer 1982); Luce Irigaray, 'Women, the Sacred and Money' in *Paragraph: The Journal of the*

divine status that the self desperately seeks to appropriate for itself now that traditional religion is on the decline.

> Men boast of having discarded their old superstitions but they are gradually sinking into an underworld ruled by illusions which become increasingly obvious. But as the gods are pulled down from heaven the sacred flows over the earth; it separates the individual from all earthly goods; it creates a gulf between him and the world of *ici-bas* far greater than that which used to separate him from the *au-dela*. The earth's surface where others live becomes an inaccessible paradise.[83]

Modern Critical Theory Group 8 (1986). While these positions reflect a genuine concern to unmask patriarchy some feminist perspectives differ considerably as to how Girardian theory should be understood. Girard's early analysis of desire appears to be male centred, however his theory of the scapegoat develops this analysis into a critique of mythic, often patriarchal, structures that have traditionally marginalized and done violence to women. On this point see Patricia Klindeinst, 'The Voice of the Shuttle Is Ours', in *Literary Theory: An Anthology*, eds, Julie Rivkin and Michael Ryan (Oxford: Blackwell, 2001), and Susan Nowak (Syracuse University), *The Girardian Theory and Feminism: Critique and Appropriation*, paper presentation at CoV&R Conference in Chapel Hill, April 22–24, 1993. Both of these thinkers in different ways draw constructively on Girard's work, the former by analysing the scapegoat theory in the context of representations of women in myth and the latter by critiquing feminist analyses of Girard for focusing too much on his implicit gender neutrality at the expense of a productive engagement with his account of differentiation. My own study is not unaware of the problems posed for Girardian theory in relation to feminism, however the 'substantive problematic' falls outside the scope of my enquiry. While not wanting to downplay the issue of gender, my main aim is to critique the absence of an ethical subject – one who can take a stand somewhere. In so far as I draw attention to the inconsistency between Girard's early and later works with respect to his treatment of desire (see Chapter 3) I hope that my work places the tension in feminist approaches to Girard mentioned above in some relief. Girard himself acknowledges the greater responsibility of men in the generative processes of collective violence, and even makes the point that when woman are made to appear responsible for such violence (as in Euripides' The Bacchae), it is probably owing to a mythological displacement on behalf of the author which exculpates men. On this point see *Violence and the Sacred*, trans., Patrick Gregory (Baltimore: Johns Hopkins University Press, 1984) p. 142. For a discussion of the significance of Girard's work in the context of the preponderance of women in myths involving sacrifice see Andrew O'Shea, 'The Lystrata Project: Intercultural Resistance and the Economy of Sacrifice', in *Intercultural Spaces: Language, Culture, Identity*, A. Pearson-Evans and A. Leahy, eds (New York: Peter Lang, 2007). For more general criticism, including the feminist critique, see Richard J. Golsan, *René Girard and Myth: An Introduction* (New York: Routledge, 2002), pp. 107–128.

83. Girard, *Deceit, Desire, and the Novel*, p. 62.

The contrast of the *postlapsarian* world to an earlier *prelapsarian* world is significant. Unlike in the earlier world, human beings are now cut off from themselves, isolated as selves that still exist among others. 'Deviated transcendence' becomes a 'historical' phenomenon. Human beings, instead of achieving self-realization or historical becoming, have left their previous state only to fall more and more into illusion.

But if the novel is now a source of truth in the absence of metaphysics, Girard is not inclined to replace the old gods with a divine humanist subject. On the contrary his whole argument is, like Barthes' *theo-auteurist criticism*, that the human being takes over the role of God *in the absence of 'God'*. But unlike Barthes, Girard believes that the consequences of this move are grave, since without a religious horizon to govern their relations externally, men will imitate each other, and instead of inner peace – which was at least a possibility within the older forms of vertical imitation, or 'external mediation' – individuals now only find increasing levels of unhappiness.

The modern autonomous subject, as well as falling prey to base obsessions, has a powerful, albeit illusory, status that can also lure people into rivalry, hatred and conflict. The unavoidable worship of these 'false gods' in a modern context is a source of profound concern for Girard, since the truth, he believes, is that the human beings are ashamed of their imitation and must hide it at all costs. The self whose vocation is to divinize itself 'refuses to recognise the fearsome problem that the presence of the other poses'.[84] It is thus this fearsome problem and human being's attempts to disguise it that generates grandiose schemes and projects. The modern subject thus must conceal its resentment under the pretence of 'originality', in the same way that traditional Christianity, according to Nietzsche, hid its 'real motivations' under a veneer of morality. The Romantic-humanist subject thus suffers from a 'slave morality' that Girard exposes as a form of self-deception.

For Girard, the intensification of the negative dynamic between self and other in the modern age occurs behind the screen of a philosophy of consciousness. The autonomous rational agent of the Enlightenment withers in the anarchic void of the underground. At the core of humanism is an extremely decadent individualism. 'The illusion present in the forms of individual thought . . . defines pride correctly by virtue of its very individualism.'[85] Pride, for Girard, is the determining characteristic of the underground – a Romantic pride that attempts to pass its divided nature off as singular.[86] The stories of Dostoevsky remind us that, wherever our 'best interest' may lie, 'the proud always prefer the most abject slavery to the egoism recommended by the false wisdom of a decadent humanism.'[87] Every enterprise of the modern individual recoils back on itself, generating more and more division. The progression of Dostoevsky's creative

---

84. Girard, *Resurrection from the Underground*, p. 94.
85. Ibid., p. 54.
86. 'Romantics want to believe they are perfectly one', Ibid., p. 62.

work charts the succession of a Promethean desire to overcome these divisions by dint of the individual's own will. Each time we find 'a new rupture that is brought about at a more elevated level than the prior one and whose aesthetic and spiritual fruits will be accordingly more remarkable'.[88] By uncovering the core structure of these dynamics with the help of the spatial metaphor, Girard shows how Dostoevsky's creative work is 'always bound to a feverish interrogation that bears on the creator himself and on his relations with others'.[89]

Any 'ethic' associated with modern individualism must sooner or later fall under the sway of a pride that continually attempts to announce its own independence even, if not especially, in the face of overwhelming evidence to the contrary – suggesting that the subject depends more than ever on the other. In this view, the modern individual will shore up it's own separation from others and assume the mantle of virtue while doing so. The ethical subject is radically undermined here, since ethics is understood ultimately as a futile ruse to justify the Romantic hero's facile sense of 'self-sufficiency'.

For Girard, historical 'becoming', without a shred of genuine consciousness, is a negative unfolding, or unravelling. The subject thus appears as utterly beyond the realm of the good. The critic relies heavily here on the ineluctability of Dostoevsky's existential insights to make his case concerning historical change. The effects of what Dostoevsky expresses so well in *Notes from the Underground*, Girard argues, have made themselves felt well before the nineteenth century. Describing where these 'concealed but recognisable' effects first emerge he says:

> Perhaps it is most suitable to seek the first traces of our malaise in the very origin of the era of the individualist, in that morality of *generosity* that Descartes, the first philosopher of individualism, and Corneille, its first dramatist, developed at the same time ... It is significant that rationalist individualism and the irrational morality of generosity appear conjointly. If one considers this 'generosity' in light of *Demons*, one will see there perhaps the beginning of an 'underground' dynamic whose moments correspond to the metamorphoses of morality and sensibility, as they work themselves out in the contemporary period.[90]

When confronted with the awesome problem of 'the Other' in the modern period (as men become gods in each other's eyes) the 'morality of generosity' is exposed as a form of attempted self-divinization. The more the subject tries to prove to itself that it is benevolent, the more it relies on 'the Other' to dignify its 'acts of kindness'. Thus the morality of generosity, for Girard, is the ultimate ruse of the Romantic hero who wants to be original – even in what he deigns to bestow on others. However, when his pride fails to be acknowledged as good, and hence to

---

87. Ibid., p. 55.
88. Ibid., p. 85.
89. Ibid.
90. Ibid., p. 94.

convince him of his 'generosity', he gropes for a 'higher' degree of confidence in, what will be yet another failed act of self-deception that leads further into the underground. According to Girard, all of history since Descartes and Corneille is an attempt to maintain an ever-shrinking distance between self and other and their competing attempts at 'self-divinisation.' An absolute distinction is hence the ultimate illusion. We shall now turn briefly to Girard's account of Dostoevsky's vision of man's failed yet prophetic attempt at historical becoming.

7. Failure to Gather: 'The Dostoyevskian Apocalypse'

If we accept that Romantic desire is responsible for the confusions that lead to the pathologies of underground existence then Girard also asks us, albeit indirectly, to acknowledge that this belief in 'spontaneity' and 'originality' is the source of the revelation of novelistic structure. Without novelists who fall under the sway of this Romantic impulse we would have no adequate spatial metaphor to guide us on our journey through literary space. It is, after all, Dostoevsky who experiences Romantic desire in its fullest and refuses to yield. Girard stresses: 'He is not a bad romantic because he lacks the essence of romanticism but, on the contrary, because he possesses it in superabundance, because he is always ready to rush into madness or genius.'[91] Indeed this is only to restate what the protagonist tells us at the end of *Notes from the Underground* 'As for me, I have never done anything but push to extremes in my life what you yourself would dare push only half way.'[92] Because of this morbid determination, to destroy oneself in order to have oneself (albeit an illusory self) Girard claims he has detected in the progression of Dostoevsky's work and thought a certain structure that pertains to all literature and consequently to all human relations. It is the 'metaphysical desire' at work in novelistic experience that, when subjected to the analysis of the critic, paradoxically yields literary substance.

The novelists themselves only obliquely intuit the triangular structure that constitutes this 'literary substance'; it requires the literary critic to make it clear. This structure reveals how desire never travels in a straight line but instead turns back on itself and on the one whose attempts to be original and self-sufficient are constantly frustrated by the very imitative nature of desire itself. This paradoxical dynamic leaves the individual seeking his own total and independent being, drawing away in an attempt to hide his desire, while becoming more and more like the other. The one who succumbs to this metaphysical desire 'wants to draw everything to himself, gather everything into his own Self but he never succeeds. He always suffers from a "flight" towards the other through which the substance of

---

91. Ibid., p. 98.
92. Ibid., p. 68.

his own being flows away'.[93] The intensity of the hero's attempts to hide his desire is only matched by the intensity of his attempts to find a model worthy of his imitation. Each failed attempt only disperses and divides him further. 'Pride goes always towards dispersion and final division, which is to say towards death. To accept this death is to be reborn into unity.'[94] The works that truly 'gather', Girard claims, are the ones that *reveal* the myth of Romantic desire and its fruitless form of 'gathering' – to these works is given the name '*Romanesque*' or new.[95]

The intersubjective crisis elaborated in *Deceit, Desire, and the Novel*, in the context of the Romantic fallacy and the extremes of underground existence, also contains elements of collective crisis that Girard, even at this early stage, begins to articulate in relation to Dostoevsky's work. The fate of the Romantic hero, like Golyadkin's 'doubling', unfolds in a broader social milieu. The ontological sickness or futile search for 'Being,' *in extremis*, leads to death.[96] This death is described by Girard as a form of 'suicide' – one that also strangely extends to the community. 'As the mediator approaches, the phenomena connected with metaphysical desire tend to be of a collective nature. This is more apparent than ever in the supreme stages of desire. Thus in Dostoevsky along with the disintegration of the individual we find a quasi-suicide of the collective.'[97] In a move that anticipates his anthropological study of collective violence, Girard argues:

> Most of the great collective scenes in Dostoevsky end in visions of chaos. In *Crime and Punishment* it is the extraordinary funeral feast in honour of Marmeladov. In *The Idiot* it is the great scenes in Lebedeff's villa, the public concert interrupted by the entrance of Nastasia Philipovna and the slap in the face to Prince Myshkin. Dostoevsky is always haunted by the same spectacle, but even in the height of his genius he seems incapable of translating its horror. It is not his imagination but the literary genre that is not capable of the task.[98]

For Girard the implications are clear: the community is undeniably claimed by the madness of negative mimesis. This is a theme that will be developed further in Girard's anthropology. If the literary genre is incapable of fully translating 'the horror', the critic will find another means. But for now, the critic gives the clearest example, up to this point, of the hero's 'vision of terror', which, once again, lays claim on the community.[99]

---

93. Ibid., p. 64.
94. Ibid., p. 140. See also Girard's comments on Matthew 12.30/Luke 11.23, 'Whoever does not gather with me scatters', *Girard, Resurrection*.
95. Girard, *Deceit, Desire, and the Novel*, pp. 16–17.
96. Ibid., p. 282.
97. Ibid., p. 280.
98. Ibid., pp. 280–281.
99. If, as Girard claims, Dostoevsky's genius is unable to transgress the 'limits of credibility', we might conclude that the critic does not hesitate to transgress these limits. Girard, *Deceit, Desire, and the Novel*, p. 281.

It is the scene from *Crime and Punishment* when torment is visited on Raskolnikov at the lowest point of his descent into hell, 'just before the release of the conclusion' and the restored unity of his conversion.

> He seemed to see the whole world laid waste by a terrible and unparalleled plague, which had swooped down on Europe from the heart of Asia. Everyone except a very few elect perished. Microscopic trichina of a hitherto unknown variety penetrated the human organism. But these corpuscles were spirits endowed with intelligence and will power. Individuals infected with them imme-diately became unbalanced and mad. Yet by a strange paradox never before had men thought they were so wise, so sure of knowing the truth. They had never had such confidence in the infallibility of their judgement, of their scien-tific theories and of their moral principles . . . Everyone was a prey to anguish and beyond understanding each other. Yet each one believed that he alone knew the truth and was grieved at the thought of the others. Each person at the sight of the other beat his breast, and wrung his hands and wept . . . they could not agree on the measures to be taken for good and evil and they did not know whom to convict and whom to acquit. They killed each other in a kind of absurd fury.[100]

This one quote from *Crime and Punishment*, depicting a 'terrible contagion', poses the whole problem that Girard's later work will seeks to address – the problem of uncontained violence.[101] It is a problem that is intimately linked for moderns like Dostoevsky with the inability to know 'whom to convict', what Girard will later describe as a sacrificial crisis *par excellence*.

The vision of terror recounted in *Deceit, Desire, and the Novel* has the charac-teristics of what Girard details in his later work *The Scapegoat*, as a collective crisis.[102] But when, as with other myths, we might expect a hero or a god to appear and to fight a monster and perhaps die, thus restoring order, what this account turns up is a 'strange paradox' that finds men 'very wise', but unable to agree. The community is left with no victim and no possibility of unanimity – in other words, left to die in an 'absurd' crisis without end. According to Girard, the 'sickness is contagious and yet it isolates individuals; it turns them against the other.'[103] The responsibility for this crisis lies with the modern individual, about whom he writes: 'Each believes he alone knows the truth and each is

---

100. Quoted in, *Deceit, Desire, and the Novel*, p. 281 (see translators note).
101. Ibid., p. 290.
102. For example, the motif of the plague is a sign that differences have broken down. In the following chapter we will explore the 'signs of persecution' in greater detail, since they form what Girard describes as a five element typology for iden-tifying myths that conceal scapegoating and are thus central to his hypothesis concerning collective violence. See Chris Fleming, *René Girard: Violence and Mimesis* (Cambridge: Polity Press, 2004), p. 80.
103. Girard, *Deceit, Desire, and the Novel*, p. 282.

miserable when he looks at his neighbours. Each condemns or acquits according to his own law.'[104] The intra-psychic divisions generated when metaphysical desire reaches its apotheosis are symptoms of individual crises that are themselves but instances of a much greater dispersion.

8. *Authentic and Inauthentic Unity: Novelistic Conclusions*

The theme of death and rebirth that we discussed at the beginning of this chapter in relation to the structuralist influences on literary criticism during the 1960s is also evident at the end of *Deceit, Desire, and the Novel*. In this section I want to explicate Girard's understanding of the meaning of novelistic experience, as evinced in the symbolic death and resurrection of the principal characters. At the end of the 'work of genius', Girard contends, spiritual resurrection has been affirmed at the expense of a Romantic individualism that inevitably leads to spiritual death. In and through the physical death of the hero in the novel life is being generated – what he sees as the common culminating motif of all 'great' novels and calls 'the unity of novelistic conclusions'. Summing up this unity, which Girard believes brought Dostoevsky his own restored humanity, we are given the following lines to ponder: 'In the second part of *The Brothers Karamazov* little Ilusha dies for the sake of all the heroes of Dostoevsky's novels and the communion which springs from that death is Balzac's and Proust's *sublime lucidity* shared by many. The structure of crime and redeeming punishment transcends the solitary consciousness.'[105] The last lines in *Deceit, Desire, and the Novel*, are the last lines from *The Brothers Karamazov* that portray a collective scene of jubilation, the Christian themes and symbols of which, Girard claims, are shared by other novelists: 'memory, death, love and resurrection.'[106] The authors, through the available index of powerfully mediating symbols, draw together the imaginary plots that all share the same basic meaning: our desires are not our own.

The contagion that Raskolnikov's vision details as a collective crisis and Girard reads as a 'suicide of the community' reflects the ontological sickness of the Romantic individual that worsens in proportion to the mediator's proximity, and ultimately leads to the complete disintegration of the subject. 'The very desire to unify oneself disperses, and here we have arrived at the definitive dispersion.'[107] In the end, what we find with many of Dostoevsky's characters is that the contradictions caused by internal mediation destroy the individual. The hero's tireless 'sadomasochistic' pursuit of what negates him leads into the most parched deserts in a paradoxical attempt to find the purest waters of self-affirmation. 'The will to

---

104. Ibid.
105. Girard, *Deceit, Desire, and the Novel*, p. 314.
106. Ibid.
107. Girard, *Deceit, Desire, and the Novel*, p. 279.

make oneself God is a will to self-destruction which is gradually realised.'[108] In the end, all the heroes in all the great novels share the same essential insight into their previously mistaken desire, and the corresponding realization of the mediator's actual power over them.

The deviated desire of the Romantic hero may indeed lead to death but according to Girard the *novel itself* leads to life. At the end of *Deceit, Desire, and the Novel* Girard claims that there are two sets of conclusions that pertain to novelistic experience: (1) two kinds of death, and (2) two kinds of conversion. Of the first set, Girard gives the following example: 'There are two antithetical deaths in the conclusion of *The Possessed*: one death that is an extinction of the spirit. Stavrogin's death is only death; Stephan's death is life. This double ending is not unusual in Dostoevsky.'[109] Physical death and spiritual death are juxtaposed in a powerfully symbolic way by the author so as to place the regenerative characteristics of novelistic experience in relief. However, the theme of 'death as life' becomes the basis of the second set of conclusions that go beyond the novel and encompass the author's own experience having traversed the literary space of his 'great work'. The two deaths – one of which is in fact life – thus correspond to the two conversions, one of which, Girard argues, represents the hero's transformation in death, while the other points to the *author's own conversion* in the act of writing the novel.[110]

The first kind of conversion is the one concerning the characters in the novels that Girard treats. The endings of these novels, whether *The Brothers Karamazov*, *Don Quixote* or *The Red and the Black*, all depict a conversion in death: a spiritual conversion, or a death that leads to life. This 'unity of conclusions' is denied by contemporary criticism, Girard claims, because it wishes to preserve (in a Romantic vein) the 'uniqueness' of the work of art.[111] But for Girard this denial overlooks the principle that can explain this unity – a principle that relates in each case to a single phenomenon. 'The unity of novelistic conclusions consists in the renunciation of metaphysical desire. The dying hero repudiates his mediator . . .'[112] And this repudiation implies renunciation of divinity and renunciation of pride.

> In renouncing divinity the hero renounces slavery. Every level of his existence is inverted, all the effects of metaphysical desire are replaced by contrary effects. Deception gives way to truth, anguish to remembrance, agitation to repose,

---

108. Ibid., p. 287.
109. Ibid., p. 291.
110. Girard tells us that the following verse from St John's Gospel could serve as an epigraph for novelistic conclusions: 'If the seed does not die after it has been sown, it will remain alone, but if it dies it will bear much fruit.' *Deceit, Desire, and the Novel*, p. 311.
111. Girard, *Deceit, Desire, and the Novel*, p. 293.
112. Ibid., pp. 293–294.

hatred to love, humiliation to humility, mediated desire to autonomy, deviated transcendency to vertical transcendency.[113]

Girard's comments here have a bearing on the two kinds of conversion, or the second set of conclusions, since it is not only the characters who give up their Romantic illusions and are reborn, but the novelist too undergoes a conversion. The principle behind the unity of novelistic conclusions suggests to Girard that there must be a real unity at work in the lives of the novelists. Something is being *wrought through the novel* that belongs to the novelist proper, constituting a *second* conversion.

Who then are the 'real heroes' of the novels Girard treats? Who are the beneficiaries of the insight that has been working itself out in the novels through the thwarted desires of the principal characters? 'The hero succumbs as he achieves truth and he entrusts *his creator* with the heritage of his clairvoyance. The title of hero of a novel must be reserved for the character who triumphs over metaphysical desire in a tragic conclusion and thus becomes *capable of writing the novel.*'[114] The author having overcoming the illusions of spontaneous desire is revealed as the real subject of literary space.[115]

In the end, the heroic characters recognize the power and influence of the mediator on their desires, and thus their dependence on him. The more the protagonists of the novels treated by Girard try to separate themselves from their model, that is, the more they attempt to convince themselves that their desires are their own, the more their pride forces them to merge with their model – where the only option left is spiritual death or spiritual rebirth (represented by physical death). This merger between hero and mediator has its counterpart in the unity of the novelist, whose own personal narrative merges with the narrative that culminates in the hero's conversion. 'The hero and his creator are separated throughout the novel but come together in the conclusion.'[116] One of the examples that Girard gives of this development is the claim by Flaubert: 'Mme Bovary, c'est moi.' What is revealed here, according to Girard is, the 'miraculous' nature of the novel

113. Ibid., p. 294.
114. Ibid., p. 296 (my italics).
115. This is the insight that Girard carries forward, as his opening remarks at the conference at Johns Hopkins in 1960 attest: 'I am personally convinced that great works of art, literature, and thought stem . . . from a genius's ability to undertake and carry out a radically destructive reinterpretation of his former intellectual and spiritual structures. Unlike lesser works, perhaps these masterpieces will pass the test of the most radical structural interpretation because they partake of the same essence, to a higher degree no doubt, than our most searching analysis.' Girard, 'Tiresias and the Critic', in *The Structuralist Controversy*, p. 20.
116. Girard, *Deceit, Desire, and the Novel*, p. 296–297.

whereby the self and other 'become one'.[117] This communion with the other is paradoxically what allows the hero to *emerge* as a new subject. By renouncing their false belief in originality they are humbled by the actual role that the other plays in their life. Girard describes this paradoxical outcome as follows:

> Victory over self-centeredness allows us to probe deeply into the Self and at the same time yields a better knowledge of Others. At a certain depth there is no difference between our own secret and the secret of Others. Everything is revealed to the novelist when he penetrates this Self, a truer Self than that which each of us displays. This Self imitates constantly on its knees before the mediator.[118]

By attempting to shore up his own separateness, the Romantic hero was only hastening his lack of difference from 'the Other'. 'Great novels always spring from an obsession that has been transcended. The hero sees himself in the rival he loathes; he renounces the "differences" suggested by hatred.'[119]

In the conclusion of *Deceit, Desire, and the Novel* we learn that the author as subject undergoes a spiritual conversion, symbolized in the conclusion of his great work as a death that the critic believes is in fact life.[120] As already mentioned Girard describes the significance of this transformation in the context of little Ilusha's death in Dostoevsky's *The Brothers Karamazov*, who dies for the sake of all Dostoevsky's heroes 'and the communion that springs from that death is Balzac's and Proust's *sublime lucidity* shared by many.'[121] The 'sublime lucidity' achieved here – as the light guiding this conversion – is, Girard believes, shared in by the 'great' novelists and 'many' others, including the readers who follow in their footsteps. It is a lucidity that stems from the author's painfully won insight into the triangle determining intersubjective relations – an implicit structure

---

117. Ibid., p. 300.
118. Ibid., p. 298.
119. Ibid., p. 300.
120. At the time of writing his first major work of criticism, *Deceit, Desire, and the Novel*, there was another surreptitious outcome of 'the conclusion' that the critic draws. It has to do with his own conversion at the end of *Deceit, Desire, and the Novel*. This 'outcome' was only revealed much later in an interview with James Williams. Girard recounts: 'When I wrote the last chapter of my first book, I had a vague idea of what I would do, but as the chapter took form I realized I was undergoing my own version of the experience I was describing. I was particularly attracted to the Christian elements . . . So I began to read the Gospels and the rest of the Bible. And I turned into a Christian,. James Williams, ed. *The Girard Reader* (New York: Crossroad Publishing, 1999), p. 285. Girard's own 'death and rebirth', and his early critical work thus parallel his analysis of the author and the novel.
121. Girard, *Deceit, Desire, and the Novel*, pp. 313–314.

governing literary space: one that (when acknowledged) generates an authentic literary community, and one that is fully articulated, as such, by the critic.

The triangular structure concealed by the Romantic fallacy is the 'true' principle governing novelistic experience. But can this structure as the logical 'result' of criticism be traced back to the author as subject prior to the scene of writing? Can the author's 'intention' be said to have any bearing on the meaning of the novelistic experience, or is it only the critic – equipped with a more sophisticated understanding of language – who can uncover this meaning, independently of all intentionality? These questions summon once again the spectre of the conscious intentional subject, forcing us to ask whether the subject that Girard so thoroughly debunks as a Romantic lie, has anything in common with the restored subjectivity discovered by great novelists 'at a certain depth'.[122] In other words, is the spiritually restored author any relation of the phenomenological and hermeneutical subject so thoroughly debunked by all those theories that influence Girard from early on?[123]

Shortly after the publication of *Deceit, Desire, and the Novel*, Girard published a shorter essay in which he clarifies the experience of religious conversion as novelistic unity with specific reference to Dostoevsky's own life. This work of criticism/biography entitled *Resurrection from the Underground* was first published in French with the subtitle: 'du double à l'unité' or *from the double to unity*. This French subtitle gives us every reason to believe that Girard's earlier insight into triangular desire has consolidated and the notion of literary space as the locus of the death of the Romantic subject and the rebirth of the author is further advanced. In it Girard clarifies the experience of conversion as the achievement of unity, with specific reference to Dostoevsky's own life. In the first chapter he sums up what he had earlier called the unity of novelistic conclusions, with specific reference to Dostoevsky's own resurrection from the underground: 'For Dostoevsky, to create oneself is to *slay the old human state,* prisoner as it is of aesthetic, psychological and spiritual forms.'[124] It is this assessment of the author's experience – when taken to the limits to which Girard takes it – that places his theory, I believe, within the family of theories that are content to debunk more traditional models of subjectivity. The old humanist subject as 'metaphysical presence', and the old 'human state' as a Romantic illusion, must die, but the author himself can return in and through literary space, as a deconstructed and now properly reconstructed subjectivity. However, we may ask, is there anything of the original subject left to substantiate the claim that it is indeed the same person? If not, might we just as easily suppose that the reconstruction is most likely an act of construction by the critic on behalf of the literary community?

---

122. Ibid., p. 298.
123. What he many years later describes in an interview with James Williams, as the 'fashionable mode' within which he is first writing.
124. Girard, *Resurrection from the Underground*, p. 31 (my italics).

9. Conclusion: The Spiritual and the Literary

Girard's early work clears a path through the underground of human experience, where we paradoxically witness the hero's sense of self-sufficiency depending more and more on a model/rival, at the cost of increasing dissonance within the self, and between self and other. This invidious dynamic becomes apparent in the novels Girard treats and is made manifest as literary substance by the critic. The structure is this substance of the novel, speaking to us of a peculiarly morbid human tendency to try and maintain a belief in our own originality, our own inherently 'valuable' desires, while our encounters with others continually threaten to confront us with the 'reality' behind all our exploits. The illusion of originality only conceals the fact that we must borrow our desires and secretly attempt to pass them off as our own, thus deceiving others, but ourselves most of all. This Romantic lie, according to Girard, is at work in all great novels, and is gradually being exposed by the novelists whose literary endeavours provide the space for an existential working out of this negative historical phenomenon. The hero's *askesis* – as the characteristically negative movement of this existential working out – is constituted by a withdrawal that is also the basis of a flight toward the other. The manifestation of 'the double' in Dostoevsky's work is an example of an extreme form of Romantic obsession with originality (what Girard calls 'metaphysical desire'). It provides an example of how unreflective imitation can lead to a kind of 'hallucination' that itself has a bearing on the social world where we confront the problem that 'the Other' poses. Personal disintegration and social disintegration become parts of the same experience.

Girard describes the historical unfolding of metaphysical desire, in the modern period, as a time when 'men become gods in each others eyes.' The loss of religious frameworks, or vertical transcendence (and the possibilities of external mediation that prevented individuals falling into rivalry) means that men now seek each other out in order to satisfy their deepest yearnings. Analogously to Barthes's '*theo-auteurist* criticism', Girard claims that the modern subject takes over the role of God from traditional metaphysics, but with this difference: the traditional picture appears more favourable to Girard, since a much more sinister form of imitation now holds sway *between* people – a condition referred to as deviated transcendence. What Girard describes as the 'Dostoyevskian apocalypse' is the culmination of this negative imitation that spreads throughout the whole organism and results in a 'suicide' of the social. When individuals strive for autonomy in the modern period they no longer know whom to acquit and whom to condemn. At the end of *Deceit, Desire, and the Novel* we learn that the spiritual death and resurrection that all great novelistic conclusions enact, also occurs in the great novelists themselves.

However, the consequence of Girard's 'debunking' of subjectivity means that the presence of a first-person perspective, as we saw above, cannot be tolerated, because such a perspective is wedded to the lie of 'originality' and thus suffers from a debilitating ontological sickness that can be only cured by the catharsis of the text brought about by the therapeutics of criticism. Even the long tradition of western spirituality does not escape the fundamental debunking of subjectivity at work here. How, for example, can we understand Christian conversion without a concept of interiority through which the soul on its searching journey meets God? When textuality is given priority over ontology in this way we lose any meaningful concept of a singular interiority or a reflective subject capable of steering a course through negative mimesis. While the critic in this scenario becomes like Tiresias pointing out Oedipus' tragic flaw, his own tragic wisdom is kept off limits – apparently irrelevant to the enquiry.[125] One imagines Augustine's self-understanding as being wholly irrelevant to his *Confessions*. Any attempt to understand how he experiences what he describes only deflects one away from the plenitude of the text towards an altogether illusory 'Author'.[126] Within a structuralist discourse the very distinction between inner and outer loses its significance.[127] What content can be given to 'internal mediation' without a developed concept of interiority? Is this not a significant point of tension in Girard's theory where it seems the primary orientation of 'internal mediation' is always towards an *external* rival? One of the chief characteristics of the hero's *askesis* is withdrawal for the sake of desire – a withdrawal predicated on the belief in the existence of a worthy rival whose desires will form the very basis of the subject's *false* identity, by providing it with a self image. When all movement is characterized thus, can

125. See Girard's commentary on the role of criticism for cultural theory, in René Girard, 'Tiresias and the Critic', in *The Structuralist Controversy*. Also, on the role of Tiresias as parallel to Oedipus – as one who knows his fault because he shares his fault – see Mark R. Anspach, 'Editor's Introduction: Imitating Oedipus', in *Oedipus Unbound: Selected Writings on Rivalry and Desire* (Stanford, CA: Stanford University Press, 2004), p. xii.

126. Speaking about what Barthes calls the 'founders of language', those authors who exceed the parameters of conventional author-text relations, Burke says: 'Barthes allows the logothethes privileges that extend far beyond those granted the author in traditional man-and-the work criticism. What Barthes will not allow to his founders, however, is any representational significance in their discourse, any content: Sade without evil, Fourier without socialism, Loyola without God, these are the postulates upon which the study commences.' Burke, *The Death and Return of the Author*, p. 41.

127. Speaking of the development of structuralist, and post-structuralist thought in contemporary culture Kearney quotes Barthes who says of the author: 'did he wish to express himself, he ought to at least know that the inner thing that he wishes to translate is itself only a ready formed dictionary, its words only explainable through other words, and so on indefinitely.' Kearney, *The Wake of Imagination*, p. 276. A little further on in this work Kearney claims: 'The imagination which is deconstructed into a parody of itself abandons all recourse to the metaphysical opposition between inner and outer.' Kearney, *The Wake of Imagination*, p. 290.

there be any ethical basis to withdrawal, or indeed can there be any form of interiority that we might claim as 'good'?

Death and rebirth is a common theme in the critical works of Barthes and Girard. The latter's early criticism charts the journey from division and disintegration, to unity and integration, and in the process begins to provide a model of subjectivity as a 'divestment of agency', whereby the work now influences the author rather than the author consciously attempting to influence the work – what Burke describes, as we discussed above (see note 27), as a new form of autobiography characterized by a movement from 'work to life'. The author, as subject, will 'reappear as a desire of the reader's, a spectre spirited back into existence by the critic himself'.[128] The spiritual symbolism that Girard draws on to explain his theory of the novel is no less evident in Barthes's criticism. As Burke observes: 'Like a Dionysus, or a Christ, the author must be dead before he can return. In a sense too, he must continue to be dead though he has returned. The text remains the "destroyer of all subjects" yet, through the twists of a silent dialectic, it also might contain a "subject to love".'[129] And a little later, in his analysis of Barthes's reintroduction of the author in the context of a new criticism and a new readership, Burke makes the point: 'As with other mythical sacrifices, resurrection and rebirth are not long in coming.'[130]

The author as 'progeny of his work' is a consequence of the debunking of subjectivity by structuralist and poststructuralist forms of criticism, but it is also a way of introducing an alternative discourse on subjectivity fully in keeping with the aims of this new criticism, which is to fundamentally undermine all 'original presence'.[131] Girard's early work achieves a manner of thinking of these developments within structuralist thought as part of a peculiarly western reflection on the self/other relation. The death and rebirth of the author, he claims, is not '. . . essentially different from that of Saint Augustine or Dante. This is why the structure of *The Brothers Karamazov* is close to the form of *The Confessions* and *The Divine Comedy*. It is the structure of the incarnation, the fundamental structure of Western art and Western experience. It is present every time artists succeed in giving their work the form of the spiritual metamorphosis that brings the work to birth.'[132] Yet without a reliable subject we must question whether it is not in

---

128. Burke, *The Death and Return of the Author*, pp. 27–30.
129. Ibid., p. 30.
130. Ibid., p. 47.
131. As Kearney observes: 'The postmodern death of the author, Barthes claims, follows from the death of God and announces that of Man. He does not bemoan this situation. On the contrary, he sees it as heralding a new kind of an-archy, and absence of origin (arche) where every act of writing traces a field which has no other origin than language itself, language which ceaselessly calls into question all origins.' *The Wake of Imagination*, p. 276.
132. Girard, *Resurrection from the Underground*, p. 140.

fact different. *Deceit, Desire, and the Novel,* and *Resurrection from the Under-ground* are both powerful meditations on the novel that lay out the groundwork for Girard's subsequent reflections on the role of crisis in the origins of human culture. However, the *symbolic* structure of 'death and rebirth' in these early works of criticism, appears, or so I shall argue, to contradict Girard's later theory of culture, when he attempts to explain how it actually conceals the *real* violence which erupts at the height of the paroxysms of negative imitation, resulting in a collective murder, or scapegoating. If this is so, we might with good reason ask: is there not also 'real violence' behind the death and rebirth of the Romantic hero?

CHAPTER 2

DIVISION AND UNITY IN CULTURAL SPACE: THE SCAPEGOAT MECHANISM

Since the idea of the sacred is always and everywhere separated from the idea of the profane in the thought of men, and since we picture a sort of logical chasm between the two, the mind irresistibly refuses to allow the two corresponding things to be confounded, or even to be merely put in contact with one another; for such a promiscuity, or even too direct a contiguity, would contradict too violently the dissociation of these ideas in the mind. The sacred thing is par excellence *that which the profane should not touch, and cannot without impunity.*[1]

Emile Durkheim

If the history of modern society is marked by the dissolution of differences, that clearly has something to do with the sacrificial crisis to which we have repeatedly referred. Indeed the phrase 'modern world' seems almost like a synonym for 'sacrificial crisis'.[2]

René Girard

1. Introduction

Girard's later work, beginning with *Violence and the Sacred* published in 1972, marks a shift in context and preoccupation. From his earlier concern with the intra- and intersubjective dynamic depicted in literary space he moves to a concern with the more collective dynamics of culture, especially in its mythic and religious manifestations. What motivates this transition? Undoubtedly, a key factor that brought this shift about is his self-confessed Durkheimianism that seems to be confirmed the more he extends his discourse into anthropology.[3] How does his work on religion and the sacred character of violence come into focus? Signs of his now more anthropological concerns are already evident in his early work when the structure of death and rebirth (with all it mythic and religious resonance)

---

1. Emile Durkheim, *The Elementary Forms of the Religious Life* (New York: The Free Press, 1915), pp. 37–57.
2. René Girard, *Violence and the Sacred*, trans., Patrick Gregory (Baltimore: Johns Hopkins University Press, 1984), p. 188.
3. For Girard, as for Durkheim, the sacred 'is not something "added to" society after it gets going, but that which arises with and is integral to society and social order' Chris Fleming, *René Girard: Violence and Mimesis* (Cambridge: Polity Press, 2004), p. 67.

is identified in literary space and attributed to the author at the end of *Deceit, Desire, and the Novel*. We can perhaps, with hindsight, think of Girard as antici-pating a move towards cultural anthropology. Yet, it was not until after the inter-national conference hosted by him and his colleagues at Johns Hopkins University in 1966, and attended by some of the central figures of the new French theory, that his interest in the area of anthropology began to take definite shape.[4] This interest comes to the fore in his second major work, *Violence and the Sacred*, which puts forward a theory of culture based on an analysis of myth and ritual, and their relationship to Greek tragedy and other historical phenomena – an analysis that brings the once literary critic into conversation with Lévi-Strauss, Herbert, Mauss and Freud, among other eminent nineteenth and twentieth-century cultural theorists. Comprehensive study of cultural systems has remained the focus of Girard's subsequent work, marking him out as an important thinker in the area of anthropology.

However, his early work, although confined to analysing the structure of the novel, contains many of the elements or themes that will re-emerge in his theory of culture. The first theme is that of a 'crisis' – caused by 'internal mediation' and the phenomenon of 'the double' – a psychological deterioration involving halluci-nations, that has a direct bearing on the social world of the sufferer. This strange condition, elaborated in one of Dostoevsky's novels, describes the process whereby the Romantic hero can no longer distinguish between the image he has of his own desires, which he always supposes to be 'original', and his alter ego, which arises from his secret imitation of a rival. When these two worlds merge, as they do for Golyadkin, the individual can no longer maintain the 'lie' that has gradually become the basis of his conscious life. Doubling thus precipitates a crisis that in Girard's later work comes to be played out at the level of the community and the wider culture, and becomes akin to Durkheim's notion of the dangerous proxim-ity of the sacred and the profane quoted above.[5] The contagiousness that besets Dostoevsky's characters, manifesting itself as division and generating disintegra-tion, is much the same illness that besets the primitive mind when the sacred and

---

4. Girard first tentatively broaches a grand theory of culture rooted in scapegoating in his 1965 essay 'Oedipus Analysed'. In this essay, which is still firmly within the discipline of literary criticism, he postulates the theory that Oedipus is a scapegoat. René Girard, *Oedipus Unbound: Selected Writings on Rivalry and Desire*, ed. Mark R. Anspach (Stanford: Stanford University Press, 2004), pp. 44–47.

5. The notion of a 'collective crisis' is also discussed, as we saw, in relation to Raskolnikov's apocalyptic vision, although the *contagious* nature of the violence is an idea that is still in embryonic form when Girard is writing as a literary critic. It does, however, re-emerge in a more developed way with profound importance for Girard's theory of sacred violence – with the result that we find a near perfect correspondence between the early intra- and intersubjective crises, and the later 'collective crisis', as will become clear in this chapter.

the profane are not kept separate.[6] Girard's initial insight thus becomes the spring for a broader analysis that takes its 'sociological' starting point from Durkheim's account of the 'extraordinary contagiousness of the sacred object'.[7]

The second theme that re-emerges in cultural space is the notion of 'death and rebirth'. As we have seen, the influence of French theory is evident on Girard's work here where the 'life of the text presupposes the death of the author'.[8] The triangular structure at work in novelistic experience is an essential aspect of this death and rebirth because, when brought to light, it reveals the true course of desire that eventually frees the hero and author from a false, destructive belief in their own originality. When viewed in light of 'novelistic conclusions' and the author's own symbolic death and resurrection, imitative desire reveals a commonly understood 'mythological' structure. In attempting to account for the prevalence of this structure in culture, Girard, as we shall see, brings forward a theory that appears to explain, from a paleo-anthropological perspective, the point(s) of origin for all narrative structures of death and rebirth – a violent eruption against one member of the group by our primitive ancestors.[9]

A third element that we find re-emerging in cultural space is the theme of unity, which as we saw is closely related to the 'death and rebirth' of the author/hero and to the life of the literary community: all works of genius share in a regeneration that makes the authors the real heroes of the novels in question. In this chapter I will continue to explore the constitutive theme of 'division and unity' with the purpose of highlighting how it is also present in his later work. By providing an exposition of Girard's theory of collective violence, developed at length in *Violence and the Sacred*, I hope to show how these same elements – crisis, death/rebirth and unity – are understood in the context of his analysis of the larger cultural space: to show, in other words, how literary space and cultural space share a similar structure. However, I will argue, that when we look back into Girard's early work in the light of his later insight into scapegoating and its concealment in so-called 'texts of persecution', we can detect that very scapegoating and concealment in Girard's own literary criticism. Hence, with no small degree of irony, Girard – the great 'de-mythologiser' – is exposed as an agent of sacred violence.

---

6. For an analysis of Durkheim's views on the 'extraordinary contagiousness of the sacred', see Cesáreo Bandera's essay entitled 'Separating the Human from the Divine', in *Contagion: Journal of Violence and Religion*, Vol. 1 (Spring, 2004), p. 85.
7. Ibid.
8. Richard Kearney, *The Wake of Imagination: Toward a Postmodern Culture* (London: Routledge, 1994), p. 274.
9. As will become clearer in this chapter, Girard maintains that this violent eruption becomes the anthropological condition for human evolution, an event that is repeated over ages and gradually gives rise to a 'signifier' and eventually a linguistic system rooted in the community and reinforced through ritual.

2. De-differentiation: The Link between Self and Sacrifice

As Girard brings his insight into the structure of the novel forward the field of enquiry no longer corresponds only to the modern period. He begins instead to consider a whole host of much earlier literature – biblical texts, mythological texts, foundational stories, texts of persecution, early Greek drama, and certain aspects of primitive religions.[10] He claims to find in these texts patterns of practice, ritual and representation that are common across all cultures. These correspondences suggest that the community, and the order that prevails in it, was founded and repeatedly restored through violence, the truth of which has been kept hidden but is now detectable in the texts just mentioned.[11] This stunning 'revelation' leads Girard to the inescapable conclusion that there must be a 'mechanism' at work within culture whereby a crisis is prevented from engulfing a community when one member is singled out to take the blame for and the brunt of the hostilities that constitute this crisis.[12]

The link between Girard's early work of literary criticism and the later work of anthropology is his central postulate concerning the erosion of differences between self and mediator, or what comes to be referred to as mimetic antagonists:[13] in the transition from literary theory to cultural anthropology the protagonists become 'antagonists'. We have already observed how rivalry between individuals can intensify, dissolving the characteristics that previously distinguished them and making them 'doubles' of each other (as evident in the case of the 'two Golyadkins'). In *Violence and the Sacred* Girard repeats this insight: 'When all differences have been eliminated and the similarity between the figures has been achieved, we say that the antagonists are doubles.'[14]

In bringing this insight forward, however, Girard moves one step beyond his initial postulate. He now claims that not only does conflict produce doubling and the erosion of differences, but, conversely, doubling and erosion produce conflict. 'At the beginning of *Violence and the Sacred*, Girard approvingly cites the psychologist Anthony Storr, who notes that nothing "resembles an angry cat or man

---

10. As with Fleming's work on Girard what cannot be replicated in this thesis is the extensive amount of ethnological, and literary particulars that Girard brings to bear on his reflections. His theoretical framework does not stand independently of these particulars. However, I am attempting to take his theory of sacred violence seriously from a philosophical perspective with the obvious limitations that follow from a mostly conceptual analysis of diverse cultural phenomena.

11. René Girard, *Things Hidden since the Foundation of the World*: Research undertaken in collaboration with J.-M. Oughourlian and G. Lefort, trans., S. Bann and M. Metteer (Stanford: Stanford University Press, 1987b).

12. René Girard, *The Scapegoat*, trans., Y. Freccero. (Baltimore: Johns Hopkins University Press, 1986).

13. Fleming, *René Girard: Violence and Mimesis*, p. 42.

14. Girard, *Violence and the Sacred*, p. 159.

so much as another angry cat or man". This endorsement of Storr is based on the psychologist's corroboration of one of the central preoccupations of Girard's work: the pervasive symmetrical patterning in forms of rivalry and agonistics.'[15] Whereas the thrust of the early work highlights the attempts of the Romantic individual to restore unity within himself, thus giving credence to his 'unique and spontaneous desire', what immediately marks out the later work is the 'symmetrical patterning' inherent in the reciprocal exchanges between partners in conflict – a dynamic that is once again detrimental to unity. In this anthropological space, 'one word borrows another' and insults fly, as a ball flies from one player to another in tennis. 'Conflict stretches out interminably because between the two adversaries there is no difference whatsoever.'[16]

This last claim appears counter-intuitive from the perspective of much socio-cultural theory, which tends to explain conflict in terms of unmanageable differences between people rather than the absence of those differences.[17] According to Girard, the truth of the situation is in fact the reverse: peace depends on clearly marked differences.[18] People do not enter into conflict because they are confronted with the difference of another that is somehow threatening *as difference*, rather they enter into conflict because the other somehow upsets an existing difference or order and thus makes everything appear *the same*. However, conflict, when reciprocal, while appearing to restore difference actually erodes it. As Fleming observes, Girard offers a wide array of dramatic examples as evidence of this thesis:

> . . . those episodes in tragic drama, for instance, in which adversaries match each other 'blow for blow': the deadly duel between the brothers Eteocles and Polyneices in Euripides' *Phoenician Women*, who imitate each others' verbal – and eventually physical – attacks, until they die simultaneously; the fatal encounter between Heracles and Lycus in Euripides' *Heracles*; the resemblances of Oedipus and Laius in Sophocles' *Oedipus the King*; and the increasingly undifferentiated rival camps of Brutus and Cassius on the one hand and Mark Anthony on the other, in Shakespeare's *Julius Caesar*.[19]

At the cultural level, the phenomenon that gives rise to such progressive de-differentiation is what anthropologists call the 'blood feud': the often catastrophic escalation of violent reciprocity.[20]

---

15. Fleming, *René Girard: Violence and Mimesis*, p. 42.
16. Girard, *Violence and the Sacred*, p. 45.
17. Fleming, *René Girard: Violence and Mimesis*, p. 43.
18. Girard, *Violence and the Sacred*, pp. 49–78.
19. Fleming, *René Girard: Violence and Mimesis*, p. 43.
20. Ibid., p. 44.

A blood feud marks the failure of a culture to direct violence along endorsed pathways, as for example in capital punishment and sacrifice.[21] When prohibitions fail to regulate behaviour, conflict can spill over into a community in unsanctioned ways, and the differences that ordinarily hold the community together break down. '[E]very move is reciprocated with "interest" in a desperate attempt to arrest violence through a frenzied administration of the same. The erosion of the identities of the warring parties and the absence of a judicial system or juridical power that transcends antagonists ensure that such conflicts remain autogenous, their singular gesture reiterated indefinitely.'[22] Vengeance, Girard tells us, turns all antagonists into doubles,[23] even as each blow attempts to establish an absolute degree of difference that will arrest violence, restore order and end the conflict. Their reciprocal violence makes them the same even though from within the system all they can see is difference – a difference that must be shored up at any cost. Because of this there is a risk that the act of vengeance will 'initiate a chain reaction whose consequence will quickly prove fatal to any society modest in size'.[24]

While a chain reaction can draw every member of the community into the conflict, vengeance, according to Girard, cannot belong to every member of society. Nor is it enough if we wish to prevent it to convince people that it is detestable 'for it is precisely because they detest it that men make a duty of vengeance.'[25] The cycles of violence in a primitive society that Girard believes the institutions of the sacred were responsible for curtailing have been largely replaced in modern society with a juridical system. This system 'does not suppress vengeance; rather it effectively limits it to a single act of reprisal enacted by a sovereign authority specializing in this particular function. The decisions of the judiciary are invariably presented as the final word on vengeance'.[26] Since primitive societies have no publicly sanctioned system of dealing with vengeance, that is, since they have no 'certain cure' once the social equilibrium has been upset, Girard believes, it is safe to assume that preventative measures will play a vital role. And so, he articulates a concept of sacrifice: 'as an instrument of prevention in the struggle against violence'.[27] The main difference between prevention at the level of the community and prevention at the level of the self is that the 'instrument of sacrifice' is only available to the community. The self lacks the cathartic resources to protect itself once a crisis arises. And from this we can presume that the self can protect itself, to the degree that it can do so at all, only by a law

---

21. Ibid.
22. Ibid., pp. 44–45.
23. Girard, *Violence and the Sacred*, pp. 12–20.
24. Ibid., p. 15.
25. Ibid.
26. Ibid.
27. Ibid., p. 17.

that has been effectively internalized; and here again, Girard might argue, we are back to an 'instrument of sacrifice'.

3. Some Characteristics of Violent Reciprocity

One of Girard's consistent claims since the publication of *Violence and the Sacred* has to do with the role of conflict and violent reciprocity in the erosion of differences and the onset of a sacrificial crisis that threatens to engulf the entire community with unthinkable consequences.[28] Greek tragedies share certain literary traits and motifs that allow us to discern this invidious dynamic if we only let go of our precious belief today in the 'originality' of the work of art.[29] Girard is reminding us in *Violence and the Sacred* of what he sees as a 'Romantic Manichean' tendency that views heroes and villains as 'good' or 'bad' without recognising how each plays off the other to generate an overall momentum, one which provides the background dynamic of culture as a whole (as the Greek tragedians knew all too well[30]).

Order and peace depend on cultural distinctions which in turn depend on the difference between impure violence, such as patricide and incest found in *Oedipus,* and purifying violence, which belongs to ritual and especially sacrifice. To collapse or efface the difference between pure and impure violence, Girard argues, is to risk the spread of reciprocal violence throughout the community.

> The sacrificial distinction, the distinction between the pure and the impure, cannot be obliterated without obliterating all other distinctions as well. One and the same process of violent reciprocity engulfs the whole. The sacrificial crisis can be defined, therefore, as a crisis of distinctions – that is, a crisis affecting the cultural order. This cultural order is nothing more than a regulated system of distinctions in which the differences among individuals are used to establish their 'identity' and their mutual relationships.[31]

When we fail to see how clearly marked differences create order and peace we fail to see how the cultural order determines every possibility with respect to identity. The loss of identity is essentially a cultural crisis. The chain reaction described

---

28. Of particular relevance to my argument are the following works by Girard, *Things Hidden*; *The Scapegoat* (Baltimore: Johns Hopkins University Press, 1986); *A Theatre of Envy: William Shakespeare* (New York, Oxford: Oxford University Press, 1991).
29. Girard's criticism here is similar to the criticism above that pertains to 'the unity of novelistic conclusions', whereby the emphasis on 'originality' obscures the shared meanings of the authors.
30. Girard, *Violence and the Sacred*, p. 47.
31. Ibid., p. 49.

earlier becomes more insidious when we consider what is now at stake in this escalation of violence. 'When the religious framework of a society starts to totter, it is not exclusively or immediately the physical security of a society that is threatened; rather the whole cultural foundation of the society is put in jeopardy.'[32] Anything that threatens the institution of sacrifice ultimately threatens the very basis of the community and therefore the preservation of human life.

From the point of view of modern freedom, which comes about with the discrediting of traditional religious frameworks, equality becomes an important principle determining the political sphere and all aspects of institutional life. However, this principle, according to Girard, tends to regard all differences as obstacles in the path of human happiness.[33] All rank, all hierarchy in the modern period is held in question and thus the very basis of cultural order and stability is perpetually undermined. Girard diagnoses this 'flattening' in anthropological terms as a 'sacrificial crisis' that pertains to the modern world.[34] When differences become 'unhinged' as they do in less sacrificially secure societies like our own, they become uncertain and potentially threatening. He believes that when people feel less secure about 'what they have and who they are', the unhinged differences generate rivalry as their potential to confer significance appears open to more and more people. This happens, for example, when in our culture the redundant titles of the nobility, access to which once adhered to strict criteria, are open to purchase by anyone who can afford them. Such 'flattening' in the modern period, Girard argues, generates mimetic rivalry and conflict because once differences no longer serve as a dam against violence they serve to swell the flood.[35]

Girard draws on Shakespeare's *Troilus and Cressida* to provide us with an interesting metaphor to help dispel our 'fashionable intellectual attitudes' that tend to see difference as a problem to be overcome. Ulysses's speech about the besieged Troy is a reflection on the role of 'Degree' in human endeavour. This Degree is the underlying principle of all order, natural and cultural, which allows individuals to find a place for themselves, '. . . it lends a meaning to things, arranging them in proper sequence within a hierarchy; it defines the objects and moral standards that men alter, manipulate and transform.'[36] Girard emphasizes the musical dimension of this metaphor and just how discordance is synonymous with collective violence.

> . . . O When Degree is shaked,
> Which is the ladder to all high designs,
> The enterprise is sick! How could communities,
> Degrees in schools, and brotherhoods in cities,

32. Ibid.
33. Ibid.
34. Girard, *Violence and the Sacred*, p. 188.
35. Girard, *Violence and the Sacred*, p. 50.
36. Ibid.

> Peaceful commerce from dividable shores,
> The primogenitive and due of birth,
> Prerogative of age, crowns, sceptres, laurels,
> But by degree, stand in authentic place?
> Take but one degree away, untune that string,
> And hark what discord follows! Everything meets
> In mere oppugnancy.[37]

Loss of differences gives rise to chaos and violence, forcing men into a perpetual confrontation that strips them of their distinctive characteristics, 'in short their identities'.[38] The consequences of this loss are similar to the mixing of the sacred and the profane, a mixing which contradict too violently the dissociation of these ideas in the mind (Durkheim). Shakespeare captures the essence of 'collective crisis' in a late Renaissance context.[39] Degree maintains balance and harmony, while lack of degree brings conflict. 'In this situation no one and nothing is spared; coherent thinking collapses and rational activities are abandoned. All associative forms are dissolved or become antagonistic; all values, spiritual or material, perish.'[40] And in a curious comment Girard asserts: 'To say that this speech merely reflects a Renaissance commonplace, the great chain of being, is unsatisfactory. Who has ever seen a great chain of being collapse?'[41] We may note that Girard is demythologizing here the ontological order canonized by western metaphysics; all cosmic order, as the basic pattern of eternal Being (following the Greek concept), when cast in these anthropological terms, is viewed as a temporal projection of the sacred. Platonic metaphysics is thus rejected. Given the significance that Girard places on 'Degree' in Shakespeare's work, and his belief that its loss illustrates how social order becomes unhinged, it is important to explore further this 'anti-metaphysical' reading if we are to grasp precisely what he means by disorder and, correspondingly, order.

4. Shakespeare's 'Mimetic Theory': The World as Stage

Girard's extended treatment of Shakespeare's work as the paradigm of his mimetic hypothesis concerning sacred violence can be found in his later critical work, *A Theatre of Envy* (1991). In this book he applies his now more developed theory

---

37. Ibid.
38. Girard, *Violence and the Sacred*, p. 51.
39. The rest of the speech just quoted, which contains common motifs of collective crisis, such as 'a flood', is emblematic of the undifferentiation that holds sway in a sacrificial crisis, as we shall see below when we outline Girard's five-element typology for identifying myths that conceal acts of scapegoating.
40. Girard, *Violence and the Sacred*, p. 51.
41. Ibid.

of collective violence to a whole range of Shakespeare's dramatic works, comedies as well as tragedies, and argues that this late Renaissance individual puts the world and its constituent forces upon the stage with greater verve and insight than many nineteenth-century anthropologists.[42] According to Girard, it is not the great chain that Shakespeare is interested in. Ulysses's speech as we saw above is no banal variation on this 'Renaissance commonplace', which must be 'fundamentally eternal and unchanging, failing which it no longer fits the definition of Being in the metaphysical and medieval sense'.[43] There may be, Girard admits, local disruptions within an order understood as a great chain, due to human sinfulness, but the order does not melt down in the way described in Ulysses's speech.[44] For this reason he believes the picture of cosmic order at work in the great chain of being does not govern Shakespeare's genius, which is, on the contrary, much more attuned to the mutability of the world. Degree exists as a function of culture and not an ontological given. As the basis of differentiation it is the primary concern of the artist in *Troilus and Cressida*. Girard describes its significance as follows:

> 'Degree', from the Latin *gradus*, means a step in a staircase or on a ladder, a nonhorizontal spacing between two entities, and more generally rank, distinction, discrimination, hierarchy, *difference*. It is also the 'endless jar' between justice and injustice, the same empty space once again that prevents any confusion between right and wrong. Justice is no exercise in exquisite impartiality, no perfect balance, but a fixed modality of imbalance, like everything cultural.[45]

When the crisis of Degree has reached fever pitch, the mimetic crisis has likewise reached its most intense point. As in the intersubjective crisis, 'formally differentiated entities have turned into undifferentiated doubles that keep colliding for no discernible purpose, like loose cargo on the deck of a storm-tossed ship. Their violence has destroyed whatever object they desire in common, depriving their struggle of its significance'.[46] Like Dostoevsky's characters, individuals imitate their rivals' desires with no sense of the proper limits within a hierarchical system – in other words, their rivals have become 'gods'. 'The destruction of degree is an

---

42. 'The difference between ancient Greek tragedy and Shakespearean tragedy, Girard believes, cannot be accounted for simply in terms of greater "aestheticism" or Shakespeare's ability for far more complex "psychological profiling". The necessary condition for the creation of Shakespeare's dramatic works resides, rather, in a cultural unveiling set in motion by the ancient Hebrews more than three thousand years before Shakespeare's birth.' Fleming, *René Girard: Violence and Mimesis*, p. 101.
43. Girard, *A Theatre of Envy*, p. 162.
44. Ibid.
45. Girard, *A Theatre of Envy*, pp. 161–162.
46. Ibid., p. 162.

influx of mimetic rivalry so massive that it resembles the plagues that never fail to show up in this kind of apocalyptic tableau.'[47] Conflict and violence thus become contagious and the differential principle that ordinarily suppresses mimetic rivalry succumbs to a 'virulent attack of the disease it is supposed to prevent'.[48]

According to Girard, the notion of 'Degree' is present in all of Shakespeare's plays.[49] However, it is more than a source of stable meaning and clearly marked differences, separating individuals in rank and station, it is also 'paradoxically' a principle of unity among people. It is thus a source of separation *and* unity, or, perhaps, more accurately, unity *in* separation, because 'when this separation is gone, when people come too near each other, hark what discord follows.'[50] The loss of Degree precipitates a sacrificial crisis.

Girard explains why, in the absence of Degree, rivalry and crisis escalate while in its presence they are, if not absent, at least containable – in other words they do not lead to destruction. Because human desires are governed by imitation, a negative example of which we saw at work in Romantic individualism, all 'order' attempts to channel desire in constructive ways. Military rank is a paradigm example of the kind of order to which Shakespeare links imitative desire. 'In a disciplined and efficient outfit, each soldier looks up to the rank immediately above his own in the hope of promotion. Each soldier takes his commanding officer as a model and guide.'[51] But when imitation ignores military rules and tra-ditions it can just as easily bring destruction as the kind of excellence accredited in the army. Describing the anthropological function of this strict rank and sta-tion Girard writes: 'Order consists of a chain of obedient imitation so pervasive that it facilitates the contagion of disorder when disorder appears.'[52] The differ-ence between 'good' imitation, and 'bad' imitation in the final analysis stems not from two types of imitation but from Degree itself: 'Imitation is "good" imitation when it conforms to the rules of Degree and respects the distinctiveness of each rank.'[53] Once again, cultural order requires clearly marked differences that can only be maintained by an underlying principle of Degree; the failure of Degree gives rise to bad imitation, whereby 'Each thing meets/in mere oppugnancy.'

This principle is central to Girard's overall theory of collective crisis. It pro-vides a more secure anthropological basis for the distinction between internal and external mediation adumbrated in *Deceit, Desire, and the Novel*.[54] As long as the

---

47. Ibid., p. 163.
48. Ibid.
49. Ibid., p. 174.
50. Ibid., p. 164.
51. Ibid.
52. Ibid., p. 165.
53. Ibid.
54. To recap on Girard's early analysis of the novel: 'We shall speak of external medi-ation when the distance is sufficient to eliminate any contact between the two spheres of possibilities of which the mediator and the subject occupy the respective centres. We shall speak of internal mediation when this distance is sufficiently

models and their imitators live in separate worlds, as in the case of Adamus and Don Quixote, they cannot become rivals. Their 'external' mediation prevents them selecting the same object. However, as these worlds overlap more and more in the modern period, they can and therefore do select the same objects, thus generating mimetic rivalry and a greater likelihood of crisis.[55]

In a system that is governed by external mediation and that therefore respects the principle of Degree the 'people on the lower steps look up to the people above them and are likely to choose them as models, but in a purely ideal sense. They must select their concrete object of desire inside their own worlds, and rivalry is impossible. The imitators would prefer to select the objects of their models, but Degree prevents them from doing so.'[56] If in *Deceit, Desire, and the Novel* the 'internal mediation' is the dominant focus, we might say that the notion of Degree in *Violence and the Sacred* and *A Theatre of Envy* provides a basis for filling out the picture of imitation more in terms of 'external mediation' – in line with a more general anthropology.

A healthy Degree means a lot of external mediation throughout the system structured by it, and therefore few internal conflicts. As soon as Degree weakens, the mediation tends to become internal, and the mimetic rivalry thus generated accelerates the incipient cultural disintegration that produced it in the first place. The breakdown of traditional institutions destroys their ability to channel desire into the non-competitive directions that prevent mimetic rivalries.[57]

It thereby opens the way to the kind of conflict that all great playwrights – and, we might add, in a slightly different context, novelists – love to portray. 'The Shakespearean notion of "Degree" includes within itself the spatial metaphor that underlies the distinction between external and internal mediation.'[58] The principle of Degree at work in Shakespeare's plays, Girard argues, is an anthropological principle essential to an ordered system of difference, and crucial to containing the rivalry that first appears in Girard's work in relation to novelistic experience. The now extended literary space is ultimately a reflection of cultural space and the dynamics that necessitate 'prohibition' – when the sacred and the profane are mixed. According to Girard, the principle of Degree is not to be confused with the metaphysical view of nature associated with traditional accounts of the great chain of being – 'a medieval idea that Shakespeare might have borrowed for

---

reduced to allow these two spheres to penetrate each other more or less profoundly.' René Girard, *Deceit, Desire, and the Novel: Self and Other in Literary Structure*, trans. Yvonne Freccero (Baltimore: Johns Hopkins University Press, 1965), p. 9.
55. Ibid.
56. Girard, *A Theatre of Envy*, p. 165.
57. Ibid., p. 166.
58. Ibid.

purely decorative purposes'.[59] We might reasonably ask, though, whether the underlying principle that gathers together 'all the particular degrees and differences' does not itself verge on the metaphysical when Girard describes it as 'a single differential principle . . . with a capital D, upon the integrity of which the stability of cultural systems and their existence depend'.[60]

5. Violence and Scapegoating: From Crisis to Resolution

So far in this chapter I have been looking at the dynamics of violent reciprocity – the loss of clearly marked differences, and the onset of a 'sacrificial crisis' that spreads throughout the community and beyond. I made the point that Greek tragedy, according to Girard, contains an insight into sacred violence made recognizable in the similarities between 'hero' and 'villain'. Moreover, I made the point that the notion of 'Degree' can be read as a way of assigning differences that are essential to order and harmony. Without hierarchy and clearly marked differences the '"modern world" is almost like a synonym for "sacrificial crisis"'.[61] I already mentioned how, on a cultural level, a phenomenon that gives rise to de-differentiation is what anthropologists call the 'blood feud'. One example of this phenomenon given by Girard allows him to compare the Greek world of tragic drama with an account of a more 'primitive' response to the threat of violence. While the former conceals the true events the latter has no such inclination. The example is taken from Jules Henry's *Jungle People*, which deals with the Kaingang Indians in Brazil, who had been moved to a reservation shortly before the author came to live among them and to observe their ways in the middle part of the twentieth century.[62]

---

59. Ibid.
60. Ibid., p. 162.
61. Girard, *Violence and the Sacred*, p. 188.
62. About Henry's work with this displaced tribe whose rituals were in decline, Girard says: 'He was thus able to observe at first hand, or through the testimony of witnesses, the process I call the sacrificial crisis.' Girard, *Violence and the Sacred*, p. 52. The whole study documents the breakdown of the society through internal feuding. Henry claims that although the group were well suited to adapt and cope with the rigours of the natural environment, 'they were unable to withstand the internal forces that were disrupting their environment and, having no culturally standardised devise to deal with them, were committing social suicide.' Girard, *Violence and the Sacred* p. 54. The 'tit-for-tat' killings were meant in a bizarre way to stop the violence but only succeeded in adding fuel to a fire. The fear generated by the 'kill-or-be-killed' attitude cannot be explained by modern psychology. Commenting on how the Indians' fears are not merely 'projections', Girard points out: 'In a universe deprived of any universal code of justice and exposed to violence, everybody has reason to fear the worst.' And in a sentence

Thus, Girard's analysis of the role of Degree in Shakespeare finds its correlate in his study of primitive societies: differences must 'stand in authentic place'.[63] Similarly, we learn that Greek tragedy is a child of the sacrificial crisis.[64] It draws its inspiration from a direct intuitive grasp of the role played by violence in cultural order and disorder, in mythology and the sacrificial crisis. Hence, 'England in the throes of religious upheaval provided Shakespeare with such an inspiration for his *Troilus and Cressida*.'[65] Once the crisis reaches a certain point the process appears to reverse itself; order is re-inscribed and the whole process begins again. Tragedy recounts these events with a certain amount of lucidity – although the insight it conveys is always 'imperfect'.[66] Yet the knowledge of cultural order and disorder is present in certain inspired texts, including tragic drama, if only the anthropologist is prepared to look for it. However, when we discover this knowledge, another question confronts us. Once the sacrificial crisis begins there seems to be no way of bringing it to a halt, and yet, Girard argues, we know from various textual accounts that either hide their inspiration or gradually reveal it that the violence does stop. What stops it, and brings the collective crisis to a halt? 'If there are really such events as sacrificial crises, some sort of braking mechanism, an automatic control that goes into effect before everything is destroyed, must be built into them. In the final stages of a sacrificial crisis the very viability of human society is put in question.'[67] What (or who) saves the community from total annihilation?

In order to explain the breakdown of differences that leads to crisis and the restoration of order that re-inscribes differences creating peace once again, Girard turns to the figure of Oedipus. Prior to the onslaught of collective violence at Thebes Oedipus, he tells us, is a 'polluted presence, a receptacle for universal shame'.[68] But another Oedipus emerges at the end of the play who becomes a

---

reminiscent of Golyadkin's 'peculiar objectivity', Girard says: 'The difference between a projection of one's own paranoia and an objective evaluation of circumstances has been worn away.' René Girard, *Resurrection from the Underground: Feodor Dostoevsky*, trans. James G. Williams (New York: Crossroad, 1997), p. 54.

63. Girard also deals with how twins are treated in Greek drama and primitive societies – how they can strike terror into the community by their undifferentiation. 'Behind the image of the twins lurks the baleful aspect of the sacred, perceived as a disparate but unified force' Girard, *Violence and the Sacred*, p. 58.

64. Ibid., p. 66.

65. Ibid.

66. Ibid., pp. 64–65.

67. Ibid., p. 67.

68. The plague motif in *Oedipus the King* conceals the presence of a sacrificial crisis. It functions like the motif of the flood in Ulysses speech in *Troilus and Cressida*, except it is hidden. Girard, *Violence and the Sacred*, p. 75/87.

'definitive' hero in the final tragedy of the Oedipus cycle, *Oedipus at Colonus*.[69] At the end of the first play we are given a clue to the hero's efficacy, with the line 'All is well.' Order and stability are restored as was intended when the violence was initially directed towards Oedipus. Therefore, it seems only logical to attribute the happy result to the victim himself.[70] This double meaning of the victim as evil *and* good is the key to the mystery of crisis and order or violence and the sacred. 'At the supreme moment of the crisis, the very moment when reciprocal violence is abruptly transformed into unanimous violence, the two faces of violence seem juxtaposed; the extremes meet. The surrogate victim serves as a catalyst in this metamorphosis. And in performing this function he seems to combine in his person the most pernicious and the most beneficial aspect of violence.'[71] The surrogate victim becomes the unrecognized incarnation of the community's own violence. If Oedipus is the saviour of the community it is only because he is a patricidal and incestuous son.

This same pattern of the poison becoming the cure[72] 'is to be found in innumerable tales from folklore and mythology; in fairy stories, legends, and even in works of literature. A source of violence and disorder during his sojourn among men, the hero appears as a redeemer as soon as he has been eliminated, invariably by violent means.'[73] All these stories point to the mechanism that Girard believes restores the stability of a community in crisis. The pervasiveness of this pattern leads him to speculate further:

> If the generating spark of religion and the transcendental force that characterises it are in fact the product of violent unanimity – of social unity forged or reforged by the 'expulsion' of the surrogate victim – then . . . we will find ourselves dealing not only with myths but with rituals and the whole question of religion.[74]

It transpires that the aim of all religion is to keep violence outside the community through ritual re-enactment of collective violence and scapegoating.[75] 'The complete explanation of the Oedipus myth – that is the determining of the precise function of the surrogate victim – permits us to understand the aim of the sacrificers. They are striving to produce a replica, as faithful as possible in every detail, of a previous crisis that was resolved by means of a spontaneously unanimous victimisation.'[76] The exemplary myth of Oedipus allows Girard to penetrate the

---

69. Ibid., p. 85.
70. Ibid.
71. Ibid., p. 86.
72. On the similarities between Oedipus and the *pharmakos* who share a dual connotation, see Girard, *Violence and the Sacred*, p. 95.
73. Ibid., p. 87.
74. Ibid.
75. Ibid., pp. 92, 140.
76. Ibid., p. 94.

'meaning of myth' and thus understand it in its properly religious context. When viewed anthropologically, in light of the scapegoat mechanism, religion itself is just another word for the surrogate victim, who reconciles the oppositions generated by the mimetic impulse.[77] It is this reconciliation that gives culture its basic structure.

The taxonomy of the scapegoat is highly elaborate. Girard devotes an entire book to exploring the various aspects of scapegoating and what makes a scapegoat suitable as a sacred object. Everything from the marks of the scapegoat, its arbitrary nature, stereotypes of persecution and the generation of unanimity are all discussed in the context of real historical phenomena – witch trials, persecution texts etc. Anyone can play the part of the victim, given the unpredictable and indiscriminate oscillations of mob behaviour. However, it is not very difficult to detect well-established patterns of persecution in cultures like our own. Summarizing aspects of Girard's work on *The Scapegoat*, Fleming writes: 'both common sense and the findings of the empirical social sciences tend to corroborate – that scapegoats or surrogate victims tend to be marginalised figures or outcasts, persons often existing on the fringes of society who, for that very reason, are vulnerable to the kinds of violence of which surrogate victimage is the most radical expression.'[78] Outrageous charges are often levelled at scapegoats:

> . . . incest as well as rape, bestiality, and parricide, is a crime which involves transgressions that level and confuse the identity of subjects and their relative loci in the social order. Scapegoats, that is, tend to be accused of exactly the kinds of acts which would contribute to the annihilation of distinctions within the community, crimes which are thought thereby to bring about the crisis of which they are accused: 'They attack the very foundation of cultural order, the family and hierarchical differences without which there would be no social order.'[79]

When we confront these stereotypes in various historical contexts we realize that the persecutors actually believed in the guilt of their victims and that real violence resulted – someone is *actually* scapegoated. This highlights another important point about the scapegoat mechanism: it functions in a non-volitional, automatic way. Nor is the fact that it operates unbeknownst to its participants 'accidental'; its very operation *requires* miscomprehension.[80]

---

77. Ibid., p. 307.
78. Fleming, *René Girard: Violence and Mimesis*, p. 51.
79. Ibid., p. 52.
80. The 'miscomprehension' here is not entirely unlike the Romantic individual's failure to see that his desires are in fact mediated. However, Girard would most likely argue that the necessary miscomprehension at the cultural level is beneficent in terms of social order while the Romantic individual seems to produce nothing but negative mimesis.

Much of the misunderstanding and mistaken belief surrounding sacred violence is stimulated by the false accounts of scapegoating, contained in mythology and other forms of representation. Girard tells us that myth, which itself is the inspirational source of much tragic drama, recounts the event of collective violence from the perspective of the restored community – the innocent victim is invariably disguised in the process as a villain, a hero, a stranger, a monster and ultimately a god.[81] Language, Girard says, cannot properly grasp hold of the sacrificial crisis. On one hand it invites anecdotal history, and on the other a visitation of grotesques and monsters.[82] All the previously terrifying and subsequently peaceful aspects of a crisis get mixed together in the process of being 'mythologized.' Tragedy then 'pieces together the scattered fragments of reciprocity and balances the elements thrown out of kilter' in the earlier process.[83] Drawing out a difference between Girard's interpretation of myth, and the traditional approach to mythology, and narrative more generally since Aristotle, Gil Bailie argues that myth actually conspires to keep silent the voice of the victim.[84] Monstrosities that recur throughout mythology are one of a number of features whose combined effect is to silence the victim and to ensure that the violent resolution of the crisis continues to be narrated from the point of view of the community. And so, 'we can only conclude that myths make constant reference to the sacrificial crisis, but do so only in order to disguise the issue. Myths are the retrospective transfiguration of sacrificial crisis, the reinterpretation of these crises in light of the cultural order that has arisen from them.'[85] Hence myth attempts to keep secret the fact of original violence.[86]

---

81. For an account of 'otherness' that is quite critical of Girard's theory of the scapegoat, see Richard Kearney, *Strangers, God's and Monsters*, (London: Routledge, 2003).

82. 'Mythology succumbs to the latter; tragedy is constantly threatened by the former.' Girard, *Violence and the Sacred*, p. 64.

83. Girard, *Violence and the Sacred*, pp. 64–65.

84. Gil Bailie, *Violence Unveiled: Humanity at the Crossroads* (New York: Crossroads Publishing, 1997), pp. 30–41. In particular: 'The Greek word for myth, *muthos*, is *mu*, which means "to close" or to "keep secret."' Bailie, *Violence Unveiled*, p. 33. We might contrast this view of *muthos* with the dominant philosophical understanding of the term *mythos* as itself a form of *mimesis* taken as 'the transformative plotting of scattered events into a new paradigm'. See R. Kearney, *On Stories* (London Routledge, 2002), p. 12.

85. Girard, *Violence and the Sacred*, p. 64.

86. On the need to forget original violence Terry Eagleton writes: 'David Hume, perhaps the greatest of British philosophers, cautions that if we investigate the origins of nations, we shall find there rebellion and usurpation . . . Blaise Pascal is quite as candid as Hume on the need to obliterate one's genesis. "The truth about the (original) usurpation", he writes conspiratorially, "must not be made apparent: it came about originally without reason and has become reasonable. We must see that it is regarded as authentic and eternal, and its origins must be hidden if

6. *Mimesis and the Monstrous Double*

At the beginning of this chapter I mentioned how the figure of the double that functions in Girard's early work to explain the loss of difference at the intra- and intersubjective level parallels the loss of difference pertaining to reciprocal violence in his later work – when antagonists become doubles. This basic dynamic is central to Girard's theory of conflictual mimesis. In *Violence and the Sacred* however, 'triangular desire', which had been deployed in *Deceit, Desire, and the Novel* as a spatial metaphor is no longer used to describe the dynamics that give rise to doubling. If the loss of differences can spread and threaten an entire community something more than a 'spatial metaphor' is needed to explain the storm that brews with such ferocity and takes the form of a collective crisis. The principle of Degree now functions to designate the space between differences in a hierarchy, and 'mimetic desire' becomes the term used to explain the hyper oscillations that lead from reciprocal violence to collective violence – from disorder to order. By using the term 'mimetic desire' Girard does not confine his analysis to the self/ other relation since the action no longer centres on the hero, as in the novel, but on the mediator who is also a rival.[87] Anyone can imitate anyone else, and everyone imitates. Collective crisis, as the logic of what can go wrong when we ignore our tendency to imitate, has replaced the intra and intersubjective crisis – cultural space thus supersedes literary space as individual concerns become eclipsed by the enormity of sacred violence.

The structure of desire discussed in *Violence and the Sacred* is essentially the same as in *Deceit, Desire, and the Novel*, except perhaps for the curious fact that what was described as 'Romantic desire', supposedly owing to the individual's 'uniqueness', is now said to 'correspond to a primary impulse of most living creatures, exacerbated in man to the point where only cultural constraints can channel it in constructive directions'.[88] The basic idea behind the escalation of violence towards crisis is the notion of the 'double bind', borrowed from Gregory Bateson's theory of schizophrenia. If desire is allowed to follow its own bent it will lead to two contradictory imperatives for the subject, who naturally imitates

---

we do not want it soon to end."' Terry, Eagleton, *Holy Terror* (New York: Oxford University Press 2005), p. 64 (quotation in text from B. Pascal, *Pensées*).

87. In *Violence and the Sacred* Girard tells us: 'Our first task is to define the rival's position within the system to which he belongs, in relation to both subject and object . . . In desiring an object the rival alerts the subject to the desirability of the object. The rival, then, serves as a model for the subject, not only in regard to such secondary matters as style and opinions but also, and more essentially, in regard to desires,' p. 145. The fact that everyone imitates and not all imitation is the same means, 'only the role of disciple is truly essential.' Girard, *Violence and the Sacred*, p. 147.

88. Ibid.

unselfconsciously until interrupted by a mediator. This double imperative: 'imitate me, I am your model/ don't imitate, I am your rival' leads to greater and greater attempts to obtain an illusory object and more intense displays of violence in the process.

> The unchannelled mimetic impulse hurls itself blindly against the obstacle of a conflicting desire. It invites its own rebuffs, and these rebuffs will in turn strengthen the mimetic inclination. We have, then, a self-perpetuating process, constantly increasing in simplicity and fervour. Whenever the disciple borrows from his model whatever he believes to be the 'true' object, he tries to possess that truth by desiring precisely what his model desires. Whenever he sees himself closest to the supreme goal, he comes into violent conflict with a rival. By a mental shortcut that is both eminently logical and self-defeating, he convinces himself that the violence itself is the most distinctive attribute of this supreme goal![89]

Violence then is self-perpetuating, since it is the motive force and the ineluctable object of our desires. Rivalry spreads, as each rival turns to even greater violence in a fatal attempt to seek out an obstacle that promises to be truly insurmountable. Mimetic desire would destroy the community if it were not for the surrogate victim, who stops the process, and the various rituals that renew the therapeutic effects of the original 'expulsion', thus preventing the crisis from beginning afresh.[90]

'The monstrous double' emerges from *within* the mechanism responsible for sacrificial substitution in a crisis-ridden community, where differences never *really* disappear, although from outside the system the symmetry appears definitive.[91] Describing the confusion that besets antagonists from within, Girard says:

> . . . the differences that seem to separate the antagonists shift ever faster and more abruptly as the crisis grows in intensity. Beyond a certain point the nonreciprocal moments succeed each other with such speed that their actual passage becomes blurred. They seem to overlap, forming a composite image in which all the previous 'highs' and 'lows', the extremes that had previously stood out in bold relief, now seem to intersect and mingle. Where formerly he had seen his antagonist and himself as incarnations of unique and separate moments in the temporal scheme of things, the subject now perceives two simultaneous projections of the entire time span – an effect that is almost cinematographic.[92]

---

89. Ibid., p. 148.
90. Ibid.
91. Ibid., pp. 158–159.
92. Ibid., p. 160.

When the collective experience of the monstrous double looms large the differences are not eliminated, as seems apparent from outside the system, but muddied and confused, leading to hallucinations.[93]

Girard provides an explication of Euripides' *The Bacchae* as a compelling example of collective violence, scapegoating and the hallucinatory effects of the monstrous double. Referring to the atmosphere of terror that accompanies the hallucination of the 'thousand headed dragon' when Dionysus springs his trap on Pentheus, Girard writes: 'When violent hysteria reaches a peak the monstrous double looms up everywhere at once. The decisive act of violence is directed against this awesome vision of evil and at the same time sponsored by it.'[94] In *The Bacchae*, the monstrous double is everywhere. From the beginning of the play 'animal, human, and divine are caught up in a frenetic interchange; beasts are mistaken for men or gods, gods and men are mistaken for beasts.'[95] As soon as the dizzying effects of the heightening mimetic antagonisms are felt, the doubling becomes decisively linked to the image of the terrifying monster. Pentheus gives us a good example of this primordial 'cyclothymia' just prior to the unanimous resolution to the tragic play when he says to Dionysus: 'I seem to see two suns, two Thebes, with two times seven gates. And you, you are a bull walking before me, with two horns sprouting from your head.'[96] When doubling becomes monstrous, the crisis has reached a critical point and the mechanism of the scapegoat is well and truly operative. What Girard adds to the intersubjective doubling explored in his early work is a more general concept that allows him to group together all the hallucinatory phenomena provoked at the height of the crisis by unrecognized reciprocity.[97] When we fail to see that our own violence erodes differences, even while it appears to us to establish them, crisis escalates.

7. *Bringing Together All Rites: The Janus Face of the Sacred*

At the end of Chapter 1 we saw how the 'unity of novelistic conclusions' brings the authors, the heroes of the novels and the literary community together in a shared unity through the structure of death and rebirth, at the end of *Deceit*,

---

93. 'To my knowledge only Dostoevsky, both in his early novel *The Double* and in the masterpieces of his maturity has set forth in concrete terms the elements of reciprocity at work in the proliferation of monsters.' Girard, *Violence and the Sacred*, p. 161.
94. Ibid.
95. Ibid., p. 162.
96. Ibid.
97. The new more expansive concept of monstrous double helps him to further explain two sets of 'puzzling' religious phenomena: possession and the ritual use of masks. Girard, *Violence and the Sacred*, p. 164.

Desire, and the Novel. In a similar way, the last chapter of *Violence and the Sacred* is entitled 'The Unity of All Rites'. In it Girard attempts to show how mimetic desire and the surrogate victimage mechanism apply to all ritual experiences, including the forms of ritual that are often regarded as aberrations. Having examined the works of Freud[98] and Lévi-Strauss in earlier chapters, Girard proceeds to connect a host of apparently anomalous practices, such as cannibalistic ritual, initiation rites, tragic catharsis and modern medicine. Even philosophical scapegoating in classical Greek culture is examined with a focus on Socrates as a victim of his people, and the poets expelled from Plato's *Republic* for tending to side with the victims of their tragic dramas over the citizens. As his study unfolds so too does the evidence of a founding event based on the formula 'unanimity *minus one.*' More and more examples are added of the prevalence of scapegoating in early cultures. Gradually, Girard begins to articulate the full scope of his hypothesis – a conclusion that seems quite staggering.

> As we bring together the various elements of our discussion, only one conclusion seems possible. There is a unity that underlies not only all mythologies and rituals but the whole of human culture, and this unity of unities depends on a single mechanism, culturally functioning because perpetually misunderstood – the mechanism that ensures the community's spontaneous and unanimous outburst of opposition to the surrogate victim.[99]

Even the modern judicial system, which, at the outset of his study, provided a method of protection by taking on the responsibility of revenge, must now be explained in the context of generative violence in the form, for example, of capital punishment. Otherwise, he says, we are back to a social contract theory that would contradict his line of argument because it would be based on rational agreement rather than misapprehension.[100]

Any elements of ritual that appear not to fit Girard's account – and hence to remain as anomalies – can be accounted for, he believes, by the inherently ambiguous nature of the sacred, and, in particular, the inherent need for the victim to appear both truly central to the community and, at the same time, utterly foreign. Girard shows this ambiguity operating in the institution of monarchy, as one institutional form of political power. The failure of modern ethnologists to understand this ambiguity, he argues, is itself a function of the sacred.

> It does not seem to have occurred to modern theorists . . . to draw together such different institutions as the African monarchies, the cannibalistic rites of the

---

98. Girard argues that Freud drew back from the mimetic hypothesis to protect his 'precious "Oedipus complex".' He also argues that it is, ironically, Freud's now discredited work in *Totem and Taboo* on the collective murder that contains some of his most brilliant insights into the origins of culture.
99. Girard, *Violence and the Sacred*, pp. 299–300.
100. Ibid., p. 298.

Tupinamba, and the sacrificial ceremonies of the Aztecs. However, each of these institutions casts light on the other. In the Aztec rites a certain time elapses between the election of a victim and his execution. During this time every effort is made to gratify his desires. The people prostrate themselves before him, fight for the privilege of touching his garments. He is treated like a king, almost like a god. Yet this reverential treatment ends in a brutal murder. The Tupinamba prisoner shares certain similarities with the African king. In each case the victim's situation combines grandeur and misery, veneration and ignominy.[101]

Discrepancies between these rites can be explained, Girard maintains, by seeing them as three different ways in which three societies look at the same process: the loss and subsequent recovery of social unity.[102]

To add credence to this theory of 'paradoxical lucidity' Girard sets it in a western context, where suddenly the 'king and the fool' become like primordial doubles of each other, holding between them the oscillating forces of mimetic desire.

> When we consider the monarchy of the Ancient Regime in France or any other traditional monarchic system, we cannot help wondering whether it would not be more profitable to consider these institutions in the light of sacred kingship than the light of modern ideas about monarchy. The concept of Divine Right is not a fiction made up on the spur of the moment to keep the king's subjects in line. The life and death of the monarchic concept in France – its sacred rites, its fools, its cure of scrofula through the royal touch, the grand finale of the guillotine – all this is clearly structured by the influence of sacred violence.[103]

The sacred character of the king is defined by his identity with the victim. The dual forces personified by the king, Girard believes, are internalized within each of us. At one level or another each of us recognizes the face of the victim behind the king and the fool in the tragic drama of human existence – the world is truly a stage, continually being set for a global cathartic performance. Whatever was missing from the 'unity of novelistic conclusions' by way of an explanation of *why* the great novelists arrived at the same conclusion, for example 'the unity of unity,' has been 'found' and articulated in *Violence and the Sacred*. 'All religious rituals spring from the surrogate victim, and all the great institutions of mankind, both secular and religious spring from ritual. Such is the case as we have seen, with political power, legal institutions, medicine, the theatre, philosophy and anthropology itself. It could hardly be otherwise, for the working basis of human thought, the process of "symbolization", is rooted in the surrogate victim.'[104] The symbolic structure of death and resurrection, as the basic structure of the novel

---

101. Ibid., p. 301.
102. Ibid., p. 302.
103. Ibid., p. 304.
104. Ibid., p. 306.

and western art more generally, when viewed in a properly anthropological light can now be understood as the Janus face of the sacred concealing the victimization and collective murder of a scapegoat. Both the unity of novelistic conclusions and the unity of all rites point in one direction: the scapegoat mechanism. This, it transpires, is not only a unifying principle that can explain the origin and function of all rites, it is also a generative phenomenon responsible for all symbolic thinking – all cultural forms all historical and political institutions, the origins of language, and the process of hominization itself. Sacrifice as a deceiving 'norm' that hides its origins in scapegoating, provides a way for societies to pass from one condition to another through a process of death and dissolution, what the philosopher Georges Bataille calls 'creation by means of loss'.[105]

8. *Beyond Structuralism: Representation and Real Violence*

From a philosophical point of view Girard's theory of collective violence as an explanation of the origins of culture appears wildly speculative. However, in order to grasp how he reaches these conclusions it is important to try to understand his relationship to a leading structuralist like Claude Lévi-Strauss whose work allows Girard to think of culture and cultural history as a system of signs designating fundamental differences based on hidden structures detectable in myth. To see him in this way is not to look first to a pre-historic event, as the 'substance' of his claim, and presume that he would have us believe that our imagination along with some archaic and often fragmentary 'texts' can be a reliable means of reconstructing an incredibly remote scenario. Rather, to acknowledge Girard's structuralist influences is to look first at language as a totality – as an all-encompassing system of signs that leads him to posit an explanation for this system that lies outside itself, as system. If we approach his theory of origins in this way it becomes easier thereafter to begin to understand how the 'system' and its 'explanation' might provide the basis of a credible *paleo*-anthropological theory of culture.[106]

---

105. Quoted in Eagleton, *Holy Terror*, p. 129. Speaking about the politically institutionalised version of sacrifice that we find in the form of the state, Eagleton argues: "[The] scapegoat maintains a metaphorical rather than a metonymic relation to the people as a whole. It is a substitute for them, rather than a signifying part of their collective life. Far from glimpsing a reflection of its own features in this traumatic horror, the community thrusts it out, thus disavowing its significance and perpetuating its own self-blindness. By displacing its own deformities onto a vilified other, it can rid itself magically of its defects. Sacrifice of this sort is a kind of social therapy or public hygiene, from which you emerge cleaner and stronger". Eagleton, *Holy Terror* p. 131. In contrast the scapegoat as a metonymic rather than a metaphorical relation to the people as a whole 'is a piece of them rather than a displacement. In this torn, twisted thing, the people come to acknowledge something of their own twisted disfigurement, contemplating themselves in the Real rather than the imaginary. They recognise in this dereliction

In *Violence and the Sacred* Girard begins to look beyond structuralism for an explanation of cultural order and disorder. However, he remains sympathetic to its basic methods, and its general antipathy towards philosophies of consciousness. 'Structural analysis cannot deal with everything,' he claims, 'but within its limits it is highly satisfactory.'[107] Fleming makes the case that 'Girard's work remains true to structuralism in several respects, not least in so far as both affirm the idea that there are generative structures which lie beneath the surface of texts that supplant authorial intention and "direct" the action of the narrative in the absence of the subject's conscious collaboration.'[108] In addition, Lévi-Strauss remains an important anthropologist for Girard since 'he is perhaps the first to appreciate the centrality of differentiation and undifferentiation in analysing the symbolic structures of mythology.'[109] Yet Girard departs from Lévi-Strauss and structuralism in general, because, in his view, both fail to give meaning to the most essential cultural structure – beyond the 'logico-semantic world of myth itself' – the polarization of all against one.[110]

Girard's mature engagement with the work of Lévi-Strauss, beginning in *Violence and the Sacred* with an analysis of 'marriage laws', continues to develop in *Things Hidden Since the Foundations of the World* where the homologies and variances between their respective theories become more apparent. In the latter of these works Girard examines two myths also examined by Lévi-Strauss in his *Totemism* – the myth from the Ojibwa Indians of North America and the myth from the Tikopia people of the Pacific.[111] His analysis of these particular myths

---

of being their own horrific double, and in doing so open themselves to a deathliness at the core of their own identity.' *Holy Terror*, p. 131.

106. See, William Mishler, 'The Question of the Origin of Language in René Girard, Eric Gans, and Kenneth Burke', in *Anthropoetics* 5, no. 1 (Spring/Summer 1999).

107. Girard, *Violence and the Sacred*, p. 241.

108. Fleming, *René Girard: Violence and Mimesis*, p. 85.

109. Ibid.

110. Ibid., p. 85.

111. Fleming provides a synopsis of both myths: 'The first depicts the origin of the five Objibwa clans from six anthropomorphic supernatural beings who came from the ocean to mix with humans. Initially, one of the six beings covered his eyes and refused to look at the humans. His curiosity, however, eventually got the better of him, and – lifting a corner of the veil covering his eyes – his gaze fell upon an Objibwan man, who was killed instantly. Although he was possessed of no malicious intent, the other supernatural beings persuaded the godly being with the deadly gaze to return to the water. The five remaining beings continued to dwell among the humans and become a great blessing to them. From these remaining five came the five great totems of clans.'

'The second myth, of the Tikopia, tells of how at one time the gods were little different from the mortal beings and even served as representatives for the various clans. It happened one day that a foreign god named Tikarau came to visit; the local gods prepared a feast for the visitor and organised some competitive "trials of speed and strength" to see whether they or their guests would triumph.

allows Girard 'not only to interpret and discuss the myths, but to engage with Lévi-Strauss – and indeed structuralist analysis itself – in more general terms'.[112] Girard interprets these myths in the manner set out in his work *The Scapegoat*, utilizing as a key to his reading what he refers to as the signs of persecution: a five fold set of criteria (what Fleming calls a 'typology') that he finds evidence for in the texts he analyses.[113] The themes or motifs that give textual evidence of sacrificial crisis are as follows:

1. A theme of disorder or undifferentiation: Girard believes that the beginnings of myths depict the crisis of degree that corresponds with the way in which intense mimetic rivalry progressively erodes all differences. As Fleming points out, most creation myths begin with a depiction of a state of the 'world' as an undifferentiated mass or an original chaos, that Girard suggests can 'also be found in mythical accounts of cosmic catastrophes, fires, floods, droughts, pestilence, and fights between people (especially twins)'.[114]

2. An individual who has committed some transgression, and is therefore guilty of a crime. Whether the offence is represented as being 'grave' or 'trivial' the actual seriousness of the crime is indicated by its grave and serious consequences.[115]

3. The presence of certain stigmata or 'victimary signs': Girard highlights how the central figures of mythology are invariably exceptional characters 'World mythology swarms with the lame, the blind, and the crippled or abounds with people stricken by the plague. As well as heroes in disgrace there are those who are exceptionally beautiful and free of all blemish.'[116]

4. A description of the killing or expulsion of the culprit. As Fleming explains, 'Myths detail events whereby a guilty party is killed or driven away, either by the whole community acting as one, or by one person who acts for the whole community. For Girard this indicates the scapegoating act stricto sensu.'[117]

During one of the races the visitor slipped and claimed to be injured; in a flash, however, he stopped limping and bolted towards the food prepared for the feast, gathered it all up and dashed away in the direction of the hills. The local gods set out after him and Tikarau slipped and fell again, enabling some of his pursuers to retrieve some of the stolen food: a coconut, a taro, a yam, and a breadfruit. Although the thief was successful in escaping with most of the food that he had gathered up, the four vegetables retrieved were saved for humans – these fruits became the basis of the totem system.' Fleming, *René Girard: Violence and Mimesis* p. 82.

112. Ibid.
113. We can find this 'typology' discussed in more detail in Girard's work *The Scapegoat*. Fleming schematizes it in a useful way in his own work on Girard, and I have further schematized it here for my purposes.
114. Fleming, *René Girard: Violence and Mimesis*, p. 80.
115. Ibid., p. 81.
116. Girard, *The Scapegoat*, pp. 31–32.

5. A return of order: The killing or expulsion has the effect of generating peace and a return to order. The negative mimesis and violence of the community are expelled along with the victim, binding the community in a restored sense of calm. Hence, 'the victims represented in myths are invariably sacralized or venerated – given the features and even the moral profile of a saviour figure – owing to the way in which they have transformed the communities under threat.'[118]

The Objibwa myth and the Tikopia myth treated by Lévi-Strauss evince the structural requirements of a scapegoat narrative, based on the above typology. Indeed, as Fleming points out, for both Girard and Lévi-Strauss the two myths mentioned here 'chart the movement from an undifferentiated state to a differentiated state via the expulsion or occlusion of a "foreign element" through which (differential) meaning is established.'[119] However, despite the similarities between Girard and Lévi-Strauss in their readings of the same myths, for the latter the 'expulsion and occlusion' are simply the 'necessary conditions' for the creation of meaning. In other words, the fragile system of signs discovers what it needs in order to organize itself into symbolic thought. The structuralist who understands language in this way, therefore only 'interprets the expulsions as exemplifying a *logic* of exclusion or elimination, which, in its exclusion, frees the mind from a certain perceptual or conceptual congestion'.[120] But the structuralist does not see the exclusion as having any bearing on a 'real event', outside the system of signs, and so there is no adequate explanation provided of the 'actual commonalities' found in the various texts.[121]

By limiting the meaning of these commonalities to their 'abstract structures', Lévi-Strauss ignores 'how the differentiation he details is established'.[122] Describing this central issue in the debate between mimetic theory and structuralism, Fleming writes: 'The difference is that for Girard, this elimination is not merely an abstract operation that somehow makes conceptualisation possible, but a historically based event, or series of events, that provides the impetus for the generation of the narrative.'[123] Moving beyond Lévi-Strauss in relation to the origins of structural thought itself, Girard contends that 'the elimination of the gods in both myths [the Ojibwa and Tikopia] suggests communal acts of violence directed at victims.'[124]

---

117. Fleming, *René Girard: Violence and Mimesis*, p. 81.
118. Ibid., p. 82.
119. Ibid., p. 85.
120. Ibid.
121. Ibid., p. 86.
122. Ibid.
123. Ibid.
124. Ibid.

If structuralism is constitutionally unable to get behind the structures it describes, it is because it always needs 'to assume that the binary oppositions it uncovers are never generated for them [structures] but are always already there; the mediation of the conflictual polarities always takes place through the system itself.'[125] This, however, does not account for the most significant aspects of the system – that is, that such 'conflictual polarities', as the basis of structural differentiation, should exist in the first place, or even *how* the 'mediation' that 'decongests' the mind is accomplished.[126] So, while structuralism of Lévi-Strauss's kind is right to claim that mythology represents the birth of human thought, it is wrong to determine this birth as having come about through an 'immaculate conception'; it is an 'intellectual blind alley' to conclude, as structuralists do, that 'from the beginning there was difference.'[127] Summing up the contribution of Girardian theory to structuralist thought, Fleming remarks:

> Part of the appeal of Girard's thinking is that it is capable of being faithful to the considerable insights of structuralism by plotting structural homologies over a broad range of cultural institutions, practices, and texts, while at the same time not resting content with these homologies, refusing to see in these complete 'explanations'. For instance, the ambiguity with which ritual holds its sacrificial victims and myth holds its heroes is amenable to a more satisfying explanation if one can actually explain – and not merely articulate – these correspondences by appeal to a singular generative mechanism that engenders both ritual and myth.[128]

Girard's explanation of the basic structures governing language and culture, therefore reaches beyond structuralism to the '*astructuralism*' (Fleming's phrase) presupposed by his scapegoat hypothesis. From a presumption of disorder comes a concept of order that cannot be explained with reference to its internal structures. It is only by positing a 'real event' outside the system of signs, Girard believes, that one can account for difference as the result of 'expulsion' and 'mythic re-appropriation' – a theory, in other words, of sacred violence.

In Chapter 1 I argued that Girard was already being influenced by structuralism when he wrote *Deceit, Desire, and the Novel,* and that the spiritual death and rebirth of the author was part of a more general debunking of the humanistic subject by a wave of new French theory. In this chapter we saw how the crisis that led to disintegration at the level of the individual in Girard's early work became the basis of a dominant motif of his later work – collective crisis. Reciprocal violence generates de-differentiation at the level of culture, giving rise to a mimetic frenzy. The principle of Degree, as examined in Shakespeare's plays, provides the

---

125. Ibid., p. 87.
126. Ibid.
127. Ibid.
128. Ibid., p. 88.

paradigm of healthy imitation and stable cultural order. However, external mediation can easily give rise to internal mediation when 'Degree' becomes threatened, leading to violence and chaos. When violence is at its most intense, Girard believes, the community is prevented from destroying itself by the scapegoat mechanism. Those caught up in the violence become polarized against a surrogate victim – an example of which he claims, can be found in the Oedipus cycle, whereby the poison and the cure become synonymous, and the ambiguous power of the sacred is conferred with grave consequences upon the King of Thebes. Evidence of a 'surrogate victim,' Girard claims, can be found in all cultures, if we are only prepared to recognize the link between de-differentiation and violence in the identifiable pattern of scapegoating in all mythological texts.

9. Conclusion: Reading Back In

The movement that we find in Girard's early work, from division to unity – from death to rebirth – is repeated in his later work. 'The Self and Other in Literary Structure' thus appears to be a proto-theory of culture. Deviated transcendence, rooted in pride and 'metaphysical desire', promises unity but leads to division. However, by renouncing the differences suggested by hatred – a renunciation that is the fruit of a 'sublime lucidity' – the 'hero' achieves a restored unity through a symbolic death and rebirth shared in by the literary community. In the later work we saw how, in death, the scapegoat becomes associated with the newly found peace and subsequently remembered and revered through myth and ritual – sacrifice being the perfect form of therapeutic re-enactment. When Girard comes to look at culture as a whole the movement once again starts with crisis or the breakdown of differences and ends with unity or restored order. However, the death and rebirth that governs the scapegoat mechanism is no mere 'mythology' or 'symbolic structure', it is rather the constituent feature of a 'real event' – one that Girard believes can explain the origins of the sacred and of culture more generally. If we read the early work – and especially its culmination in this 'unity of novelistic conclusions' – in light of the central theme of *Violence and the Sacred* (the scapegoat mechanism), it appears that something of a 'sacrificial crisis' is at work in literary space, that is differences break down (doubling, mimetic crisis) and are then restored through a quasi-mythic death and rebirth. And if 'real violence' against an innocent victim is the proper explanation of this structure, who or what, we might ask, functions as the 'scapegoat' – the generative element that guarantees unity, at the end of *Deceit, Desire, and the Novel*?

To try to answer this question I want to consider the implications of Girard's later theory for his early theory. Specifically, I want to look at the structuralism of literary space in light of the *astructuralism* of cultural space. This will involve taking the five-element typology mentioned above, which claims to uncover myths of persecution that point to acts of real violence against real victims, and applying it to Girard's own analysis of novelistic space in *Deceit, Desire, and the Novel*; it will involve, in other words, treating his literary criticism as a mythological text and thus conducting a kind of Girardian reading on Girard. Once again, the themes that occur in myths, and provide textual evidence of sacrificial crisis and scapegoating, are: (1) a theme of undifferentiation and disorder, (2) the presence of an individual who has committed a 'transgression' (and thus is responsible for the crisis), (3) the presence of certain signs on the culpable individual, (4) a description of this killing or expulsion and (5) the return of order. When these themes remain hidden, the text functions in a mythological capacity to conceal collective violence by displacing the responsibility for the crisis onto an innocent victim – unity has thus been achieved on the basis of a lie, that implicitly perpetuates the original act of violence.

When we consider these themes in relation to *Deceit, Desire, and the Novel*, we find an unusual correspondence between Girard's own theory of the novel and what he goes on to describe in an anthropological context as the constitutive features of a scapegoat myth, that is crisis, expulsion and restored order. For example, the first theme of crisis can be readily identified in the fraught intersubjective relation between self and other, particularly in the way imitative desire leads to internal mediation and obsessive rivalry. We find the fullest expression of this crisis in what Girard calls 'The Dostoyevskian Apocalypse' where Raskolnikov's vision of a plague of deadly flies descending on Europe provides the background explanation of how the culmination of internal mediation in metaphysical desire leaves the individual not knowing whom to condemn or whom to acquit, in other words, in a state of undifferentiation. This 'cultural contagion' thus becomes a fuller account of the disease – referred to at the beginning of the book as an 'ontological sickness' – that ends in the suicide of the social.[129] When read in light of the first theme that gives textual evidence of scapegoating, we can conclude with Girard the anthropologist that such 'pestilence' and 'plague' invariably represent displaced depictions of the process of undifferentiation, 'the annihilation of specificities symptomatic of a sacrificial crisis'.[130]

The second theme proposed by Girard as hidden evidence of a scapegoat myth is a blameworthy individual, someone who is seen as having caused the disintegration. This theme is once again obvious in *Deceit, Desire, and the Novel*, where the Romantic hero is depicted as the archetype of all characters whose failed exploits are owing to the mistaken belief in their own originality. The Romantic hero is thus deemed responsible by Girard for the crisis in the self-other relation, and literary space more broadly. He is the one who would be god, but who in fact requires a resurrection from the underground. Like Oedipus, he is both good and evil; he is the poisonous presence in literary space and ultimately the basis of a restored unity.

The third theme, the presence of certain marks or signs on the victim, is perhaps more obscure in Girard's early work, though I would argue it is nonetheless evident. In describing these 'stigmata' Fleming suggests that the central figures of

129. Girard, *Deceit, Desire, and the Novel*, p. 279.
130. Fleming, *René Girard: Violence and Mimesis*, p. 80.

world mythology are invariably highly unusual characters, 'aliens, monstrous creatures or gods; these all bear obvious signs of physical or moral exceptionality'.[131]
The fact that these exceptional human beings are usually depicted as 'heterogeneous mixtures of god, human and animal' is also indicative of the very crisis
brought about by mimetic rivalry – the loss of difference. Thus, in *Deceit, Desire,
and the Novel*, when Girard tells us that 'men become gods' is he not at once
exposing the problem for cultural systems of this kind of 'heterogeneous mixing',
and also reinforcing the attendant problem of scapegoating by making modern
individualism guilty of 'self-divinisation' – of being responsible for the mixing?
In other words, does he not offer an account of a type which in his own later
analysis, must be considered mythic? When he formulates his scapegoat theory,
men do 'become gods', not because of individual crisis, but because of collective
crisis. But unlike the images from world mythology, Girard does not represent his
Romantic 'god' uncritically, he does not believe the hero is an exceptional figure,
at least not until the *genius* is revealed at the end of the first work of criticism as
the fruit of novelistic experience. What he describes in terms of 'ontological sickness' is a condition and a dynamic in which the hero believes himself to be both
debased and divine. The signs of divinity are thus part of the hero's own interpretation of desire, and it is this attribute *that makes him guilty*. Girard's early understanding of the victim in *Deceit, Desire, and the Novel* revolves around the
Romantic hero as 'victim of triangular desire',[132] 'victim of internal mediation',[133]
'victim of metaphysical desire'[134] and 'eternal victim'.[135] What strikes a reader as
odd, having learned that the later work reveals the hero of structural violence as
'innocent', is the manner in which the Romantic hero is referred to as a 'victim',
but one who is actually guilty for the crimes of literary space. By making the hero
of the novel the 'victim of desire' Girard also, ironically, makes him guilty of the
one crime that will justify his expulsion from literary space. Unlike more archaic
myth perhaps in which the victim was driven out and then in his absence seen as
a god, in the myth that pervades literary space the hero wants to be god, and is
hence expelled. Yet like archaic myth, in and through his absence he is revered as
a 'genius' and a 'true hero'.[136]

In a manner reminiscent of the way Oedipus is marked with the stigmata of a
'club foot', we find in Girard's early description of Descartes, the father of modern individualism, a depiction of his 'divided nature', in other words his pride, as
somehow symbolic of the way in which the philosopher walked with 'unbalanced
gait' due to the 'great weakness on his right side on which he was unable to support himself'.[137] Should this description of a physical manifestation of a spiritual

---

131. Ibid., p. 81.
132. Girard, *Deceit, Desire, and the Novel*, p. 3.
133. Girard, *Deceit, Desire, and the Novel*, p. 177.
134. Ibid., p. 283.
135. Ibid., p. 299.
136. Ibid., p. 296.
137. Ibid., p. 92.

disease not rightly be declared a kind of mythologizing by the literary community that justifies the subject's expulsion?

The fourth theme, a description of the killing or expulsion of the culprit, signifies for Girard the act of scapegoating. It is what Mircea Eliade calls the 'creative murder' that establishes the community or polity,[138] and I want to suggest it is represented at the end of *Deceit, Desire, and the Novel* by the spiritual death of the Romantic individual, a death that Girard believes is itself depicted in the great novels by the physical death of the principal character. However, when the critic, like a Dr. Kevorkian,[139] assists with this textual suicide, we have to wonder whether his own invisible intentions do not conceal a more sinister desire to tidy up the literary scene at any cost. Either way, the physical death as the basis of a spiritual death can be seen as a kind of 'killing' of the old Romantic self, in which the literary critic and the literary community participate. The culpable party must be expelled.[140]

If the previous four themes and their appearance in *Deceit, Desire, and the Novel*, fail to persuade us that mythological displacement is at work in Girard's own criticism (based on his later criteria for identifying such mythological displacement), then perhaps conviction will be finally secured when we consider the fifth and last theme in relation to what Girard describes as 'the unity of novelistic conclusions'. This theme, 'the regeneration or return of order', relies on the above-mentioned 'killing' to engender peace and unity. The death and rebirth of the author that we find at the end of the literary theory functions in the terms of what Girard later calls 'double transference', associated with the ambiguity of the victim who is both monstrous and godlike. The 'secondary displacement' (from being a polluted presence that must be expelled, to being raised up to divine status) ensures that victims become heroes/gods, 'owing to the way in which they have transformed the crisis and "saved" the communities under threat.'[141] The novelist thus undergoes regeneration because, for Girard, the unity of novelistic conclusions points to the truth of literary space. The hero who is capable of writing the great work, that is, every author and every novelistic genius, and every great critic for that matter[142] – must put to death his or her Romantic self. Thus order is restored, and a community is born (once again).

---

138. Fleming, *René Girard: Violence and Mimesis*, p. 81.

139. Former American pathologist who claims to have assisted 130 patients with their 'right to die', and who served eight years of a prison sentence between 1999 and 2007 for second-degree murder. See Ellen Piligian and Monica Davey, 'Dr. Kevorkian, assisted-suicide advocate, is released from prison.' *International Herald Tribune, Americas* (June 1, 2007).

140. This expulsion can be seen as both 'metaphoric' and 'metonymic' after Eagleton's analysis (see note 105 above).

141. Fleming, *René Girard: Violence and Mimesis*, p. 82.

142. In an interview with James Williams at the end of *The Girard Reader*, Girard relates how when he started working on *Deceit, Desire, and the Novel* in the late

Girard's five-element typology for identifying myths that conceal scapegoating, when applied to his own early theory, actually reveal this work as mythological. By his own later diagnosis of collective violence and its evidence in myth, we can unmask his literary criticism as a form of scapegoating that charts the crisis, resolution and unity of the literary community around the Romantic hero, and what might be called philosophy of consciousness (in all its various guises). For all Girard's analysis of the Oedipus story, does he not himself embody here something of its tragic spirit? By identifying with Tiresias is the critic not reinstating the paradox of the blind seer who tries to warn Oedipus, but ends up hastening the violent resolution that he himself participates in? The following chapter will examine how this blind spot in Girardian theory forces him to merge the 'Romantic Fallacy' and the 'Scapegoat Mechanism' so as to fatally undermine subjectivity and all meliorist accounts of historical change.

1950s it was very much in the mode of the atheistic intellectuals of the time. René Girard, *The Girard Reader*, (ed.) James G. Williams. (New York: The Crossroads Publishing Company, 1996), p. 283. In the same interview Girard recounts how he identified with the novelist's conversion when he wrote the conclusion of *Deceit, Desire, and the Novel*. Girard recounts: 'When I wrote the last chapter of my first book, I had a vague idea of what I would do, but as the chapter took form I realized I was undergoing my own version of the experience I was describing. I was particularly attracted to the Christian elements . . . So I began to read the Gospels and the rest of the Bible. And I turned into a Christian,' p. 285.

CHAPTER 3

NEGATING SUBJECTIVITY AND HISTORY: PROBLEMS WITHIN GIRARDIAN THEORY

By evoking the notion of metaphysical desire, I am not in any way giving in to metaphysics. To understand this notion, we have only to look at the kinship between the mimetic structure . . . and the part played by notions of honour or prestige in certain types of rivalry that are regulated by society: duels, sporting competitions etc. These notions are in fact created by the rivalry; they have no tangible reality whatsoever. Yet the very fact that there is a rivalry involving them makes them appear more real than any object . . . In our world [a world not stabilized by victimage mechanisms], we end up with an 'infinite' measure of desire – what I have called ontological or metaphysical desire.[1]

René Girard

. . . for the course of History is predictable in the degree to which all men [sic] love themselves, and spontaneous in the degree to which each man loves God and through Him his neighbour.[2]

W. H. Auden

1. Introduction

The first quotation above, taken from *Things Hidden Since the Foundation of the World*, describes the conditions that give rise to the modern sacrificial crisis. In it Girard makes the point that what, in the past, appeared to be 'real' marks of distinction were only conferred with meaning by desire itself. Within a traditional world view, ordered hierarchically by the principle of Degree, desire, and hence rivalry (and hence violence), is contained. But in our world, a world that does not even have the appearance of the real, these forces are being unleashed. However, what may strike a reader who has been persuaded by my argument so far – that there is an important difference between Girard's early and later works – is that Girard continues to use terms from his early explanation of crisis (as 'metaphysical desire') to explain the modern sacrificial crisis. When the protections that once formed part of the sacred, are no longer available, an 'infinity' of desire goes unchannelled. This assimilation of an already suspicious view of history into an

---

1. René Girard, *Things Hidden since the Foundation of the World: Research Undertaken in Collaboration with J.-M. Oughourlian and G. Lefort*, trans. S. Bann and M. Metteer (Stanford: Stanford University Press, 1987b), pp. 296–297.
2. Quoted in Anthony Hecht, *The Hidden Law: The Poetry of W. H. Auden* (New York: Harvard University Press, 1994).

anthropological account of cultural disintegration results in a thoroughly dystopian position that gives no quarter to 'humanism'. The apocalyptic tone of his most recent work, *Achever Clausewitz,* confirms this.[3] Indeed, Auden's poetic insight into a 'spontaneous History' brought about by each individual's capacity to love God and neighbour, cited in the second quotation above, must be considered, in Girard's account, yet another illusion of the Romantic fallacy.

In Chapter 2, I discussed how literary space and cultural space share the same basic elements with regard to crisis and resolution (division and unity). Yet, I argued, Girard's early work *does not share* with the later work the same explanation of this resolution – namely the scapegoat mechanism – since this latter explanation properly belongs to this later work. When we read the early work in the light of the theory of the scapegoat and the five-element typology that Girard claims provides the interpretative key for identifying myths that conceal acts of scapegoating, we find evidence of such 'scapegoating' in *Deceit, Desire, and the Novel* – or so I have argued. The renunciation of the Romantic individual at the hands of the critic functions in the same way as the victim's immolation at the hands of the community, that is, as the catalyst of a restored unity. But the unity achieved at the end of *Deceit, Desire, and the Novel* is not the same as the unity achieved at the end of *Violence and the Sacred*. The 'unity of novelistic conclusions'[4] provides the basis of an identity between the author and the critic, while the 'Unity of All Rites' exposes all apparently unifying activity as a form of division – 'unanimity minus one'. Hence, in Girard's work we find two different and conflicting accounts of unity: the unity of the literary community at the end of *Deceit, Desire, and the Novel*, which is 'true', and the unity at the end of *Violence and the Sacred*, which is 'false'.

The first strand of my critique of Girard, then, exposes his own scapegoating of the subject under the terms of the Romantic fallacy. This certainly places his early work in question as a credible account of subjectivity and the self/other relation, since we can now readily see that the rebirth of the hero has more to do with

---

3. The picture on the cover of this work is a mushroom cloud from a nuclear bomb. René Girard, *Achever Clausewitz* (Paris: Carnets Nord, 2007a). Also, in a recent interview with Robert Doran, Girard asserts, 'I personally think that [9/11] represents a new dimension, a new world dimension. What communism was trying to do, to have a truly global war, has happened, and it is real now.' René Girard, 'Apocalyptic Thinking After 9/11', in *SubStance*, No. 115, Vol. 37, no. 1 (2008), p. 21. Girardians often use the term apocalypse when referring to the 'unveiling' or 'disclosure' of violence. See Robert Hamerton-Kelly, *Politics and Apocalypse: Studies in Violence, Mimesis, and Culture* (East Lansing: Michigan State University, 2007).

4. 'The unity of novelistic conclusions consists in the renunciation of metaphysical desire.' René Girard, *Deceit, Desire, and the Novel: Self and Other in Literary Structure*, trans. Yvonne Freccero (Baltimore: Johns Hopkins University Press, 1965), p. 293, 294.

legitimating the literary community than the actual integrity of a restored selfhood. But there are two other related strands of critique that I wish to develop in this chapter – so that in all I am bringing forward three lines of argument against Girardian theory. The second strand has to do with the fact that Girard continues to employ his early work to help explain and buttress his theory of the scapegoat and in particular his application of this theory to the modern period. The third strand (constituting my most sustained critique) focuses on the consequences of this continued employment of his early work for explanatory purposes in his later work (I shall identify three significant – and significantly problematic – consequences). While there is a good deal of interdependence between them, for the sake of my overall argument these three strands can remain broadly independent.

I have already elaborated the first strand in Chapter 2. In the following section of this chapter I proceed to the second strand showing how Girard relies on some central insights from his early work to explain the modern crisis in cultural space (and hence considers the later work as unproblematically continuous with this early work). While I do not wish to attack his theory of the scapegoat in his later anthropology, I do want to question its apparent continuity with his early work and the suggestion that this anthropology *requires* the absence of a meliorist view of human development. In the remaining sections of this chapter I proceed to the third strand of my overall argument, highlighting the problems for Girard's theory – by way of inconsistency and tension – that derive from his continued concealment of the early act of scapegoating in his account of a 'debunked' subject.

The first consequence, as I will show, of Girard's relying on his (now problematic) early theory to explain his later theory is that it commits him to two incompatible accounts of violence: one (in the early theory) stressing the need for violence to be kept *hidden*, and the other (in the later theory) claiming that the true allure of violence lies in its being made *manifest*. By examining the influence of Alexandre Kojève on Girard's formulation of desire as mimetic, I make the case that Girard's later understanding of how crisis escalates is not compatible with his early theory, and that his reliance on his early account of mimetic desire to explain collective violence is by no means straightforward. The second consequence of Girard's dependence on his early theory is that a moral subject is given no space to emerge in his or her own right. I will consider how the Girardian view of 'interdividual psychology' further alienates the perspective of a thinking feeling subject, by divesting it of any positive sense of interiority. The third consequence of Girard's continued use of the problematic theory concerns where (in the absence of a moral subject) he is pushed when trying to account for 'agency'. Having outlined how *desire* ends up with more status and agency than a moral subject, I will argue that such reifying of desire is more characteristic of Schopenhauerian 'Will' than Christian *agapē,* and is thus at odds with Girard's own stated belief in the Christian *kerygma*.[5] The final section in this chapter makes an ancillary, but nonetheless important, point concerning Girard's understanding in *Deceit, Desire, and the Novel* of the limits of the author's insight into his own world. I argue that

Girard's hypostatizing of desire translates as a kind of irrationalism that cannot account for – and consequently must deny – for example, Dostoevsky's *own critique* of the determining and reductive forces of nineteenth century Russia; this critique is dismissed – unwarrantedly, I shall claim – in favour of a primarily psychological reading of the author's development. If Dostoevsky's own analysis of culture matters prior to any 'novelistic conclusions' – which of course would indicate a pre-apocalyptic lucidity on his part – perhaps Girardian theory need not dispense with an ethical subject altogether when confronted with the peculiar dynamics of desire.

2. *Explaining Cultural Space by Reference to Literary Space*

As I have attempted to show through my analyses of the literary and the cultural spaces, Girard's early criticism can be understood as a form of scapegoating, whereby the Romantic hero is symbolically put to death, and the genius who is consecrated through this 'slaying' is partaken of by the literary community: unity is established. There is nothing particularly problematic about this for Girard's later theory so long as this theory does not in any significant way depend on it in explaining subjectivity and historical change. To use the earlier work – and what has now been shown (if my argument in the previous chapter holds good) to be its spurious account – to validate his anthropological claims would be incompatible with the spirit of Girard's later work exposing the scapegoat mechanism.[6] The aim of this section is to show where Girard is still trading off his early theory when he attempts to explain the relevance of his later mimetic theory for the modern period.

But before I examine this use of the early theory, I want to discuss briefly Girard's more explicit pronouncements, in the context of his theory of collective violence, on individualism and the modern period. The modern individual, while

---

5. On the problematic nature of Girard's mimetic theory for certain strands of Christianity see Gavin Flood, 'Mimesis, Narrative and Subjectivity in the Work of Girard and Ricoeur', in *Cultural Values*, vol. 4, no. 2 (April, 2000), especially the following passage, concerning the absence of subjectivity in Girard's work: '[T]he subjective response, and the subjective appropriation of the Christian narrative, is central to a sense of Christian narrative identity. While Girard might not object to this conception of subjective response, he arguably underestimates its importance in history, for subjectivity is overwhelmed by the more powerful force of mimetic desire,' p. 213.

6. On the need to reveal distortions that conceal scapegoating, Girard writes, 'These distortions must be identified and corrected, in order to reveal the arbitrary nature of the violence that persecution texts present as justified.' René Girard, 'The Scapegoat as Historical Referent', in *The Girard Reader*, ed. James G. Williams (New York: Crossroads Publishing, 2003), p. 105.

not seen as directly to blame for the crisis in cultural space, is nonetheless not granted any capacity to come to terms with mimetic desire in a manner that could resist violence or be deemed creative and transformative. This is so, Girard believes, broadly for two reasons: first, individualism is rooted in sacrifice, and, second, the individual lacks a cathartic mechanism. In *Violence and the Sacred*, he claims that sacrifice is a social institution, of which modern psychology can be understood as a much later development, 'contrary to its original spirit'.

> In ritual sacrifice the victim, when actually put to death, diverts violence from its forbidden objectives within the community . . . If the transfer is purely personal, as it is in psychoanalysis, then sacrifice cannot be a true social institution involving the entire community. But sacrifice as we know it is essentially a communal institution. 'Individualisation' marks a later, decadent stage in its evolution.[7]

In *Things Hidden Since the Foundation of the World*, Girard extends his hypothesis of the scapegoat, and sacrifice as a ritual re-enactment of an original violence, into the fields of biblical studies and psychology, as part of his sustained engagement with French psychoanalysis; individuality is further undermined as having any reliable agency that does not depend on the social institution of sacrifice. Without 'clearly marked differences' that are socially prescribed, individuals do not act; 'Desire' now acts for them.

> Desire is the mimetic crisis itself; it is the acute mimetic rivalry with the other that occurs in all circumstances we call 'private', ranging from eroticism to professionalism or intellectual ambition. The crisis can be stabilized at different levels according to the individuals concerned, but it always lacks the resources of catharsis and expulsion.[8]

Without a capacity to act positively and non-violently, the modern subject who believes in her own individuality or rational agency must be seen as effectively contributing to what Girard claims is the sacrificial crisis of the modern world.

Girard's hypothesis of the scapegoat as the cornerstone of the human community brings forward a theory of transcendence by violence re-enacted through ritual as a means of harnessing the protective, restorative and, ultimately, preservative forces of an original act of violence. This hypothesis marks a transition in his overall work from an analysis of death and rebirth that results in a completely new subject in his early criticism, to an analysis of death and rebirth that results in a new quasi-community in his later anthropology. In contrast to his early

---

7. René Girard, *Violence and the Sacred*, trans., Patrick Gregory (Baltimore: Johns Hopkins University Press, 1984), p. 101.
8. Girard, *Things Hidden*, p. 288.

criticism, transcendence in his later work is not an individual but rather a collective phenomenon. The self's prospects of overcoming, of letting go, of experiencing peace, or indeed identity and unity, it transpires, are functions of the sacred – which is always and everywhere rooted in the community – and arises out of the protective and restorative need to preserve life amidst crisis (uncertainty, loss of difference and death). Modern psychology intuits this function but cannot nearly replicate it to the same extent, since the mechanism that is generated by unanimous violence is not available to the individual. The individual, as individual, lacks the cathartic resources that belong to the community and therefore in our world the 'processes of desire' do not ever give rise to a 'collective crescendo'.[9]

I have been arguing up until now that there is nothing particularly problematic about Girard's early scapegoating for his later theory as long as he does not use the early work to explain aspects of this theory. Nor is there any obvious problem with his later theory of individualism as a 'decadent stage of sacrifice' if this theory is plausible within the terms of his account of the sacred. We might say that Girard is perfectly entitled to a 'happy coincidence' between his earlier antipathy toward the Romantic hero and his later profound suspicion of individualism – provided that this later suspicion is not based on the earlier antipathy, which (if my argument holds water) is deeply problematic.

We saw in Chapter 1 that the explanation of modern individualism revolves around triangular desire. This explanation allows nothing in the action of the self or the movement of history except a form of 'self-divinisation' that comes about with the loss of transcendence in the modern period: outside of a religious framework, 'men become gods in each others' eyes.' Not only does the other appear more powerful with the toppling of traditional hierarchies, each individual must produce 'Being' from within him or herself. Each must actively seek to take over the role of God from medieval theology, while secretly looking to the other for guidance. Historical change is negatively determined by the intra- and intersubjective dynamics of desire and the modern belief in each individual's originality. Self-divinization, or metaphysical desire, is based on the lie of horizontal transcendence, and as such it is an extreme manifestation of the individual's Romantic illusions.

In the scenario just outlined, in which 'men become gods', any ethic of 'generosity', as we saw in Chapter 1, is co-opted into a relentless self-deception, which Girard detects in what he considers the more or less equivalent perspectives of Descartes and Corneille – who both appear as ominous harbingers of modern individualism. This deceived and deceiving subject, short of a radical conversion, is helpless to resist negative mimesis through independent moral choice. While imitative desire has of course negative consequences for the subject in Girard's early work, it also has negative consequences for the subject in his later work,

---

9. Ibid., p. 287.

since it is now the catalyst of a sacrificial crisis that can be stopped only by some external cultural mechanism. By privileging imitative desire over human agency in both cases as an explanation of crises (literary, cultural), the individual, by default, is held responsible for the crises by Girard; either by pursuing her Romantic illusions (early work), or indirectly, by following her desires and hence contributing to mimetic escalation (later work). Thus, the individual crisis in the modern period treated in Girard's literary criticism is made to appear symptomatic of the crisis in cultural space, that is, as a condition arising from the lack of a cathartic mechanism when the sacred and the profane are mixed. These two theories of individualism that we find in Girard's work (one in his literary criticism and the other in his anthropology) appear to be aspects of one continuous and consistent theory. Might Girard plead ignorance of the correspondence here and once again invoke a 'happy coincidence'?

This possibility seems unlikely when we carefully consider Girard's later work, because when we do we are forced to acknowledge that his cultural anthropology is in fact trading off his early theory. Not only does he not renounce his early problematic theory of the Romantic fallacy, as the source of crisis in a modern context, he actually employs this theory of crisis to help validate his later theory of crisis.[10] As we saw in Chapter 2, when he develops his anthropology he holds onto a theory of imitation developed in the literary work (one that brings the 'false' desire for originality to light), and he places it in the context of Degree to provide an example of the collective crisis that now pertains to cultural space. The internal mediation, or 'inner division', experienced by the underground man (as the paradigm case of Romanic illusion), is thus supplemented in the later work by a fuller 'anthropological' account of the external mediation facilitated by a healthy measure of Degree and a harmonious order free of unchannelled rivalry and desire. Thus, internal mediation and external mediation are seen to explain loss of order and order respectively (the former coming to dominate in the modern period). It is not simply a 'happy coincidence' that the individual appears responsible for the crisis in both literary and cultural space. Girard actively promotes the idea that both 'spaces' are interdependent and quite naturally continuous; what follows from this interdependence and continuity in assessing modern individualism – that it is responsible for crisis – is not mere chance. It suggests that the 'lack of a cathartic mechanism' can now explain how 'men become gods in each others eyes', and this in turn appears to explain why the modern world is synonymous with a sacrificial crisis. The literary space and the cultural space

---

10. In a much later interview with James G. Williams he actually confirms the theoretical status of his early analysis with one small amendment: he now claims the author is 'scapegoating' the 'wicked' hero of the novel (without any reference to his own scapegoating of the Romantic hero). See, René Girard, 'The Anthropology of the Cross: A Conversation with René Girard', in *The Girard Reader*, ed. James G. Williams (New York: Crossroads Publishing, 2003a), p. 284.

are run together as if both analyses of death and rebirth, crisis and unity, are unproblematically parts of one unified theory of culture.[11]

By relying on the early criticism as still valid, Girard draws conclusions from it that help him explain crisis and unity in cultural space. When the early and later works appear to be part of one overarching theory, the Romantic individual is seen as somehow intrinsic to the cultural order and disorder that characterizes the sacred. And since the principle of Degree can no longer apply in the absence of traditional hierarchy in the modern world, negative mimesis, as a symptom of the false belief that one's desires are original, becomes the predominant experience of so-called freedom. When 'men become gods in each others' eyes,' it appears they are attempting, in the absence of a cathartic mechanism, to generate a unity that seems no longer possible, for Girard, once religious horizons, and their ritual functions, fade. The Romantic fallacy (that purports to debunk all philosophies of consciousness) is thus seen to explain the failed logic of history and human deve- lopment in the absence of religious frameworks, as if cultural space is a natural continuation of literary space.[12]

But what is remarkably ironic about Girard's retrospective anthropologizing of his early literary work is that it involves him in committing the very 'crime' (scapegoating) that he himself has both given us the most penetrating account of and made a career out of exposing in the work of other authors![13] The early

---

11. Other evidence of Girard's reliance on the early theory can be found scattered throughout his later work, often as references to the explanatory power of literary space. See, Girard, *Violence and the Sacred*, p. 146, 161; Girard, *Things Hidden*, p. 288.

12. For one thing it discounts the minimum condition of subjective agency, that is, being able to take a stand in relation to the world: as Girard himself says when he is asked where he is speaking from, 'I do not know and I do not care.' Girard, *Things Hidden*, p. 435.

13. 'Crime' does not seem too strong a word here when we bear in mind Girard's own explicit recognition that scapegoating can occur in theorizing, amounting to what he calls symbolic violence. This violence also occurs with respect to how some modern thinkers understand what follows from Nietzsche's 'Death of God' as an insight that actually implicates people in an original crime. The madman of Nietzsche's oft-quoted tract, Girard claims, hits on the essential truth of the mat- ter when he says, 'we have killed him' (Girard, 'Nietzsche versus the Crucified', in Williams, James G., ed. *The Girard Reader* (New York: Crossroads Publishing, 2003b), p. 256). Those who ignore this anthropological insight in favour of an atheistic reading of this passage (in other words as the 'death of metaphysics'), Girard believes, only reiterate a 'harmless cliché for what Nietzsche is really saying' (*The Girard Reader*, p. 257). Indeed, those who ignore the significance of the theme of the murder are themselves guilty of perpetuating 'real' violence since, 'the text of the death of God functions as one more murder of God as long as the theme of the murder remains unacknowledged' (*The Girard Reader*, p. 258). Quotation by Nietzsche taken from *The Gay Science*, aphorism 125.

theory of crisis – when made to appear congruent with his later work – generates a number of problematic consequences which I will be examining in the remainder of this chapter.

3. History as Negating Negativity: The Legacy of Alexandre Kojève

The influence of Alexandre Kojève's interpretation of Hegel on a generation of French thinkers, including Girard, has been widely noted.[14] Describing the broad contours of Girard's and Kojève's relationship, George Erving remarks: 'For both, desire is constitutive of human subjectivity, operates concretely at the level of anthropology and psychology, is concerned with existential recognition, is socially mediated, and is ineluctably bound up with violence.'[15] Erving argues that, while Kojève's reading of Hegel is based on an explicit assessment of the 'master and slave' dialectic, he follows Marx's humanistic turn, and incorporates Heidegger's notion of authenticity, in which 'true subjectivity emerges only by its willingness to overcome the living biological self.'[16] The human agent transcends itself (its own biological givenness) by transforming the natural order. 'Consequently, for Kojève, the self is a finite being, though, paradoxically, it is not an objective entity or *thing* that, as Kojève remarks "is always identical to itself". The self is rather an *action* such that "the very being of this I will be becoming, and the universal form of this being will not be space but time."'[17] Erving tells us that Kojève's dual ontology, which attributes true being to the non-natural self who must overcome its natural self, privileges difference over identity, and thus breaks with Hegel's Absolute *Geist*. However Kojève holds onto Hegel's dynamic concept of desire. 'For Kojève, desire creates the condition by which consciousness becomes *self*-consciousness (and thus human rather than animal consciousness), for desire is what makes the subject aware of himself *as such* by drawing attention to the fact that he is not that which he contemplates.'[18] The individual's being thus presupposes desire.[19]

---

14. Girard has gone some ways to disavow Kojève's influence on his central insight. Eugene Webb claims that Girard related to him in a conversation that he had been reading Kojève at the time he was writing *Deceit, Desire, and the Novel*, but that he 'did not believe Kojève or Hegel to have made a contribution toward what he himself considers his major original insight, the theory . . . of the resolution of violence through its polarization onto a single victim; both Kojève and Hegel, he says, remained bound to the idea of a perpetual dialectic of violence'. Eugene Webb, *The Self Between: From Freud to the New Social Psychology of France* (Washington: University of Washington Press, 1993), p. 116.

15. George Erving, 'René Girard and the Legacy of Alexandre Kojève', in *Contagion: Journal of Mimesis and Culture*, ed. Andrew McKenna, Vol. 10 (Spring 2003), p. 113.

16. Ibid.

17. George Erving, 'René Girard and the Legacy of Alexandre Kojève', p. 114.

18. Ibid.

The subject constituted by desire is a 'negating negativity', that is an emptiness in search of a fullness. 'It is a negativity that seeks positive content by negating and appropriating for itself the desire, that is, the being of another.'[20] Only in such a way does a subject gain recognition, and thereby say 'I am'. 'It is only as a creature who desires to have the sovereignty of its non-natural self recognised that man becomes aware of his pre-eminence over an animal consciousness that is given, fixed and incapable of self-reflection.'[21] Desire reveals the emptiness that the object of desire fails to satisfy, and as such it becomes conscious of itself as 'other than the static given real thing that stays eternally identical to itself'.[22] Therefore, what it must seek to appropriate if it is to be satisfied is the desire of the other, which inevitably gives rise to conflict and violence since in order to fully appropriate the other's desire the subject must destroy the other.[23] For Kojève, the other is a function of my being; therefore human society is 'necessarily contentious'. Erving quotes Kojève on this point: 'The I of Desire is an emptiness that receives a real positive content only by [a] negating action that satisfies Desire in destroying, transforming, and "assimilating" the desired non-I. And the positive content of the I, constituted by negation, is a function of the positive content of the negated non-I.'[24] Thus desire as a negating negativity creates the conditions whereby the other maintains the integrity of the I. The 'ineluctable violence' of desire forms the basis of Kojève's master and slave dialectic, and it is worth noting

---

19. Such a conclusion was anathema to the ancients. In a world ordered to the Good, being did not depend on appetite. 'Aristotle argued that humans, as rational beings, could decide to follow the commands of reason or to ignore these commands and follow their desires.' Lauren Swayne Barthold, 'Towards an Ethics of Love: Arendt on will and Augustine', in *Philosophy and Social Criticism*, vol. 26, no. 6 (London: Sage, 2000), p. 3. Barthold also argues: 'Although, one could not find any explicit notion of the will in Aristotle, he developed a notion that concerned the deliberation over which is the best means to reach a certain end. Thus his notion of *"prohairesis"*, which refers to the mediation between thinking and desire, could be described in terms of the faculty of choice' (Ibid. p. 3). When as Kojève claims, 'man's very being implies and presupposes Desire', this 'faculty of choice' has become what Girard describes as 'internal mediation', or negative mimesis. Thus, any rational, and thereby positive, content is held in doubt.

20. Erving, 'René Girard and the Legacy of Alexandre Kojève', p. 115.

21. Ibid.

22. Ibid.

23. On the anthropological conditions of conflict that gives rise to the master and slave dialectic, Kojève claims: '[it] does the man of the Fight no good to kill his adversary. He must overcome him "dialectically." That is, he must leave him life and consciousness, and destroy only his autonomy. He must overcome the adversary only in so far as the adversary is opposed to him and acts against him. In other words, he must enslave him.' Alexandre Kojève, *Introduction to the Reading of Hegel: Lectures on the Phenomenology of Spirit*, ed. Allan Bloom, trans. James H. Nichols, Jr. (Ithaca, NY: Cornell University Press, 1980), p. 15.

24. Erving, 'René Girard and the Legacy of Alexandre Kojève', p. 115.

the parallel between this intersubjective violence and the collective crisis depicted by Girard. In both cases, the other and the surrogate victim function to generate unity and identity where there was none. Erving's analysis suggests that in both instances violence is central to the process – the negating 'I' becomes a dim reflection of the negating community. However, as I have already shown, while the early and later forms of unity through negation are structurally the same, different conclusions are drawn by Girard from each. Thus, the early unity is seen as 'true', while the later unity is seen as 'false' (as unanimity minus one).[25]

Kojève's main postulate of desire as 'negating negativity' foreshadows Girard's theory of mimetic rivalry. In particular Kojève's comments on the mediated nature of desire are significant in anticipating Girard's concept of 'triangular desire'. Erving quotes the key passage in Kojève's text that might be seen as the starting point of Girard's mimetic theory. 'Desire directed toward a natural object is human only to the extent that it is "mediated" by the Desire of another directed toward a natural object: it is human to desire what others desire, because they desire it . . . human history is the history of desired Desires.'[26] Arising from this analysis, Erving outlines five characteristics that Girard's mimetic model has in common with Kojève's, including the observation that desire is constitutive of human subjectivity. However, he goes on to point out:

> The most fundamental point of comparison is that for both, Desire and being form an identity relation. It is axiomatic for Girard not only that desire is mimetic, but that 'Imitative desire is always a desire to be another.' Thus while Girard's model of triangular desire describes the apparent role of the model as the mediator of an ostensible object-related desire, this turns out to belie a submerged desire to possess the being of the mediator/model itself. As with Kojève, desire for Girard is not finally directed at objects *per se*, at what Kojève refers to as the 'given' and 'thingish', but rather at 'the spectacle of another real or illusory desire' for desire is aimed at the mediator's being.[27]

The autonomous subject who desires self-sufficiency is delusional in so far as he believes that he can succeed, but his desire as such is truthful since by desiring he rightly senses that he lacks being, and while Girard's subject despairs at this fact Kojève's simply 'shrugs' and resumes his negating activity.[28] For both thinkers I come into being as a human subject only through the other who becomes the

---

25. What we find when we read back in to Girard's appropriation of Kojève's dynamic concept of desire in his (Girard's) early work, is that the centre of negating activity shifts from the author as ontological subject to the text, which now contains any possibility of unity through a catharsis of Romantic originality – and hence, original presence.

26. Erving, 'René Girard and the Legacy of Alexandre Kojève', p. 116.

27. Ibid.

28. Erving, 'René Girard and the Legacy of Alexandre Kojève', p. 117.

substance of my 'being': this analysis (as we shall see a little later) paves the way for Girard's articulation of 'the interdividual' as a subject existing between self and other.

The similarities between Kojève and Girard are surely striking. However, there are differences between them that highlight the tension discussed above with regard to the incompatibility between their distinct views of conflict.[29] Girard's analysis of Hegel in his literary criticism appears to mark a break with Kojève concerning what the assertion of violence signifies. To hide his violence is the superior achievement of the one who inhabits the underground. Thus *deceit* becomes the operative term for Girard (and of course it is highlighted in the very title of his first major work) in a way that surpasses the more straightforward intentions of Kojève's dialectical partners.[30] Erving quotes the passage that underscores Girard's 'break' in this regard: 'The Hegelian dialectic rests on physical courage. Whoever has no fear will be master, whoever is afraid will be slave. The novelistic [i.e., Girardian] dialectic rests on hypocrisy. Violence, far from serving the interests of whoever exerts it, reveals the intensity of his desire; thus *it is a sign of slavery.*'[31] Deceit, as the crucial postulate for Girard, and the chief characteristic of the Romantic fallacy, is in the service of desire, which must not show itself as such for fear 'being' will dissipate. Violence is the foil for the hero's *askesis* – it reveals his deepest secret – whereas his withdrawal (his concealment of desire and violence) allows the masquerade of his 'being' to pass unnoticed. Furthermore, this masquerade allows him to attract potential rivals.

---

29. Kojève's influence was wide reaching, especially among French phenomenologists. According to Herbert Spiegelberg, French phenomenology takes it for granted that Husserl's phenomenology belongs together with Hegel's *Phenomenology of Spirit* and even originated from it. In Kojéve's lectures on Hegel in Paris in the 1930s, attended by many young French theorists, he simply asserted that 'Hegel's phenomenology was "phenomenological description in the Husserlian sense of the word". Such an interpretation became possible because to Kojève the Hegelian method, in contrast to the reality which it tried to explore, was "by no means dialectical; it is purely contemplative and descriptive in the phenomelogocal in the Husserlian sense of the term."' Spiegelberg, H., *The Phenomenological Movement: A Historical Introduction* 3rd Revised and Enlarged Edition (London: Kluwer Academic Publishers, 1994), pp. 440–441. In both Kojève's and Girard's interpretation of Hegel's phenomenology, the genuinely dialectal aspects of spirit, so important to the hermeneutical tradition of Gadamer, Ricoeur and Taylor, are played down.

30. Deceit is the negative characterization of inwardness that haunts the Girardian subject. It constitutes the process of internal mediation whereby the subject is all the time confronting a negative image of himself as a reminder of his lack of originality. Kojève's subject is too busy moving on to the next 'project' to feel any great internal dissonance.

31. Quoted in, Erving, 'The Legacy of Kojève', p. 120 (my italics).

The 'zero-sum' logic ensures that the subject operates with a sense of inadequacy, shame and self-hatred, while simultaneously regarding the other with envy. In its bid for mastery, the Girardian subject, according to Erving, 'attempts to dissimulate its feelings, but its strategies inevitably fail. Its fundamental delusion regarding desire and subjectivity results in a self-defeating, unreflective mimesis. Thus Girard's postulate of the romantic fallacy ensures that deceit becomes the subject's modus operandus [*sic*], for the self is both deceiving and deceived.'[32] For Kojève the self has nothing to hide. Since it does not strive for Romantic autonomy it is not motivated by a sense of shame nor does it approach the other with envy. 'It has no need for deceit' because its struggles for ontological recognition are overt, depending as they do on courage and violence rather than the dissimulation of one's 'true' intentions. Kojève's 'struggle' is thus a 'psychologically straightforward engagement – one imagines, for example, two knights jousting – where the goal of satisfying desire, of achieving mastery and thus human consciousness, is understood from the outset to be wholly dependent upon the Other.'[33]

Girard's and Kojève's subjects appear to differ considerably on the basis of what they publicly exhibit since the latter asserts its violence while the former conceals it. Yet Erving does not quite say this. Indeed, he initially states that for both Girard and Kojève 'desire is constitutive of human subjectivity . . . is concerned with existential recognition, is socially mediated, and is ineluctably bound up with violence'.[34] He sees Girard's break with Kojève coming with respect to the former's crucial postulate concerning the deceptions of Romantic self-sufficiency, which, as discussed, Kojève's subject does not share. If, as Erving claims, the two subjects share violence, it cannot be the same kind of violence; in other words, it cannot be outward violence – a violence that is put on display. While Erving's point is that the Romantic subject differs from the Hegelian and Kojèvian subject in terms of deceit, he does not make an explicit link between the deception and what is in fact hidden in the way that Girard does in the passage quoted above ('violence is a sign of slavery'). If, in Girard's early work, 'violence is a sign of slavery' then the subject is loath to put it on display.[35] When Girard posits a Romantic fallacy (as self-deception), he automatically discounts himself from sharing with Kojève a theory of 'violent struggle' as the motive force of history. Thus Erving is right to point out an important difference between Girard and Kojève with respect to the former's key postulate of deceit, but he is surely wrong to say they both share a theory of violent struggle as the motive force of

---

32. Erving, 'René Girard and the Legacy of Alexandre Kojève', p. 120.

33. Ibid., p. 121.

34. Ibid., p. 116.

35. One of the examples that Girard gives of this concealment relates to Julian de Sorel in Stendhal's *The Red and the Black*, who puts down the weapon 'whose decorative role is symbolic' when he notices Mathilde's eyes 'shine with joy'. Girard, *Deceit, Desire, and the Novel*, p. 112.

history – unless, that is, Erving does not distinguish between Girard's early and later work. It is, once again, Girard's later work that maintains a theory of outward violence, which (unlike the Kojèvian dialectic), is not a self-overcoming, but rather a gradual escalation of apocalyptic violence. Therefore, Girard's negative view of human effort in history marks another point of divergence with Kojève.

Erving tells us that Girard ultimately rejects Kojève's progressive view of history because this view is, effectively, an anthropologizing of the Christian idea of transcendence that involves an 'immanent but absolute self-understanding'.[36] Bringing the Christian idea of transcendence within a temporal horizon implies, for Girard, 'the pernicious illusions of "horizontal transcendence" and "metaphysical desire" that trigger mimetic crises and their resolution through legitimized murder.'[37] Erving is certainly correct in his analysis here, but he conflates Girard's early theory of crises with Girard's later theory of crisis; (metaphysical desire is thus the 'trigger' of mimetic crisis, and scapegoating). However, the idea of 'horizontal' or 'deviated' transcendence (and its relationship to metaphysical desire) is developed in Girard's early work. It explains the individual's attempt to acquire the other's 'being', and in this sense it is only truly appropriate to explaining the dynamics of triangular desire and the intra- and intersubjective crisis. When Girard writes *Violence and the Sacred* he then develops a theory of mimetic desire that is adequate to explain the collective crisis that culminates in scapegoating – one that relies on an outward display of violence that can account for the contagion that ends in violent opposition. But as we saw this theory cannot emanate from the early work without some difficulties. For, first, the early work, when viewed in light of the later work, must be seen as a form of unacknowledged violence; and, second, Romantic self-deception cannot generate the conditions of the sacred, that is crisis on a collective scale while maintaining the secrecy of its own violence and desire.

Like other philosophers using Girardian theory, Erving does not sufficiently distinguish between the early and later work.[38] He simply reflects the understandable tendency within this theory to believe that the early explanation of crisis also works for the later explanation of crisis.[39] Only when the sacred is understood to be responsible for cultural order does the *explicit* nature of violence becomes self-evident. Violence, Girard claims, in his later work, is 'that beautiful totality'

---

36. Erving, 'René Girard and the Legacy of Alexandre Kojève', p. 123.
37. Ibid.
38. 'Girard's theory of history builds directly upon the premise of the subject's romantic fallacy, where unreflective mimesis as a source of violence formed an ever-present threat to primitive communities.' Erving, 'René Girard and the Legacy of Alexander Kojève', p. 121.
39. For example, see Stephen L. Gardner, 'The Ontological Obsessions of Radical Thought', in *Contagion: Journal of Violence, Mimesis, and Culture*, Vol. 10. (Spring 2003), p. 21.

that men seek to possess.[40] It is 'the signifier of ultimate desire, of divine self-sufficiency . . . whose beauty depends on its being inaccessible and impenetrable.'[41] Deceit, as the basis of an illusory subjectivity, cannot remain a central postulate of Girard's theory once an account of scapegoating is introduced. Why then does he bring a theory of self-deception forward to explain a theory of violent escalation? Perhaps to do otherwise would be to acknowledge that his early treatment of subjectivity was unduly severe, constituting as it does an act of symbolic violence.

4. Interdividual Psychology: A Loss of Positive Interiority?

The influence of Kojève's conception of desire, as negating negativity, and of the other as a function of the self, has a considerable impact on Girard's thought as it develops. With Kojève's emphasis on 'violent struggle', and Girard's early emphasis on 'self-deception', an ethical subject can neither advance nor retreat with any degree of certainty. Hence when we consider Girard's later anthropology, which has absorbed Kojève's understanding of desire, what we actually find is a subject who is constantly moving *between* self and other. In the absence of an intentional rational agent there appears to be no way for this subject to locate itself, to take up a position, and commit itself; in Girardian theory ethical agency can only be the servant of negating negativity and/or self-deception. Jean-Michel Oughourlian (one of the significant interlocutors in *Things Hidden Since the Foundation of the World*) conceptualizes the subject of mimetic theory as the 'interdividual self'. Commenting on how desire brings this self into existence, he says:

> Because desire is the only psychological motion, it alone . . . is capable of producing the self and breathing life into it. The first hypothesis I would like to formulate in this regard is this: *desire gives rise to the self and by its movement animates it*. The second hypothesis . . . is that *desire is mimetic*. This postulate, which was advanced by René Girard as early as 1961, seems to be capable of serving as the foundation of a new, pure psychology – that is, one unencumbered by any sort of biologism. We have chosen to call this *interdividual psychology*.[42]

---

40. Girard continues: 'The victim of this violence both adores and detests it. He strives to master it by means of a mimetic counter violence and measures his own stature in proportion to his failure. If by chance, however, he actually succeeds in asserting his violence over that model, the latter's prestige vanishes. He must then turn to an even greater violence and seek out an obstacle that promises to be truly insurmountable.' Girard, *Violence and the Sacred*, p. 148.
41. Ibid.
42. Quoted in, Webb, *The Self Between*, p. 7.

The implications of this view for our understanding of human motivation and traditional concepts of the self are radical. For one thing it suggests that we do not value objects because of their intrinsic worth, but rather we value and thus reach for them because of some vaguely felt sense of insufficiency that requires a remedy. This view thoroughly debunks any possibility of rational evaluation on the part of the subject since our desires are now acutely dependent on other people – a fact that our 'deceived' consciousness wholly ignores in its bid for 'rational' agency. Oughlourian's two hypotheses, building as they do on mimetic theory, require that we revise earlier psychologies. 'They demand that one renounce the mythical claim to a self that would be a permanent structure in a monadic subject.'[43]

In opposition to this mythic self that we must renounce, Oughlourian says that the interdividual self is an 'unstable, constantly changing and ultimately evanescent structure'.[44] Mimetic desire (the imputed ruler of the human world) means that no object can be trusted and no subject can be reasonably discerning – reason loses its bearings. According to Girard, the modern shift to the subject, with the unleashing of desire that accompanies it, coincides with the erosion of traditional hierarchies that functioned in a protective capacity against the potential for uncontrollable mob violence. Our efforts to free desire in constructive and creative ways today are ultimately stifling.

> Some people equate the proliferation of desire with a loosening of the bonds of culture, which they deplore; they link it to the levelling of 'natural' hierarchies on a broad front, and the wreckage of all values worthy of respect. In the modern world, these enemies of desire are ranged against the friends of desire; the two camps pass judgement on each other in the name of order against disorder, reaction against progress, the past against the future, and so on. In doing so they oversimplify a very complex state of affairs. In contrast to what the 'enemies' of desire are always telling us, our world shows itself to be quite capable of absorbing high doses of 'undifferentiating'.[45]

What would have destroyed other societies, Girard tells us, is transformed into an engine of development that can assimilate (well neigh all) cultures and populations that had remained outside this 'engine's' sphere. By this means premodern culture becomes modernized. However, the expansion of human potential that the friends of desire expect never truly materializes: 'Either the liberated desire is channelled into competitive directions that, though enormously creative, are ultimately disappointing, or it simply ends up in sterile conflict and anarchic confusion, with a corresponding increase in the sense of anguish.'[46] As religious taboos

---

43. Quoted in, Webb, *The Self Between*, p. 9.
44. Ibid.
45. Girard, *Things Hidden*, p. 284.
46. Ibid., p. 285.

and cultural prohibitions are toppled, the individual believes that its desire will blossom, 'its wonderful innocence will finally be able to bear fruit.'[47] The problem with this form of flattening and equalizing is that the external obstacles that traditionally prevented desire from spreading no longer function in a protective capacity.

As the key markers of difference erode, the effects of mimesis will ensure that another obstacle is found to take the place of the prohibition that no longer works.[48] But something in the nature of this process has fundamentally changed.

> Men lose the kind of obstacle that is inert and passive, but at the same time beneficent and equal for all – the obstacle that for this reason could never really become humiliating or incapacitating. In place of this obstacle established by religious prohibition, they have to reckon increasingly with the kind of obstacle that is active mobile and fierce – the model metamorphosed into a rival, interested in personally crossing them and well equipped to do so.[49]

The loss of hierarchies brought about by modern freedom has increased the likelihood of negative mimesis because it has replaced external obstacles with obstacles that mediate internally in a much more uncertain and potentially chaotic manner. The more people give in to their desires the more difficult it is for them to negotiate their relationships to others. Hence, the more people invest in ideas of freedom and liberation 'the more they will in fact be working to reinforce the competitive world that is stifling them.'[50] Everything since the Enlightenment it seems constitutes a loss of differentiation that is assimilated for the time being so long as the tentacles of desire have something to grasp. The self as part of the historical play of mimesis and the growing undifferentiation is, from the Girardian viewpoint, inextricably caught in the nets of the sacred without any truly effective way of protecting itself from crisis. The 'interdividual self' thus attempts to take account of this 'undifferentiation' by treating its interior life as mythic but, with such a thorough debunking of consciousness and intentionality, we are left wondering if there is any subjectivity left reliably to mediate otherness, or constructively reflect on its own negative mimesis.

Girard's work articulates a 'concern for victims', and underscores the importance of the other, and of getting beyond the confines of ego psychology, or a narrow view of consciousness. However, as Webb highlights, 'in the absence of a fully developed philosophical anthropology', the centrality of the other 'seems to depend more on the personal good instincts of the thinker than on a well-developed theoretical foundation'.[51] A persistent difficulty in understanding Girard's philosophical position lies in his unwillingness to attribute any positive dimension to

47. Ibid.
48. Ibid., p. 286.
49. Ibid.
50. Ibid.
51. Webb, *The Self Between*, p. 225.

the notion of inwardness. Reading Girard in conversation, in *Things Hidden Since the Foundation of the World,* one gets the impression that his partners in dialogue do not help him in this regard.[52] Having tried to distinguish 'that obscure thing named desire' as something that 'must only occur in a world in which barriers are pulled down and differences eradicated', in other words the modern world, Oughourlian turns to the question concerning where all the mimetic desire now goes, without the previously effective religious channels.

> Desire can, in fact, be defined, in similar terms (to ritual activities) as a process of mimesis involving undifferentiating; it is akin to the process of deepening conflict that issues in the mechanism of re-unification through the victim. Yet in our world the processes of desire do not ever give rise to the collective crescendo that marks the ritual activities; at no stage are they concluded by an act of spontaneous expulsion.[53]

Girard accepts this analysis, desire has become localized. But he elaborates: 'As a state, it corresponds not so much to mimetic crises as they occur in primitive societies, but to something at once similar and different, which is linked to the lasting enfeeblement of founding violence in our own world.'[54] He attributes responsibility for this 'enfeeblement' to the Judeao-Christian texts. The church's sacrificial reading of the gospels allows this founding violence to remain, albeit in a weakened state, and therefore the 'mimetic crisis . . . has been enormously slowed down and lengthened, in the individual historical context.'[55]

Running parallel to Girard's analysis of culture and his hypothesis of founding violence is his interpretation of the Judeao-Christian scriptures. He understands these texts as unique in definitely exposing the innocence of the victim, from whose immolation through mob violence, and putative 'guilt', culture emerges. After the Christian event, the world can no longer be founded by violence against victims. And for this reason, Girard believes, wherever the Christian culture takes root it becomes increasingly difficult for violence against victims to ensue. All other accounts, to a greater or lesser extent, continue to cover-up the innocence of the victim and the guilt of the perpetrators. A consequence of the Christian

---

52. At the beginning of the chapter on 'Mimetic Desire', which opens the section entitled 'Interdividual Psychology', in *Things Hidden,* Girard and his interlocutors discuss the process of 'hominization' and how desire 'evolves' in a peculiarly human manner.
53. Girard, *Things Hidden,* p. 287.
54. Ibid., p. 288.
55. Oughourlian summarizes Girard as follows: '[In our world] in which the mechanisms of culture are exposed to the slow but inexorable subversion of a Judeao-Christian element tempered by the sacrificial interpretation, the mimetic crisis must be lived out in this modified modern version, by each individual in his [*sic*] relationships with others.' Girard, *Things Hidden,* pp. 288–289.

event is the 'gradual effacement of the victimage mechanism',[56] and the loss of the once cathartic effects of the sacred; what contemporary culture experiences in an acute way.

In Girard's account of the transition to the modern world we find every indication that the site of the 'collective crisis' has shifted from the external cultural world of the community to the internalized cultural world of the individual. However, he clearly sees this as something ultimately *negative* for the individual and all of his or her relationships.

> Desire is what happens to human relations when there is no longer any resolution through the victim, and consequently no form of polarisation that is genuinely unanimous and can trigger such a resolution. But human relationships are mimetic none the less. We shall be able to discover beneath the 'underground' (in the Dostoevskyan sense) and always deceptive form of individual symptoms, the dynamic style of the sacrificial crisis. In this instance, however, there can be no ritualistic or victimary resolution, and, if and when it becomes acute, the crisis ensues – what we call psychosis.[57]

The dynamics of the modern sacrificial crisis are still worked out through 'internal mediation' – which, as we saw in Chapter 1, is fundamental to understanding the intra- and intersubjective crisis. Once the scapegoat mechanism is revealed, all that this inner world can muster (any overt conception of subjectivity being precluded by the structuralist framing of this whole analysis) is thwarted desire. This world of the Romantic subject (the personification of all philosophies of consciousness) is hollowed out by 'Desire' that is without openness to reasonable intervention. This inner world is a world of frustration, self-loathing, resentment, hallucinations, and eventual psychosis. Nietzsche and the figure of the madman loom large.[58]

How are we to be clear about Girard's view of subjectivity? If we take the Romantic fallacy as the precondition of consciousness the corruption of the inner psychic life of the experiencing subject is a *fait accompli* – an example of which we find in Girard's analysis of the underground man. The difficulty with this position when it continues to be a part of Girard's over all theory is that it reduces all psychologies of the subject and all philosophies of consciousness to the control of a single entity called Desire. An example of this reduction can be found in the following formulation by Girard: '. . . far from being unconscious in Freud's sense and only appearing in its true form in our dreams, desire not only observes but

---

56. Ibid.
57. Ibid., p. 288.
58. According to Girard, it was the cumulative effects of resentment as 'weakened vengeance' in a mind that understood the significance of sacred violence and its loss of efficacy in a Christianized world that finally drove Nietzsche mad. Girard, 'Nietzsche versus the Crucified', in *The Girard Reader*, p. 252.

never stops *thinking about* the meaning of its observations. Desire is always reflection on desire.'[59] Here as Paisley Livingston points out, it would appear as if 'desire . . . were what pulled the strings of the human marionette . . . a kind of homunculus equipped with . . . cognitive faculties.'[60] Is the inevitability of such a reifying of desire not unnecessarily written into the structure of the subject within Girardian theory from the beginning?[61]

In the end, giving desire more status than a thinking feeling subject undermines Girard's discourse because he believes, as a Christian thinker, that there *is* a 'real human subject', who emerges out of 'the rule of the kingdom of God'.[62] Webb brings out the incongruity of maintaining, as Girard attempts to do, a structuralist notion of the subject (one that refuses all interiority) as part of a Christian commitment, by highlighting a key gospel term: the kingdom of god. 'It is perhaps worth mentioning that in all the places in the New Testament that speak of the "kingdom of God," the term in Greek is *basileia tou theou*, which means literally, the "rule" or "reign" of God – not a place, that is, or even a community, but a condition of being governed *inwardly* by the will of God.'[63] Outside this kingdom 'the only subject is the mimetic structure' – the individual who desires is simply a crisis without a resolution. When the 'inner' is thus construed *only* as Romantic or disorderly desire that later becomes synonymous with the lack of a sacrificial mechanism it appears that the Kingdom of God is nowhere near at hand.

---

59. Girard, *Things Hidden*, p. 328 (my italics).
60. P. Livingston, *Models of Desire: René Girard and the Psychology of Mimesis* (Baltimore: The Johns Hopkins University Press, 1992), p. 25. According to Frank Richardson and Kathy Frost, Livingston suggests that in order to clarify a number of matters about the nature and operations of mimetic desire, we have to use many of the ideas and terms of an 'intentionalist psychology' (usually discouraged by Girard's structuralism), and that we can do so without lapsing into subjectivism or individualism. 'Girard and Psychology: Furthering the Dialogue', p. 7. Paper presented at an international meeting of the Colloquium on Violence and Religion (CoV&R), in June 2006.
61. Another example of Girard's tendency to reify desire arises in a chapter entitled 'Desire without Object'. After a discussion about how mimetic desire generates 'doubles', which, as we saw, leads to hallucinations and crisis at the intersubjective level, Oughourlian asks: 'You are saying that "desire" does this and that . . . Would you not agree that you are tending to give desire a false identity?' Once again Girard refuses to give any legitimacy to a first-person perspective: 'If desire is the same for all of us, and if it is the key to the system of relationships, there is no reason not to make it the real "subject" of the structure – a subject that comes back to mimesis in the end. I avoid saying "desiring subject" so as not to give the impression of relapsing into a psychology of the subject.' Girard, *Things Hidden*, p. 303.
62. Ibid., p. 199.
63. Webb, *The Self Between*, p. 176, Chp. 6, note 4 (my italics).

The loss of positive interiority in Girard's work as it develops is in part understandable when we consider how he explains the Romantic hero's 'spiritual askesis' in his literary criticism. As we saw in Chapter 1, the analogy between the literary quest and the spiritual quest is developed in *Deceit, Desire, and the Novel* when the critic compares the Romantic hero's search for divine self-sufficiency with Augustine's reflective search for God, the eternal essence. With this analogy – between the lover of the eternal essence, and the lover of the world, between the Saint and the Romantic – we have not *two different loves* (what we find in Augustine's theory of the will), but rather two entirely different kinds of subject, one internal and the other external. The question I posed in that same chapter (can there be any form of interiority that we might claim as 'good'?) appears even more relevant when we consider the extent of the spiritual crisis that Girard is now arguing confronts humankind. We are left wondering whether Girard's early atheism-inspired debunking of modern subjectivity, which undergoes no significant revision, does not altogether run aground in a discourse that attempts to include 'extra-textual' claims of 'real' violence and also a Christian concept of the good as love (*agapē*). The lack of an available subject due to Girard's early scapegoating in literary space thus gives 'desire' and even 'violence' more status in his theory than the very conditions of Christian conversion.

5. *'The Death of Desire': Mimesis and the World as Will*

A precedent for the tendency to hypostatize desire, and, in doing so, to hopelessly undermine the subject is to be found in the work of the German philosopher, Arthur Schopenhauer, who is arguably the first major thinker to emphasize 'the abstract category of desire itself'.[64] Like Girardian 'Desire', which is, in the end, more 'entitive' than a thinking feeling agent, Schopenhauerian 'Will' ensures that the subject becomes the blind servant of an even more blind force, the self-replication of which, Eagleton tells us, is its own sole purpose. In the context of early nineteenth century 'bourgeois society' we discover that the determinative role and frequency of 'appetite' permits a dramatic theoretical shift.[65] 'With Schopenhauer,

---

64. Terry Eagleton, *The Ideology of the Aesthetic* (Cambridge: Basil Blackwell Press/ Cambridge University Press, 1990), p. 158. Girard does make the point that desire is never fully abstract since it is fundamentally relational (*Deceit, Desire, and the Novel*, p. 178). However, as he moves away from a first-person perspective, and all positive forms of subjectivity, gaining one's bearings within such an intra- and interrelational world becomes increasingly difficult. And when in *Things Hidden* desire becomes 'hypostatized' we have to wonder whether 'relationality' itself has not become abstract for Girard's discourse.

65. The regularity of desire in bourgeois society permits a dramatic theoretical shift. What follows is: "[t]he construction of desire as a thing in itself, a momentous

desire has become the protagonist of the human theatre, and human subjects themselves its mere obedient servants or underlings.'[66] The emerging individualism of the social order is furthered by the now apparent 'infinity of desire', where the only end of accumulation is yet further accumulation.[67] In a neo-Marxist vein, Eagleton provides an analysis of these developments that parallels Girard's literary account of the movement from vertical to horizontal transcendence.

> In a traumatic collapse of teleology, desire comes to seem independent of any particular ends, or at least as grotesquely disproportionate to them; and once it thus ceases to be (in the phenomenological sense) intentional, it begins monstrously to obtrude itself as *Ding-an-sich*, an opaque unfathomable, self-propelling power utterly without purpose or reason, like some grisly caricature of the deity.[68]

The modern period, as a kind of fatal rupture (Girard), is the same period that witnesses the articulation of Schopenhauer's philosophy of the 'World as Will', where the subject is now the site of an irremediable fissure, helpless in its attempts to recover any positive resources within itself that might bring about greater clarity or indeed satisfaction.[69]

The will is not simply 'an absence in search of a fullness' as when the subject is construed as a 'negating negativity' (*a la* Kojève). The self is now at the mercy of an agency that inscribes its diabolical presence on the body. Because of this integral link with the human organism, when desire becomes hypostatized in the modern period, it is possible to see it, as the Romantics did, as supremely positive. However, Schopenhauer provides the 'sting in the tail' to all idealist philosophies of this kind, since

> ... the preconditions of such Romantic affirmation are also the preconditions of the Schopenhauerian denunciation of desire *tout court*, accepting the categories

---

metaphysical event or self-identical force, as against some earlier social order in which desire is still too narrowly particularist, too intimately bound up with local or traditional obligation, to be reified in quite this way', Eagleton, *The Ideology of the Aesthetic* p. 159.

66. Ibid., p. 159.
67. Ibid.
68. Ibid.
69. According to Schopenhauer, 'The world as idea, the objective world, has ... as it were, two poles; the simple knowing subject without the forms of its knowledge, and a crude matter with form and quality. Both are completely unknowable; the subject because it is that which knows, matter because without form and quality it cannot be perceived.' Arthur Schopenhauer, 'The World as Will and Idea', quoted in A. Hofstadter and R. Kuhns, eds, *Philosophies of Art and Beauty: Selected Readings in Aesthetics from Plato to Heidegger* (Chicago and London: University of Chicago Press, 1976), p. 449.

of Romantic humanism but impudently inverting the valuations. Like Schopenhauer, you can retain the whole totalizing apparatus of bourgeois humanism at its most affirmative – the singular central principle informing the whole of reality, the integrated cosmic whole, the stable relations of phenomena and essence – while mischievously emptying these forms of their idealised content.[70]

If Freud's transformation of what Girard calls the 'eternal kingdom of ideas' into 'false essences' is a modern form of mythological thinking,[71] for Schopenhauer this 'transformation' is simply the naturally recurring tendency of the will. When, as Eagleton claims, you drain off the ideological substance from the system ('freedom, justice, reason, progress') you can then simply 'fill the system, still intact, with the actual degraded materials of everyday existence.'[72] Desire can now latch on to anything it sees fit to desire in a kind of negative competition since there is no discernible hierarchy of 'goods'. Whether desire is its own end or there is some notion of the sacred at work here is secondary. The main point that Girard and Schopenhauer agree on with respect to desire is that, independently of any intentional subject, *it directs itself.*

In the absence of any discernible objective truth, one 'lie' replaces another slightly more 'honest lie' as the subject takes on the myth-making function that was once the prerogative of the community. Schopenhauer's notion of the will . . .

> . . . structurally speaking serves just the same function as the Hegelian Idea or the Romantic life-force, but is now nothing more than the uncouth rapacity of the average bourgeois, elevated to cosmic status and transformed to the prime metaphysical mover of the entire universe. It is as though one retained the whole paraphernalia of the Platonic Ideas but called them Profit, Philistinism, Self-Interest and so on.[73]

In this terrifying vision, the whole world, 'from the forces of gravity to the rumblings of the gut' (Eagleton), are invested with a futile craving. Human beings in the market place are divine forces, writ 'repellently' large; their 'self-divinisation', to use a Girardian term, projects their 'sordid appetites as the very stuff of the cosmos'.[74] The grander his gestures the sooner they fall flat. The naturalizing effect of this debunking removes any hope of an historical alternative. Like the modern 'friends of desire' whose 'liberation', Girard claims, is ultimately stifling,

---

70. Arthur Schopenhauer, 'The World as Will and Idea', quoted in A. Hofstadter and R. Kuhns, eds, *Philosophies of Art and Beauty,* pp. 159–160.
71. Girard, *Things Hidden*, p. 251.
72. Eagleton, *The Ideology of the Aesthetic*, p. 160.
73. Ibid.
74. Ibid.

Schopenhauer's vision suggests that every attempt to affirm life is a further step towards undermining the very thing that makes such an affirmation meaningful. 'The forms of the Hegelian system are turned against that system with a vengeance; totalization is still possible, but now of a purely negative kind.'[75] It is this negative kind of totalization that is easily recognizable in the dynamics of underground existence.

The Romantic hero's desire for 'originality' can be understood as a dim reflection of the now unassailable inner will. To be in touch with this inner will, to make my 'spontaneous desire' an expression of my unique individuality, is at root a dangerous naivety. In reality there can be no personal purchase on such an impersonal inner force. 'What makes me what I am, the will of which I am simply a materialization, is utterly indifferent to my individual identity, which it uses merely for its own pointless self-reproduction.'[76] This self-reproducing will, like desire, becomes the puppet master of a deceived and deceiving ego, all the time 'strategizing' at the expense of a thinking, feeling agent.[77] Schopenhauer's distrust of what is most fundamentally human can be seen as anticipating Girard's own distrust of the individual's belief in his or her 'unique identity', or selfhood.

> At the very root of the human subject lies that which is implacably alien to it, so that in a devastating irony this will which is the very pith of my being, which I can feel from the inside of my body with incomparably greater immediacy than I can know anything else, is absolutely unlike me at all, without consciousness or motive, as blankly unfeeling and anonymous as the force which stirs the waves. No more powerful image of alienation could be imagined than this malicious parody of idealist humanism.[78]

There is no longer any authentic 'transcendence' or 'unity' within the self that is not already circumscribed by the implacable will, announcing itself in the modern period as the absolute enemy of our conscious life. This enemy thus functions like an intolerable weight of meaninglessness that 'we bear inside ourselves as the very principle of our being, as though permanently pregnant with monsters'.[79] And, not incidentally, 'the monstrous'[80] is the very form of the crisis for the individual given over to blind mimetic desire. In Schopenhauer's scheme, subjectivity as the basis of a renewed transcendence through internalization and individuation becomes hopelessly and irreparably flawed. The creative self, as the spoiled child of a Romantic idealism, must renounce its claims to transformative potential.

---

75. Ibid.
76. Ibid., p. 161.
77. Girard, *Things Hidden*, p. 301.
78. Eagleton, *The Ideology of the Aesthetic*, p. 161.
79. Ibid.
80. Girard, *Violence and the Sacred*.

It must accept once and for all that our flawed subjectivity makes us forever strangers to ourselves. 'It is this which touches on the guilty secret or impossible paradox of bourgeois society, that it is exactly in their freedom that men and women are most inexorably enchained, that we live immured in our bodies like lifers in a cell.'[81] And if we develop Eagleton's metaphor here with a certain nod to Girard's reading of the sacred character of all legal systems (as essentially sacrificial), we might indeed go so far as to wonder whether such 'free' individuals are not in fact on death row.[82]

Both Girard and Schopenhauer draw similar conclusions from their respective negative assessments of desire, and both thinkers would appear to adopt explicitly 'religious' solutions to the apparently hopeless human condition. While Christian conversion provides the basis of reflective mimesis for Girard, thus pointing us (in the absence of any inner haven of the self) towards 'good models', for Schopenhauer the category of the 'aesthetic' provides a temporary escape from the prison-house of subjectivity. Unlike the Romantic individual, Schopenhauer's aesthetic individual harbours no illusions concerning his self-sufficiency. Nor is it a question of trying to deceive anyone by trying to hide his desires. In Schopenhauer's world 'the detachment we attain for a precious moment in contemplating the artefact is an implicit alternative to appetitive egoism.'[83] The whole point of Schopenhauer's 'solution' is to see the self and the world as they are in all their futility: 'only by somehow piercing the veil of Maya and recognising the fictional status of the individual ego can one behave to others with true indifference – which is to say, to make no significant difference between them and oneself.'[84] My own individual self, like all other individual selves, is a false construal of what is only an effect of an indifferent malevolent will.

The solution to the crisis wrought by Schopenhauerian 'Will' is similar to Girard's own solution to the crisis at the end of *Deceit, Desire, and the Novel*, for which Flaubert provides the motto – 'Mme Bovary c'est moi!'[85] The Romantic hero who successfully overcomes his metaphysical desire achieves a kind of transcendental detachment, whereby he realizes that 'at a certain depth there is no difference' between self and other.[86] Both the Romantic hero and the Schopenhauerian

---

81. Eagleton, *The Ideology of the Aesthetic*, p. 161.
82. This is how Eagleton describes the 'death of desire' in the modern period: 'The Schopenhauerian aesthetic is the death drive in action, though this death is secretly a kind of life, *Eros* disguised as *Thanatos*: the subject cannot be entirely negated as long as it still delights, even if what it takes pleasure in is the process of its own dissolution.' Eagleton, *The Ideology of the Aesthetic* p. 164.
83. Ibid.
84. Ibid., p. 165.
85. Girard, *Deceit, Desire, and the Novel*, p. 299.
86. Ibid., p. 298. Cf. Erving's last note on the loss of difference at the end of Girard's first major work, which Girard posits as the basis of a new unity for the Romantic hero, and the way it is oddly characterized as the source of crisis in Girard's later work.

subject must forfeit their former status and let go of their fictional selves that otherwise keep them 'immured' in their false egos, believing that they are in fact 'different'. Thus, like the symbolic regeneration of the author at the end of *Deceit, Desire, and the Novel*, the aesthetic individual achieves a similar rebirth, as Eagleton points out: 'Just as all true knowledge springs from the death of the subject, so too does all moral value; to act morally is not to act from a positive standpoint, but to act from no standpoint at all. The only good subject is a dead one, or at least one which can project itself by empathic indifference into the place of every other.'[87] However, it remains impossible *to know* whether my 'empathy' for you is not just another ruse of the will.[88]

When desire becomes hypostatized in Girard's later work we are left wondering how to understand the solution offered (to the problem posed by 'desire'), which is to 'imitate good models' since once again knowledge and action appear ironically at odds. Girard himself recognizes the difficulty here. Speaking of mimesis in the modern world, he says: 'there is no way of distinguishing on an objective basis, no way of making a systematic overall distinction, between forms of behaviour that are "good" to imitate and those that are not.'[89] If Girard's hypostatizing of desire is the offspring of Schopenhauer's bleak vision then any claim to a 'positive' form of mimesis to counteract the 'negative' mimesis that leads to crisis, can only sound hollow.[90] His attempt to reinscribe a positive act that can be genuinely grasped by the subject is thus open to a similar critique as Schopenhauer's 'sublime disinterestedness', the source of which Eagleton puzzles over: 'It can obviously not be a product of the will, since it involves the will's momentary suspension; but it is hard to see how it can be the work of the alienated intellect either, and in Schopenhauer's drastically reduced universe there are really no other agents available.'[91] If reason cannot influence the ravenous will,

---

87. Eagleton, *The Ideology of the Aesthetic*, p. 164.
88. Eagleton puts the dilemma this way: 'All practice for Schopenhauer inhabits the domain of illusion; to prosecute my pity for you is in that moment to dispel it, to find myself writhing instead in the toils of self-interest. Only by transcending the diseased category of subjecthood altogether could one individual feel for another; but this very proposition cancels itself out.' Eagleton, *The Ideology of the Aesthetic* p. 165.
89. Girard, *Things Hidden*, p. 290.
90. Eagleton puts the problem of practice as follows: 'To fight injustice is to desire, and so to be complicit with that deeper injustice which is human life . . . Every bit of the world, from doorknobs to doctoral dissertations to modes of production and the law of the excluded middle, is the fruit of some stray appetite locked into the great empire of intentions and effects . . . The world is one vast externalisation of a useless passion, and that alone is real.' Eagleton, *The Ideology of the Aesthetic*, p. 162. Girard would perhaps argue that desire is indeed useful if it is generative, but without the possibility of unanimity in the modern world we have to conclude that desire in Girardian theory is made redundant.
91. Eagleton, *The Ideology of the Aesthetic*, pp. 165–166.

and the fictional nature of identity only exposes one's actions as futile, then any ethical solution of the kind that Girard and Schopenhauer propose is impossible. And if their theory is able to dissect the insidious workings of the will, or the violence that pertains to mimesis, then 'reason to that extent must be capable of curving back on itself, scrutinizing the drives of which it proclaims itself the obedient servant.'[92] Either both have somehow given desire the slip in their theorizing, or 'that theorizing is just another of its futile expressions and so quite valueless'.[93]

The contradiction that Schopenhauer's work shares with Girard's work is a kind of 'transcendentalism without a subject' (Eagleton). This is the case, because to be *subject to* the 'agency' of desire is to accept that "the place of absolute knowledge is preserved" though lacking all 'determinate identity'.[94] The knowing subject has been dislocated and its former space made utterly inscrutable: 'There can be no subject to fill it, for to be a subject is to desire, and to desire is to be deluded. An idealist philosophy that once dreamt of finding salvation through the subject is now forced to contemplate the unspeakable prospect that no salvation is possible without the *wholesale immolation of the subject itself*, the most privileged category of the entire system.'[95] The insight into scapegoating that Girard brings forward in *Violence and the Sacred* pertains more than ever to his own analysis of modern freedom. By bringing out some of the comparisons with Schopenhauerian 'Will', we discover that Girard's debunking of the subject and his hypostatizing of desire can be understood in line with a tradition that rejects one of the central tenets of western spirituality. This tenet pertains to personal experience and the new significance it comes to have within Christian spirituality from the sixteenth century onwards, a development we will have a chance to examine in more detail in the second part of the book.

6. *Dostoevsky's Conscious Attack on Rationalism*

Bringing out the affinities as I have just done, between Girard's projects and the philosophical developments that have sought to hypostatize desire at the expense of 'reason' and 'subjectivity', makes it easy to understand why Girard can be seen as an ally of modern forms of irrationalism. His analysis of Dostoevsky in particular adds substance to this view when it claims that the central insight of novelistic experience must pertain to the psychology of the author himself even when the 'irrationalism' of his characters can be understood as reflecting the

---

92. Ibid., p. 167.
93. Ibid.
94. Ibid., p. 168.
95. Ibid, (my italics).

'irrationalism' of the social world. As we saw in Chapter 1, the Romantic fallacy, as the basis of inner division, is something that the individual must get beyond. It provides the primary source of conflict, which will get played out in literary space by the great novelists. Hence, the individual must overcome himself ('slay the old human state'). Regardless of where the social forces are pushing him, the Romantic hero pushes himself, thereby achieving, in the great works, a restored unity and vertical transcendence. The starting point for the critic is thus the largely irrational exploits of the principal characters. In the end, desire knows more than an illusory subject, characterized by 'envy, jealousy, and impotent hatred'.[96]

But does Girard's critique of Dostoevsky not perhaps place too much emphasis on the psychological unravelling of the author through his characters at the expense of the author's own understanding of his creative work in the context of the period in which he is writing? In other words, by overplaying the structuralist debunking of subjectivity, does he not gravely downplay the author's own deliberate depiction of the reductive social forces of his time? Dostoevsky's himself had a quite developed critique of these forces and if this critique is to be accorded any significance then analysis must bear on more than the hidden structure of the author's desires. It must also at least consider what the author is attempting to depict prior to the ending of his 'great work'. Here, arguably, we find a very acute subjectivity attempting to reflect the irrational spirit of the age, at least as much as, if not more than, he is trying to work out his own hateful relationships. Has Girard made too much of the 'Romantic fallacy' in Dostoevsky's work?

From 1700 onward, particularly in France and England, there was a comprehensive effort to replace the classical philosophical understanding – much indebted to Aristotle – of human nature, society and history. Because of the success of a new scientific stance to the world associated with Isaac Newton, the methods of the natural sciences came to be regarded as the only valid methods of arriving at truth. In the eighteenth century, many thinkers aspired to be 'Newtons of the Mind', who would apply that scientific approach to developing a new foundation for the entire range of human existence.[97] Dostoevsky's *Notes from the Underground* represents a vigorous attack on the influence of this 'scientific temper' on the intellectual and cultural attitudes of nineteenth century Russia. *Notes from the Underground* is written by a man desperately trying to overcome a profound sense of loneliness, isolation and alienation, brought on by his contemporary intellectual culture. As Lev Shestov, an early twentieth-century Russian philosopher remarked, the *Notes* are 'an existential critique of pure reason'.[98]

---

96. Girard, *Deceit, Desire, and the Novel*, p. 41.
97. Peter Gay, *The Enlightenment: An Interpretation*. Volume II: 'The Science of Freedom' (London: Weidenfeld and Nicholson, 1970), p. 174.
98. See, E. V. Cherkasova, 'Kant on Free Will and Arbitrariness: A View from Dostoevsky's Underground', in *Philosophy and Literature* 28.2 (2004) 367–378.

Dostoevsky himself comments on the plight of the principal character in the preface of this work as follows: 'In the chapter entitled "Underground," this person introduces himself and his views, and as it were, tries to explain the causes that brought about, inevitably brought about, his appearance in our midst.'[99] In a style that Mikhail Bakhtin refers to as 'polyphonic', Dostoevsky writes the definitive counter-Enlightenment story.[100]

Dostoevsky's main attack is on what he sees as the 'wall' of closed rationalism that turns the human's consciousness of himself or herself into a kind of disease. The 'wall' that the thinking feeling subject confronts here is the utterly unquestionable status of scientific dogma. There simply is no thinking through the human's baser instincts: as the main character of the *Notes* points out, when an individual being is left only with the feeling of revenge, he 'dashes straight for his object like an infuriated bull with its horns down, and nothing but a wall will stop him'.[101] The almost mystical 'iron laws' of nature are summed up in the formula "$2 \times 2 = 4$".[102] The hero of Dostoevsky's masterpiece pushes this equation as a formula for *human nature* to its logical conclusions.[103] The more self-absorbed

---

99. Fyodor Dostoevsky, *Notes from the Underground/The Double*, trans. Jessie Coulson (Harmondsworth, Middlesex: Penguin Books, 1972).

100. In the new 'polyphonic' novel the characters are 'free people who are capable of standing beside their creator, of disagreeing with him and even rebelling against him. The plurality of independent and unmerged voices and consciousnesses and the genuine polyphony of full-valued voices are in fact characteristics of Dostoevsky's novels. It is not a multitude of characters and fates with a unified objective world, illuminated by the author's unified consciousness that unfolds in his works, but precisely the plurality of equal consciousnesses and their worlds, which are combined here in the unity of a given event, while at the same time maintaining their unmergedness'. Mikhail Bakhtin, *Problems of Dostoevsky's Poetics*, trans. R. W. Rostel (Ann Arbor: Ardis, 1973), p. 4.

101. Dostoevsky, *Notes from the Underground*, p. 20.

102. Ibid., p. 40.

103. 'As soon as they prove to you, for instance that you are descended from a monkey, then it is no use scowling, accept it as a fact. When they prove to you that in reality one drop of your own fat must be dearer to you than a hundred thousand of your fellow-creatures, and that this conclusion is the final solution of all so-called virtues and duties and all such prejudices and fancies, then you have to accept it, there is nothing to be done about it, for twice two is a law of mathematics. Just try refuting it . . .' Dostoevsky, *Notes from the Underground*, p. 23. Part of the cultural background to Dostoevsky's critique of the '$2 \times 2 = 4$' formula was the publication some years earlier of Nikolia Chernyshevsky's essay, *The Anthropological Principle in Philosophy* (1860), which expressed similar sentiments to those embodied later in the characters of Chernshevsky's novel *What is To Be Done*, a work that was to have a major influence on Dostoevsky. 'In general, it is necessary only to examine more closely an action or a feeling that seems to be altruistic to see that all of them are based on the

modern human's are, the more conscious they become, and the more aware they are of the utter futility of conscious existence. Consciousness thus becomes similar to a disease, making everything that was once 'noble' and 'true', appear debased and artificial. The more enlightened and educated we become according to nineteenth-century standards the more we discover that we are physically or physiologically determined. Dostoevsky brings out the fact that we experience this 'being determined' as a degradation of our being. The underground man, who, having committed a loathsome action that at first appears shameful, ends up taking an unusual pleasure in this degradation: bitterness, thus turns into 'a sort of shameful accursed sweetness'.[104]

To understand what we might call this 'guilty pleasure' in self-abasement is to grasp the irrationalism that Dostoevsky appears to suggest is at least more authentically human than the 'closed rationalism' of 2x2=4. Referring to where the degradation leads when one becomes *aware* that one is pushed to the 'wall' by the *laws* of 'acute consciousness', the narrator says that you realize then that there is no escape for you, 'that you never could become a different man',[105] and therefore if you are a scoundrel then you are not to blame for being a scoundrel. Hence a peculiar problem faces the 'irrationalist', since nineteenth century scientism does not quite manage to remove our consciousness of responsibility.[106] So we end up conscious of being inexorably determined *and yet to blame*. 'The worst of it, look at it which way one will, it still turns out that I was always the most to blame in everything. And what is most humiliating of all, innocently to blame.'[107] The underground man spells out the bizarre contradictions of this reductionist determinism: the human person, despite all he is told, still feels anger at this contempt for his humanity, yet, because he accepts what science is telling him, knows that he should not feel that anger. He is aware that the new scientism fundamentally erodes the categories of moral existence, for example good, evil, guilt and forgiveness.[108]

---

thought of personal interest, personal gratification, personal benefit; they are based on the feeling that is called egoism' Edie, J. Scanlan, and M. B. Zeldin, eds, *Russian Philosophy*, Vol. II, (Chicago: Quadrangle Press, 1965), p. 49.

104. Dostoevsky, *Notes from the Underground*, p. 19.

105. Ibid.

106. I am grateful to Brendan Purcell of the Philosophy Department in University College Dublin whose lectures and conversation helped me to understand Dostoevsky's own critique of nineteenth-century Russia.

107. Dostoevsky, *Notes from the Underground*, p. 19.

108. 'I should certainty have never been able to do anything with my generosity of soul – neither to forgive, for my assailant would perhaps have slapped me from the laws of nature, and one cannot forgive the laws of nature; nor to forget, for even if it were from the laws of nature, it was still an affront. Finally, even if I wanted to be anything but magnanimous, had desired on the contrary to revenge myself on my assailant, I could not have revenged myself on anyone for anything because I should certainly never have made up my mind to do anything, even if I had been able to.' Dostoevsky, *Notes from the Underground*, p. 20.

When applied to human reality, scientific rationalism denies the individual the prospect of a genuine act, leaving him to feel in a kind of inertia, a depersonalized experience of what is most fundamental to his sense of self. Is Girard's 'alienated Christianity' not reflected here in Dostoevsky's fierce though brilliant assessment of the social forces of nineteenth-century Russia?

Perhaps. But unsurprisingly, in opposition to the general critical assessment of Dostoevsky's 'Notes' as constituting in part, but primarily, a devastating attack on the prevalence of utilitarianism in nineteenth-century Russia, Girard makes the case that the author is in no way identical with the protagonist who asks rather sourly: 'what's the point in wishing by numbers.'[109] What Girard wants to emphasize instead of Dostoevsky's attack on modern scientism and rationalism, is that the author can only be identified with the hero at the end of the work of genius, when he has overcome his 'metaphysical desire' in the miracle of writing the novel.[110] 'It is true,' he tells us, 'that Dostoevsky shares his hero's disgust for the mediocre utopias of the end of the nineteenth century. But we should not mistake this partial agreement with total agreement . . . the underground Dostoevsky is not Dostoevsky, the genius, but rather the romantic Dostoevsky of earlier works.'[111] Girard, as we saw in Chapter 1, privileges a structuralist approach to literary space. Dostoevsky the genius, the one who overcomes his metaphysical desire and his illusory self, does so in the process of writing. However, if Dostoevsky's attack on utilitarianism is only 'partial', not the serious work of the novel, the implication is that the real problem lies in the psychology of the individual. The structuralist reading, then, minimizes the effects of the reductive socio-cultural forces at play in nineteenth-century Russia – and, more to the point, discounts Dostoevsky's own strong rejection of them in and through his novel.

Similarly, Girard maintains, the contagion that besets Europe in Raskolnikov's vision is owing to a form of metaphysical desire, or pride, whereby 'men condemn or acquit according to their own law' (something we also explored in Chapter 1). Girard's focus on the individual's 'Romantic fallacy' is so strong that it does not admit of anything that might mitigate the fact that our desires are borrowed, that is, Girard's budding mimetic theory. In terms of the project of the early work this seems understandable: it does after all concern 'the self and other in literary space'.

---

109. Reflecting an anti-rational view, the protagonist from *The Notes* says: 'As a matter of fact . . . if the formula for all our desires and whims is some day discovered – I mean what they depend on, what laws they result from, how they are disseminated, what sort of good they aspire to in a particular instance, and so on – a real mathematical formula, that is, then it is possible that man will at once cease to want anything, indeed I suppose it is possible that he will cease to exist. Well what's the point of wishing by numbers?' Dostoevsky, *Notes from the Underground*, p. 34.
110. Girard, *Deceit, Desire, and the Novel*, p. 300.
111. Girard, *Deceit, Desire, and the Novel*, pp. 259–260.

The dynamics of desire in structuring our relationships have an important significance here. However, a critique of rationalism is an attack not only on social engineering, but also on the undermining of human beings and their relationships, brought about by this engineering. It is arguably this aspect of the critique of utilitarianism that comes through when Dostoevsky presents his devastating attack on the 'wall of closed rationalism'. If scientism stifles and cramps human freedom it is because it also undermines human relationships, making any alternative to a bland instrumentalism or a negative imitative desire difficult in the extreme. If men do 'condemn or acquit according to their own law' then perhaps the 'law' here has as much to do with a narrow form of rationalism that soaks the good out of life leaving us alienated from each other and from our selves, unmotivated and uncaring.

Dostoevsky's radical critique of utilitarianism forces us to contemplate nineteenth-century scientism as a project that undermines what is fundamental to being human. His attack does not preclude a critique of negative mimesis, but it does make some of the conclusions drawn from Girard's analysis more difficult to sustain. For example, if rationalism is the driving force behind the worst excesses of the dehumanizing tendencies of the modern project then the transition from vertical to horizontal transcendence is not as easily explicable solely in terms of pride. The explanation now has to include an account of epistemologically driven societal changes, as much as the psychological dynamics of individuals. Viewed in an existential light, the problem of rationalism and scientism can be recognized as the 'law' that makes it impossible to know who is responsible in every instance, because our inner life, our passions, our consciousness, etc., are not reducible to rational methods of analysis and application. If we are all 'innocently guilty' because of an exaggerated confidence in $2 \times 2 = 4$, as the protagonist in *Notes* spitefully insists, then no one is really to blame. Is this not the dilemma that Dostoevsky is hinting at when he has Raskolnikov proclaim that 'nobody knew whom to condemn or whom to acquit'? It is a stumbling block perhaps to our will to scapegoat, but an all too human problem nonetheless, that certainly is not at odds with Girard's later theory of the sacred. We may justly ask, from the outset of his early theory, does Girard really need to do away with an ontological subject altogether in order to account for the 'resurrection' of an already quite lucid author?

7. Conclusion: Beyond Literary Space

In this chapter I have developed three main lines of argument against Girardian theory. I began by first reiterating the theoretical anomaly that, as I had argued in Chapter 2, exists in his early work. This anomaly was identified from the structural similarities between the early and later works, which present two different accounts of unity: the first a 'true' unity and the second a 'false' one. When the anomaly was further explored by reading back into Girard's early work in light of his later work, I suggested that he himself was guilty of scapegoating the Romantic hero for the sake of the literary community – so that the early 'unity' is exposed also as false. This I outlined as the first main strand of my argument against Girardian theory.

The second strand of my argument concerns evidence that Girard's later work employs the early theory to help validate the latter account of crisis, showing that not only does Girard not renounce the problematic early work but actually draws on key aspects of it to bolster and support his account of crisis in the modern world. As his theory evolves he attempts to maintain what is (according to the first strand of my argument) a mythological account of literary space alongside a demythologizing account of anthropological space – a form of scapegoating *and* a rejection of scapegoating – with three significant consequences for his theory.

The third and final strand of my argument details these consequences flowing from Girard's attempt to maintain two incompatible theories under the one explanatory umbrella of crisis in the modern period. If Dostoevsky's 'Underground Man' pushes to extremes what others will only push half way, then we might say Girard himself is pushed to extremes when he is forced to maintain a view that pits 'Desire' against the individual to such a degree that the only conceivable interpretation of the modern world is that it becomes 'synonymous with a sacrificial crisis'. By negating subjectivity and history and making the later work appear continuous with the early work, Girard's overall theory generates a number of profound tensions: first, incompatible accounts of crisis that purport to cohere in one unified theory of subjectivity and history; second, the loss of interiority and a first-person perspective, and hence the possibility of true, or positive spiritual *askesis*, to counter the negative mimesis of internal mediation; and, third, the hypostatizing of desire, and hence the aligning of 'Mimetic Desire' with 'Blind Will.' In sections three through five above I attempted to elaborate these consequences.

The problems are most readily identifiable here when we draw out the implications of Kojève's theory of desire for Girard's work. While he is clearly indebted to Kojève, Girard maintains a view of historical development as a negative unfolding in which the self in all its struggles is condemned to futility – a view which is clearly at odds with Kojève's progressive concept of history. As we saw the self is governed by deceit and therefore must hide its desires and violence from the other out of fear that its lack of originality will be noticed. The early theory thus contradicts the later view in which violence is the ultimate goal and the basis of a divine self-sufficiency – less a neurotic need to hide itself and more an outward activity that is always in danger of becoming contagious. The tension between the early and later work is now exposed, since we can readily see that the Romantic fallacy cannot be responsible for the collective crisis as Girard suggests in his later work when he places internal mediation and external mediation in the context of Degree as the underlying principle of all order, whose failure triggers a sacrificial crisis. Internal mediation, which generated the crisis in literary space, is thus viewed by Girard as an essential component of the crisis in cultural space, as if the explanation of cultural space is but the extension of the explanation of literary space.

Section four set out to highlight how Girard's concept of the 'interdividual self' is left without anchorage on a sea of mimetic desire. I outlined there how this self, whose ontological insufficiency corresponds to a lack of catharsis, forces Girard into a construal of desire as having more agency than an individual self with an inwardly generated personal identity (a central tenet of Christian faith). In the following section I drew a comparison between Girardian 'Desire' and Schopenhauerian 'Will' in order to demonstrate how such a reifying of desire ends up doing violence to the subject; this demonstration strengthens the case already made against Girard's own scapegoating tendencies,[112] but perhaps more significantly it points to a danger that runs counter to the Christian spirituality to which he himself is committed.

Finally, in addition to elaborating the tensions and inconsistencies arising as consequences from what I address in the first two strands of my argument, I attempted in the immediately preceding section above to draw out the irrationalism implicit in the reifying of desire. In doing so, I made the case that while such an attack on the subject and reason may appear to be the substance of Dostoevsky's work as analysed by Girard, Dostoevsky *himself* presents a well-worked out critique of the social forces that 'produce' the irrationalism at work in *The Notes from the Underground*, and the nineteenth century more generally. In other words, he is not simply a slave to mimetic forces until he gradually works through these dynamics in his novels but is rather capable of analysing with profound insight the broader social picture that gives rise to various forms of obsession. This fact reminds us that we need not dispense with a subject altogether when confronted with the peculiar dynamics of desire.

Now that we have outlined the problems in Girard's theory we can perhaps consider how Taylor might come to his aid by addressing them. If Taylor is genuinely to be of help here he can do so only by taking seriously Girard's key concern – a concern whose significance and urgency, I believe, is in no way diminished by the *aporiai* into which Girard himself has been led in trying to deal with it. This concern is: the loss of difference and the consequent crisis that arises for communities and individuals in their attempts to generate unity and identity. Why is this a deep and troubling concern? Quite simply because in these very attempts the creation of victims and scapegoats by some form of violence seems to be unavoidable. Girard's career has been characterized by a determined effort to expose the source of division and violence in cultural systems. Beginning with his early criticism, he has charted and attempted to explain the processes of

---

112. Girard's 'scapegoating tendencies' have been addressed elsewhere. See R. Kearney, *The Poetics of Modernity: Toward a Hermeneutic Imagination* (Atlantic Highlands, NJ: Humanities Press, 1995), especially part three, 'Current Debates'.

undifferentiation and crisis. Regrettably, as I have tried to show, his explanation has involved a radical undermining of any viable conception of subjectivity or historical change. Despite his final restoration of a transcendent subject at the end of *Deceit, Desire, and the Novel* (a restoration that, for reasons I that have been at pains to elaborate above, does not work), his insistence on the 'Romantic lie' as the *modus operandi* of the modern self has made it impossible for a subject to occupy a genuinely ethical space. We cannot hope to offer an account of how the challenge to contemporary culture, so powerfully identified by Girard, is to be met without a nuanced conception of an ethical subject who is capable of successfully traversing a space from division to unity – and of doing so in a post-religious age. Is such an account available? I hope to answer this question affirma-tively when I turn now in the second part of the book to explore key aspects of Taylor's thought.

PART II

FROM SACRIFICE TO SELF: TAYLOR'S PHILOSOPHICAL ACCOUNT

CHAPTER 4

THE EARLY MODERN PERIOD: TRANSPOSING THE OLD COSMIC ORDER

As in Greek tragedy and primitive religion, it is not the differences but the loss of them that gives rise to the violence and chaos that inspires Ulysses' plaint. This loss forces men into a perpetual confrontation, one that strips them of all their distinctive characteristics – in short of their 'identities.' Language itself is put in jeopardy. 'Each thing meets in mere oppugnancy': the objects are reduced to indefinite objects, 'things' that wantonly collide with each other like loose cargo on the decks of a storm tossed ship . . . To say this speech merely reflects a Renaissance commonplace, the great chain of being, is unsatisfactory. Who has ever seen a great chain collapse?[1]

René Girard

There was of course a traditional 'organicism' in the old views of order: the different things in the universe depend on each other and support each other. But where that mutual dependence once flowed from the fact that each holds its ordered place in the whole, which would otherwise revert to chaos . . . now the support takes direct efficient-causal form . . . This new order of interlocking natures arises to take the place of an order predicated on ontic logos. As the metaphysical basis of the earlier view erodes, in particular with the growing success of mechanistic science, the new vision can step into the vacuum.[2]

Charles Taylor

1. Introduction

A cursory glance at the quotations above alerts the reader to a contrast between what appear to be two very different accounts of order and transition in the human world. Girard's theory, captured succinctly here in the first quotation, purports to explain order from an anthropological perspective that appears profoundly suspicious of ontology and the capacity of a historical subject to survive the decomposition, which, for him, characterizes the modern period. For Taylor, however, this period need not be seen as a case of terminal decline; as he observes, 'something new arises'. His immense enquiry in *Sources of the Self* reveals that modern selfhood in all its anthropological, epistemological, aesthetic and political

---

1. Girard, Violence and the Sacred, trans. Patrick Gregory (Baltimore: Johns Hopkins University Press), p. 51.
2. Charles Taylor, *Sources of the Self: The Making of the Modern Identity* (New York: Cambridge University Press, 1992c), pp. 275, 276.

implications, also has its roots in ideas of the human good, that form part of a perennial quest of human cultures. These ideas of the good, as an aspect of life and yet somehow beyond life, help shape our group and individual identities and, Taylor believes, as the human story evolves they gradually become clearer and more articulate. He argues that the modern emphasis on universal and equal respect is the result of a long effort to define and reach the good, so that gradually the conception of selfhood becomes the locus of dispute, contestation and recognition in the working out of our value commitments. Hence, gaining orientation to the good through telling and retelling our stories becomes paramount to having an identity – something we will return to in greater detail in the final chapter. At the heart of 'the good' as it comes to be construed in the modern period is what Taylor calls the 'affirmation of ordinary life'. a value that has decisively if not completely replaced an earlier conception of reason as still connected to an hierarchy based on 'death and rebirth' – in other words, to a sacrificial world view – as a phenomenon somehow grounded in nature. His analysis of the aims of 'ordinary life' as superseding the older neo-Platonic view of hierarchy presents a rebuff to Girard's account of the great chain as playing only a marginal and 'decorative' role in the maintenance of order. The new view 'fills the vacuum' (that Girard otherwise *rightly* sees as) resulting from the loss of traditional hierarchy.

While dealing with a shorter anthropological timeline than Girard, Taylor has a more positive view of the modern period, borne out in his analysis of developments in the west. His aim in *Sources of the Self* is, on one hand to provide a historically grounded account of what our western notions of respect consist in today, and, on the other hand, to provide an ontological analysis of the basic conditions of human agency. The former account then is his 'philosophical history', while the latter analysis is his 'philosophical anthropology'.[3] While these two are never truly separate, for the sake of responding adequately to Girard's own 'bi-focal' analysis (literary/cultural), I will, for now, consider them as distinct: in Chapters 4 and 5 I will, for the most part, explore the relevance of Taylor's philosophical history for Girard's work, taking up then the relevant aspects of his philosophical anthropology in Chapter 6.

Unlike Girard, Taylor believes that there is a real moral basis to modern culture that can be reclaimed from the background of its key concerns, although articulating its significance is increasingly difficult. Breaking out of the structures of violence is a historical project that requires a depth dimension to human experience that is difficult to fathom in Girard's work due to, as I have argued, the persistent 'effects' of structuralism. The latter's reaction to existential and historical depth is, as Kearney observes in the context of certain strands of postmodernism, a form of 'surrender to the prevailing positivism which declares that things

---

3. Nicholas H. Smith, *Charles Taylor: Meaning, Morals, and Modernity* (Cambridge: Polity Press, 2002), p. 8.

are the way they are and cannot be otherwise'.[4] By contrast, Taylor's account of the developments in modern culture, as we shall begin to see in this chapter, attempts to confront the human tendency towards 'sacrifice' in a self-conscious way, while providing a morally meliorist view of the self and its historical developments. Unlike Girard, who sees the collapse of a theocentric concept of hierarchy and the unleashing of desire as a definitive loss for the individual, Taylor believes by placing the individual at the centre of the ordering process the early modern period provided the conditions of a new kind of authentic selfhood. His philosophical history highlights how an internalization of the good first becomes radical around the sixteenth century, and begins to mirror the differentiating role of the traditional cosmic order.

In light of Taylor's work, I attempt to establish, in this second part of the book, whether a workable model of human agency can be formulated that does not necessarily entail the rejection of Girard's theory of the sacred. I will begin in this chapter by considering Taylor's more historical account, and the way it responds to a number of specific issues that I have already outlined with respect to Girard's account of the transition to the modern period. I will try to show how Taylor's work can address some of these issues that, left as they are, tend to undermine the possibility of any positive account of human agency or historical development. The main issues, already outlined in Part One, are: (1) the loss of positive interiority as an aberration of Augustine's concept of the will, (2) the historical veracity of conflating the views of Corneille and Descartes and (3) the inability of modern culture to replace the traditional sacred order when the community can no longer effectively resort to violence. These 'undermining motifs' in Girardian theory can be strongly contested, as I shall attempt to show, by reference to Taylor's account.

The first such motif concerns the Romantic hero's spiritual *askesis* which, as we saw, is a kind of futile withdrawal by the individual for the sake of a more 'worthy' obstacle to excite his desire, something that Girard juxtaposes with the Saint's spiritual journey inwards in search of God. I suggested that the analogy, between the lover of the eternal essence, and the lover of the world – between the 'Saint and the Romantic' – presents, not two different kinds of love (as is the case with Augustinian *caritas* and *cupiditas*), but rather two entirely different subjects. Rather than one subject and two tendencies of the will (which, as we shall see more clearly in this chapter, is Augustine's position), Girard separates 'literary space' from 'spiritual space', with the result that his concept of the self involves two entirely different subjects and two entirely different wills. The Romantic thus becomes preoccupied with 'originality', as a futile expression of his own desire, while the Saint, becomes preoccupied with 'originality', as the place of his home

---

4. Richard Kearney, *The Wake of Imagination: Toward a Postmodern Culture* (London: Routledge, 1994), p. 393, 397.

in the eternal essence. By explicating Taylor's work on 'Augustinian inwardness' I will argue that his interpretation of Augustine allows for a less dichotomous view, while also recognizing how the subject can become divided through a certain *objectifying* stance to the world.

The second but related problem with Girardian theory that we will revisit in this chapter has to do with his understanding of modern individualism as pure egoism or 'pridefulness'. By explaining Descartes' appropriation of the Augustinian subject, Taylor draws out the continuity between the premodern and the modern experience, and in the process he shows how the moral sources that once belonged to a cosmic order defined by the Greek concept of Being, begin to be redefined and further internalized as rational, in the seventeenth century. What for Girard is a negative unfolding (discussed in chapter one), rooted in the individual's self-deception concerning his own 'originality', has for Taylor a moral import, and is part of an incarnational mode of life. We see the difference here discussed with respect to both Girard's and Taylor's comparisons between Descartes and Corneille. As we noted in chapter one, for Girard, pride announces itself in the modern world as the inability to admit that we imitate others. Its effects are recognizable in 'the morality of "generosity" that Descartes, the first philosopher of individualism, and Corneille, its first dramatist, develop at the same time.'[5] Thus the ethic of 'individualism' for Girard is just a ruse of the ego in its bid for divine self-sufficiency. In its attempts to avoid the reality of its own imitative desires, it seeks out 'proof' to convince itself of its own superiority. Later in the chapter we will show how Taylor's reading of the *difference* between Descartes and Corneille challenges Girard's view that both early modern thinkers *share a similar ethic*, and highlights what is new and radical about the beginning of the modern period.

The third and perhaps most significant problem to which we will address Taylor's philosophical history in this chapter is Girard's later anthropological analysis of the modern world as 'synonymous with a sacrificial crisis'. For Girard, as we saw in Chapter 2, the movement from vertical to horizontal transcendence – what he describes in his early work as a period when 'men become gods' – is characterized as a transition from external to internal mediation, whereby the negative imitation that pertains to the Romantic fallacy now holds sway. The anthropological principle of Degree is privileged by Girard over the philosophical doctrine of the 'great chain of being', in order to explain how external mediation holds internal mediation in check – who after all 'has ever seen a great chain collapse'. A traditional hierarchical order thus functions to contain violence by channelling mimetic desire in non-rivalrous ways, while the absence of hierarchy, and hence Degree, releases desire in competitive and ultimately destructive ways. Without Degree, Girard argues, there is crisis, and, since Degree is an inherently

5. René Girard, *Resurrection from the Underground: Feodor Dostoevsky*, trans., James G. Williams (New York: Crossroads Publishing Company, 1997), p. 94.

anthropological and social principle, the individual in the modern world does not have any capacity to keep the destructive forces in check.

In Part I, I argued that in order to understand how this anthropological principle fails to restore order in the modern world, Girard relies heavily on 'internal mediation', or the negative dynamics that arise from the Romantic fallacy. The problem with making the later theory appear continuous with the early theory is that it further masks Girard's early mythological account, concealing his own act of scapegoating the subject. What follows from this when we *look again* at the anthropological principle of Degree is that the Romantic hero is now held responsible not only for the crisis in literary space but also for the crisis in the modern world: once 'Degrees are shaked', hierarchies are flattened and thus it appears 'men become gods in each others eyes.' From the Girardian perspective the older order simply cannot function to contain violence once the individual's pride gains a foothold. As long as the early mythological account that appears to explain crisis so well, is still intact and apparently continuous with the later theory there is no way for Girard to conceive of an alternative to the total loss and deterioration of order in the modern period. But is all order really so fundamentally undermined when the individual attempts to gain some autonomy? When Girard himself is seen to be scapegoating the modern individual, for the sake of the literary community (and to be merging two separate theories as if they were somehow a unified theory), are we not now in a position to speak to Girard's strongest claims concerning violence and religion, and to do so from the perspective of a historical and ontological subject? Later in this chapter we will consider Taylor's analysis of how the traditional order associated with Degree is transposed onto a Providential order that places the individual at least partly in control of the design in nature that had been, prior to the modern period, a socially determined hierarchically arranged cosmic order. At the heart of this transposition is Taylor's central idea concerning the affirmation of ordinary life, a largely Protestant revolution in thought that presents the strongest challenge yet to Girard's thorough debunking of subjectivity and historical development in the name of Christian anthropology.

2. Taylor's St. Augustine: 'In Interiore Homine'

In her work entitled *Love and Saint Augustine*, Hannah Arendt describes how, for Augustine, whose every experience is conditioned by death, our striving after future goods is something we must always fear. Arising from this, 'only a present without a future is immutable and utterly unthreatened.'[6] It is here in the 'futureless present' that we find the absolute good, which Augustine calls eternity.

---

6. Hannah Arendt, *Love and Saint Augustine*, ed. Joanna Vecchiarelli Scott and Judith Chelius Stark (Chicago and London: University of Chicago Press, 1996), p. 13.

Human life does not endure; each day we lose it a little more. While only the present appears real there seems no way of measuring it – no space in which to take a stand. 'Life is always either – no more or not yet.'[7] However, humans do measure time.[8] Arendt puts Augustine's question as follows: 'Perhaps man possess a "space" where time can be conserved long enough to be measured, and would not this "space", which man carries with him transcend both life and time?'[9] The space that permits us to measure time turns out to exist in our memory where things are being stored up.

Memory contains the trace of all our past experiences – even our anticipated experiences, and all things imagined whether realized or not. It is here that the true space of the subject opens.

> Memory, the storehouse of time is the presence of the 'no more' (*iam non*) as expectation is the presence of the 'not yet' (*nondum*). Therefore, I do not measure what is no more but something in my memory remains fixed in it. It is only by calling past and future into the present of remembrance and expectation that time exists at all.[10]

Hence it is only in the 'now' of the present made possible by memory that the past and the future meet; it is here in the 'now' that time is measured backwards and forwards. However what prevents humans from living in this now, that is, in eternity, is life itself, which never 'stands still.'[11] This is so, Arendt tells us, because it takes an object to determine and arouse desire. Life itself (human existence, temporality, createdness) is defined for Augustine by what it craves because craving, by drawing us away from the now, does not permit time to stand still.

Memory, thus, opens the space of temporality within which the search for God takes place, and as such it holds a central place in Augustine's philosophy. The structure of craving that Arendt discusses in relation to Augustine's conception of

---

7. Arendt, *Love and Saint Augustine*, p. 14.

8. The idea of the sacred articulated here is not purely that of an anthropological function, *a la* Girard, but rather lies in what *is*, timeless existence. Speaking of religious perspectives as a search for the rediscovery of man, Ruth Nada Anshen writes, 'By emphasizing timeless existence against reason as a reality, we are liberated, in our communion with the eternal, from the otherwise unbreakable rule of "before and after." Then we are able to admit that all forms, all symbols in religions, by their negation of error and their affirmation of the actuality of truth, make it possible to experience that knowing which is above knowledge, and that dynamic passage of the universe to unending unity.' M. Hades and M. Smith, *Heroes and Gods: Spiritual Biographies in Antiquity*, ed. R.N. Anshen (London: Routledge and Kegan Paul, 1965), pp. x–xi.

9. Arendt, *Love and Saint Augustine*, p. 15.

10. Ibid.

11. Ibid., p. 16.

love, a structure that depends on the possession of the object craved, is determined by the space of memory where past and present meet. Human beings in turn help constitute the earthly world by what they crave or love for 'it is the love of the world that turns heaven and earth into the world as a changeable thing. In its flight from death, the craving for permanence clings to the very things sure to be lost in death.'[12] And so, we learn that the wrong kind of love craves the wrong kind of object, which continually disappoints, and correspondingly the right kind of love craves the right kind of object – thereby directing us on the path to eternity, and to the ultimate Good. To these different kinds of love Augustine gives the terms '*cupiditas*' and '*caritas*' respectively.

Taylor's analysis of Augustine is indispensable to his understanding of modern freedom and how the 'good life' has come to be expressed in and through our various horizons of significance – horizons, which as we shall see in Chapter 6, have meaning within a temporal context and require personal commitment. What Augustine unequivocally establishes for later thinkers like Descartes is the irreducible notion of 'reflexive self-presence.' In the section in *Sources of the Self* entitled 'In Interiore Homine' Taylor presents a detailed account of the striking elements of continuity between Plato and Augustine, while at the same time highlighting what he sees as an important *difference*. While both thinkers hold to the same oppositions – that is, between spirit/matter, higher/lower, eternal/temporal, immutable/changeable – Augustine, Taylor claims, 'centrally and essentially' describes these oppositions in terms of 'inner/outer'.[13] Here is how Taylor, following this early Church Father, describes the difference between the two realms: 'the outer is the bodily, what we have in common with the beasts, including even our senses, and our memory storage of our images of outer things. The inner is the soul.'[14] For the person concerned with his or her spiritual well-being a crucial shift in direction is articulated here. The road from the 'lower to the higher' now passes through our attending to ourselves as inner.[15]

Taylor, however, wants to stress another important facet of this inward person, indeed of this whole mode of inwardness, which has to do with a different kind of self-presence than, he claims, we find in Plato – one that is intimately connected with God. The image of the sun as the 'highest good' or the ultimate principle of

---

12. Ibid., p. 17.
13. Taylor, *Sources of the Self*, p. 129.
14. Ibid.
15. Taylor's own main textual source for his reading of Augustine is E. Gilson, *The Christian Philosophy of Saint Augustine*. John Millbank critiques Taylor's analysis of Augustinian inwardness, by arguing that to see it as a 'deepening' of an already existing Socratic turn to interiority (which he thinks Taylor does) is an 'oversimplification'. However, to pursue this further and respond cogently on behalf of Taylor, which I believe could be done, is beyond the scope of my analysis here. See, J. Millbank, *The Word Made Strange: Theology, Language, Culture* (Oxford: Blackwell, 1997), p. 207.

Being plays a central role for both Plato and Augustine. For Plato we discover the highest good by 'looking at the domain of objects, which it organises in the field of Ideas.'[16] The power of seeing the good that resides in the eye of the soul does not have to be put into this metaphorical 'eye' – rather the eye just has to be turned. As with Augustine, the right *direction* is crucial – except with one important difference. For Augustine, while God is also more likely to be known through His created order, our principal route to God, Taylor argues, is not through the object domain but *in* our selves.[17] The Good is now very much rooted within, defined primarily as a way of seeing. In other words, the light of God is not just out there illuminating the order of being, as we find with Plato's vision, it is now the very light in the soul, referred to in John's Gospel as the 'light that lighted every man that cometh into the world.'[18] In an important sense, the light of the good is now at either end of our experience – in the 'what' experienced and the 'who' experiencing.

By shifting the focus from the field of objects known to the activity itself of knowing, where God is now found, each of us can begin our own particular search for knowledge. By doing so each of us takes up a reflexive stance. In an attempt to draw out the significance of this turning to the self, Taylor contrasts it with the way the ancient moralists would have viewed reflexivity. He tells us that they often gave advice about 'caring for one's soul', which was reflexive in so far as they wanted to stress the foolishness of getting wrapped up in things that essentially do not matter. As with our modern day over-zealous businessperson to whom we might say, 'take care of yourself', the point was that 'showing a profit' or 'getting ahead,' or whatever might be driving you, is not worth a heart attack.[19] The injunction here, Taylor suggests, calls us to a reflexive stance but not a radically reflexive one; the latter first comes into play with Augustine and the adoption of a first-person standpoint.

Taylor explains this radically reflexive first-person standpoint in the following way. The world that is known by me is there for me – is experienced by me. Our emphasis on objectivity leaves out just this dimension of the first person – what it is like to be a certain kind (just *this* kind) of experiencing agent. By being radically reflexive we can turn and make our own experience an object of attention, we can become aware of our awareness. Describing this reflexivity, Taylor writes: 'Radical reflexivity brings to the fore a kind of presence to oneself which is

---

16. Taylor, *Sources of the Self*, p. 129.
17. The reason for this is: ". . . because God is not just the transcendent object or just the principle of order of the nearer objects, which we strain to see. God is also and for us primarily the basic support and underlying principle of our knowing activity. God is not just what we long to see but what powers the eye which sees.' Taylor, *Sources of the Self*, p. 129.
18. Ibid.
19. Ibid., p. 130.

inseparable from one's being the agent of experience, something to which access by its very nature is asymmetrical: there is a crucial difference between the way I experience my activity, thought, and feeling, and the way you or anyone else does. This is what makes me a being that can speak of itself in the first person.'[20] Augustine's turn to the self was radically reflexive in this way and what followed, we might say, 'instinctively', was a language of inwardness; the inner light that shines in our presence to ourselves instantiates our first person standpoint. Unlike the outer light it illuminates the *space* where I am present to myself.[21] In this space where I am aware of my own activity of sensing and thinking, I am made aware of this activity's dependence on something beyond it, which provides the standard for all reasonable activity – something that I should look up to and revere; 'By going inward I am drawn upward.'[22]

The idea that God is to be found within is crucial to Augustine's account of our search for self-knowledge; this is so because even when the soul is present to itself it can fail to know itself, it can be mistaken about its own nature. Our search is doomed to failure unless we *already* have some understanding of ourselves – a knowledge that lies implicit in our memory. Augustine, Taylor tells us, breaks from the Platonic theory of prenatal experience and develops a concept of memory that comes to include matters that have nothing to do with past experience.[23] Just as God is the source of light behind the eye of the soul that draws me inward, God is also the source of memory that leads me to true self-knowledge. Once again, in going inwards where I strive to make myself more fully present to myself, I am drawn upwards to the awareness that God stands above me. 'At the very root of memory the soul finds God . . . And so the soul can be said to "remember God".'[24] By going within I find the truth, but I find it *in* God. This, for Taylor is the ultimate 'reflexive move' that Augustine articulates, whereby we now grasp the intelligible not just because our soul's eye is directed to it, but primarily because we are directed by the Master within.[25] Indeed, what greater theory of 'positive mimesis', that turns against rivalrous desire, can there be than one that takes its lead from this inner 'singular' domain?

---

20. Ibid., p. 129.
21. Ibid., p. 131.
22. Ibid., p. 134.
23. Describing this development that was decisive for Descartes' later theory of innate ideas, Taylor shows how inwardness is given further scope and significance: 'Deep within us is an implicit understanding, which we have to think hard to bring to explicit and conscious formulation. This is our "*memoria*". And it is here that our implicit grasp of what we are resides, which guides us as we move from our original self-ignorance and grievous self-misdescription to true self-knowledge.' Taylor, *Sources of the Self*, p. 135.
24. Ibid.
25. Ibid., p. 136.

Augustine places the focus on our activity of striving to know and he makes us aware of this in a 'first-person perspective'.[26] God is found in the intimacy of my self-presence, where knower and known are one. As well as being behind the eye of the soul God is the One whose Ideas the eye strives to see. God is 'closer to me than I am to myself', but it could never be the case in this view that my pride is 'more exterior [to me] than the external world' as Girard argues is the fate of the Romantic hero. Because even when I am drawn outward through *cupiditas* it is still *me* who is searching for permanence, for God; for my origins in the eternal essence. The movement inward through *caritas*, is the basis of Augustine's attempt to discern his relationship with God in the soul and its activity. In this striving for the good, humans show themselves most clearly and uniquely as the image of God through their inner self-presence and love. Thus we can see how essentially linked this doctrine of inwardness is to Augustine's whole conception of the human being's relationship to God.[27] Our inwardness, however potentially corrupting it may be, is also our route to God. Arising from Augustine's thought, Arendt and Taylor stress different but complimentary aspects of 'memory': for the former it opens the space of temporality, while for the latter it is the soul's implicit knowledge of itself.[28]

I already mentioned that, depending on what the object of our love is, our soul can potentially face two ways: 'towards the higher and immaterial, or towards the lower and sensible' – or towards the 'inner or outer' (Arendt). Our attention is directed in two ways in accordance with the two directions of desire, *caritas* or *cupiditas*. Once again, Taylor points out the similarity and the difference between Augustine and Plato on this crucial issue of two directions, or two loves. The key difference, he tells us, resides in Augustine's developed notion of the will. From Stoic thinkers like Chrysippus, there developed a notion of the will based on moral choice (*prohairesis*), or our power to give or withhold assent, which through Christian interpretation came to place an emphasis on personal commitment,

---

26. Ibid.
27. Ibid., p. 137.
28. Taylor explains how the soul comes to know itself from its implicit knowledge of God, and how this move becomes the basis of Augustine's attempts to discern the image of the trinity in the soul and its activity. "The mind comes to know itself and, in that, love itself [first trinity]. The same basic idea underlies the second trinity, of memory, intelligence, and will . . . In this, the basic movement of the trinity in the soul is made even clearer. 'Memory' is the soul's implicit knowledge of itself . . . But to make this explicit and full knowledge I have to formulate it. In the particular case of the soul, the true latent knowledge I have of myself will be overlaid by all sorts of false images. To dissipate these distorted appearances, and to get to the truth, I have to draw out the implicit knowledge within (which also comes from above) . . . But to understand my true self is to love it, and so with intelligence comes will, and with self-knowledge, self-love." Taylor, *Sources of the Self*, p. 136.

and, as Taylor claims, had a deep influence on early modern thinking. But a second change emerged out of a Christian outlook that was given paradigmatic formulation by Augustine.[29] 'Where for Plato, our desire for the good is a function of how much we see it, for Augustine the will is not simply dependent on knowledge.'[30] This view argues that human beings are capable of two radically different moral dispositions. Unlike the Socratic/Platonic doctrine of right action, where seeing the good is tantamount to doing the good, 'Augustine's doctrine of the two loves allows for the possibility that our disposition may be radically perverse, driving us to turn our backs on even the good we see.'[31]

And so, the Christian view insists that knowledge alone is not enough – the will must first be healed through grace before we can function fully on the Socratic model.[32] We do not get around the problem of the divided will by claiming that only Romantics choose the worse half and mistake it for the 'totality'.[33] Romanticism, as Girard characterizes it, is determined by a fundamental disposition of the will, but Augustine would no doubt argue that this does not sum up the constituent force of subjectivity, since it is still the subject who struggles with this weakness, knowing all the time of his own failing (as Augustine surely did). To annex all of subjectivity, and characterize it as 'Romantic', based on an evaluation of one constitutive tendency of the will, is to misrepresent an important strand of western spirituality.[34]

The Christian development of the will weaves together two 'master ideas' which struggle to coexist: 'The will as our power to confer or withhold all things considered assent, or choice; and the will as the basic disposition of our being.'[35] This development complicates the Socratic model where we always act for the good we see and introduces a potential conflict between 'vision and desire'. The significance of this conflict for us is that 'in the zone in which we live, of half understanding and contrary desires, the will is as much the independent variable, determining what we can know, as it is the dependent one, shaped by what

---

29. Ibid., p. 128.
30. Ibid., p. 137.
31. Ibid., p. 138.
32. Ibid.
33. René Girard, *Resurrection from the Underground: Feodor Dostoevsky*, trans. James G. Williams (New York: Crossroad, 1997), p. 62, 63.
34. Augustinian spirituality is not easily amenable to mimetic theory. By highlighting how mediated desire is always object related, and does not (pace Girard) need a third object, or (pace Kojève) become its own object, Arendt points to what we might see as a significant source of tension between Augustine's model of desire and Girard's model of desire. 'Even *caritas* mediates between man and God in exactly the same way as *cupiditas* mediates between man and the world. All it does is mediate. It is no revelation of an original interconnectedness of either man and God or man and world.' Arendt, *Love and Saint Augustine*, p. 30.
35. Taylor, *Sources of the Self*, p. 138.

we see.'[36] The circularity here, Taylor claims, can lead us to dominate and possess the things that surround us. The danger is that we make ourselves into what is most detestable in ourselves. As in the case of the 'underground man', and other Dostoyevskian 'heroes', we then become slaves to our own obsessions, and dominated by a fascination with the sensible – including the spectrum of negative relationships.[37]

What we find described in Girard's theory of internal mediation – as the quintessential underground disease – arguably has its source in what Taylor calls Augustine's radical reflexivity, with one important qualification. Radical reflexivity is central to our moral understanding, but if it were only a source of evil, as internal mediation appears to be, the solution, as Taylor argues, might simply be to turn away from the self, and become absorbed in impersonal ideas or indeed an external model. But for Augustine 'it is not radical reflexivity which is evil, on the contrary we show most clearly the image of God in our fullest self-presence. Evil is when this reflexivity is enclosed within itself. Healing comes when it is broken open, not in order to be abandoned, but in order to acknowledge its dependence on God.'[38] Here, overcoming evil is not simply dependent on seeing the good, but involves something also in the dimension of the soul's sense of itself, which as we noted, belongs to 'memory'. Where for Plato the eye has the capacity to see, for Augustine it has lost this capacity and must be restored through grace.[39] For Girard, 'novelistic experience' might be said to draw out the conflict between vision and desire in the context of the self-other relation.[40] We saw, for example, that the pride of the Romantic hero is based on a belief in originality, a form of inverted Augustinianism. However, we also pointed out that this analogy to Augustinian desire ends up creating a dichotomy between the 'Saint and the Romantic', which we can now see more clearly is false, since Augustine's notion of the will is neither *caritas* nor *cupiditas*, but both. That is, two tendencies of the same will, at play in a human drama whose stage is the inner person. God who is found in the intimacy of my self-presence can be thought of 'as the most fundamental ordering principle in me.'[41] This new ordering principle becomes a defining feature of the transition to the modern period.

---

36. Ibid.
37. Taylor, *Sources of the Self*, p. 139.
38. Ibid.
39. Ibid.
40. In *Deceit, Desire, and the Novel* Girard claims: 'The subjective and objective fallacies are one and the same; both originate in the image which we all have of our own desires.' René Girard, *Deceit, Desire, and the Novel: Self and Other in Literary Structure*, trans. Yvonne Freccero (Baltimore: Johns Hopkins University Press, 1965), p. 16.
41. Taylor, *Sources of the Self*, p. 136.

3. *Disengaged Reason and the Affirmation of Ordinary Life*

Augustine's 'schismatic will' provides the template for seminal concepts that Taylor believes come to characterize much of the modern outlook – will as our moral choice, and will as the basic disposition of our being. The former acts with greater rational consistency towards empirical data, the latter feels somehow cut off from the world, isolated yet still longing for unity with the whole. Both have their source in the experience of lack associated with Augustinian 'radical reflexivity' and 'self-presence'. In terms of 'moral choice', the lack can be remedied by a certain rational control, whereas in terms of 'our basic disposition' the lack seems almost like a terminal weakness. In the following chapter we will consider in greater detail the developments of the will as 'our basic disposition' and in particular how the Romantic tradition attempted to remedy the weakness, but for now we shall focus on the developments of the will that sought greater rational control.

We saw how *lack of permanence* 'manifests' itself as an absence for Augustine – a fear of death associated with the loss of the 'wrong' object of desire. But 'fear', as the *very experience of loss*, also takes on rational significance for Augustine in terms of 'negation', which he translates into one of the basic modes of argument for the existence of God in the western Christian tradition.[42] A variant of this 'ontological argument' inhabits Descartes' proof in the Third Meditation. The proof that I exist turns out to be derivative from the proof that God exists. However, negation is expressed in *The Meditations* in terms of doubt and in relation to the idea of Descartes' own finite nature, since if he did not also have implanted 'within him' an idea of infinity and perfection, how would he even know he was doubting? Whether or not the argument that God exists actually convinces is not the issue here. According to Taylor, what is at stake is the significance of this 'lack' that Augustine experiences. Drawing explicitly on Cartesian language, Taylor phrases developed reflexivity in this way: '. . . to understand myself as doubting and wanting is to see myself as lacking in some respect, and hence as finite and imperfect. So *my most basic and unavoidable modes of self-understanding* presuppose the idea of infinity.'[43] What stands out here within a modern rational framework is the 'mode of self-understanding' that is 'lacking' and 'imperfect', a mode that is constitutive of the very notion of radically reflexivity. The Romantic

---

42. Taylor rehearses the typically Augustinian form of proof: 'The démarche which is common to . . . all (proofs) is something like this: my experience of my own thinking puts me in contact with a perfection, which at one and the same time shows itself to be an essential condition of that thinking and also to be far beyond my own finite scope and powers to attain. There must then be a higher being on which all this depends, i.e. God.' Taylor, *Sources of the Self*, p. 140.

43. Ibid., p. 141 (my italics).

hero, it seems, was not the first to experience insufficiency in the face of Being; but this insufficiency, although it may lead to a conversion to 'vertical transcendence' within literary space, still does not provide materials for a rational proof – in Augustinian/Cartesian mode – for God's existence.

Girard's antipathy toward the modern period discounts any continuity between Augustine and Descartes, whom he describes as 'the first philosopher of individualism'.[44] Unlike Taylor, Girard sees Descartes as the instigator of modern 'self-divinization', but he ignores the philosophical import of the move to radical reflexivity, and more specifically its source in Augustinian inwardness. As we discussed in Chapter 1, his use of St. Mark's text, 'Whoever does not gather with me scatters,'[45] places the emphasis on novelistic experience as the place of 'gathering' by the author who successfully renounces metaphysical desire. Here the critic once again eschews a first-person perspective.[46] The deep structures of the text replace the depths of the soul, and the critic replaces God as the minister of effective therapy. This break with Augustine is further reinforced when Girard characterizes the Cartesian ethic, which begins with self-reflexivity, as a form of 'proof' that the individual requires in order to convince himself of his ontological sufficiency, in other words as a means of 'self-divinization'. It is this 'proof' of the individual's superior being, masked under the veil of 'generosity', that Girard believes Descartes shares with his contemporary Corneille.[47] However, for Taylor, it is precisely this ethic of generosity that is quite radical with respect to the

---

44. Girard, *Resurrection from the Underground*, p. 94.

45. Ibid., p. 64.

46. In making the case for Augustine's 'proto-cogito', Taylor draws our attention to another remarkably modern fact about Augustine's thinking – he not only used the word 'cogito' but also singled it out for comment. 'To focus on my own thinking activity is to bring to attention not only the order of things in the cosmos that I seek to *find* but also the order I seek to *make* as I struggle to plumb the depths of memory and discern my true being. In the *Confessions*, Augustine reflects how our thoughts "must be rallied and drawn together again, that they may be known; that is to say, they must as it were be collected and gathered together from their dispersions: whence the word 'cogitation' is derived". And Augustine goes on the point out the etymological link between "*cogitare*" and "*cogere*" = "to bring together" or "to collect."' Taylor, *Sources of the Self*, p. 141. Disengaged subjectivity was, of course, not what Augustine had in mind, but the influence of the whole language and experience of inwardness is undeniable.

47. As we discussed in Chapter 1, Girard claims (quoted from Chapter 1), 'Perhaps it is most suitable to seek the first traces of our malaise in the very origin of the era of the individualist, in that morality of *generosity* that Descartes, the first philosopher of individualism, and Corneille, its first dramatist, developed at the same time . . . It is significant that rationalist individualism and the irrational morality of generosity appear conjointly.' Girard, *Resurrection from the Underground*, p. 94.

modern emphasis on rational subjectivity, what he refers to as the Cartesian stance of self-generating, 'methodological ordering of evident insight.'[48] For Taylor, *distinguishing* between Descartes and Corneille is crucial if we are to properly understand the shift from the older hierarchically ordered world of the 'honor ethic' to the modern world of the 'disengaged subject'. Generosity undergoes a transposition with Descartes whereby it becomes an emotion that accompanies my newly discovered sense of my human dignity as a rational self.[49] It is not simply a thickly disguised justification for the individual's superiority; rather it becomes part of what I owe to myself, if I am to fulfil my capacity as a rational agent. What we have, Taylor tells us, 'is a virtually total transposition of the notion of generosity from the defense of honor in warrior societies (portrayed by Corneille) to the Cartesian ideal of rational control'.[50] Taylor believes that this modern theme of the dignity of the rational agent, which has such a considerable place in modern ethical and political thought, arises from an internalization of moral sources at the beginning of the modern period.[51]

In my bid for control I may no longer meet the personal God of Augustine, but I am nonetheless driven inwards by 'doubt' to where I now achieve a clarity and fullness of self-presence that was lacking before.[52] What appears to be significant to Girard's conversation with philosophy is not so much the way God is replaced

---

48. Taylor, *Sources of the Self*, p. 157.
49. Ibid., p. 154.
50. Ibid.
51. Taylor's most recent work *A Secular Age* (which I will address more fully in the Epilogue) also draws our attention to this important distinction between Descartes and Corneille, with even more relevance for our conversation on the way in which 'rank' (for Girard, 'external mediation') is internalized in the modern period, that is in terms of the transition from one kind of order to another. Speaking once again about what Descartes added to the ethic of 'generosity', Taylor suggests that, the word 'meant something different in the seventeenth century. It designates the lively sense one has of one's rank, and of the honour which attaches to it, which motivates one to live up to the demands of one's station. Corneille's heroes are always declaring their "générosite" as the reason for the striking, courageous and often gruesome acts they are about to commit. But Descartes takes the notion out of the public space, and the field of socially defined ranks, into the internal realm of self-knowledge . . . The rank I must live up to is the non-socially defined one of rational agent . . . In other words, the central place, the virtue which can uphold and sustain the others, which Socrates gave to wisdom, for instance, and others have given to temperance, for Descartes falls to generosity. The key motivation here is the demands laid on me by my own status as a rational being, and the satisfaction is that of having lived up to the dignity of this station.' Charles Taylor, *A Secular Age* (Cambridge, MA and London: Belknap Press of Harvard University Press, 2007), p. 134.
52. Taylor, *Sources of the Self*, p. 157.

as the way the locus of control (what Taylor also calls 'the centre of gravity') has shifted.[53] What we are left with after Descartes is a mechanistic view of the world, which comes to characterize so much of Deism, and is part of the new Reforming Movement. Hence, the distinction between Descartes and Corneille is a sign for Taylor of a 'transvaluation' that emphasizes the dignity of the rational agent. 'Control' rather than 'proof' is the motivating force. Individualism here is generating more than the multiple divisions that come to flourish in underground existence. Properly understood, it will soon inspire a new attitude towards nature and the social world, initially under the banner of a reaction against the traditional metaphysical order.

The affirmation of ordinary life holds a central place in Taylor's analysis of modern freedom. It marks a decline in a metaphysical view, and its attendant values, and the rise of a new religious view, the aims of which were largely compatible with the concurrent revolution in the sciences. Prior to this 'transvaluation of values', theoretical contemplation and the participation of the citizen in the life of the polity generally thought to out-rank ordinary life.[54] The transition that Taylor details upsets the older hierarchies by displacing the locus of the good life from 'some special range of higher activities' to 'life itself'. The consequence of this change, he tells us, is that 'full human life', which for Augustine is still synonymous with eternal Being and the well-ordered soul, 'is now defined in terms of labor and production, on the one hand, and marriage and family on the other'.[55] The sixteenth and seventeenth centuries see the locus of value begin to shift from an other-worldly sphere of 'immutable substances', which excluded ordinary human concerns, to 'this world' as somehow holding the key to happiness and human flourishing. As a result of the affirmation of ordinary life 'higher activities come under vigorous criticism'.[56]

The Scientific Revolution, most notably in the work of Francis Bacon, discredits the Aristotelian ideal of *theōria* as involving contemplation of the order of the cosmos. Taylor argues that Bacon constantly points out that the older sciences have sought some satisfying overall order in things rather than being concerned to see how things function. As a result, they have not borne fruit or 'adduced a single experiment which tends to relieve and benefit the condition of man'.[57]

---

53. 'The thesis is not that I gain knowledge when I turn towards God in faith. Rather the certainty of clear and distinct perception is unconditional and self-generated. What has happened is rather that God's existence has become a stage in my progress towards science through the methodological ordering of evident insight. God's existence is a theorem in my system of perfect science.' Taylor, *Sources of the Self*, p. 157.
54. Taylor, *Sources of the Self*, p. 212.
55. Ibid., p. 213.
56. Ibid.
57. Ibid.

The goal of the new science was just the opposite.[58] With the change in values came the reversal of the older hierarchy. What was previously seen in a negative light as being lower is raised and valued as the new standard. Conversely, what was previously seen as higher is frowned upon as vanity and presumption. Practical benevolence and the reduction of suffering begin to take centre stage, thus implicit in the affirmation of ordinary life, then, is an inherent bent towards social equality – the centre of the good life is something that everyone, and not just the privileged few, can share and have a part in.[59]

Taylor argues that the scope of this social reversal can best be measured by looking at the critique launched against another hierarchical view, one we looked at briefly in distinguishing between Descartes and Corneille – the honour ethic with its roots in the citizen life. This ethic reflected the then rigidly stratified social structures and particularly the distinction between aristocrats and commoners.[60] While the social dimension of this challenge was not immediately evident, the goals of the 'ethic of honor and glory' were denounced outright as the worst forms of vanity. The promotion of ordinary life eventually gives this critique its historical significance as an engine of social change. In the latter part of the seventeenth century, we learn . . .

> The critique is taken up and becomes a commonplace of a new ideal of life, in which sober and disciplined production was given the central place, and the search for honour condemned as fractious and undisciplined self-indulgence, gratuitously endangering the really valuable things in life. A new model of civility emerges in the eighteenth century, in which the life of commerce and acquisition gains an unprecedentedly positive place.[61]

Whereas commerce had previously been thought to lead to a demeaning preoccupation with material, worldly things – and in some societies engaging in trade had been seen as a violation of aristocratic values – commercial life now came to be seen in a positive light as a civilizing force.[62] Now too, the aristocratic search for military glory came to be seen as wildly destructive and even piratical. By contrast, commerce came to be understood as constructive and polite, binding people together in peace and forming the basis of proper values.[63]

---

58. Taylor describes it as follows: 'Science is not a higher activity that ordinary life should subserve; on the contrary, science should benefit ordinary life. Not to make this the goal is not only a moral failing, a lack of charity, but also and inextricably an epistemological failing. Bacon has no doubt that the root of this momentous error is pride . . . "We impose the seal of our image on the creatures and works of God, we do not diligently seek to discover the seal of God on things."' Ibid.
59. Taylor, *Sources of the Self*, p. 214.
60. Ibid.
61. Ibid.
62. Ibid., p. 213.
63. Ibid., p. 214.

Within traditional hierarchies there were, of course, differing conceptions of value: in the case of contemplation, a world order structured by the Good, and, in the case of the ethic of honour and glory, fame and immortality, as the spur to great deeds. Furthermore, hierarchy, as Girard reminds us, kept order in check by ensuring that imitation remained 'external'. However, to understand the moral source driving the ethic of ordinary life that reacts against the older honour code, Taylor claims that we have to look to Judeo-Christian spirituality and in particular the transformations wrought by the Reformation. Common to all Reformers was a rejection of the kind of mediation involved in forms of worship that eclipsed personal commitment. Tied to this rejection of mediation was a rejection of the mediaeval understanding of the sacred that flowed from the most fundamental principle of the Reformers – that fallen humanity could do nothing to effect their own salvation. And so we find one of the most powerful ideas influencing the new Protestant movements: 'that of an unaccountable salvation by an almighty and merciful God, against all rational human hope and utterly disregarding our just deserts'.[64] To have faith is to acknowledge how utterly helpless we are.

Of course the whole Catholic understanding of the sacred, as well as the mediating role of the church, ran counter to this view of faith and therefore had to be rejected. This rejection included not only the Mass, as a human attempt to effect communion with God, but also a vast panorama of traditional Catholic rituals and pieties designed to mediate God's grace and enrich the common life. Indeed the Catholic understanding of the church as the locus and vehicle of the sacred ceased to make any sense within a Reformed view; now each person 'stands alone in relation to God: his or her fate – salvation or damnation – is separately decided'.[65]

In rejecting the sacred and the idea of mediation, Protestants also rejected the monastic life and the view (mistaken according to Taylor) that these vocations supposed a hierarchy of nearness to the sacred, with the religious life being seen as 'higher' than the secular life, and in particular productive life and the family.[66] For the Reformers, such a hierarchical understanding of monastic life undermined the personal commitment of the Christian, permitting lay persons only *half involvement* in their own salvation, because it left them dependent on those more fully committed to the Christian life for mediating grace and, as less dedicated than those with special vocations, prepared to settle for a weak commitment of faith.[67] Thus, the same movement through which the Reformers rejected the Mass and the various forms of Catholic mediation also brought a rejection of special

---

64. Ibid., p. 215.
65. Ibid., p. 216.
66. Ibid., p. 217.
67. Taylor describes the 'half-involvement' and the Protestant response in this way: 'I (the Catholic) am a passenger in the ecclesial ship on its journey to God. But for Protestants there can be no passengers. This is because there can be no ship in the Catholic sense, no common movement carrying humans to salvation. Each believer rows his or her own boat.' Ibid.

vocation to the monastic life and an affirmation of the spiritual vocation of lay life. 'By denying any special form of life as a privileged locus of the sacred, they were denying the very distinction between sacred and profane and hence affirming their interpenetration.'[68] This affirmation of ordinary life had the effect of hallowing what had been hitherto considered profane. And we can readily see how, with the collapse of hierarchies and greater 'interpenetration', the rites of 'making sacred' (in the Girardian sense), are brought under increasing pressure – but as part of a development that understands itself as inspired by an incarnational mode of life. If, as Durkheim claims (see above, beginning of Chapter 2, note 1), crisis results for primitive peoples from too great a contiguity of the sacred and the profane, for the modern mind this 'contiguity' becomes a moral imperative.

4. Right Use, Right Order: Innerworldly Asceticism

The challenge to monasticism was partly seen as a challenge to a Christian church that had been overtly influenced by a Greek ideal – in particular the Platonic notion of the Good. This Greek/Christian synthesis (which, Taylor argues, was worth supporting) helped Augustine to go beyond his Manichean phase by providing a justification for seeing all of being as good.[69] However, while many people influenced by Platonic oppositions renounced worldly things *as a means to* salvation, the early Protestants saw this form of asceticism as presumption. In affirming the good in the here and now, the Reformers spurned any 'oppositions' that placed our ultimate standards elsewhere – namely in a cosmos ordered for the Good. As a result of such 'other-worldly' theories, Greek philosophy gave rise to a view of self-abnegation that brought the wholeness and integrity of the human good into question. Doctrines such as Stoicism, that preached the foolishness of loving things in this world, were hard to reconcile with the Jewish-Christian doctrine of creation found in the first chapter of Genesis that claims *all* of creation is good.[70] According to Taylor, the two views of self-denial or asceticism provide a contrast between Greek and Christian notions of the good: the former gives up what is without value while the latter gives up what *has* value – and for that very reason. He describes this important difference as follows:

> For the Stoic, what is renounced is, if rightly renounced, *ipso facto* not part of the good. For the Christian, what is renounced is thereby affirmed as good – both in the sense that the renunciation would lose its meaning if the thing were indifferent and in the sense that the renunciation is the furtherance of God's will, which precisely affirms the goodness of the kinds of things renounced: health, freedom, life.[71]

---

68. Ibid.
69. Ibid., p. 220.
70. Ibid., p. 218.
71. Ibid., p. 219.

By giving up a good in order to follow God, the Christian becomes an instrument of God's hallowing of life. There is no need to renounce part for the sake of the whole, or to mutilate the very thing we are attempting to affirm – hence the rejection of pagan sacrifice by Christianity is a related idea. 'In the restored order that God is conferring, good doesn't need to be sacrificed for good. The eschatological promise in both Judaism and Christianity is that God will restore the integrity of the good.'[72] The Christian sense of loss at renunciation is profound *because it is a real loss*, and in this it follows Christ's own death, which was not a rejection of the world on his behalf, but a consequence of evil in the world.

The Christian/Greek synthesis constantly justifies a certain notion of hierarchy that placed the integrity of the good in question, allowing some to appear more deserving of salvation, and consequently it was a natural target for the challenges of Protestantism. Where the Greek view of renunciation dominated, ascetic vocations could appear 'higher' and of course this gave succour to the Reformers arguments that the ordinary good was being perverted – a correction that became urgent in their view. As the movement spread, the hallowing of mundane life could not be reconciled with notions of hierarchy: at first of vocation and later even of social caste. But how was ordinary life to encompass the new spiritual purposes of 'exalting the humble and humbling the exalted?'[73] And how was it to do so in light of God's ends and for his glory? This is where Augustine's theory of 'two loves' provided something of a solution, not because he necessarily favoured the things of this world and everyday life, but because his notion of inwardness provided a way of seeing things in a new light.[74] The new order that started to emerge with ordinary life involved understanding where the things of this world belonged. 'God placed mankind over creation and made the things of this world for humans. But humans are there in turn to serve and glorify God, and so their use of things should serve this final goal.'[75] Just as the right object orders our craving and our relationship to God, the right use of things helps God put shape on that order in our everyday lives. Likewise the wrong object leads to the wrong use, which manifests itself in sinful attachment. 'The consequences of sin is that humans come to be concerned with these things not for God's sake but for themselves. They come to desire them as ends and no longer simply as instruments for God's purposes. And this upsets the whole order of things.'[76]

To be Reformed meant to take one's proper place in God's creation and to do this one had to avoid, on the one hand, the error of asceticism, and, on the other

---

72. Ibid.
73. Ibid., p. 221.
74. Arendt claims, that '[t]he road to "happiness" is pointed out by desire and leads to "enjoyment" by way of "usage." The right object of enjoyment determines the objects of right usage: "Things to be enjoyed make us happy. Things to be used help us who tend toward happiness."' *Love and Saint Augustine*, p. 33; internal quotation taken from Augustine, *Christian Doctrine I*.
75. Ibid.
76. Ibid.

hand, the error of becoming absorbed in things, or taking them for our end.[77] 'It was not the use of things that brought evil, Puritan preachers constantly repeated, but our deviant purposes in using them.'[78] Taylor describes the Puritan intention in quasi-Augustinian terms: 'we should love the things of this world but our love should as it were pass through them to their Creator.'[79] With the Reformation we now love worldly things, but with the love of God in our hearts. This right relationship to things restores God's creation. The ethic of ordinary life introduces a new vigour into the notion of inwardness, whereby God's grace opens human being out to participation and belonging through an instrumental relationship to things.

The *interpenetration* of the 'sacred and profane' that is so necessary to a Reformed order where older hierarchies are displaced, comes with a certain distance from things that one would otherwise seek to possess. This distance is not a renunciation in the traditional sense, but rather seeks to affirm what earlier ascetics tended to renounce. The key is to affirm it in the right spirit, which involves putting it 'under our feet' rather than seeing it as having no place in the order of the good. It is the inner person that makes this transposition, giving rise to what Weber calls the Puritan's 'innerworldly asceticism'.[80] We separate ourselves from the world in order to better understand God's creation. 'The answer to the absorption in things which is the result of sin is not renunciation but a certain kind of use, one which is detached from things and focused on God.'[81] Drawing on the work of Perry Miller, Taylor recognizes the paradox in an aspiration to hallow ordinary life not by connecting it to the sacramental life of the church in the manner of the Catholic tradition but rather by living it in a way that is both 'caring and not caring'. 'It is a caring and not caring, whose paradoxical nature comes out in the Puritan notion that we should use the world with "weaned affections". Use things, "but be not wedded to them, but so weaned from them, that you may use them, as if you use them not".'[82]

This understanding of the role and place of 'the ordinary' extended to thinking about one's own position in life – as part of God's plan. The term vocation was no longer just associated with the priesthood or monastic life; for Puritans

---

77. When the right order is restored through grace human beings turn from things back to God, but not through asceticism or rejection of the world. We stem our sinful craving and attachment to the wrong thing by enjoying the things of God's creation *while* remaining detached from them. That is, by enjoying them in a certain spirit, which might be described in more direct Augustinian language as using them while not craving for them or seeking to possess them.
78. Ibid., p. 222.
79. Ibid.
80. Ibid.
81. Ibid., p. 223.
82. Ibid. Taylor is quoting here from, Perry Miller, *The New England Mind: The Seventeenth Century (Cambridge, MA: Harvard University Press, 1967).*

everyone had a particular calling, the specific form of labour to which God summoned him or her, and every calling, whether judge, blacksmith or midwife, was considered valuable in God's eyes.[83] And as with our use of things, our primary aim in working at whatever we are called to do must be to serve God. However, we do this by serving others through our calling: 'a central feature of any valid calling was that it be of benefit to humans.'[84] Marriage too was affirmed as a vocation through the hallowing of ordinary life, and its new spiritual significance was also tempered by the same rules that applied to use: 'it must never become an end in itself, but serve the glory of God.'[85] Without losing the essential spirit of Augustine's Hellenized philosophy, we can say that the rule for the Puritan was 'to have but *not* to hold'.[86]

Using things as God intended requires knowing the mind of God which now must be '(re)discovered' in our fallen state. Scientific probing becomes part of a religious effort to use things according to God's purposes because it helps us to discover just what those purposes are. Thus an instrumental stance towards the world takes on spiritual significance. It not only 'allows us to experiment and obtain valid scientific results . . . which gives us rational control over ourselves and our world. In this religious tradition it is the way we serve God in creation'.[87] We do this, once again, through our calling (which is both for God's order, and ourselves) and through an instrumental stance that protects us from treating things as ends valuable in themselves whereby we become absorbed in things that

---

83. The phrase that best captures this change, occurring as the title of the first section of the chapter by Taylor in *Sources* on 'ordinary life', is the Puritan expression 'God loveth adverbs.' What matters is not *what* one does (the verb) but *how* one does it (the adverb); 'it all turns on the spirit in which one lives whatever one lives, even the most mundane existence.' Taylor, *Sources of the Self*, p. 224. Once again, we can critically advert to Girard's theory by saying that it is not our place, or 'rank', in a hierarchy that is significant in the early modern period, but the way we live our life, aided of course by our inner connection to God.

84. Ibid., p. 225.

85. Ibid., p. 226.

86. Taylor discusses the Puritan strand of Reformed Protestantism at length because it provides an extreme example of the affirmation of ordinary life: a movement, he believes, that has profoundly shaped the modern identity. From the beginning what helped to define ordinary life as a movement for change was that its purposes were largely conducive to those of the scientific revolution a connection that proved more than a coincidence. Both movements appealed to 'living experience' be that personal conversion or direct observation. They stood together in their opposition to the traditional Aristotelian view of nature and order, and in their belief that knowledge should be useful – for the general good and benefit of mankind. On a deeper level, Taylor argues, the connection comes through in the religious outlook that suffuses Bacon's work. Taylor, *Sources of the Self*, p. 231.

87. Ibid., p. 232.

could wrench us away from God. We can readily see that by the time Descartes conducts his meditations the ground is already fertile for his 'disengaged reason'. The whole modern world view begins to take shape around a set of ideas that view detachment as the correct mode of existence – a mode that is only made possible by a certain inwardness that can put things in their proper place by adopting an instrumental stance to the world.

Taylor credits John Locke with developing ordinary life into a more productive form, and further rationalizing Christianity. 'Where in the Reform variant it was a matter of living *worshipfully* for God now it is becoming a question of living *rationally.*'[88] Procedural reason, whereby we remain 'disengaged' from things, raises us from destructive illusion, whether blind custom or superstition, to beneficence and so 'from wild disordered egoism to the productive search for happiness which confers benefits on others as well.'[89] From reason flows the 'beneficent potentiality of self-love'.[90] John Locke builds on the rejection of the traditional hierarchy of values whereby reason was substantive (enabling us to see the order of the good), and puts forward a view of reason that allowed us to *do* good. 'The rationality in question is now procedural: in practical affairs, instrumental; in theoretical, involving the careful, disengaged scrutiny of our ideas and their assembly according to the canons of mathematical deduction, and empirical probability. This is how we participate in God's purposes. Not through blind instinct, like the animals, but through conscious calculation, we take our place in the whole.'[91]

The act of 'taking our place' thus begins to supplant a religious cosmogony in which a sense of helplessness naturally prevailed among the many with a greater likelihood of collective crisis. Greater rational control meant 'right order' through participation by all, or most, thus giving each a stake in greater stability and the furtherance of Gods plan. This vision of a 'rationalized Christianity' furthered the aims of ordinary life. God's goodness is shown in his designing the world for our preservation and in making sure the various parts of it are 'conducive to reciprocal conservation.'[92] The parts that work together with common purpose sustain the whole – each part has its place, and is benefited by, and benefits other parts. Locke thus helps shape the growing Deist picture of the world. However, with the emphasis on 'instrumental, maximizing reason' the traditional understanding of faith comes under attack. The good that God wills comes more and more to be centred on the natural good and therefore grace and revelation become unnecessary for directing individual action. Through disengaged, procedural reason we can know God's design and therefore what ought to be done, and God only wills

---

88. Ibid., p. 242.
89. Ibid.
90. Ibid., p. 243.
91. Ibid.
92. Ibid., p. 244.

what can be done. By the end of the seventeenth century the fully rational Deist picture of the cosmos is all but complete.

5. Deism and the New Providential Order: Re-marking Difference

The view of a cosmic order reflected in nature comes under attack in the modern period, under the broad banner of 'ordinary life'. A great chain of being, as our quotation from Girard at the outset of this chapter indicates, is discredited as a metaphysical illusion. However, within new more rationalized Christianity inspired by the development of Protestantism the notion of a great chain is given a new more dynamic meaning, as we shall see below. The order that, since Plato, had belonged to a hierarchical vision of the universe is redefined in a more instrumental way with the advent of Deism.

According to Taylor, the form of Deism that Locke inspired, in which a 'punctual self' places priority on disengagement, operates by objectifying the domain of experience in question. Arising from its close relationship with voluntarism (a freely willing unaccountable God), this new outlook inherits a command theory of law and morality.[93] Reward and punishment as an underlying motivation for action ensures that 'law' determines what is good. In a rationally ordered world it is ultimately God who wills our good and dispenses our just deserts. To avoid pain we must keep our passions in check or keep them in their proper place. Within this scheme of things an ethic can be constructed whereby each person maximizes his or her own good, and the 'higher good' becomes just the maximization of individual goods. The law as a function of the state can then be seen to regulate competing goods – in the extreme as an arm of a 'Leviathan'.[94]

The idea of love, or desire directing us internally to our proper end (which was central to traditional philosophies of motivation) plays no part in this rational scheme. However, before a rationalized Christianity was transposed into secular law, the absence of any positive role for our feelings in relation to the good was being rigorously questioned. Taylor comments on how a group of seventeenth century thinkers called the 'Cambridge Platonists' rejected a religion of external law 'in the name of one which saw humans as intrinsically attuned to God'.[95] The contrast is described as a religion of fear versus one of love, 'a servile or forced devotion versus a free one'.[96] The imagery of the Cambridge Platonists in their

---

93. Ibid., p. 249.
94. Ibid.
95. Ibid.
96. In this analysis of external law there are echoes of how Jacques Derrida describes the God of Abraham as the 'one who sees in secret'. J. Derrida, *The Gift of Death*, trans. David Wills (Chicago: University of Chicago Press, 1998). Indeed, when we consider Kierkegaard's 'fear and trembling' in face of ultimate commitment, we

attack on 'mechanical Christians', and their celebration of an 'inner nature', was prescient. With such language as 'the organic versus the artificial' and 'the living versus the mechanical' Taylor notes how some commentators were right to see these thinkers as significantly prefiguring later Romanticism: 'The battle lines are already drawn.'[97]

From these 'battle lines' the key idea develops that morality is not just a matter of arbitrary extrinsic decree with no bidding from our natural inner sentiments to guide us towards the good. The new idea suggests that the highest good does not lie in an arbitrary will, as with voluntarism, but in the very nature of the cosmos, 'our love for it isn't commanded under threat of punishment, but comes spontaneously from our being.'[98] According to Taylor, Shaftesbury, followed by Hutcheson, develops a rival to Lockean Deism that stressed 'natural affection' and saw disengaged reason as standing in the way of our love for the whole that the good person longs to grasp.[99] The challenge to the older Deism is clear: the *motive* of benevolence must be the key to goodness. But Hutcheson went further by holding that we must also *believe* in and trust our own moral inclination. 'In acknowledging the mainsprings of good in us, we rejoice in them, and this joy makes them flow stronger.'[100] Once again, after Augustine, 'we turn within to retrieve the true form of our natural affection; or our benevolent sentiments; and in doing that we give them their full force.'[101] What the two forms of Deism – mechanistic and proto-Romantic, respectively – seem to share, according to Taylor, is the notion of a great 'interlocking universe' in which parts are designed to be conducive to their mutual preservation and flourishing.

In Deism the traditional cosmic order that took paradigmatic shape with Plato noticeably shifts towards a providential order whereby God is now concerned with maximizing human happiness.[102] Taylor argues that the impact of this shift can be felt most forcibly in the widespread belief in the affirmation of ordinary life. It translates as a dramatic change from a hierarchical understanding of the good as a vision of rational cosmic order to a view that sees each person participating in the good through a providential interlocking order based on universal benevolence. The idea that Hutcheson added to the more disengaged,

---

can grasp how thinking in relation to ethics was foreshadowed by this earlier debate. 'Humans approach God in fear as an inscrutable law giver whose judgments are utterly beyond human comprehension, and may have already, indeed, condemned us, regardless of our present aspiration to reform.' Taylor, *Sources of the Self*, p. 249. Further to this, what preoccupies the Father of existentialism is a certain loss of qualitative distinctions (see main Introduction, note 15).

97. Ibid., p. 250.
98. Ibid., p. 253.
99. Ibid., pp. 254–255.
100. Ibid., p. 262.
101. Ibid., p. 265.
102. Ibid., p. 267.

instrumental view of ordinary life was that the fullest human happiness is attained when we give full rein to our moral sentiments and feelings of benevolence.[103] What makes God good is that he brings about our happiness, and our happiness thus brings about the general good; self-fulfilment can be seen as having a moral dimension. However, the Deist conception of happiness, Taylor points out, is defined purely in creaturely terms. Our soul still needs God to be integrally good. 'But what our goodness seems to consist in is a "determination . . . towards the universal happiness"; and what God's goodness consists in seems to be his foster-ing this same end.'[104] Happiness, as a non-theocentric notion of the good, plays a central role in this outlook. What ordinary life fosters is a view that focuses on the human, since it is now *human* happiness that really matters in the universe.[105] Practical benevolence, the reduction of suffering, becomes paramount.

The crucial point about Deism that Taylor stresses is that it was not just a staging post for atheistic humanism. On the contrary, it was based on a deeply held religious world view embedded in the Protestant affirmation of ordinary life. The fact that it was human-centred certainly marked a change from the ancient model and may indeed have inspired later atheistic theories. But despite this, what gave Deism its affinity with Christianity was the fact that 'once more a *cosmic order* was at the centre of spiritual life.'[106] To best illustrate this interlocking order in which ordinary life plays a central role Taylor draws heavily from Alexander Pope's *Essay on Man*. In continuity with a long tradition, Pope describes the new order as a 'great chain of being'.[107] But what differs about Pope's 'Vast chain' is that it no longer functions within the neo-Platonic theory of emanations, but is rather 'that interconnection of mutual service which the things of this world of harmonious functions render to each other'.[108] The chain is here based on a provi-dential order. Taylor notes that there was a traditional 'organicism' in the older views of order whereby mutual dependence held everything in check: a theory of 'correspondences'. If each thing did not hold its ordered place in the whole it was believed that things would revert to chaos, and here we find a close resemblance to how Girard describes the sacrificial crisis in *Violence and the Sacred*.

In the context of my book, it is striking that Taylor illustrates the deli-cate balance of the traditional *ontic logos,* where 'each thing holds its ordered place', with the *same* example of Ulysses's speech in *Troilus and Cressida* that Girard cites: 'Take but one degree away, untune that string, / And hark what discord follows.'[109] However, Taylor does not focus, as Girard does, on the effectiveness of this older order – so long as all degrees remain harmonious – in holding crises in

---

103. Ibid.
104. Ibid. Taylor is quoting here from, Francis Hutcheson, *A System of Moral Phi-losophy, facsimile reproduction of the posthumous 1755 edition (Hildesheim: Georg Olms, 1969)*, p. 217.
105. Taylor, *Sources of the Self*, p. 268.
106. Ibid., p. 272.
107. Ibid., p. 274.
108. Ibid., p. 275.

check. Rather he wants to stress *what has changed* with the arrival of a more mechanical view of the universe. In the new interlocking order, the mutual support takes 'direct efficient-causal form' – things work together to form a whole.[110] One couplet from Pope's *Essay* will suffice to illustrate the transformation that Taylor wants to convey: 'Nothing is foreign: Parts relate to whole; / One all-extending, all preserving Soul.'[111] As long as the 'sacred' and the 'profane' were kept apart, as they were in the older *ontic* order, the system remained delicately balanced. But with the advent of a providential order, order is now 'preserved' when each individual takes up his or her calling. Order, and hence benevolence, is something we all actively have a stake in. For Taylor the decisive change relates to how one order replaced another:

> As the metaphysical basis of the earlier view erodes, in particular with the growing success of mechanistic science, the new vision can step into the vacuum. It is fully compatible with the modern conception of the nature of a thing as made up of forces which operate *within it*. Each thing is seen to have its own purpose or bent.[112]

Here is a radically new conception that is ready to be transposed into a self-regulating economic system.[113] The goodness of the order consists in the fact that these purposes do not run counter to each other but rather mesh with and feed each other. Finding one's own purpose, the source of one's happiness, has become part of a Design.[114]

Thus the ethic of ordinary life stands in sharp contrast to the mainstream of ancient thought. Certain activities are singled out not because they are hierarchically ordered in light of the human's rational nature, but because they are part of God's plan. The new activities (work in a calling and family life) 'are marked as

---

109. William Shakespeare, *Troilus and Cressida*, ed. Kenneth Palmer (London and New York: Methuen and Co. 1982) 1:3, 109–110. Quoted in, Taylor, *Sources of the Self*, p. 275–276.

110. Ibid., p. 276.

111. Alexander Pope, "An Essay on Man", in *The Poems of Alexander Pope*, ed. John Butt (London: Methuen and Co Ltd., 1968). Quoted in, Taylor, *Sources of the Self*, p. 276.

112. Taylor, *Sources of the Self*, p. 276 (my italics).

113. Ibid., p. 286.

114. Taylor describes the new order as follows: 'Instrumental reason intervenes in two ways . . . First, it shows us that the best policy, for the maximization of our gains, is to fit into our proper place in the order. Everything is made so that the good of each serves the good of all; so our best interests must be to act for the general good. But second, this whole itself is a magnificent creation of instrumental reason, now that of God, which has encompassed a universal maximization. Our powers of reason which enable us to see this, can lift us to a grasp of the whole and in this way bring us to want more than our particular interest.' Taylor, *Sources of the Self*, p. 280.

significant, because they define how God intends us to live, what he designed us for when he made us. It follows that to see what we ought to do we need an insight not into the hierarchical order of nature but into the purposes of God'.[115] The 'clearly marked differences' of the older sacred order, that had to be carefully circumscribed so as to avoid crisis, are given a new understanding since now the purposes of God *reveal the marked character* of what activities we are called to. Acknowledging this becomes important because in doing so we are acknowledging God's plan for us. This has to do with our own personal relationship to God, and the higher good, and the role each individual plays in discovering his or her calling rather than simply filling a pre-existing slot in some natural ranking, which if not properly filled (or somehow breached) could see the whole operation revert to chaos. What makes the proper way of life good is now found in the new significance of each thing. The unity of the overall design – the concord – is achieved through the interlocking purposes. The specific design of each thing, what marks it out as different, is also what brings it into sync with other things and the greater design. Now living by nature is living by an ethic, not of hierarchical reason, but of marked activities, fully continuous with the affirmation of ordinary life that gave rise to it.[116]

6. Conclusion: 'Self-Love and Social'

Having considered 'the affirmation of ordinary life' and its influence on Deism, we can now respond to Girard's anthropological concerns when he asks 'who has ever seen a great chain of being collapse?' by saying that nobody has seen a great chain collapse because 'the chain' as it was originally understood is transposed onto a new, more efficient interlocking system, fully in accordance with a 'rational' and 'benevolent' form of Christianity; this form emerges as a reaction to the traditional Catholic view of the sacred and is itself a new order filling the vacuum generated by the decline of the older order. The point here is not to argue against the traditional 'ontic' order, however its 'metaphysical status' is viewed, nor to attempt to completely discredit Girard's anthropological principle of 'Degree'. Rather, what Taylor highlights is how order is *re-imagined* in the modern period, as something that has its locus in a more human and less theocentric view of nature. Furthermore, the massive effort to formulate this new perspective is initially driven by a Christianity-inspired incarnational mode of life. The advantages of the new Deist order are such that each person living out the differences marked as significant for him or her could now assume some responsibility for initiating and maintaining a new order to supersede the older view (with its emphasis on maintaining order as a meaningful whole through the contemplation

---

115. Ibid., p. 278.
116. Ibid., p. 279.

of succeeding levels of hierarchy). The new providential order passes through the space of radical reflexivity. Gathering ourselves in from dispersion, we discover God's design and our place in it. By giving ordinary life greater significance in cosmic affairs, this internalization helped offset the likelihood of the 'chaos' that threatened a traditional social order, and, of course, earlier more archaic forms of order. Each part is now indispensable to the whole and, furthermore, is our route to universal harmony and happiness. In Pope's words: 'true SELF-LOVE and SOCIAL are the same.'[117]

We saw how Taylor gives a central role to Augustine's notion of inwardness in helping to shape the early modern identity. Augustine's 'two-loves' theory provides a developed notion of the will, and places a certain primacy on the self and its inner relationship with God that resists the formulation that Girard gives it. Within an Augustinian perspective, the 'Saint and the Romantic' are not separate subjects but constitutive tendencies of the same dynamic experience of interiority. Arising from this, the notion of inwardness paves the way for both the modern disengaged stance of rational control, and the more expressivist theories of nature that develop out of what I have called the proto-Romantic reaction to the mechanistic universe (met in the previous section) and that I shall explore in the following chapter. Instrumental reason allows us to play our part in the design of nature, but our way of contact with this design also lies within us in another way – namely in our natural sentiments of sympathy and benevolence. Exploring my own sentiments (including my desires and inclinations) takes on moral importance since what is right and good is what fits a design, of which my sentiments are an integral part, and to which they are inwardly attuned.[118] As our feelings become normative, our access to the whole domain of good and evil, while still subject to correction by reason, depends more and more on our moral sense to help us uncover *the right* inner impulse.[119]

I have been arguing, after Taylor, that Girard's theory of 'self-divinization', which makes 'generosity' and 'proof' a double-sided attribute of pride, fails to acknowledge the internalization of moral sources that takes definite shape in the modern period. The emphasis on rational control is a development on Corneille's notion of generosity, which, Taylor explains, still belongs to an older ethic of honour and glory. Having looked at Augustine in greater detail, we can now see how the *cogito*, as the locus of gathering and the basis of Descartes' first-person stance, is in continuity with the Augustinian move inward. And, having once again considered the role of Degree, but this time in the context of the interlocking purposes that the Deist picture introduces, we can begin to imagine how the great chain is transformed from a delicately balanced 'ontic order' into one that takes 'direct efficient causal form'. Clearly marked differences are *still* part of this

---

117. Pope, 'An Essay on Man', quoted in, Taylor, *Sources of the Self*, p. 280.
118. Ibid., p. 282.
119. Ibid., p. 284.

order, though, these 'differences' are no longer understood as belonging solely to an externally ordered hierarchical system, but instead become constitutive of our own disengaged stance to the world, a stance that also comes to include an important role for our sentiments.

According to Taylor, unity and identity are thus preserved and, *pace* Girard, not completely undermined in the modern period; the new Deist vision can 'step into the vacuum'.[120] In an interlocking order things work together to form a whole whereby individual ends feed each other. Within this benevolent design that places priority on ordinary life the individual must take up a calling for his or her own good and for the sake of the whole. By taking rational control of oneself and one's place in this order, a lot less was left to chance, and so one's dependence on worldly things was thought to decrease. It is here, perhaps, that the Protestant interpenetration of the sacred and the profane has its greatest anthropological significance, since it radically undercuts a world that could more easily be given over to superstition, and indeed crisis.

The affirmation of ordinary life thus transforms the notion of degree into one that the human now has a share in determining. The great chain of being is no longer understood as reflecting an *ontic* order hierarchically ascending through-out nature and the cosmos, but is instead brought down to earth – a transition that Arthur O. Lovejoy refers to as the 'temporalization' of the great chain of being.[121] God's benevolence means human happiness must prevail and so, in ful-filling his or her purpose, the individual assumes a certain responsibility for gen-erating the order and harmony of the whole. How we access the new order will depend on the importance we give to the different kinds of moral sources.[122] However, after Shaftesbury and Hutcheson, it is no longer simply a rational proc-ess as it was for Locke. Knowing good and evil now depends on our moral sense and feelings as much as on our reason; and these come to awareness within us. The horizontal axis of transcendence that Girard describes as 'deviated', resulting only in the pernicious illusions of metaphysical desire, and later referred to as the basis of a sacrificial crisis, can be fruitfully reconsidered in light of Taylor's analysis of the modern period. 'Ordinary life' and the reduction of suffering are two powerful early modern ideas that give a peculiarly Christian significance to the 'interpenetration of the sacred and the profane'. Whereas for Girard, this interpenetration is a source of crisis, in the perspective that I have been elaborat-ing in this chapter it can become *part* of a worthy struggle to realize an incarna-tional mode of life. In the following chapter we will consider, with the help of Taylor's work on Hegel, how this struggle becomes the catalyst of modern subjec-tivity as it attempts to understand division and unity as the very basis of historical reality.

---

120. Ibid., p. 276.
121. Arthur O. Lovejoy, *The Great Chain of Being: A Study of the History of an Idea* (New York: Harper and Row Publishers, 1965), p. 246.
122. Taylor, *Sources of the Self*, p. 283.

CHAPTER 5

RETHINKING DIVISION AND UNITY: SUBJECTIVITY, RELIGION AND THE CURRENT OF LIFE

The new place of sentiment completes the revolution which has yielded a modern view of nature as normative, so utterly different from the ancient view. For the ancients nature offers us an order which moves us to love and instantiate it, unless we are depraved. But the modern view, on the other hand, endorses nature as the source of right inner impulse. Nature as norm is an inner tendency; it is ready to become the voice within, which Rousseau will make it, and to be transposed by the Romantics into a richer and deeper inwardness.[1]

Charles Taylor

In that the good to which nature conduces is now a purely natural, self-contained good, and in that the proximate moral source is a self-subsistent order of interlocking beings, to whose principles we have access within ourselves, the stage is set for another independent ethic, in which nature itself will become the prime moral source, without its Author.[2]

Charles Taylor

1. Introduction

In the previous chapter we traced, with the help of Taylor's work in *Sources of the Self*, what he describes as a massive shift in the notion of the constitutive good connected with nature. While we did not give any considerable space to the pre-Christian Greek context, which Taylor of course does, we nonetheless sketched the transition from a hierarchical notion of reason to a conception of providential design that marks certain activities as significant. The affirmation of ordinary life preceded and energized the new providential order that presented a picture of nature as a vast network of interlocking beings. The design in nature 'works towards the conservation of each of its parts', whereby the age-old principle of order, 'is now understood as conducing to the life and happiness of the sentient creatures which it contains'.[3] Taylor's analysis of these developments gives us a way of further understanding, in the context of our discussion concerning crisis, how a more primitive order – one based on 'clearly marked differences', externally organized and maintained through sacrifice – might gradually come to be

---

1. Charles Taylor, *Sources of the Self: The Making of the Modern Identity* (New York: Cambridge University Press, 1992c), p. 284.
2. Ibid., p. 315.
3. Ibid.

re-imagined in a manner that places the centrality on the individual's rational control and basic moral sentiments, as the constitutive aspects of a new order.[4] In this way, Taylor's philosophical history can be seen as partially in agreement with Girard in so far they both acknowledge that an older order is radically challenged in the period that becomes known as modern. But for Taylor, the Augustinian notion of inwardness is one of the defining moves that pave the way for ordinary life and the emphasis on practical benevolence. If, by the time Descartes' wrote his *Meditations*, the social world was still greatly threatened by sacred violence and the propensity for it to escalate into crisis, as Girard claims is characteristic of all cultures, then individuals themselves were soon to begin functioning to generate the order and control (once the preserve of the social), in the name of a new, religiously inspired motivation towards universal respect.

However, having argued that the modern period involves a kind of internalization of moral sources and a re-marking of difference by the individual (rather than the whole society), as something that Girard perhaps dismisses too easily when he describes the 'modern world as being synonymous with a sacrificial crisis', we are still left with an important question. The question concerns whether the individual has the capacity to sustain the moral dimension of this internalization when this dimension becomes disconnected from a recognizable form of Christian theism.[5] In other words, what happens to the 'divisions' that, as we saw in chapter one, Girard argues are constitutive of the Romantic individual's 'pride', when the more obviously transcendent order of Deism is replaced more and more by the individual's subjective powers alone? Might Girard's thesis concerning 'self-divinization' still be relevant to an analysis of modern individualism once the initial inspiration of ordinary life, as a historical development, loses its momentum? In this chapter we will consider how the problem of division (the catalyst of 'crises'), relates to the whole notion of 'inwardness' as it continued to make its influence felt. Once again, Taylor's philosophical history will be rallied in a selective and focused way to respond to Girard's damning critique of modern individualism. My argument here does not dispute the central Girardian insight

---

4. Marcel Gauchet also explains the development of transcendence as a process of increased differentiation through internalization, highlighting the specificity of Christianity and the Reformation in this process. '[T]ranscendent religion's basic characteristic is to be found . . . in its innovative attempt to provide increasingly sophisticated versions of God's difference and to display their consequences. The reality of the process initiated by the advent of the Christian concept of the Deity should not be sought in something that appeals to an explicit continuity with tradition. We must rather look for it in what broke with institutional repression in the Church – that is, the Reformation – in response to the structural split contained in the notion of a unique creator god.' *The Disenchantment of the World: A Political History of Religion by Marcel Gauchet*, trans., Oscar Burge (Princeton: Princeton University Press, 1997), 61.

5. Taylor, *Sources of the Self*, p. 315.

that religion is essentially violent and that, arising from this fact, social and cultural order relies on a measure of violence to quell destructive mimesis and restore harmony. However, I want to offer a critique of Girard's analysis of 'originality' as the source of 'internal mediation' and all the problems that beset the modern world – what he understands as the default position of those who fail to see that their desires are not their own. Following Taylor, I want to argue that 'originality' has a moral basis. This argument will attempt to show that 'self-divinization' is a possible but not inevitable tendency in modern forms of freedom (as *cupiditas* for Augustine is a possible but not inevitable tendency of the will).

By once again addressing Taylor's philosophical history to the central problem of division in Girard's work, as it is articulated in the context of literary space and cultural space – as Romantic pride and sacrifice respectively – I will outline how Taylor understands the Romantic emphasis on 'inner nature' as a source of good and the precondition of originality. Girard explicitly argues that individualism is a form of separation and fragmentation.[6] However, I hope to show in this chapter, with Taylor's help that the philosophies of nature in the eighteenth century reveal that our being in touch with our inner nature keeps us connected to the benevolence postulated by moral sense theory – so that connection and unity, rather than separation and fragmentation, characterize the individual in whom this inner nature flows.

In section two we look at how Romantic expressivism, as a development of this strand of Deism, is from its inception preoccupied with a notion of 'illusory substitution', arising from the conception of a 'divided will' that can be traced back to Augustine's 'two-loves' theory. The problem of being 'deceived', then, was explicitly thematized within Romanticism from the beginning and so cannot simply be construed, *a la* Girard, as an overdetermined 'inevitability' of an unreflective individualism.[7] In an attempt to respond to the charges of 'self-divinization' that Girard levels at modern individualism for its 'mistaken' preoccupation with 'originality' I will outline, in section three, how originality comes to the fore in the modern period as, in part, a reaction to a more rationalist view that sought to

---

6. 'The structure of crime and redeeming punishment redeems the solitary consciousness,' René Girard, *Deceit, Desire, and the Novel: Self and Other in Literary Structure*, trans. Yvonne Freccero (Baltimore: Johns Hopkins University Press, 1965), p. 314, and again, 'I am alone and they are everyone – this is the underground motto.' p. 260.

7. I am referring here to the tendency within Girardian discourse to associate Romanticism exclusively with the 'self-deceiving subject' who mistakenly believes in his own originality, when in actuality his identity is mediated by an other. This also gives rise to anachronistic claims concerning what historical figures could be deemed 'Romantic'. So for example, Chris Fleming and John O'Carroll in their essay, 'Romanticism', claim, 'Augustine was not a Romantic' in, *Anthropoetics 11*, no. 1 (Spring/Summer 2005). The implication here of course (which I am contesting) is that Augustine could ever have been a Romantic.

objectify the self and the world, leaving human beings divided and hence cut off from an authentic unity. In section four, I will consider how what Girard and others see as a form of self-divinization can be understood as an attempt to meet the demands of authentic expression and heal the subjects 'rift' with nature. Section five will draws out the religious implications of this move for the subject who must now confront the challenges of division and unity as a new historical project, albeit one with significant antecedents in the long tradition of western thought. By drawing out further what Taylor sees as the religious context of subjectivity in section six we will highlight how Girard's concerns are not dissimilar to Hegel's; the latter's attempts to overcome division, I shall suggest, can be fruitfully compared to the scapegoat theory. Finally, we will consider again some of Taylor's analysis from *Sources*, in particular how he understands the expressivist movement as giving rise to the shadow side of modern humanism in the aftermath of the scientific developments of the seventeenth century. This shadow side comes about when the 'current of life' is reinterpreted (with peculiarly dire consequences) as 'blind will' – connected now, ominously, to *homo religiosus.*

2. Sentiments and the Voice of Nature

With the advent of Deism, a new and paradigmatic route of access to the design in nature is now gained through our *feelings*.[8] When sentiments become 'normative' in this way we discover what is right, partly by coming to experience our normal sentiments. 'This may involve our overcoming the distortive effects of vice or false opinion – Hutcheson constantly points out how the extrinsic theory makes us fail to appreciate our moral sentiments, and this dampens them.'[9] Thus 'sentiment' becomes the touchstone of the morally good ". . . because undistorted, normal feeling is my way of access into the design of things, which is the real constitutive good, determining good and bad. This sentiment can be corrected by reason when it deviates, but the insight it yields cannot be substituted for by reason'.[10] Unlike in the theories of rational order that preceded it, sentiment and its role in a providential order is here part measure of the good, a measure that reason must take account of.

By placing greater value on the private sphere, including conjugal marriage[11] and family bonds – as well as the range of emotional experiences wrought

---

8. Taylor believes that the revolution in the philosophical understanding of sentiment in the seventeenth century is reflected in a change of vocabulary: 'the word "sentiment" itself, partly replacing "passion", bespeaks the rehabilitation the life of feeling has gone through' Taylor, *Sources of the Self*, p. 283.

9. Ibid., p. 284.

10. Ibid.

through the new medium of the novel – the emphasis on sentiment has a massive influence on the culture of modernity.[12] This emphasis is also found in the growth of the feeling for nature in the eighteenth century and, more particularly, the sentiments that nature awakens in us.[13] Taylor once again reminds us of what is new about this reverence for nature by highlighting how it differed from the earlier conception of 'correspondences' (found, as we have seen, in Shakespeare) between natural phenomena and human affairs.[14] He gives the example of the portends prior to Duncan's murder (in the play Macbeth) to illustrate these correspondences: 'On the previous Tuesday a falcon had been killed by a mousing owl, and Duncan's horse turned wild in the night.' These 'signs' refer to a disturbance of order in nature that was at the time well understood as a 'public language of reference'.[15]

> Nature is here in some way in tune with human affairs. But the relation is utterly different and in fact incompatible with the modern one we inherit from the eighteenth century. Shakespeare draws on some notion of ontic logos, more precisely on the correspondences of Renaissance thought. The same hierarchical order manifests itself in different domains, the human, the avian, the animal; and so these are attuned: the disorder in one is reflected in the disorder of

---

11. Taylor explains the changes in the following way: 'What changes is not that people begin loving their children or feeling affection for their spouses, but that these dispositions come to be seen as a crucial part of what makes life worthy and significant' Taylor, *Sources of the Self*, p. 292.
12. Taylor, *Sources of the Self*, pp. 286–296.
13. Ibid., p. 298.
14. In Chapter 2 we looked at Girard's anthropological account of the great chain as a phenomenon to which he refuses to grant any metaphysical status, stressing instead the notion of 'Degree' as the underlying principle of all order and hierarchy. In the previous chapter I spoke about the great chain and the 'correspondences' by referring to difference between Girard's and Taylor's account of 'the chain', which Taylor's analysis of Deism brings out. The chain itself does not cease to exist, nor does it stop acting as a useful metaphor; rather (for Taylor at least) the order it had maintained as part of an *ontic* order is transposed in the modern period onto an interlocking order with greater subjective control. My point here is to draw out how these different interpretations of order are working in respect to Girard's and Taylor's thought.
15. Taylor refers to R. M. Rilke's *Dunio Elergies*, as an example of how, in the modern period, the poet no longer has the same gamut of references available to him or her as was once available in an *ontic* order. Hence, his or her poetry embodies the modern sense of alienation from nature and God. 'Who if I cried out will hear me among the order of angels?' Charles Taylor, *The Ethics of Authenticity* (Cambridge, MA: Harvard University Press, 1992a), pp. 84–85.

the others. Duncan's murder is the negation of all hierarchy, as is the killing of a falcon by a mousing owl or the rebellion of animals against mankind.[16]

We have already seen how the principle of 'Degree' is central to Girard's notion of cultural crisis, and how when this is disturbed 'what discord follows'. While Girard underscores the anthropological aspects of Degree and hierarchy etc., we can nonetheless recognize the similarity here between what Girard describes as a cultural order and what Taylor describes as an *ontic* order – in both cases chaos can occur.

However, we can also recognize a difference that can help explain why Girard sees this order as something that becomes defunct in the modern period, while Taylor sees it as something that is transposed onto a new interlocking order. This difference comes through in how each describes the premodern order itself: for Girard we might say this order is 'tuned' (hence his emphasis on Shakespeare's musical metaphor), while for Taylor it is 'attuned' (hence his emphasis on the correspondences). Girard thus views the order as quite static to begin with, the harmony having to do with the various pre-existing slots, or 'ranks', being filled, and crucially maintained, while the disorder in the various spheres that we find for example in Lear or Macbeth represents a loss of difference between these slots (what he calls a 'crisis of degree'). While stressing the delicate balance of this order, Taylor also draws our attention to our *connection to nature*, a form of contact that was, already within an *ontic* order, a kind of participation, whereby individuals (by keeping their proper places) felt invested in the whole – a whole that greatly transcended them in status and power. This difference between Girard and Taylor opens up two divergent construals of the transition to the modern world: as heralding *either* a sacrificial crisis *or* a new mode of being. Whichever of these construals we opt for will determine whether we see our relationship to nature and order being sundered in the modern period, or somehow being reconstituted.

The greater emphasis on sentiment in the eighteenth century and the importance of nature, and its power to awaken our moral sentiments, Taylor believes, belongs to an order that is being reconfigured. Beginning with the moral sense theories in the seventeenth century, the older cosmology is gradually replaced by a view that values inner experience and feeling in a way that is very different from the order in nature depicted by Shakespeare:

> . . . the meaning that the natural phenomena bear is no longer defined by the order of nature in itself or by the Ideas which they embody. It is defined through the effect of the phenomena on us, in the reactions they awaken. The affinity between nature and ourselves is now mediated not by an objective rational order but by the way that nature resonates in us. Our attunement with nature

---

16. Taylor, *Sources of the Self*, pp. 298, 299.

no longer consists in recognition of ontic hierarchy, but on being able to release the echo within ourselves.[17]

And this new way of thinking about nature as somehow having a resonance or 'voice within' becomes a key insight for a whole wave of expressivist theories of nature and human life around this time.[18] Being in touch with this inner 'echo' or 'voice' becomes a crucial issue for the subsequent generation of Romantic thinkers from Rousseau onwards, since it is precisely their concern with being cut off from nature and the current of life through an overemphasis on mechanical and instrumental control that causes them to react vehemently against dominant modes of rationalism.

According to Taylor, Rousseau more than any other thinker of this period, gives us a way of understanding the internalization of moral sources as somehow in continuity with the earlier doctrine of nature articulated by Augustine[19] – with one important difference: 'grace' no longer has to break through as it does for Augustine.

> In the orthodox theory, the source of the higher love is grace; it is the God of Abraham, Isaac, and Jacob. For Rousseau (without entirely ceasing to be God, at least of the philosophers), it has become the voice of nature. The doctrine of original sin, in its orthodox understanding, has been abandoned. Nature is fundamentally good, and the estrangement which depraves us is one which separates us from it. An Augustinian picture of the will has been transposed into a doctrine which denies one of the central tenets of Augustine's theology.[20]

'Grace' now comes to us quite naturally from being in touch with the 'voice of nature' within, and hence the importance of nature as a source of goodness and the corresponding dangers of corruption from *without*. What we find in Rousseau's *Emile*, for example, is an affirmation of the original impulse of nature, our contact with which becomes lost due to a depraved culture. 'We suffer this

---

17. Ibid., p. 299.
18. Ibid., p. 355.
19. Much of the reforming spirit of the Enlightenment had an over confidence in human nature that Rousseau did not share. Unlike the Encyclopaedists, for example, Taylor tells us, 'Rousseau was drawn to a view in which there was a place for a real notion of depravity. Human evil was not the kind of thing that could be offset by an increase of knowledge or enlightenment. Indeed the belief that it could be was itself part of the distortion, and reliance on it could only aggravate things. What was needed was a transformation of the will. Rousseau brought back into the world of eighteenth century Deism the fundamentally Augustinian notion that humans are capable of two loves, of two basic orientations of the will.' Taylor, *Sources of the Self*, p. 356.
20. Ibid., p. 357.

loss because we no longer depend on ourselves and this inner impulse, but rather on others, and on what they think of us, expect from us, admire or despise in us, reward or punish in us. We are separated from nature by the dense web of opinion which is woven between us in society and can no longer recover contact with it.'[21] By comparing ourselves negatively with others we are led away from our true nature and into illusion and rivalry, not because our 'originality' is false, as Girard maintains, but because we mistake an externally induced image of our desires for some original impulse – an image that Taylor refers to elsewhere as an 'illusory substitute'.[22]

By placing such an important emphasis on our inner nature over and against the corrupting influences of the external social world, Rousseau, Taylor argues, takes the revolution in sentiment that was a central feature of Deism farther than had been previously conceived. 'For a moral sense theorist like Hutcheson, our own moral feelings are an important source of understanding the good, but they only serve in combination with our grasping our setting within a providential order.'[23] Thus our instinctive approval of benevolence serves to bring about both our own good and the universal good. However, the definition of conscience that Rousseau articulates as an inner sentiment could be viewed as more potent than the earlier moral sense theory. 'Not just that I have, thanks be to God, sentiments which accord with what I see through other means to be the universal good, but that the inner voice of my true sentiments *define* what is good: since the élan of nature in me is the good, it is this which has to be consulted to discover it.'[24] Our inner nature is thus unmoored from a *pre-existing* order, while our first point of reference becomes our own inner nature: 'Rousseau immensely enlarges the scope of the inner voice. We can now know from within us, from the impulses of our own being, what nature marks as significant.'[25] It is this potential that is fully embraced by the expressivist theories of nature, and hence can be seen as the starting point of a further transformation in modern culture towards a deeper inwardness and a radical autonomy.[26]

This radicalizing of moral sense theory by Romantic expressivism highlights a related problem to the one discussed above as to whether and/or how order is transposed in the modern world. We saw that Girard does not attribute any value to inwardness as a peculiarly western development, and so when traditional hierarchy begins to wane it simply has nowhere to be transposed to. The move to

---

21. Ibid.
22. Charles Taylor, "Foucault on Freedom and Truth", in *Philosophy and the Human Sciences: Philosophical Papers 2* (Cambridge, MA: Cambridge University Press, 1985b) p. 161.
23. Taylor, *Sources of the Self*, p. 362.
24. Ibid.
25. Ibid.
26. Ibid., p. 363.

individualism marks a decline in culture and order. And because questions of 'the Good' are at best secondary to the functional requirements of a cultural system 'the Good' as something valuable *in itself,* is reduced by Girard to a healthy measure of 'Degree'. The notion of hierarchy, which was understood within a Greek and Christian context, up until the modern period, as something that existed *for the sake of* the Good, is within an anthropological setting, something that exists *in order to* protect and preserve. Here lies the problem of having a static view of order since it forecloses all questions of what *moves us* to love and instantiate the Good, or the will of God, above and beyond the immediate scene or context, filled as it often is with anxiety. What the principle of 'Degree' fails to explain is *what makes* the order in nature good, or fulfilling or worthwhile . . . something worthy of our love and allegiance. And in relation to our discussion of 'inner nature', the problem concerns precisely Girard's capacity to take seriously the Romantic understanding of nature as a source of good.

For example, we have seen how Girard's characterization of the Romantic individual depicts someone always divided within himself by his so-called 'mechanical' reactions to the other that are designed to protect his 'originality'.[27] Yet crucially for Girard, unlike Rousseau, the individual's pride, although a form of negative imitation, is not ultimately something socially induced; rather it springs from his own mistaken belief in originality.[28] The social world, at least in his later work, is fundamentally a source of protection from the paroxysms of mimetic contagion. However, for Rousseau, the pride that makes us compare ourselves and imitate negatively belongs solely to the state of society. He calls this socially induced pride, *amour-propre.* His state of nature on the other hand, is characterized by a peaceful self-love, *amour de soi,* that does not lead to violence because it is a solitary self-love with no need for others and therefore supposedly 'without mimesis'.[29] For Girard, the Romantic belief in 'spontaneous desire', or a desire that is somehow immune from mimesis, is synonymous with *separation,* as a mark of one's own 'originality', which leads to further pride and the multiple divisions of the underground.[30] The problem for understanding Girard's refusal

---

27. Girard, *Deceit, Desire, and the Novel,* p. 298.
28. In a typical comment that aligns Rousseau with the 'deviated transcendence' of the Romantic hero's 'spiritual askesis' Girard says: 'Rousseau affirms that he will present himself armed with *The Confessions* before the supreme tribunal. The Book of Life is displaced by the book of his life.' Girard, *Resurrection from the Underground,* p. 96.
29. Wolfgang Palover, 'Mimesis and Scapegoating in the Works of Hobbes, Rousseau and Kant', in *Contagion: Journal of Violence, Mimesis, and Culture.* Vol. 10, (Spring 2003), p. 143.
30. What Girard's analysis of literary space teaches us is that the falseness of the social world is based on what he sees as the mistaken belief that there is any original impulse that the individual can gain access to through his or her inner experience.

to grant inwardness any value comes back in the end to his characterization of separation as a form of pride, when, as we have seen, for Rousseau, being in touch with our inner nature is in no way meant as a form of separation but rather *authentic connection.*

All the tensions that beset Girard's theory I would argue stem from the fact that he deems inner nature to be devoid of goodness. Desire is the master that makes sentiment its underling. But, as we have seen, an important strand of western spirituality, beginning in the modern period with moral sense theory and culminating with the Romantic voice of nature within, considers this inner nature to be fundamentally good (and with some claim to be in continuity with the Judea-Christian inheritance).[31] By missing the commonality between Deism and Romantic expressivism, and by characterizing Rousseau's move toward the self as a form of 'separation', hence divine self-sufficiency, pride etc., Girard fails to recognize a significant moral dimension in the transition from a premodern order. To try and explain how what counts as 'separation' for Girard can become the basis of actual 'connection' for Rousseau, and Romantic expressivism more broadly, we will now turn to Taylor's *Hegel* and the defining ideas of the eighteenth century, ideas that sought to respond to the problems posed by separation, or 'division', and the requirements of unity.[32]

3. Expression and Originality: Combining Two Views of Nature

The Augustinian turn inward, toward the self, makes explicit the two tendencies of the will and their manifestations in *caritas* and *cupiditas*. The doctrine of the 'two loves', as we saw, allows for the possibility that the human disposition may be radically perverse. The Christian development of the will thereby weaves together two 'master ideas' that struggle to co-exist: 'the will as our power to confer or withhold all things considered assent, or choice; and the will as the basic

---

31. Taylor makes the point: 'There is a divine affirmation of the creature, which is captured in the repeated phrase in Genesis I about each stage of the creation "and God saw that it was good". *Agapē* is inseparable from such a "seeing-good"'. Taylor, *Sources of the Self*, p. 516.

32. Taylor attempts to explain the continuity in the philosophical tradition as follows: 'The philosophy of nature as a source was central to the great upheaval in thought and sensibility that we refer to as "Romanticism", so much so that it is tempting to identify them. But as the mention of Goethe and Hegel shows, this would be too simple. My claim is rather that the picture of nature as a source was a crucial part of the conceptual armoury in which Romanticism arose and conquered European culture and sensibility. The word has a bewildering number of definitions, and some have even doubted that there is such a thing as a unified phenomenon, as against a conceptual muddle hidden in a single term.' Taylor, *Sources of the Self*, p. 368.

disposition of our being.'[33] We also saw how, broadly speaking, the power to confer or withhold consent more or less comes to the fore as a developed idea with the notion of a disengaged subject and the centrality given to ordinary life. Even when the picture is filled out in relation to our sentiments, our choice for the good is but the fulfilment of a right inner impulse. And as we discussed above, Rousseau's challenge to what we might call this one-sided view of natural benevolence as *simply* tending toward the good, ensures that the Augustinian notion of a 'divided will' gets taken up again and revivified in terms that place an even greater significance on our inner impulses than the theory of moral sentiments had emphasized. The source of our unhappiness and our sense of alienation – in short our inner division – can now be understood to arise from the external world which generates the most malign forms of vanity and illusion.[34] Can the voice of nature become a reliable source of order, a way of putting shape on the world when the extent of our inner division becomes evident?

Whereas the disengaged stance to nature seemed to stress rational choice often at the expense of a robust notion of human depravity, Romantic expressivism took seriously the notion of human will as the basic disposition of our being. The new formulation of our inner nature still meant that there could be a potential conflict between vision and desire.[35] We can be cut off from our inner source of good, a condition, moreover, which our new scientific knowledge, so far from ameliorating, may only exacerbate. And so, the expressivists followed Rousseau in propounding a 'two-loves' view:

> The inner voice is our mode of access, but we can lose contact with it; it can be stifled in us. And what can stifle it is precisely the disengaged stance of calculating reason, the view of nature from the outside, as a merely observed order. The filiation with earlier theories of grace is evident. Nature stands as a reservoir of good. In the stance of disengagement, we are out of phase with it, cut off from it; we cannot recover contact with it.[36]

The continuity with the older tradition is borne out in the way that different currents of eighteenth-century thought come to characterize humans' powers, their

---

33. Ibid., p. 138.
34. An important figure on Taylor's own understanding of the modern period was Isaiah Berlin. See C. Taylor, 'The Importance of Herder', in *Isaiah Berlin: A Celebration*, eds, Edna and Avishai Margalit (London: Hogarth Press, 1991b). Also, Isaiah. Berlin, *The Roots of Romanticism*, ed. Henry Hardy (London: Chatto and Windus, 1999).
35. As we mentioned in the previous chapter, the significance of this conflict for us under the formulation of 'two loves' is that 'in the zone in which we live of half understanding and contrary desires, the will is as much the independent variable, determining what we can know as it is the dependent one shaped by what we see.' Taylor, *Sources of the Self*, p. 138.
36. Ibid., p. 370.

limitations and the source of those limitations. While not in agreement with the Augustinian conception of original sin, the Romantic tradition did share with the older Catholic theology the belief that nature was fundamentally good. And unlike Descartes' self-transparent *cogito*, Rousseau insisted that human depravity posed a fundamental problem to true self-knowledge – since it was beyond the scope of a disengaged stance, coming to us as it often did unnoticed through the mediations of the external world. He did not disconnect from meaningful engagement with the world like his Calvinist predecessors. His was not the stance of 'objectification' that we associated with the aims of ordinary life in the previous chapter.[37] Hence, from the age of Enlightenment there evolved an anthropology which combined two perspectives that were not entirely consistent: 'the notion of self-defining subjectivity correlative to the new objectivity; and the view of man as part of nature, hence fully under the jurisdiction of this objectivity'.[38]

Johann Gottfried Herder is identified as one of the key figures in the development of a post-Enlightenment climate in Germany – a climate that was critical of some aspects of the modern revolution, while at the same time striving to incorporate much of its spirit. According to Taylor, Herder reacts against the 'objectification' of human nature and the division of 'the human mind into different faculties, of man into body and soul, against a calculative notion of reason, divorced from feeling and will'.[39] In addition to his reaction against what we can broadly call 'dualism', he is largely responsible for developing an alternative anthropology centred on 'expression', a term that Taylor borrows from the domain of art.[40] What Herder adds to the older Aristotelian concepts is a self-unfolding

---

37. Speaking about the Protestant influence on the modern period, Taylor writes: 'It is probable that the unremitting struggle to desacralize the world in the name of an undivided devotion to God waged by Calvin and his followers helped to destroy the sense of creation as a locus of meanings in relation to which man had to define himself'. Charles Taylor, *Hegel* (New York: Cambridge University Press, 1977a), p. 9. Taylor uses the terms 'disenchanted', desacralized and sometimes 'objectified' to describe the 'denial of the world of inherent meaning'. Ibid.

38. Ibid., p. 10.

39. Ibid., p. 13.

40. In saying that the central notion here is of human action or life as expression, Taylor is not harking back to the premodern view of the 'world as text' in which ideas and corresponding terms express or embody the same ideal order. Rather what he attempts to explain is the force at work here. In the older view we are expressing what already exists, the meaning of which our expression somehow captures. However, Taylor suggests there is another sense in which we speak of expression as giving vent to something we feel or desire. When someone expresses anger by cursing or striking the table 'what is expressed is a subject, or some state of a subject, or at a minimum some life form which resembles a subject.' Taylor, *Hegel*, p. 14. Taylor's use of the term 'expression' is closer to this latter sense, although he claims something of the first is incorporated as well.

subject, a subject that can recognize his self-realization as his own – as having unfolded from within himself, and from his own particular contact with nature.

> It was Herder and the expressivist anthropology developed from him which added the epoch-making demand that my realisation of the human essence be my own, and hence launched the idea that each individual (. . . and each people) has its own way of being human, which it cannot exchange with that of any other except at the cost of distortion and self-mutilation.[41]

This notion of having one's own singular and unique way of being becomes a hugely influential moral source for contemporary forms of freedom. By tracing the predominant moral impulses of contemporary western culture, Taylor argues that the quest for authenticity has its most significant historical antecedents in the eighteenth century and in Herder particularly.[42] As we already discussed, Rousseau had paved the way for this radical view by giving the voice of nature an unprecedented primacy.[43]

Central to human development and the realization of human form in an expressivist view is the manifestation of an inner power striving to realize and maintain its own shape against those the surrounding world might impose. Taylor describes it as follows: '. . . the ideal realisation is one which not only conforms to an idea (as with Aristotelian form), but is also internally generated; indeed these two requirements are inseparable in that the proper form of a man incorporates the notion of free subjectivity.'[44] With the emergence of a self-unfolding subject the older teleological notion of the human changes to incorporate a fuller model of subjective expression whereby in realizing an essence or form, our life does not just embody this form in reality but also defines in a determinate way what it is.[45] Taylor stresses that the idea a person realizes, the form of her life, is not something wholly determined beforehand; it becomes fully determinate only *through*

---

41. Taylor, *Hegel*, p. 15.
42. See also: Charles Taylor, *The Ethics of Authenticity* (Cambridge, MA: Harvard University Press, 1992a).
43. Thus expressivist views differed from other formulas that were still common at the time, such as: 'To thine own self be true . . .', familiar to us from Shakespeare's Hamlet. While we do find an emphasis on inwardness here, it is still very much in the old world orbit of 'not being false to anyone'. With Herder, and 'expressivism', the very notion of a 'false world', or a world where the question of falseness between people emerges, is undercut. Unlike an *ontic* order, an expressivist view held that an individual is not simply responsible for his honesty – being right with himself *in order to* be right with the world, whereby the delicate *ontic* balance might otherwise be upset. The individual's 'honesty,' his unfolding self-realization is now a world-transforming act.
44. Taylor, *Hegel*, p. 15.
45. Ibid., p. 16.

its own unfolding. The affinity here with the older notion of an inner voice help-ing to 'define' what is significant is clear: authenticity has a moral dimension.

> Hence the Herderian idea that my humanity is something unique, not equiva-lent to yours, and this unique quality can only be revealed in my life itself. 'Each man has his own measure, as it were an accord peculiar to him of all his feelings to each other'. The idea is not just that men are different; this was hardly new; it was rather that the differences define the unique form that each of us is called to realise. The differences take on moral import, so that the ques-tion could arise for the first time whether a given form of life was an authentic expression of certain individuals or people. This is the new dimension added by a theory of *self*-realisation.[46]

In this new formulation the human subject comes to know himself by expressing and thereby clarifying what he is and recognizing himself in this expression. According to Taylor, this twofold expression – both realization and clarification of purposes – is one of the key ideas underlying the revolution of the late eighteenth century and, more significantly for our study, it is one of the founda-tional ideas of the civilization which has grown up since then and shaped our contemporary world. Behind externally induced illusions lies a moral source if only individuals can discover and express it. Contra Girard, 'originality' has a moral significance.

Under Herder's influence the new expressivist view of the subject as self-unfolding, through the realization and clarification of purpose, has a profound effect on language and art toward the end of the eighteenth century. Language is no longer only referential sign, it is also expression, and in this aspect it is seen as continuous with art. Both are vehicles of expression that define and clarify human feelings, and transform them into something higher. In the case of art, in its highest form, the feeling must be recognised by the artist as her own; 'subjectivity at its highest is self-awareness.'[47] A certain quality of feeling is an essential com-ponent, a feeling of self that is also a vision of self, expressed in our highest activi-ties, language and art. By achieving self-clarity, we express our full selves and hence are free. Essential to our fulfilment is the feeling and vision we have of our-selves at our fullest, 'as natural and spiritual beings, as subject of natural desires and of the highest aspiration to self-clarity and freedom and expressive form, and all of these in harmonious unity'.[48] This view of the subject and his relationship to the world can be found in the Romantic poetry of the age, in its reverence for nature and awe of the sublime. We can also recognize in this view how our natu-ral inclinations should be affirmed as truer forms of expression while our negative feelings can be properly understood only in relation to a corrupt society.[49]

---

46. Ibid., pp. 16–17.
47. Ibid., p. 21.
48. Ibid., p. 22.

Taylor reminds us however that the expressivist anthropology was a response to the atomist, mechanist and utilitarian picture of human life. What flowed from philosophy and poetry associated with this anthropology at the time was a rift within nature: that is, between nature as plan or instrument and nature as the will that acted on this plan. The rift was intolerable for the originators of the expressivist theory (Rousseau, Herder and other Romantics). They experienced the Enlightenment conception of nature as a tearing apart of the unity of life in which nature should be at once the inspiration and motive force of thought and will.[50] This emphasis on unity and wholeness, which is accessed through a purer state of nature, is one of the central moral sources of contemporary freedom that Taylor identifies in *Source of the Self*. It stresses that nature is more than just a template for the will; to overcome the dichotomy that accompanies objectification the voice of nature must speak through the will.[51]

We find emerging here two dominant views of nature. Whereas one sees the objectified world as proof of the subject's self-possession, the other feels it as imposing exile or inner cleavage, amounting to a denial of life, communion with nature and the possibility of self-expression.[52] An integrative expressivist view included a passionate demand for unity and wholeness. Proponents of this view rejected the dichotomies of the Enlightenment conception of nature and the distortions of the human's true nature as self-expressive being. Since the human is expressive in this way, such a distorted view is an obstacle to human fulfilment. As Taylor explains in a manner that echoes the objections of the Cambridge Platonists to strict Lockean Deism: 'A man who sees his feelings as in another category from thought, as facts about him to be explained mechanistically, cannot rise higher to a transformed expression of them.'[53] In such a world humans are thus alienated from a vital part of themselves, in a manner similar to how in Girardian theory the community becomes alienated from its own source.

Another kind of abstraction, owing to the Enlightenment conception of human being introduces a false world of representation that cuts people off from the real living sources.[54] The individual's self expression is distorted because 'his life does not express him, but rather an illusory substitute for his real feelings

---

49. Once again Rousseau, one of the first to articulate this insight, sums up this basic Romantic idea in the opening lines of *Emile*: 'God makes all things good; man meddles with them and they become evil.' Taylor, *Sources of the Self*, p. 357. See also: *The Ethics of Authenticity*, p. 29.
50. Taylor, *Hegel*, p. 23.
51. Taylor, *Sources of the Self*, pp. 357–358.
52. Taylor, *Hegel*, p. 23.
53. Ibid., p. 24.
54. This concern with being 'cut off' is a further development of what we discussed in the previous section in relation to Rousseau; namely, the way human beings can lose touch with their inner nature and come to identify with an internalized 'illusory' image of themselves from the external world.

and aspirations'.[55] So, while human's are cut off from nature and denied full expression they are also fed a false picture of the world that stands in for their true aspirations and thereby fails to fulfil the promise (that these aspirations hold) of unity and wholeness. Taylor attributes the original articulation of this 'illusory substitution' to Augustine,[56] but clearly it is a concern close to his own heart. Indeed Taylor takes Foucault to task for not being critical enough when denouncing liberation through expression as just another form of illusion. The point is a subtle one since Foucault also sees 'self-expression' as succumbing to 'illusory substitution' through the regimes of control associated with knowledge/power.[57] Taylor's defence of authenticity is based on his belief that there is always an impulse towards the good, or what is higher, at work in our struggles. In the case of Foucault this good might include an impulse towards greater equality, but, according to Taylor, it remains implicit, unexpressed and therefore inaccessible. Thus we can never decide what values should remain off limits, or what should be given full expression. Taylor attributes this confusion to Foucault's Nietzsche-derived stance of neutrality between the different historical systems of power, which ironically appears to neutralize the evaluations *that arise out of his own analysis.*[58]

Over and against the objectified view of the world as proof of the subject's self-possession, expressivism offers us a strongly anti-dualist philosophy. In addition, it makes freedom a central value of human life. This freedom is seen as consisting of genuine self-expression rather than the standard Enlightenment view which stressed the independent self-defining subject.[59] Reminding us of the persistence of 'illusory substitutions' Taylor says that freedom experienced as authentic self-expression is threatened not only by external invasion but also by all the distortions that expression itself is menaced by. It can fail by a *mis*-shaping that is ultimately external in origin, but may become anchored in the self.[60] This is, of course, another reference to Rousseau and his theory of *amour-propre.* But we can also detect here the kinds of 'distortions' that are addressed in Girard's own theory of triangular desire.

As already indicated, Girard shares with Rousseau certain insights into the forms of mimesis that generate so many of the distortions, alluded to above, that expression is menaced by. Pride, in all its various guises, helps to explain for both thinkers how the 'gentlest of passions receives sacrifices of human blood',[61] Yet Girard's

---

55. Ibid.
56. Taylor, *Sources of the Self,* p. 356.
57. Taylor, 'Foucault on Freedom and Truth', pp. 152–184.
58. Ibid., p. 163.
59. Taylor, *Hegel,* p. 24.
60. Ibid.
61. Rousseau, it seems, also had an acute anthropological intuition, and was aware of how 'negative mimesis' could lead to collective violence: 'People become accustomed to judging different objects and to making comparisons; gradually they

view of human nature is closer to Hobbes's rather than Rousseau's assessment of humans in their natural state. For the source of pride for Girard, does not, in the end, come from the social world. It is not then an *externally* produced image of desire that causes the Romantic hero so much trouble by becoming anchored in the self, pulling her outward away from the essential goodness of her natural impulses. Rather, all the distortions that the individual is beset by belong to and arise from a compulsive belief in a unique spontaneous identity. So while Girardian theory holds no possibility of a self-reflexive first-person perspective in the mode of an Augustinian subject, he does however maintain a view of nature that is closely aligned to Augustine's concept of evil as inherent in our natural disposition. However, as I have already argued, this view of nature as evil is only part of the Augustinian picture. For Augustine, the human hearts' capacity to quest for God in the end permits us to think of human nature as redeemable. Is Girard too selective in his reading of Augustine?[62]

The Romantic objection to the more disengaged forms of freedom, Taylor claims, was based precisely on the fear that humans were being cut off from nature and hence from the possibility of unified integral expression. Freedom experienced as authentic expression cannot be realized in a world where the subject is separate. The 'freedom' of the rational subject of control only works to keep humans alienated from full expression – from 'the realisation and clarification of his feelings and vision'. This static view of freedom also generates 'illusory substitutes' for the individual's true aspirations that not only fail to fulfil, but make one unaware of one's true nature.[63] Taylor seems convinced, as Rousseau was before him, that these illusions are 'ultimately external in origin', though they can indeed become anchored in the self.[64] However, notwithstanding the expressivist critique of disengaged reason, the central motivating force of the whole

---

acquire ideas of merit and beauty, which in turn produce feelings of preference. As a result of seeing each other, people cannot do without seeing more of each other. A tender and sweet sentiment insinuates itself into the soul, and at the least obstacle becomes an inflamed fury; jealousy awakens with love; discord triumphs, and the gentlest of passions receives sacrifices of human blood.' Jean Jacques Rousseau, *A Discourse on Inequality*, trans., Maurice Cranston (Middlesex: Penguin Books, 1984) p. 114.

62. 'Le trois quarts de ce que je dis sont dans saint Augustine' ('Three quarters of what I say can be found in Saint Augustine'). René Girard, *Quand ces choses commenceront . . .*, Entretiens avec Michel Treguer (Paris: Arléa, 1994), p. 224.

63. The Romantic hero of literary space, whose mechanical reactions send him rushing toward a model/obstacle or resentfully holding on to his divided nature for the sake of desire, is in Taylor's analysis *misnamed*. While Girard attributes the Romantic impulse to Descartes 'deceptive' ethic of generosity, we can perhaps now more clearly see that Descartes was rather the father of modern rationalism, and of a mechanistic view of the universe.

64. Taylor, *Hegel*, p. 24.

Romantic tradition, as it took shape for Herder and others at this time, was not separation, or 'self-divinisation' as Girard maintains, but rather the wholeness of integral expression through greater contact with the 'current of life'. Indeed, in so far as Girard is actually concerned with 'separation' and the multiple divisions of 'internal mediation' that for him characterize the Romantic individual's various 'illusions', he can be seen as sharing with this whole tradition an important insight into the overarching significance of unity.

4. 'Self-divinisation' or the Demands of Expression?

It should be acknowledged that Girard is not eccentric in reading much of modern thought as an attempted move towards and legitimation of 'self-divinisation'. In this section I will look at a quite similar reading, focused especially on Kant and Hegel as thinkers confronting and attempting to reconcile deep tensions bequeathed by the stand-off between the Enlightenment and Romanticism. Here the internalization that Taylor claims began as a religious development is thought to take a more radically humanistic turn as humans set out on their own to resolve their inner conflicts. Both Kant and Hegel are seen as attempting to resolve the problem of the divided nature of human being by first understanding it as a dichotomy between subject and object and then bringing the shortcomings within the self into relationship (through reason or spirit) with a more idealized self. For Kant then, 'moral dignity' is achieved by overcoming the phenomenal self under the compulsion of the moral will to be perfect – or to strive to realize its noumenal self. For Hegel, finite spirit and the limitations of the objective world are overcome through a dialectical movement towards Absolute Spirit. Speaking about Kant's concept of freedom as a form of inner 'bondage', Robert Tucker claims:

> He maintains that practical reason compels man to form a picture of himself as a being of godlike perfection and to regard this idealized person as his 'real self' . . . This *hubris* is the pathology of human selfhood. Man falsifies his identity as finite man when he arrogates to himself absolute attributes and powers . . . in his attempt to realise the unrealisable, he necessarily becomes divided in himself. His soul becomes the arena of a war between *homo noumenon* and *homo phenomenon*.[65]

A little later Tucker describes the same tendency toward self-divinization in Hegel as follows:

> . . . The Kantian dichotomy . . . reappears in Hegelianism writ large as a dichotomy between noumenal world-self and phenomenal world-self. The division of

---

65. Robert Tucker, *Philosophy and Myth in Karl Marx*. Second edition (New York: Cambridge University Press, 1972), p. 38.

Kantian man against himself in the quest for moral perfection has turned into spirit's division against itself, or self-alienation. And just as Kant pictures the divided man as being at war with himself in the effort to eliminate the two selves, so Hegel represents self-alienated spirit as locked in conflict with itself: 'Thus spirit is at war with itself; it has to overcome itself as its most formidable obstacle. That development, which in the sphere of nature is a peaceful growth, is in that of spirit, a severe, a mighty conflict with itself. What spirit really strives for is the realization of its ideal being . . . Its expansion, therefore, does not present the harmless tranquillity of mere growth, as does that of organic life, but a stern reluctant working against itself'.[66]

When this project of self-divinization becomes the philosophical solution to internal division, we can readily grasp why Marx, in a letter to his father while still a student of Hegel, wrote: 'If previously the gods dwelt above the earth, now they were at the centre of it.'[67]

As Tucker makes clear, there is already an acknowledgement of modern philosophical humanism as a form of 'self-divinization', if not explicitly by Kant or Hegel, certainly by Marx. Tucker sees such 'self-divinization' as negative, as 'pathological', and Girard's own reaction against 'originality' – his account of how 'men become gods' – sits comfortably within this reading. However, there is another way of thinking of this whole philosophical development, which Taylor gives us: one that does not see pride as the dominant motif, but rather emphasizes instead the genuine concern to respond to the pressing need to reformulate the subject's relationship to the world in face of rapidly changing socio-historical forces. While Taylor's analysis of the eighteenth century does not minimize the significance of the 'divided self' for modern thought, it does however stress the religious dimension of this struggle for unity. Thus, his analysis highlights not so much the various modern solutions to the problem of inner division (Kantian, Hegelian, Marxist etc.). Rather, it underscores the significance of the *impulse* towards wholeness or unity itself, which is understood as being in continuity with the Judeo-Christian religion, and from which arises all philosophical problematizing about 'division', as separation or alienation.

As we have seen, expressivism contained an inspiration to unity with nature that the atomizing theories of the Enlightenment were thought to undermine. Objectified nature was experienced as an exile and, what is more, the demands for a whole, fully expressed life could not be satisfied with overcoming the Cartesian 'mind/body' dualism. This desire for union between body and soul, thought and sense, that was in no way fulfilled by the self-possessed rational subject, could not stop at the limits of the body:

If I am not satisfied with myself as a mind confronting internal and external nature, but must think of myself as life in which nature speaks through thought

---

66. Tucker, *Philosophy and Myth in Karl Marx*, p. 50, internal quotation taken from Hegel's Lectures on the Philosophy of History.
67. Tucker, *Philosophy and Myth in Karl Marx*, p. 73.

and will, if therefore I as a subject am one with my body, then I have to take account of the fact that my body is in interchange with the greater nature outside. Nature knows no fixed boundaries at the limits of the body, and hence I as a subject must be in interchange with this greater nature.[68]

The desires of the subject cannot be purely individualistic. The subject is here connected in a complex and intimate way with nature. If I am to be authentic, if my feeling/vision of myself is to adequately express my true nature, my real existence, then my feeling/vision has to go beyond the limits of myself to encompass the 'great current' of life that somehow runs through me. And if there is to be unity in the self (which of course is essential to the Romantic spirit of the eighteenth century) then it is this 'greater current', not just my own bodily life, which has to be united with higher aspiration to freedom and expression. 'Thus one of the central aspirations of the expressivist view was that man be united in communion with nature, that his self-feeling (Selbstgefühl) unite with a sympathy (Mitgefühl) for all life, and for nature as living.'[69]

We can readily see how being connected in this way allows all our bodily feelings and experiences to take on greater significance. The subject as the locus of all possible unity and wholeness becomes crucial to our experience of the body and the natural world; this experience is different from an 'objectified world of mechanical relations'. For the expressivist view and the Romantic Movement in general this latter scientific world could only be experienced as dead; as a place of exile, devoid of that universal sympathy which obtains between people.[70] Against this alien world, nature is now seen as a great stream of life of which we are a vital part. Therefore, our way of contact, Taylor explains, is by sympathetic insertion into this stream, whereby we seek interchange with a larger life in a quest for unity and wholeness.

Much of the expressivist emphasis on unity was inspired by nostalgia for the premodern period, and in particular by the avowed fascination with classical Greece. To the thinkers of this age, the ancient Greeks represented a mode of life in which the highest human aspiration was at one with human nature and with all of nature. This mode of life was the perfect exemplar of the expressivist desire for union and communion. The Greek era, Taylor tells us, was one 'of unity and harmony within man, in which thought and feeling, morality and sensibility were one, in which the form which man stamped on his life, whether moral, political or spiritual flowed from his own natural being, and was not imposed on it by the force of raw will'.[71] Behind this picture of Greek 'unity and harmony' we can, with hindsight, detect a deep division between a rarefied space and what was not

---

68. Taylor, *Hegel*, p. 25.
69. Ibid.
70. Ibid.
71. Taylor, *Hegel*, p. 27.

considered worthy of inclusion. Equipped with our ethic of 'dignity' and 'equality', we must see this pure classical space as quite small and exclusive.[72] However, what the expressivists did recognize in their aspirations for freedom and fulfilment was that in early Greek culture the great current of life in nature was not alien to the human spirit. On the contrary, nature 'was inhabited by gods of human shape', with whom humans sustained communion, and who drew from them their 'highest feats.'[73] So, while perhaps naïve about the violence that pertained to the generative forces of Greek religion, the Romantics nonetheless recognized a truth in the unifying power of this form of expression.

Yet there was something else uneasy about the expressivists' longing, since their much-valued new subjectivity, and the freedom that it brought, was won largely *at the expense of the unity* of the old cosmic order to which the 'Greek way' was so intimately connected. The nostalgia for this 'Greek way' was therefore deeply fraught. The yearning personified by Schiller, among others, sang of a past when 'Life's fullness flowed through creation.' But it also sang of the *irretrievable loss* as humans now stand before a 'Godless nature', a nature devoid of its generative force (it was this sense of loss of course that fuelled Romantic *nostalgia*).

Another characteristic of the expressivist movement related to its sense of communion with nature is its aspiration to brotherhood or communion with other human beings. The Enlightenment vision of society made up of atomistic, morally self-sufficient subjects provokes a sense of outrage among those who held to an expressivist view. This vision promotes the idea of a subject who enters into external relations with other subjects seeking either advantage (*a la* Locke), or the defence of individual rights (*a la* Kant). For the expressivists the connection between people has to run deeper, not least because it has to channel the great current of life. 'They seek for a deeper bond of felt unity which will unite sympathy between men with their highest self-feeling, in which men's highest concerns are shared and woven into community life rather than remaining the preserve of individuals.'[74] This desire to unite in sympathy and be united in a common concern has had a powerful influence on the modern imagination, as the story of

---

72. Indeed, Girard's mimetic theory, and its explication of the role of generative scapegoating, reminds us of the huge price of 'unity and harmony' in ancient societies. 'Even in fifth century Greece', he claims, '– the Athens of the great tragedians – human sacrifice had not, it seems, completely disappeared.' (René Girard, *Violence and the Sacred*, trans. Patrick Gregory (Baltimore: Johns Hopkins University Press, 1984, p. 9). And to see how this unity was achieved and how intuitively the 'generating spark of religion' (Girard, *Violence and the Sacred*, p. 87) was understood (Girard gives us many examples). In Chapter 2 we discussed the function of tragedy that draws on the religious impulse, and outlined Girard's analysis of Oedipus and Pentheus as scapegoat figures.

73. Taylor, *Hegel*, p. 26.

74. Ibid., p. 28.

nationalism in the twentieth century can attest. For the expressivists it was an ideal inspired, once again, by the ancient Greek *polis* where the gods of the city and the gods of nature were two sides of the same coin, bringing together the fullest freedom with the deepest community life. Overall, the four demands – for inner unity, freedom and communion with others and with nature – reflect the aspirations of expressivist consciousness; and incorporating such a strongly felt need for integral expression – a need once again met in the pantheistic culture of ancient Greece – they gave the modern subject an unavoidably sacred character. However, it could not be guaranteed that the subject alone could find the resources to generate the much sought after unity.

To the expressivist mix of fusion and creation Kant added an emphasis on the moral freedom of the subject – a freedom that reinforced the subject's self-possession while at the same time distancing her from her natural inclination. For the expressivists, Kantian autonomy, while compelling in its account of human freedom, merely reflected a more profound inner cleavage. Kant developed the idea that the individual should 'draw his moral precepts out of his own will and not from any external source, be this God himself'.[75] Yet, however much Kantian freedom might inspire individuals to buck external demands and received authority, it could not deliver on the much hoped for integral expression. To the contrary, because of its emphasis on the independent self-choosing subject, this radical freedom seemed possible only at the cost of a disjunction with nature. This disjuncture, as Taylor points out is

> . . . a division within myself between reason and sensibility more radical than anything the materialist, utilitarian Enlightenment had dreamed, and hence a division with external nature from whose causal laws the free self must be radically independent, even while phenomenally his behaviour appeared to conform.[76]

Here lie the seeds of modern existentialism: a break with external nature and all that it might entail for the individual. 'The radically free subject was thrown back on himself, and it seemed on his individual self, in opposition to nature . . . and on to a decision in which others could have no share.'[77] An individual's 'unique measure' is not being expressed here through a self-unfolding subject, or in the Kantian sense, by 'submitting nature to law', but rather was being exercised in and through an infinite choice, a choice that ultimately pitted the subject *against* the world.[78]

---

75. Ibid., p. 30.
76. Ibid., p. 33.
77. Ibid.
78. Taylor, *Sources of the Self*, p. 450.

The way of dealing with the *aporia* of radical freedom and integral expression that Taylor explores is not the existentialist way, but rather the way of history – where the highest challenge to historical reflection is to reconcile what is greatest in ancient and modern cultures. The paradigm of expressive perfection that many eighteenth and nineteenth-century thinkers found in ancient Greece was based on a belief that this classical period had achieved the most perfect unity between nature and the highest human expressive form.[79] However, the price of the development of reason to that higher stage of self-clarity, which is essential to our realization as radically free beings, was that this beautiful unity, which came so naturally to the early Greeks, had to die. And this was so because humans *had to be inwardly divided in order to grow.*[80] The growth of reason and hence radical freedom required a disjunction from the natural and sensible. The 'sacrifice' of primal Greek unity was necessary if humans were to develop to their fullest self-consciousness and free self-determination.[81] For while there was no hope of a return to the lost beauty of Greece, there was hope of a higher synthesis once humans had developed their faculty of reason. 'If the early Greek synthesis had been unreflective, and had to be, for reflection starts by dividing man within himself, then the new unity would fully incorporate the reflective consciousness gained, would indeed be brought about by this reflective consciousness.'[82] This at least was the hope of reconciling the division that modern subjectivity both inaugurated and contained, and the primary tasks of thought and sensibility were seen as the overcoming of profound oppositions – oppositions between the two ideals of radical freedom and integral expression.[83] In the end, Kantian autonomy does not overcome these oppositions but deeply exacerbates them. The only way for cosmic spirit to reach unity and wholeness was to somehow include a place for reason – reason that is essentially divisive. And this could only happen, as Hegel most fully grasped, if humans are seen as the vehicle of this spirit *while still retaining* their autonomy.[84]

5. Religion and the History of Division

The Enlightenment insistence that nothing should be believed but what reason licences failed to dispel the belief that religion is a source of unity as the early

---

79. Taylor, *Hegel*, p. 35.
80. Ibid.
81. Ibid.
82. Ibid.
83. Ibid., p. 36.
84. Ibid., pp. 48–49.

Greek synthesis had amply demonstrated.[85] A 'religion of the people' appeared indispensable to the kind of unity that could restore an individual's relationship with nature and reconcile the opposites that so divided him, or her. For Hegel, the public religions of ancient Greece provided an important model of *Volksreligion*. These public religions were 'an integral part of social life, inseparable from the other aspects of the city's common existence, and essential to its identity'.[86] In short, Hegel sought a regeneration through religion whereby one could achieve radical freedom while at the same time a wholeness of integral expression – undivided. Following Rousseau's rejection of the traditional hierarchy of preferences that obtain between human beings in a social context, and acknowledging the need for recognition that arises from our other dependence, Hegel saw the Greek festival as a way of affirming subjectivity and the current of life as somehow other than and yet integral to each other.[87] Caring about myself in this context is compatible with freedom and social unity.[88]

According to Taylor, in order for religion to achieve Hegel's aims it must be fully subjectivized '. . . that is, it must be more than an external allegiance to certain doctrines and practices, and become a living piety in order to unite man within himself: and it must be more than the religion of some individuals, it must be woven into the life of the people, and linked with reformed political institutions if it is to unite men with each other.'[89] Here the Enlightenment picture of the human is not rejected but integrated into a larger vision where reason and sensibility are not opposed. Hegel's requirements for regeneration thus meet the

---

85. In his work on Hegel, Taylor shows how the Enlightenment in Germany was interwoven with religion and could never be contained in one of two opposed camps, as in France. Ibid., p. 12.

86. Ibid., p. 54.

87. By breaking with the older hierarchical view of the universe, Rousseau is at the origin of a new discourse about honour and dignity. 'To the traditional ways of thinking about honor and pride he adds a third, which is quite different. There was a discourse denouncing pride . . . which called on us to remove ourselves from the whole dimension of human life and be utterly unconcerned with esteem. And then there was an ethic of honor, frankly nonuniversalist and inegalitarian . . . Rousseau borrows the denunciation of the first discourse but he doesn't end up calling for a renunciation of all concern with esteem. On the contrary, in his portrait of the republican model, caring about esteem is central. What is wrong with pride or honor is its striving after preferences, hence division, hence real other-dependence, and therefore loss of the voice of nature, and consequently corruption . . . The remedy is not rejecting the importance of esteem, but entering into a quite different system, characterised by equality, reciprocity and unity of purpose.' Charles Taylor, 'The Politics of Recognition', in *Multiculturalism: Examining the Politics of Recognition*, ed. Amy Gutmann (Princeton: Princeton University Press, 1994). p. 49.

88. Charles Taylor, 'The Politics of Recognition', p. 48.

89. Taylor, *Hegel*, p. 55.

requirements of a *Volksreligion* such as the Greeks enjoyed. However, Taylor claims us that Hegel is very much concerned with understanding and expressing this regeneration in Christian terms. To this end Hegel becomes preoccupied with the distinction between 'pure' or 'natural' religion and 'positive' religion that the teaching of Jesus and its subsequent distortions make clear. Taylor maintains that in his essay, *The Positivity of the Christian Religion,* Hegel sets out to explain what happened to the religion of Jesus so that it 'degenerated into present-day Christianity' with the original emphasis on the integral movement of the heart replaced by rules and dry formulae. A 'positive' religion is grounded on authority rather than postulated by our own reason directed by our heart and supplemented by the forms our devotion takes.[90]

The sad truth of Christianity is that it was forced to become a positive religion. Jesus' teachings could not reach a generation of people oriented so much to the law and command. So Jesus was forced to rely on the messiah myth and to give this myth a higher sense.[91] The result was ultimately that the followers who were unable to live up to the standard of the heart, who were incapable of living the full unity of reason and will preached yet another positive religion founded on belief in Christ, rather than a recovery of God's will in one's own heart.[92]

While preserving the original teaching of Jesus, this religion did not meet the requirements of a regenerated *Volksreligion*. For one thing, the unity between autonomy and wholeness is still unattainable by anyone but the man-god. Worse, not only does this ideal become external (a Christ to whom men pray, or an after-life beyond this world) but, as Taylor points out: '[t]he sense of separation and inadequacy is all the crueler in that the ideal is higher than its predecessors, not just compliance with the law of external observances, but a purity of intention, against which men must sense uncleanness of the heart, a vice of the will.'[93] The perfect example of a natural religion that combines a radical freedom and integral expression must now somehow recover this 'unclean heart' and 'corrupt will' and in an act of transformation reach a higher standard of intention. All this appears too tall an order. Hegel's reflections on the problem give rise to the theme of the 'unhappy consciousness'. Once we grasp the original teaching of Jesus, Christianity becomes a failed religion – a realization made all the more dramatic by the fact that Jesus had to die, so unprepared was the world to hear his message.[94]

As a result of this failure we find a sadness at the heart of the new religion that, Taylor claims, did not attend the earlier *Volksreligion*. 'Already this [failure] marks the subsequent life of Christianity with a certain melancholy, that at the

---

90. Ibid.
91. Ibid., 57.
92. Ibid.
93. Ibid.
94. Ibid.

centre of its worship is the Crucified One, and this starkly contrasts with Greek religion in which the divine is woven into the self-affirmation of the community.'[95] What was a celebration for the older pagan religions becomes a source of profound sadness for the Judeo-Christian faith.[96] Girard unlike Hegel describes this sadness as a failure to properly unite around the victim.[97] However, Hegel does suggest that this melancholy could be further understood as arising from the deep division that Christianity was meant to heal, that is – between radical freedom and integral expression. In *The Spirit of Christianity and It's Fate*, Hegel discusses his paradigm of the original 'unhappy consciousness' – the religion of the Jews as founded by Abraham. Taylor tells us that for Hegel 'separation from' and 'domination of' nature were defining features of this religion from the beginning. With the sacrifice of Isaac, Abraham tore himself loose from the original unity with nature and with his tribe. 'Nature became for him so much neutral matter, which could not be united with spirit but rather had to be dominated by it.'[98]

Taylor claims that Hegel interprets the spirit of Abraham as a spirit of 'objectification' and 'disenchantment' that – as already discussed in relation to Enlightenment reason – divides humans internally and externally. This divisive spirit of 'separation' and 'domination' ceased to see nature as 'an embodiment of sacred or spiritual order in relation to which man must define himself, and came to be seen as raw material to be shaped by human will'.[99] Here Taylor takes issue with Hegel regarding the source of this objectification. While Hegel sees it as belonging properly to Judaism, Taylor argues it is more accurately viewed from a historical perspective as characteristically Christian.[100] According to Taylor, by seeing the essential *connection* in this objectification between separation from and domination of nature, Hegel is 'projecting one of the central strands of

---

95. Ibid.
96. Hegel develops the idea of the 'unhappy counsciousness' as something also experienced by spirit when it encounters the objective world. 'In its confrontation with an apparent object, spirit feels imprisoned in limitation. It experiences what Hegel calls the "sorrow of finitude".' Tucker, *Philosophy and Myth in Karl Marx*, p. 53, internal quotation taken from *Hegel's Science of Logic*.
97. For Girard, the melancholy of Christianity arises from the unavoidable innocence of the victim, whereas the 'self-affirmation' of the Greek religion was bought at the expense of the victim – the one deemed guilty. Hence, Girard too sees Christianity as a 'failed religion', but unlike Hegel's account this is its triumph since it provides all cultures with a way out of violent mimesis and the human tendency to unite around a victim. Girard, *Things Hidden*, pp. 141–179.
98. Taylor, *Hegel*, p. 58.
99. Ibid.
100. Girard also claims that the spirit of Christianity is 'divisive'. He quotes Matthew's gospel, 'Don't think I have come to bring peace on earth; I have not come to bring peace but a sword.' René Girard, *I See Satan Fall Like Lightning*, trans. James G. Williams (Maryknoll, NY: Orbis Books, 2001), p. 159.

modern consciousness back onto the father of the Jewish faith'.[101] In effect, the division between 'radical freedom' and 'integral expression' comes to have a religious character very different from the shining example of the Greeks. In the Greek model, religion – when properly woven into the life of the city – is responsible for creating only unity. The religion of the Jews on the other hand is seen as a source of *division* that comes to have an important resonance for the individual's relationship to the world in the modern period.

While Taylor is careful to point out that Hegel's analysis may not be historically accurate he does not disagree with Hegel's essential argument, namely that the division is a religious one. He simply relocates the significant moment of 'religious division' onto Christianity. Regarding Hegel's projecting back 'too far' (and recalling his own analysis of the affirmation of ordinary life that we have already met) Taylor writes: "Historically this is hard to sustain; but if I am right in holding that Christianity and particularly its Calvinist form had an important role in the forming of the modern consciousness of objectification, Hegel's thesis here may be insightful *even if misplaced*."[102] The difference between the two thinkers as to the source of the objectification and disenchantment becomes significant when we consider, as we already have, Taylor's philosophical history in *Sources of the Self*. The radical reflexivity that comes to play a defining role in the early modern period, as a new mode of inwardness that values ordinary life, is central to Taylor's argument concerning modern freedom; for it suggests that the divisions within the self are driven, at least in part, by an incarnational mode of life whose primary inspiration is the Christian gospels. Abraham's sacrifice may be understood as the source of a break with nature and a clinging to God, but its occurrence is still very much within an externally ordered social world. In anthropological and historical terms, Abraham's 'break', while radical, does not fundamentally challenge the law of sacrifice that permits the community to bond as a community (a people), and to re-establish difference at the expense of a victim. Thus, modern objectification becomes sacrifice by another name, whereby even the innerworldly asceticism of the Puritan (the 'putting under foot') can be seen to reflect the older Abrahamic adherence to the law.

Taylor claims that Hegel more or less made the same point about Christianity overcoming the older forms of division with respect to human beings and nature, and thereby becoming an 'agent of disenchantment'. He quotes Hegel: 'Christianity has depopulated Valhalla, hewn down the sacred groves and rooted out the phantasy of the people as shameful superstition, as a diabolical poison.'[103] Of course for Taylor this is not a secondary point – and cannot be if his intuitions about inwardness and ordinary life are to have currency. Hegel thus understands

---

101. Taylor, *Hegel*, p. 58.
102. Ibid, (my italics).
103. Ibid., p. 58. Here Taylor is quoting from: H. Nohl (Ed), Hegel's, *Theologische Jugendschriften*.

Christianity as having an anthropological and historical import by generating in individuals a greater sense of independence and self-possession in a life generated by the internal law of the heart rather than the external 'positive' law of command.[104] Hegel's comments above suggest that he shares with Girard a similar insight into religion. With deference to Girard's hermeneutical key, however, we might say that Jesus does not so much 'root out the poison' as expose the whole process of 'rooting out poison' as no more than scapegoating – an exposure achieved only by his own subjection to this process, by his own willing assumption of the scapegoat-victim role.[105] Thus the failure of sacred violence to generate a cleansing unity, which Jesus' life and death expose once and for all, can be understood to propel the whole notion of modern disenchantment. In this way the flattening of hierarchies for Girard becomes synonymous with a 'sacrificial crisis', while for Hegel it becomes synonymous with a form of expression and self-realization that can meet the requirements of radical freedom and integral expression through the self-conscious regeneration of order.[106]

6. Division and the Unity of Life: 'Unanimity Plus One'

Religious developments in the sixteenth and seventeenth centuries provide the impetus for a variety of ways of rethinking the order inherent in nature.

----

104. Reading disenchantment as a form of division, and separation from the sacred, also helps explain why Taylor does not reduce Weber's analysis of the modern world to a 'knee-jerk' atheism that equates the loss of religion with the loss of metaphysics – what Girard refers to as 'the loss of the suprasensible in the Platonic sense'. Girard, *The Girard Reader*, p. 259.

105. That the 'phantasy of the people' is 'rooted out' as a 'diabolical poison' reflects Girard's comments on the *pharmakon*, which he articulates in terms of sacred violence. With respect to this old Greek festival it is explained in *Violence and the Sacred* that the poison is part of the cure in the same way that pure violence protects against impure violence in ritual sacrifice. Girard, *Violence and the Sacred*, pp. 288, 296, 297.

106. The hierarchy that Hegel introduces is not based on an *ontic* order, or a purely 'anthropological' notion of degree. It is more horizontal than these formulae, which are both characterized by vertical succession. However, Taylor argues that Hegelian hierarchy is *also* historical and temporal: 'The general structure of the universe . . . is thus determined by virtue of its being the embodiment and expression of *Geist*. It includes a hierarchy of beings from the lowest inanimate forms through various kinds of living species to man. And then of course, for the realisation of *Geist*, man has to develop . . . So that there is also a hierarchy of cultural forms and modes of consciousness which succeed each other in time and make up human history.' Taylor, *Hegel*, p. 91. See also: Arthur O. Lovejoy, 'The Temporalization of the Great Chain', in *The Great Chain of Being: A Study in the History of an Idea* (New York: Harper and Row Publishers, 1965).

Whereas previously the good was conceived in terms of a hierarchically ordered universe, by the eighteenth century it comes to us quite naturally if we can only somehow reach beyond the illusions of socially induced pride and make contact with its 'inner voice'. Rousseau is an important hinge figure in the transition to modernity because of the way he maintains a 'two-loves' view of nature, and hence a theory of how human nature can be deceived and even depraved. However, because of the essential goodness of nature the Romantic individual's turn inward can be construed not as a separation in the manner of Girard's literary hero, but rather as a form of genuine connection to the great current of life – the basis of an identity that is both individual and social.[107] Herder develops the notion that each individual or people has his or her own unique way of being that is to be discovered, clarified and made determinate, in the actual process of its own unfolding and so cannot be determined beforehand, for example by the requirements of a hierarchically ordered universe. The more those influenced by Herder confront the need for integral expression *and* the historical conditions of their separateness (the radical freedom so valued by Kantians) the more impossible seems the task of unification. It is precisely to this fundamental aporia that Hegel responds, and provides something of a solution.

Hegel's turn to Judaeo-Christian religion was not meant simply as an allegorical device to help articulate his philosophical system, but actually provides the anthropological basis for the working out of his theory of master and slave.[108] By breaking with nature and his tribe, Abraham clung to God in servitude and, in return, God put nature at human being's disposal. The 'unhappy consciousness' is the consciousness of this break in which unity and mutuality is replaced by domination and servitude – 'between man and nature, nature and spirit, and ultimately also between man and man'.[109] As already mentioned, the religion of Jesus, which emphasized a movement of the heart, was replaced by another 'positive' religion based on law and command. The result was that the primary movement of Jesus' disciples became that of retreat, of turning inward.[110] In this movement, we might argue, Augustine and Dostoyevsky (in their somewhat different ways) excel.

Taylor shows how Hegel comes to see the initial break with nature and attempted reconciliation through Jesus in the context of the Kantian ideal of moral autonomy and the aspiration to expressive unity. However, from early on, Hegel refuses to accept the separation of morality and inclination that was central to Kant's position. With his more anthropological account of religion, he comes

---

107. Taylor, 'The Politics of Recognition', p. 49.
108. While Girard's 'original scene', like Freud's, is based on the violence of 'all against one', Hegel's 'original scene' is based on the violence of 'one against one'. Hobbes, another main 'scenic' thinker, suggests the primary threat is 'all against all', which is perhaps the first phase in the Girardian scene.
109. Taylor, *Hegel*, p. 59.
110. Ibid.

to see that this separation was inevitable, and in many ways culminates in Kantian autonomy with its division between duty and desire. Taylor describes this realization by Hegel as follows: 'Against the Kantian separation of duty and desire, Hegel sees Jesus' vision of their union, in which the spirit of their reconciliation . . . replaces, goes beyond and hence fulfils the law with its particular measured prescriptions.'[111] This presents a strong case against those like Tucker (and of course Girard) who, as we saw at the beginning of the previous section, argue that Hegel's development on the Kantian theme of 'inner division' is just a bolder form of self-divinization. Taylor's account allows us to see this development as one that attempts to fulfil the requirements of freedom – as the very essence of Christianity.

By contrast with a religion based on love – as a union of opposites – Kantian morality remains one of division, and what is perhaps worse, despite its claims to the contrary, it retains an 'indistinguishable residue of positivity'.[112] However, rather than being dominated by a master outside ourselves – through rules and commands etc. – we are now dominated by a master within: we become slaves to the rational moral law. Against this division created by Kantian autonomy, 'Hegel holds fundamentally to the expressivist view of nature: the self is the inner single source which expresses itself in the unfolding of reason and inclination alike. Thus the imposition of an alien law on one of these sides of our being is a kind of (partial) slavery.'[113] This analysis of Kantian morality, according to Taylor, fits with Hegel's discussion of Abraham and how his separation from nature cannot but lead to relations of domination and servitude. With this morality we now become masters of inclination and servants of reason, whereas before we were masters of nature and servants of God. Thus, the Kantian moral individual is the successor of Abraham who (in Taylor's words) 'internalizes his jealous law-giving God and calls him reason'.

The unity of life, the precious goal of Romantic expressivism, is near impossible to achieve under the rule of law – external or internal. Positivity, separation and objectification remain persistent yet apparently necessary obstacles in our search for the full unity of integral expression. This unity encompassing our actions and what befalls us in history is captured by Hegel's notion of 'fate', understood as 'the reaction unto us of our own trespass against life'.[114] To sin against life is to separate and divide the living whole within and between humans, or between humans and nature. Like the Eastern notion of 'karma', or indeed the Greek notion of 'nemesis', it is to call down a certain fate upon the sinner. For Hegel, to see this, that is, to see fate as the other side of our act, is to see the possibility of reconciliation by ceasing to act in ways that divide. To act in this reconciling way, is to act out of love, as Jesus did.

---

111. Ibid., p. 60.
112. Ibid.
113. Ibid.
114. Ibid., p. 61.

However, according to Taylor, Jesus does not, in the end, provide the model of the perfect religion for Hegel – namely a teaching that can transcend the limitations of autonomy, and combine radical freedom with integral expression, because Jesus does not ultimately escape fate (this is the very reason for the melancholia, as already noted, which at least for Hegel is inextricable from Christianity). 'Fate can catch *even the innocent* who is drawn into transgression against his will. Suppose I am attacked, and I have to fight for my life or let injustice be done. In either case I must transgress against the unity of life, by what I do or what I suffer.'[115] In one sense then Hegel interprets Jesus' fate as a transgression against the unity of life. In another sense Jesus dies willingly in order not to be divided from others, and hence from love.

Despite the ambiguity that Taylor highlights here in Hegel's account of Jesus' death, what is revealing, in terms of our conversation with Girardian theory, is the way fate is used to explain how an innocent person can die and how his death can be justified in relation to 'the unity of life'. Fate was of course notorious for cutting down Greek heroes – heroes who were never truly 'innocent', who always suffered from some 'tragic' flaw that would justify the 'revenge of the gods': their murder, or expulsion from the *polis*. If, as Girard claims, Jesus is a scapegoat, the victim of his people, like Job (and many others) before him,[116] then the community depends on his guilt, because it is the very guilt of the victim that allows the community to form as a community (the unity of the community is always divided – it is always unanimity *minus* one). As we have seen, according to Girard, the only thing that can restore unity when a violent crisis escalates is the scapegoat mechanism – a process that requires the 'unanimous guilt' of the victim. If Jesus does appear to transgress against 'unity', as Hegel suggests, then following Girard we can assert that he 'transgresses' rather against the unanimity that is always generated at the expense of the surrogate victim – the one who, relative to the collective 'sin', Girard tells us, is always innocent. Hence Jesus acts for the sake of *authentic unity*, even though fate 'catches him' the way fate has caught every victim 'since the foundation of the world' – through an act of collective violence.[117]

Perhaps, in the end, it is Hegel's model of Jesus that is flawed. But we can nonetheless begin to see how a theory of sacred violence as a form of 'unity'

---

115. Ibid., p. 62 (my italics).
116. René Girard, *Job: The Victim of His People*, trans. Yvonne Freccero (London: Athlone, 1987a).
117. Describing how the 'tragic flaw' functions in Greek drama, as a 'shadowy similitude' of religious experience, Girard says, the hero 'must be neither wholly good nor wholly bad. A certain degree of goodness is required in a tragic hero in order to establish sympathy between him and the audience; yet a certain degree of weakness, a "tragic flaw" is needed, to neutralise the goodness and permit the audience to tolerate the hero's downfall and death'. Girard, *Violence and the Sacred*, p. 291. Fate like 'chance' in primitive ritual is a way of unburdening the community from the consequences of what happens next. Girard, *Violence and the Sacred*, pp. 312–314.

(as unanimity) that is itself a 'division', can be understood within the context of the eighteenth-century search for the wholeness of integral expression. Separation no longer needs to be simply managed with a binding inner law as in the Kantian ideal. For Hegel it is rather to be overcome through the self-positing nature of spirit, of spirit's own desire to know itself. If we accept Taylor's argument concerning a religiously inspired internalization of moral sources, then it is a short step to acknowledging why the problem of division and unity might become paramount for the subject. It is after all a problem implicit in the socio-cultural world, which according to Hegel finds its early expression in Abraham's break with nature. It does not take too much further speculation, helped by Girardian theory, to see this archetypal separation as having its anthropological bearing in sacrifice, or in collective murder and scapegoating, a point implicit in the Hegelian dialectic.[118] The Romantic divisions of Girard's early work and the community's separation from a part of itself through scapegoating in his later work bespeak a very 'Hegelian' problem.

The persistent yet mistaken belief in one's own 'uniqueness', Girard claims, is responsible for self-divinization and all the historical and human 'developments' that flow from this concealed desire to be God. However, as we saw above, following Herder, the subject as unique and original is the paradigm for the expressivists – in this view it could never be the case that the subject's identity was simply his own, since it was also an integral expression of the whole. Subjectivity may indeed divide us and separate us, but at a higher level it was thought to also generate a greater unity. If 'uniqueness' is the 'mechanism' of division (which is how it appears in Girard's literary criticism), might it not rather be understood as the source of unity in line with Girard's later work? In other words, in and through the community's initial coming together and separation (unanimity *minus* one),

---

118. While Hegel does not posit a 'founding event' as Girard does, and arguably justifies violence by making conflict necessary – as if human beings are God's scapegoats (His means of becoming whole) – we do find in Hegel a preoccupation with sacrifice as somehow efficacious. 'Itself is its own object of attainment and the sole aim of spirit. This result it is, at which the process of the world's history has been continually aiming; and to which the sacrifices that have ever and anon been laid on the vast altar of the earth, through the long lapses of ages, have been offered.' Quoted in Tucker, *Philosophy and Myth in Karl Marx*. p. 48. Reflecting a more nuanced view of Hegel on sacrifice, Taylor writes: 'From the very beginning . . . Hegel does not take up the standpoint of the more austere Enlightenment about religion, that nothing can be believed but what reason licences. He does indeed condemn superstition, where men act in order to bring about a response from the supernatural, say, sacrifice in order to placate an angry God. But he is far from holding that sacrifice has no place in a purified religion if it is done . . . as an expression of dependence on God, rather than a means of avoiding punishment (as Hegel rather unrealistically saw Greek sacrifice).' Taylor, *Hegel*, p. 54.

is there not an implicit identity with the one set apart, the surrogate victim (the source of a unanimity *plus* one)?

7. Conclusion: A Post-Romantic Vision

Both Girard and Taylor place Christianity at the heart of modern division, 'disenchantment' and 'objectification' and yet, as we have seen, they both hold quite different views on how this crisis should be understood. Girard believes that differences belong to the community through original violence; disenchantment erodes the externally mediated 'Degree' of difference because it flattens hierarchies and sends the individual into himself, where degree cannot be maintained simply because the individual lacks the cathartic resources to re-inscribe these differences in an efficacious manner. Hence, '"Individualisation" marks a later, decadent stage in [sacrifices'] evolution, a development contrary to its original impulse.'[119] Taylor argues in a different vein entirely. His preoccupation is with the philosophical developments in western culture, covering a shorter time-span than Girard – from early Greek to Christian, to modern, and then to contemporary periods – and giving primacy to the depth of human experience. These developments he claims have brought about a massive shift in the notion of a constitutive good, an internalization of moral sources based largely on the Protestant affirmation of ordinary life, and subsequently a new and important role for sentiment that gets taken up by the Romantics and articulated as the voice of nature within.

The tensions that I outlined above, arising from the ideals of freedom and expression, are the same tensions that Taylor articulates in *Sources*. The division at the heart of modern freedom – a liberating form of independence at odds with an impulse towards unity and wholeness – is the same division that leaves the modern subject in *Sources* 'constitutionally in tension'.[120] To follow the way of rational control, for which Kant provides the moral template, is to adopt a stance of disengagement from one's own nature and feelings. This in turn impedes the exercise of the creative imagination – so essential for full expression. Kant, as the modern Abraham who 'internalises his jealous law-giving god and calls him reason', becomes emblematic of this conflict and division. When understood historically and culturally it seems that division is indissociable from any concept of identity or unity – because once we begin to reflect (on our experience, our relationships etc.) we are *already divided*. Whether ultimately grounded in the self or the community, absolute unity is predicated on separation, as Hegel acknowledges. We can perhaps now see more clearly that 'division and unity' are written into the modern subject from its inception. The individual, as separate, is

---

119. Girard, *Violence and the Sacred*, p. 101.
120. Taylor, *Sources of the Self*, p. 390.

both *apart from* and *a part of* the whole. This insight finds peculiar anthropological expression in the Judeo-Christian tradition, and gains a positive shape in the modern period with the affirmation of ordinary life. However, as religious horizons begin to fade, the subject's unifying power is increasingly revealed, and not without problems.

The critical aspect of the revolution that took shape in the European imagination was a new mode of inwardness that wanted to include the demands of disengaged rational control and integral powers of expression. Arising out of the early modern disputes that rejected the hierarchical view of nature is a view of *inner nature*, made potent by the expressivist idea of articulation: the inner domain of the self can now be construed as having depth, that is, reaching further than we can ever articulate.[121] Comparing this new domain to what was previously available, Taylor writes:

> That examining the soul should involve the exploration of a vast domain is not, of course, a new idea. The Platonic tradition would concur. But this domain is not an inner one. To understand the soul, we are led to contemplate the order in which it is set, the public order of things. What is new in the post-expressivist era is that the domain is within, that is, it is only open to a mode of exploration which involves the first-person stance. That is what it means to define the voice or impulse as 'inner'.[122]

Up until the eighteenth century the subject that had emerged from the religious developments of the sixteenth century in opposition to the traditional view of cosmic order, was largely defined by disengaged rational control. From the eighteenth century on, according to Taylor, the modern subject is no longer defined by just these powers of instrumental reasoning, but by the new power of self-articulation as well – the power which has been ascribed since the Romantic period to the creative imagination.

Rousseau reminds us that being in touch with ourselves, our 'inner nature', can involve illusion – it can involve a misshaping by the pride and false images that come from the social world but eventually became anchored in the self. His attempt to break with the older hierarchical system of 'preferences' makes him an important hinge figure for Taylor, between the traditional 'honour' system and the modern system of 'dignity'.[123] The key point here for Taylor is that, while having a socially derived identity is no longer an option, the need for recognition by others of one's identity still persists. The difference today is that the fulfilment of this need is no longer guaranteed by social categories that everyone takes for

---

121. Ibid., p. 389.
122. Ibid.
123. Taylor, 'The Politics of Recognition', p. 49.

granted, categories whose meaning is still inscribed within a larger cosmic order.[124] Selfhood has a moral significance for Taylor precisely because of *what is at stake* in having an identity today. While 'the means' of expressing it may be subjective, 'the matter' – what it is about – is tied to the very process of generating meaningful categories that can help replace the significances that were once embedded in a public order of reference.[125]

Exploring the depths of our being need no longer lead us to God, as it did with Augustine. By the mid-nineteenth century a preoccupation with the current of life in the modern period brings a new danger. To the extent that we are taken beyond ourselves in this exploration it is to the larger nature from which we emerged. This nature, while contactable through 'the voice within', cannot offer us a *higher* view of ourselves.[126] With the advances in modern science (evolutionary theory, micro biology, astronomy) that make any special place for humans in the universe ever more questionable, the voice of nature becomes correspondingly uncertain. Our inner sentiments, which thinkers from the moral sense theorists to the Romantic expressivists believed could provide us with a moral compass to help us navigate in an essentially corrupt social world, cease to be trustworthy.

Beginning with Schopenhauerian 'Will', the Romantic 'voice of nature', and the notion of 'inner depths', becomes emptied of its 'idealized content'.[127] By the late nineteenth century our inner depths are seen as amoral and impossible to measure. They amount to no more than a 'blind will' that is indifferent to our basic concerns for happiness and the preservation of life. A master image of this new sense of the human condition is found in Joseph Conrad's *Heart of Darkness*, when Marlow sees the natives for the first time:

> The earth seemed unearthly. We are accustomed to look upon the shackled form of a conquered monster, but there you could look at a thing monstrous and free. It was unearthly, and the men were – No, they were not inhuman. Well, you know, that was the worst of it, – this suspicion of their not being inhuman. It would come slowly on one. They howled and leaped and spun, and made horrid faces; but what thrilled you was just the thought of their humanity – like yours – the thought of your *remote kinship* with this *wild and passionate uproar*. Ugly. Yes it was ugly enough; but if you were man enough you would admit to

---

124. '. . . inwardly derived, personal, original identity doesn't enjoy this recognition *a priori*. It has to win it through exchange, and the attempt can fail. What has come about with the modern age is not the need for recognition but the conditions in which the attempt to be recognised can fail' Taylor, 'The Politics of Recognition', p. 34.
125. Taylor, *The Ethics of Authenticity*, pp. 81–82.
126. Taylor, *Sources of the Self*, p. 390.
127. Terry Eagleton, *The Ideology of the Aesthetic* (Cambridge: Basil Blackwell Press/ Cambridge University Press, 1990), p. 160.

yourself that there was in you just the faintest trace of a response to that terrible noise, a dim suspicion of there being a *meaning* in it which you – you so remote from the night of first ages – could comprehend. And why not? . . . What was there after all? Joy, fear, sorrow, valour, rage – who can tell? – but truth – truth stripped of its cloak of time.[128]

This passage, which Taylor quotes, illustrates the shadow side of the modern story.[129] In a premodern world, religion provides a reliable means of transcendence, whereby certain actions can be deemed good, noble, virtuous etc. The instruments of the Church, informed by religious doctrines, can protect and renew the congregation of faith. However, within the new modern landscape brought about by 'science and progress', the very act of transcendence, that was an unquestioned good in Christian Europe, is opened to the same scrutiny as archaic religion, a scrutiny prompted by our 'remote kinship' with more primordial forms of transcendence. Taylor takes up this theme of 'dark origins' and it's relationship to the pre-Axial sacred in *A Secular Age* – something I will explore in greater detail in the Epilogue.

What Conrad's 'master image' confronts us with, according to Taylor, is a radically post-Romantic vision, one that no longer sees nature as a source of goodness, but rather as the source of 'a wild and passionate uproar' that finds its purest expression in *homo religiosus*. It has one overriding consequence for our 'all too human' nature that is powerfully formulated by Nietzsche in his concept of the will to power: we cannot escape it's meaning for us, however dark and unimaginable. What began as a religious affirmation of ordinary life in the sixteenth century – one that maintained a central place for the good – had by the early twentieth century followed internalization to its ultimate conclusions. Thus, this 'affirmation' unmoors itself from any concept of the good beyond the subject, only to find its human powers struggling on the edge of an abyss. How does the self proceed in a post-Romantic age when the inner depth of the creative imagination – our contact with nature as a reliable source – is so thoroughly cast in doubt? This question is equally relevant to Taylor's own work and how he attempts to recover a historical self. How he goes about answering this question perhaps is the defining move that allows him to respond positively to Girard's anti-subjectivism. The problem posed here for Taylor has to do with the way the self in the modern period can avoid the stance of pure objectivity and rational control, while remaining sufficiently connected or attuned to others and to the world so as to have a meaningful identity-maintaining life. Expression remains for him an indispensable condition of selfhood, even though our modern sources are not wholly reliable

128. Joseph Conrad, *Heart of Darkness and the Secret Sharer* (New York: Bantam Books, 1981), p. 51.
129. Taylor, *Sources of the Self*, p. 417.

after the 'Schopenhauerian turn'. However, despite if not because of the transformations in modern culture, Taylor is a philosopher of the good. The modern subject, in being radically resituated in relation to her moral sources, may be left in uncertain waters with no possibility of returning to the warm gulf stream, or to the peculiar comfort of a dry and ordered topographical landscape. But there is nonetheless a potential to shape the horizon within which one finds oneself and hence to see beyond the danger. The quest is still open. While we may no longer have completely reliable maps to navigate, and while the future may be as much an act of will as a fact of circumstance, Taylor thinks there is still hope for the self. It is to his reasons for this hope that I now turn in the following, final chapter.

CHAPTER 6

CRISIS AND UNITY IN MORAL SPACE:
IDENTITY AND THE GOOD

From the very beginning of the human story religion, our link with the highest, has been recurrently associated with sacrifice, even mutilation, as though something of us has to be torn away or immolated if we are to please the gods.[1]
Charles Taylor

In many cultures, [the] sense of the special importance of the human being is encapsulated in religious and cosmological outlooks, and connected views of social life, which turn it in directions antithetical to modern rights doctrine. Part of what is special about humans is that they are proper food for the gods; or that they embody cosmic principles differently between men and women ... The rights doctrine presents human importance in a radical form, one that is hard to gainsay. This affirmation can be taken on several levels. Just empirically there seems to be something to it, although establishing this is not just a matter of counting heads, but of making a plausible interpretation of human history.[2]
Charles Taylor

1. Introduction

At the end of *Sources of the Self*, having mapped the conflicts of modernity, Taylor confronts a fundamental problem at the heart of the human story. Traditionally, humans managed to survive only within a religious world view, and this world view revealed very early the price of such survival – some significant element of human sacrifice – a price that perhaps we have no good grounds to suppose will cease to be exacted even when we have made the transition to a post-religious world view.[3] Taylor's insight in the first quotation, into the price of human culture

---

1. Taylor, *Sources of the Self: The Making of the Modern Identity* (New York: Cambridge University Press, 1992c), p. 519.
2. Charles Taylor, 'Explanation and Practical Reason', in *Philosophical Arguments* (Cambridge, MA: Harvard University Press, 1995), p. 56.
3. Derrida confronts the problem of sacrifice from a philosophical perspective in his book *The Gift of Death*. Also in his essay 'Faith and Knowledge' he refers to the crisis of thought and decision in the context of sacrifice, as involving a 'price that is priceless'. J. Derrida, *Religion*, eds, J. Derrida and Gianni Vattimo (Oxford: Polity Press, 1998), p. 51. While Derrida highlights the impossibility of deciding in situations that include the trace of religious violence, and hence making transitions (between self and other, or even historically from past to present to future), Taylor

and community, reveals his concern with the forces of religious violence. Something in the very constitution of the human condition suggests that we are separated from ourselves, for better and for worse. Arising from this, both thinkers also share a belief that modern culture rightly reacts against more traditional forms of transcendence that do violence to marginal individuals and or groups. And, somewhat surprisingly, they both agree that this reaction relies on a universalist assumption about the source of our concern for others, albeit an assumption that is often left unarticulated. For, as they both see it, secular culture opposes traditional forms of transcendence, while at the same time drawing inspiration from the older moral and spiritual sources.[4] However, as I argued in Chapter 4, Taylor, unlike Girard, believes that there is a real moral basis to modern culture, although articulating its significance is increasingly difficult. His philosophical history highlights how an internalization of the good first becomes radical around the sixteenth century, and helps to bring about a transformation in values from a hierarchically ordered world, where the supreme good was very much beyond this life, to an order that centred on the individual, thereby giving him or her greater scope to define what the good actually consists in.

But Taylor's story is not by any means an entirely positive one for the individual. What comes about with the loss of the older 'well-ordered' world is a form of 'atomism',[5] not because the individual chooses to live solipsisticly, without social bonds, but rather because the new scientific paradigm dominates to such an extent that one's deepest and highest aspirations towards fulfilment become difficult to express, or to make meaningful. The scientific revolution in its relentless tendency towards reductive materialism does not just cramp human fulfilment, it distrusts all appeals to transcendence. This curtailment on human potential and happiness, according to Taylor, is itself a kind of 'mutilation' that still tends to run very deep in our culture; and, as a result, that individuals experience the profound absence of the earlier deeper and higher form of significance

---

highlights the albeit fraught possibility, of making such decisions/transitions – non-violently – through interpretation and narrative.

4. Charles Taylor, *Sources of the Self*, p. 104. From Girard's point of view modern atheism and talk of the 'death of God' are simultaneously correct and naïve. 'What is in fact dying' Girard tells us, 'is the sacrificial concept of divinity preserved by medieval and modern theology'. Girard, *Things Hidden*, p. 135. Atheism, he believes, is correct in opposing, for the most part, the God of transcendent violence, but naïve in thinking that this is the God of Christian faith. Eugene Webb, *The Self Between: From Freud to the New Social Psychology of France* (Washington: University of Washington Press, 1993), p. 186. The failure to recognize this on behalf of modern atheism means: 'Modern anti-Christianity is merely the reversal of sacrificial Christianity and as a result helps to perpetuate it' Girard, *Things Hidden*, p. 226.

5. Charles Taylor, 'Atomism', in *Philosophy and the Human Sciences: Philosophical Papers 2* (Cambridge: Cambridge University Press, 1985b), p. 187.

without any obvious way of connecting to it and making it their own. This is the source of a general malaise and a profound crisis for the self.[6] Towards the end of Chapter 5 we saw a deepening of the problem of sacrifice as a form of inner division whereby the self for all its good intentions to generate unity is left in dark and uncertain territory.

Hence, both Taylor and Girard share the view that the modern world is a source of crisis, but for Taylor the need for a concept of the good is stronger that ever. As Guy Vanheeswijck points out, 'Girard focuses on what has been lost in the constitution of the modern subject; Taylor does not undervalue such a loss, but is precisely in search of an articulation of moral sources which have constituted the modern subject in order to *compensate for* this loss.'[7] For Taylor the crisis in modern culture is a 'crisis of identity' centred on the self, developing in history – a self as the locus not only of the crisis but also of any attempted resolution of it. For Girard, modern culture is a crisis of difference – a sacrificial crisis – that has its origins in a world whose restorative resources are in decline. For him the modern 'divisions within the self' are *non*-recuperable because the individual lacks the necessary cathartic mechanism that properly belongs only to the community. Within a functioning sacred order this mechanism helps maintain what Girard calls the anthropological principle of Degree as salutary preserver of differences, thereby channelling violence creatively to protect against crisis. In its search for self-fulfilment modern individualism fails to realize that its freedom is ultimately stifling. But as we saw Girard's own theoretical attempt to merge his later work with his early work only compounds the difficulty of forging a conception of the self that, in the absence of the earlier 'anthropological principle', can withstand the loss of hierarchy; and this difficulty is further reinforced by the anti-subjectivist import of what I have called his 'reifying of desire' – thereby creating even greater problems for any ethical attempt to confront religious violence.

In outlining Taylor's philosophical history in Chapters 4 and 5 I argued that Taylor can respond positively to a number of problematic motifs in Girard's theory, which (if left as they are) prevent us from understanding Girard's anthropology in a context of human development. These motifs, addressed in Chapter 4, are: (1) the loss of positive interiority as an aberration of Augustine's concept of the will, (2) a conflation of two distinct concepts of generosity that misses what is radical about modern reflexivity and (3) an account of order that focuses only on what is lost – to the exclusion of early modern religious developments. Taylor's account of early modern developments, and in particular the ethic of ordinary

---

6. As Taylor is aware this crisis has been recognized by a number of important thinkers in different ways: for example, classic thinkers of modernity such as, Weber, Tocqueville and Nietzsche, and more recent cultural critics such as Christopher Lash and Allan Bloom.

7. Guy Vanheeswijck, 'The Place of René Girard in Contemporary Philosophy', *Contagion: Journal of Violence, Mimesis and Culture.* Vol. 10, 2003, p. 107.

life, allows us to re-imagine the transition to the modern period as containing an inspiration to greater individual participation in the ordering process – in the name of benevolence and the reduction of suffering (broadly: human flourishing). Many of those thinkers preoccupied with a providential order in nature were also concerned with our inner sentiments and our connection to nature as a source of good. The Romantic Movement took this development a stage further through its tendency to an identifiable form of theism with a conception of inner depths. These depths prompt us to be in touch with the 'current of life', and to put shape on our own life, thereby avoiding socially induced illusions. However, this deepening of the initial transposition of order brought new dangers. At the end of the previous chapter, I broached the problem that arises for modern theory when subjectivity becomes unmoored from a reliable concept of the good and then carried into the treacherous waters of blind will. Taylor's own solution to this problem is articulated in his philosophical anthropology, which attempts to take seriously the historical concerns that pertain to the internalization of the good, and, following from this, the emergence of the individual's creative powers. Thus his philosophical history and his philosophical anthropology are interrelated – interpretation at one level informs interpretation at the other and *vice versa*. As we shall explore in this chapter, the transcendental conditions of subjectivity, that form the basis of his philosophical anthropology, open out onto a broad narrative and the deeply historical self already discussed in Chapters 4 and 5.[8]

Even when we can show that Taylor successfully meets the challenges posed by Girard – by demonstrating that order is transposed rather than eroded in the early modern period – we are still left with the even greater challenge of showing how Taylor's conception of selfhood can respond positively to the problems posed for this self by the 'Schopenhauerian turn'. These problems concern a kind of 'impenetrability' (Conrad), a radical alienation from ourselves and, therefore, the impossibility of knowing and doing the good. If we are to convince Girardians that their anti-subjectivism is in danger of adding to these Schopenhauerian forces that leave individuals at the mercy of a primal agency that can erupt in violence, we need also to convince them of an alternative to reifying desire: we need to show that Taylor's philosophical anthropology is also equipped to tackle Girard's concerns about 'ontology'.[9] In other words, we need to make the case that Taylor's philosophical anthropology can deal with crisis (both individual and cultural) more thoroughly and, perhaps, more convincingly than Girard does. For Girard, as I have argued, presents a flawed conception of subjectivity (one that conceals an unfounded dichotomy), a subjectivity which he then alleges is unable

---

8. Describing Taylor's project, Smith writes: 'Transcendental analysis must be refracted through historical understanding.' Nicholas H. Smith, *Charles Taylor: Meaning, Morals, and Modernity* (Cambridge: Polity Press, 2002), p. 7.
9. These concerns, discussed in Chapter 1, relate to Girard's analysis of modern subjectivity as the form of an 'ontological illness', 'self-divinization', etc.

to cope with the 'modern sacrificial crisis'. This internal problem in Girard's theory, as I have argued in Chapters 2 and 3, stems from the 'unity of novelistic conclusions' at the end of *Deceit, Desire, and the Novel,* and the exclusion of the Romantic hero and hence any genuine condition of subjectivity. As I have shown, Girard's early and later works are *not* continuous. And his own scapegoating of the subject precludes any alternative – more positive – account of the self. How might Taylor's conception of selfhood avoid the initial problem that pertains to Girard's conception of subjectivity, and then proceed to tackle, in a serious – because now self-conscious – manner the 'burning concerns' that the latter has about modern individualism and its inability to cope with undifferentiation and crisis?

In the context of our overall discussion thus far of selfhood and sacrifice (crisis and unity), we might identify Girard's key concerns as, (A) the vicissitudes of desire, (B) the inability of the individual to 're-mark' difference, (C) the modern loss of difference, and (D) the need for unity as a still enduring, though deeply fraught, need today. In light of Girard's later theory of religious violence, and the centrality of the scapegoat mechanism in the generation of human culture and order, the self simply does not have the resources to meet these concerns in a satisfactory manner. The greater part of this chapter will be given over to analysing some of the key concepts of Taylor's philosophical anthropology and to arguing that they can meet these Girardian concerns. My aim is to argue that Taylor is also a thinker of crisis, which, for him, as we have seen in the previous two chapters, has deep historical roots. I hope to show that his analysis of the self as a human agent, and its capacity to cope with crisis in a more subjective space of reflexivity, is all the time informed by the broader background of contemporary culture. Thus the two spaces of crisis that, as we saw in part one, pertain to Girard's account of the self/other relation, and the communal space of ritual and Degree, for Taylor can never be separated out.

Section two of this chapter, then, will tackle the first two of Girard's key concerns, namely 'the vicissitudes of desire', and 'the inability of the individual to "re-mark" difference', by considering Taylor's conception of 'strong evaluation' as a way of breaking out of the circularity of imitative desire, and 'moral space' as a space of reflection and orientation through which we can make the kinds of distinctions that provide meaning, thereby compensating for the loss of the earlier now more contested categories of difference. In this section the issue of identity also arises in a way that will enable me to show that it is crucial to the whole *aporia* of difference that we meet in Girard's theory. Section three, then, will tackle Girard's third key concern, namely, 'the modern loss of difference', by considering the importance that Taylor places on modern 'disenchantment' and the centrality he gives to understanding the loss of meaning that can attend the subjectivizing of order, while still maintaining the viability of moral space for the formation of individual identity. Section four will tackle Girard's fourth key concern, namely, 'the need for unity as a still enduring, though deeply fraught, need today', and will do so by considering Taylor's conception of a human life driven by a craving or quest that – while allowing for certain kinds of death and rebirth – can be gathered (more or less) into a narrative unity over the whole life-course.

2. Moral Space: Strong Value, Identity and Gaining Orientation

The factors that generate crisis for the self in the modern period, discussed in Chapters 1 and 2 in the context of literary and cultural space, have to do with the strictly imitative and reactive nature of the subject's desires albeit that they appear all the time to be seeking to establish the Romantic hero's identity as *separate*.[10] The illusions of literary space are only confirmed for Girard by his later analysis of cultural space when imitative desire – *in extremis* – is explained as the catalyst of cultural crisis; the individual's belief in originality, her 'metaphysical desire', is now seen as the effect of her broader culture, and the deterioration of this culture's organizing power – the scapegoat mechanism. However, as I argued in Chapter 5, Girard's analysis of the Romantic concern with originality as somehow preoccupied with separation is in fact mistaken. The Romantic Movement itself, as it developed from its initial impetus in 'moral sense theory' to its central doctrine of 'nature as source', was preoccupied with *connection* rather than separation – a connection to self, to others, to nature and to the cosmos – and through this connection, with the possibility of integral expression. Girard's account of the imitative and reactive nature of the modern individual's desires – and his or her quest for original identity – appears grossly overdrawn. Is Girard's conception of desire really credible or helpful for thinking about human agents and their experience of crisis today?

By describing desire as 'mimetic', Girard makes a distinction between human and animal (or non-human) needs and desires.[11] Fleming explains this as

---

10. In *Deceit, Desire, and the Novel*, Girard understands the Romantic view as 'mech-anistic' and 'divisive', while for Taylor, as we have seen in Chapter 5, it is precisely the reaction against these characteristics that distinguishes Romanticism and, in particular, expressivism from other forms of modern freedom that embrace mech-anism, atomism and technical control. See René Girard, *Deceit, Desire, and the Novel: Self and Other in Literary Structure*, trans. Yvonne Freccero (Baltimore: Johns Hopkins University Press, 1965) pp. 188–298. See also Charles Taylor, *The Ethics of Authenticity* (London: Harvard University Press, 1992a), chap. 1.

11. Webb draws our attention to this distinction between what he refers to as 'appe-tites and needs' and 'desires', which is discussed by Girard and Oughlourlian in *Things Hidden*, p. 283, and *To Double Business Bound: Essays on Literature, Mimesis, Anthropology* (Baltimore: Johns Hopkins University Press), p. 90. Webb's own contention is that this distinction "is of more fundamental importance than the authors realize, and has not yet been fully developed". Eugene Webb, *The Self Between: From Freud to the New Social Psychology of France* (Washington: University of Washington Press, 1993), p. 8 (also see footnote, p. 8).

follows: '. . . although animal needs for hydration, shelter, rest and nutrition persist at the human level, they do not in themselves constitute "desire" *per se*. Any of these needs may serve as pretexts for the formation for desire, but by themselves, are not sufficient for it.'[12] Unlike human 'needs', which, being biological and arising from particular situations, can at least be met, 'desire', from a Girardian point of view, 'can emerge in the absence of any genuine appetite at all'.[13] Thus, unlike human or animal needs, it is 'indeterminate', and so prone to 'fascinations with objects and figures that possess not only use values, but symbolic values as well'.[14] The key difference is perhaps that we can imagine an individual satisfying his or her needs regardless of belonging to a group, but we cannot in the Girardian scheme imagine desire even arising for the same individual without the presence of others.

Such an apparent disjuncture in Girard's theory between 'needs' and 'desires' is not part of Taylor's understanding of human agency. Human beings desire, and have a capacity for reason and hence agency, by virtue of reflection. Desires are not 'grafted on to the needs and appetites of animal life'[15] as if the apparent symbiosis here is actually determined by the collective. To be a human agent (whatever about a hominoid) is, as an individual, to reflect on and evaluate one's desires. This reflection, and what Taylor calls the 'strong evaluation' accompanying it, underpins a distinction between 'first order' and 'second order' desires that Taylor borrows from the moral philosopher Harry Frankfurt.[16]

> First order desires are desires that human beings share with other animals. Animals desire food, a mate, to avert danger and so forth and their behaviour can be explained in terms of whatever is required to satisfy their desires. Human beings have similar 'first order' desires or appetites, but their behaviour is also motivated by positive or negative feelings about the desires themselves. Human beings have the capacity to evaluate their desires accordingly, and they are often motivated to act on the basis of such evaluations. 'Second-order' desires, then, are desires about desires, desires which enable us to arbitrate between motives and so to act in a way that is distinctive of human agency.[17]

Admittedly, the distinction between first and second order desires depicted here appears to align with the distinction we have just seen between what Girard terms 'needs' and 'desires'. However, Taylor believes, if we fail to ask the important

---

12. Chris Fleming, *René Girard: Violence and Mimesis* (Cambridge: Polity Press, 2004), p. 11.
13. Ibid.
14. Ibid.
15. Ibid.
16. See Charles Taylor, 'What is Human Agency?', in *Human Agency and Language. Philosophical Papers, 1* (Cambridge: Cambridge University Press, 1985b).
17. Smith, *Charles Taylor: Meaning, Morals, and Modernity*, p. 89.

question concerning what we do when we evaluate different desires we will miss the more significant feature of human agency that reflection on desire brings out. Smith explains the distinction through which Taylor gets at this significance.

> On the one hand, we can weigh up which of the desires will, as a matter of fact, provide the most satisfaction. Faced with the choice, say, between desirable flavours of ice cream, I can compare the strength of the desires I happen to have and I can choose on the basis of my stronger desire. The decisive issue in my evaluation is just what I happen to feel like. Taylor calls this 'weak evaluation'. But a quite different issue is at stake, Taylor remarks when we find ourselves evaluating desires in terms of their *worth*. So, for instance, petty feelings of spite might incline me one way, but I am also aware that I can be moved by a more generous spirit. What counts now is the way I locate or interpret the feelings, that is, how I characterise them as something base and petty, or as something higher and more admirable.[18]

For the human agent, as strong evaluator, the world is charged with significance. By discerning the worth of her desires she can help make them part of a worthwhile life.[19] With this distinction between weak and strong evaluation we are better able to grasp Taylor's concept of the self and how we come to possess an identity, and, importantly, we can begin to see the role of our desires and motivations in this process.

For Taylor, reflection on desire always takes place within a moral framework. An individual's identity, then, as strongly valued, can be understood as being defined by the fundamental commitments and identifications that go into providing the 'frame' within which he or she can try to determine in each case what is good or valuable, or what should be done.[20] One's framework becomes the horizon within which one is capable of taking a stand.[21] On this understanding of identity, a Catholic, anarchist, an atheist or a Jew, is not just strongly attached to a particular spiritual view or background; rather this view or background provides the frame within which they can determine where they stand on questions

---

18. Ibid.
19. According the Smith, 'Taylor is not just claiming that the strong evaluator is more articulate about his options . . . For he is also claiming there can only be said to be a range of options on account of their "desirability-characterizations". The range of possibilities facing the strong evaluator does not pre-exist the articulation of his desires or purposes, as if the weak evaluator had simply overlooked them. The nuance and depth with which the strong evaluator reflects upon his desires and purposes finds its way into the desires and purposes themselves.' Smith, *Charles Taylor: Meaning, Morals, and Modernity*, p. 90.
20. For further discussion of 'strong evaluation' see Taylor, 'Explanation and Practical Reason'. In this important essay, Taylor already anticipates much of the core of his argument in *Sources of the Self*.
21. Taylor, *Sources of the Self*, p. 27.

of what is good, worthwhile or of value. Conversely, if they were to lose this commitment or identification they would be lost with regard to a range of important
questions in determining the significance things have for them. We call this
condition, which is tied to a loss of meaning, an 'identity crisis'. In not knowing
who they are, people who experience this condition lack a frame or horizon
within which things can take on a relatively stable significance and have value.[22]
According to Taylor this painful and terrifying experience brings to light the
essential link between identity and a kind of orientation.[23] 'To know who you are
is to be oriented in moral space, a space in which questions arise about what is
good or bad, what is worth doing and what is not, what has meaning and importance for you and what is trivial and secondary.'[24] Our framework then is our
limit, our horizon, within which we take a stand and gain orientation. The question of identity ('who am I?') and its relationship to orientation, are part of a particularly modern discourse. The frameworks that were embedded in nature –
and taken for granted by human beings – no longer provide a viable set of
co-ordinates for personal meaning. Today, our identities, as defined by whatever
gives us our fundamental orientation, have been 'disembedded' from such older
ontic orders and have become complex and many-tiered.[25]

The 'who' question, presupposes a subject who can answer this question for
him or herself, an interlocutor among others, someone with his or her own standpoint or position.

> But to be able to answer for oneself is to know where one stands, what one
> wants to answer. And that is why we naturally tend to talk of our fundamental
> orientation in terms of who we are. To lose this orientation, or not to have
> found it, is not to know who one is. And this orientation, once attained, defines
> where you answer from, hence your identity.[26]

Speaking for oneself has a moral accent. One's identity, which allows one to find
one's bearings and plot a course through strong evaluation, is largely constituted

---

22. The frameworks, within which these values reside, whether, for example, British,
    Catholic, anarchist or combinations of all three, are not simply dispensable inter-
    pretations, a point that often appears muted in Girard's discourse. In fact, Taylor
    argues that doing without the frameworks that constitute our qualitative distinc-
    tions is utterly impossible. The horizons within which we live our lives and make
    sense of them have to include these strong qualitative distinctions: living within
    these strongly qualified horizons is constitutive of human agency. Taylor, *Sources
    of the Self*, p. 27.
23. Taylor, *Sources of the Self*, p. 28.
24. Ibid.
25. Ibid., p. 29.
26. Ibid.

in moral space. This space, for Taylor, is 'ontologically basic'.[27] The question for his enquiry into selfhood thus becomes: through what framework-definition can I best find my bearings in this moral space. To live in a space of questions to which strong value and framework definitions provide answers is to have a number of co-ordinates. The qualitative distinctions that we make in order to arrive at these co-ordinates provide a quasi 'map of moral space'; they permit us to find the precise horizon within which we know where we stand, and what meanings things have for us.[28] Hence our identity, as an active process of discernment and deliberation, is inextricable from orienting ourselves in a space of concern, and of meaning. In other words, by incorporating the qualitative distinctions that need to be clarified within this space, our identity is both defined by strongly valued preferences and also defines the space of qualitative distinctions within which we live and choose.[29] Making qualitative distinctions, discovering meaning and 'marking difference' for oneself, has (*pace* Girard) a subjective dimension. Moral space provides the conditions for working out the personally nuanced solutions to a range of problems whose solutions were once presented impersonally as 'readymade' by a religious world view.

Within the picture just outlined we cannot choose to be lost or have an identity crisis, because being lost or in crisis results from a failure to make qualitative distinctions and to find meaning. To be able to choose in this context means to be able to make just such qualitative distinctions. The issue of having an identity is thus closely tied to the issue of not being in crisis, since working on your identity is the very process of getting clear on the things that are of significance to you. Moral space, for Taylor, thus provides the conditions for helping to resolve a fundamental problem concerning selfhood in the modern period. Our frameworks arise from attempts to answer questions that inescapably exist for us today in the absence of a traditional religious world view. The person who chooses poorly is still operating within a framework unlike the person who is experiencing what we commonly call an 'identity crisis'. 'To be without any sense of strong value, as Taylor depicts it, is to suffer a painful and frightening emptiness.'[30] It is because frameworks can fail, while at the same time they are of such defining importance for us, that Taylor believes we ought to define them as best we can:

> One orients oneself in a space which exists independently of one's success or failure in finding one's bearings, which makes the task of finding these bearings

---

27. Ibid. Smith makes the point that Taylor's hermeneutics (especially his explication of moral space) owes a dept to Heidegger. See Nicholas H. Smith, 'Taylor and the Hermeneutical Tradition', in R. Abbey, ed. *Contemporary Philosophy in Focus: Charles Taylor* (New York: Cambridge University Press, 2004), p. 34.
28. Ibid.
29. Taylor, *Sources of the Self*, p. 30.
30. Smith, *Charles Taylor: Meaning, Morals, and Modernity*, p. 93.

inescapable. Within this picture, the notion of inventing a qualitative distinction out of whole cloth makes no sense for one can only adopt such distinctions as make sense to one within one's basic orientation.[31]

Once we begin to reflect on our desires we are already in a space of concern that presupposes some sense of 'higher or lower', in other words a space that gives meaning to our choices. Without some implicit sense of a standard, we cannot, on Taylor's account, be said to be operating within the terms of an 'identity'. Hence even a desiring subject disoriented by false imitation, to the extent that he is making distinctions at all, is still orientating himself within the parameters of a personally derived identity. The limits that we draw (if and when we do draw limits) are drawn from our knowledge of what we actually do.

It follows from Taylor's account of frameworks as 'necessary', that the many different religious accounts of 'the shape of the divine' are not simply answers to questions that might one day disappear from human concern. Modern identity does not presuppose or imply the loss of religious frameworks. And just as traditional religious claims should not be written off as 'ontologically queer', orientation should not be thought of as the answer to an artificial, dispensable question concerning 'who I am'. Rather it is impossible to conceive of a form in which this question is not 'always already' there, demanding an answer: as a moral subject, I can no more do without some orientation in moral space than as a moving body I can do without some orientation – some sense of front and behind, left and right, above and below – in physical space.[32] For Taylor, any epistemological position that fails to take account of this question (an actual failure bearing on a widespread identity crisis in western culture today) ignores or suppresses what we actually do when we try to make sense of our lives on a whole range of questions concerning our identity and its relationship to the good. The subject within Girardian theory, caught up as she is within an entirely imitative and reactive space, cannot locate herself within a space of questions concerning the good and hence cannot even begin to evaluate in a strong way with respect to the significance of her life. In the space that Girard articulates, it is unclear how the 'framework definitions' can provide the basis of an identity that might help the subject in the throes of crisis to gain orientation. Moral space, as ontologically basic (or existentially inescapable), permits subjects to gain such orientation to the good, by evaluating their desires and purposes in a strong way (thereby working through illusions to the greater clarity afforded by qualitative distinctions).

3. *Disenchantment: Modern Crisis, and Being Lost in Moral Space*

For Girard, human beings, as individuals, lack a cathartic mechanism, and thus the loss of degree in the modern period ushers in a sacrificial crisis. Taylor's

---

31. Taylor, *Sources of the Self*, pp. 30–31.
32. Smith, 'Taylor and the Hermeneutical Tradition', p. 39.

philosophical history allows us to see that the breakdown of traditional forms of order and clearly marked differences is partly brought about by the establishing of a new providential order. But Taylor also tells of a crisis that is brought about by the loss of what he calls traditional religious frameworks. The sense of meaning that such hierarchical and otherworldly views once imparted appears impossible to replace. Yet the very thing that makes human life valuable is tied up for Taylor with the possibility of finding or making such meaning. The moral world of moderns is made significantly different from previous civilizations by our sense today that human beings command our respect. This can readily be seen in the importance we place on avoiding suffering.[33] The notion that we ought to reduce suffering to a minimum is an integral part of what respect means to us today. Girard refers to this new value as arising from what he describes as the modern concern for victims.[34] For Taylor, the importance of reducing suffering can be explained by the decline of belief in a cosmic order that required us to ritually undo a terrible crime often with an equally terrible punishment. In the past 'suffering' was often institutionalized in a set of practices that were concerned with balancing the books. To punish someone was in some ways to pay a debt to nature. 'In the language of the time the criminal must make *amende honorable*.'[35] In his essay on Foucault, Taylor draws our attention to the 'radical discontinuity' between such organized violence and the sense that modern democratic societies normally have of themselves.[36] Such 'punishment', described by Foucault in the context of its own time as a kind of 'liturgy', seems to moderns a form of sadism.[37] 'Human beings are set in a cosmic order, or constituted by a hierarchy of beings which is also a hierarchy of goods. They stand . . . in a political order, which is related and in some sense endorsed by the cosmic order.'[38] If this was once the case, our notions of respect now are emphatically opposed to orders of this kind that require human beings to suffer, and in a sense to be sacrificed.

---

33. Taylor, *Sources of the Self*, p. 12.
34. René Girard, *I See Satan Fall Like Lightning*.
35. 'Certain kinds of crime – parricide is a good example – are offences against this order . . . They do not just represent damage done to the interests of certain other individuals . . . They represent a violation of the order, tearing things out of their place, as it were. And so punishment is not just a matter of making reparations for damage inflicted . . . The order must be set right.' Charles Taylor, 'Foucault on Freedom and Truth', in *Philosophy and the Human Sciences: Philosophical Papers 2*, p. 154.
36. Ibid.
37. Ibid. The bigger the crime the more that time was 'put out of joint' (to paraphrase Shakespeare's Hamlet), and therefore the greater the punishment required to set things right. Taylor discusses the meaning of organized violence in a premodern context – the significance it had for a public order. See also, Taylor, 'Explanation and Practical Reason', p. 55.
38. Ibid.

But regardless of how brutal these older orders could be, and however much they, in today's view, unjustly restricted and excluded other than dominant groups, the meaning that they provided was a stabilizing force. Both Taylor and Girard agree that the loss of this older 'transcendent' order, as the basis of a meaningful whole, is the main challenge of the modern age. For Taylor, providential Deism provided something of a solution (as we saw in the context of the initial breach with an *ontic* view). However, he believes that the problem is exacerbated today because of strongly naturalist tendencies deeply entrenched in the human sciences as well as the natural sciences themselves that deny *tout court* any validity to transcendent frameworks.[39] When this denial then gains a further foothold in a great deal of influential philosophical discourse some of our most important moral distinctions are left inarticulate and unexpressed. It is these distinctions that might otherwise step into the vacuum created by the eclipse of the earlier 'meaningful' order(s) and open the way to other possibilities of meaning.

Largely for this reason Taylor, in *Sources*, explores the sense we make of moral intuitions that have for millennia provided meaning and standards for action. In doing so, he attempts to retrieve the moral ideal behind the self's motivated search.[40] Since, as long as the true motivation of our actions and beliefs remains implicit, unexplored and even hidden – as tends to happen within a narrow range of scientific, instrumental and procedural criteria – questions about substantive meaning and 'the good' likewise remain inaccessible. Even modern rights doctrines eschew our motivational connection to the good.[41] Hence, the background

---

39. Taylor's quarrel here is not just with naturalism but also with a great deal of contemporary political philosophy which, under the banner of a procedural or neutral liberalism (Dworkin, Scanlan, Rawls), seeks to exclude substantive moral issues (other than those concerning distributive justice) from the domain of 'public reason'.

40. Broadly, Taylor's claim here is that what begins as a mode of 'access' to the world, once objectified through language, becomes a discernible set of ontological claims that can be rationally argued. It is this argument or conversation that he attempts to cultivate in *Sources of the Self*, with such diverse historical thinkers as Plato, Augustine, Rousseau, Descartes, Locke, Shaftsbury, Hutcheson and a range of modern literary figures, some of whom we encountered in Chapter 4.

41. On the 'priority of the right over the good' in contemporary moral philosophy see Charles Taylor, 'Iris Murdoch and Moral Philosophy', in Maria Antonaccio William Schweiker, ed. *Iris Murdoch and the Search for Human Goodness* (Chicago and London: Chicago University Press, 1996b). The kind of problem that arises here can perhaps be seen in the following example: I believe in capital punishment, as both punitive and preventative, but also feel, at a deeper unexpressed level, that the taking of human life is a violation of a person's inherent dignity. The suppression of moral frameworks adds to the confusion here, and ignores the substantive issue (what constitutes a person's inherent dignity). The silence the more proceduralist views promote runs counter to an ethics that would reclaim its moral sources and come clean about its moral frameworks.

picture that might provide a plausible interpretation of our journey so far – and what drives out highest aspirations and our deepest concerns – remains fraught and unclear.

In other words, there is a lot of 'suppression' today of what it means to be a self.[42] Taylor's concern about this suppression, and the silence that it breeds, is focused on the lack of fit between what people officially and consciously believe and what they need to make sense of their actual moral reactions.[43] We draw on frameworks when we have to make sense of our responses and when we have to defend these responses as the right ones. In the past, when moral frameworks enjoyed unquestioned allegiance, the process was more straightforward. Within the contemporary liberal philosophical climate that cramps our impulses toward more substantive ends, people often remain unaware of the constituents of their beliefs and unclear about their true motivations. 'Many of our contemporaries deny ontology altogether.'[44] This denial, and not the denial of 'Romantic originality', is, for Taylor, the cause of crisis today because – operative in the 'soft-relativism' prevalent through much of contemporary thought – it refuses to even engage in deliberations about what makes for a worthy, fulfilled, or meaningful life.

The undermining of our sense of the cosmos as a meaningful order, what Weber calls the 'disenchantment of the world,' has destroyed the 'taken-for-granted' horizons in which people previously lived their moral and spiritual lives.[45] The question of meaning, or of thinking about the point of one's life, never arose for people prior to the modern age. Today, by contrast, 'dignity' (the basic condition of a self-derived identity) is on everyone's lips but achieving it is more and more difficult. As Taylor observes, the older horizons that satisfied this human longing – in the case of, for example, Corneille – have disappeared, a fact well captured by Nietzsche's madman.[46] This loss of traditional frameworks generates a sense of disorientation, one that appears very close to what Girard describes as 'the breakdown of difference' – although it is never total or absolute for modern

---

42. Taylor, *Sources of the Self*, p. 10.
43. Ibid., p. 9.
44. Ibid., p. 10.
45. Ibid., pp. 16–17.
46. By evoking Nietzsche here Taylor, unlike Girard, links disenchantment to 'the death of God' in a way that is less directly tied to sacrifice and more tied to a definite loss of meaning in the modern period. Girard sees this as the quintessential move by modern atheism, the loss of the 'suprasensible in the Platonic sense', and argues that when compared to the full-blooded collective murder that it actually masks, it should be seen as a 'harmless cliché.' René Girard, 'Nietzsche versus the Crucified', in Williams, James G., ed. *The Girard Reader*, (New York: Crossroads Publishing, 2003b, p. 257. Such a criticism would be wrong-headed in the context of Taylor's analysis of the modern period, since he is clearly not interpreting disenchantment as a form of atheism.

culture as it perhaps was in local contexts for earlier societies. Describing the crisis that threatens the modern seeker, compared to his premodern precursor, Taylor writes 'the world loses altogether its spiritual contour, nothing is worth doing, the fear is of a terrifying emptiness, a kind of vertigo, or even fracturing of our world and body space.'[47] People's sense of emptiness, futility and lack of purpose today is well documented by psychoanalysts and is arguably related to the dissolution of their horizons of meaning.[48] While some individuals may suffer the consequences of this crisis more than others, Taylor argues that we still '[need] frameworks to know where we stand on issues'.[49]

For many people an ultimately believable framework is the object of an uncertain 'quest' that can fail, and to fail in this respect is to fail to find meaning, to fail to make sense.[50] The quest then, is always a quest for sense.[51] This sense is found or made through articulating it, and because, for us moderns, so much here depends on our powers of expression, what we find, by way of a framework, is interwoven with what we invent. More and more today, we attain meaning by making sense through our expressive powers. To put it bluntly, the point of our lives is bound up with our attempts to find just such a point.[52] As older horizons

---

47. Taylor, *Sources of the Self*, p. 18.
48. Taylor, *Sources of the Self*, p. 19. It has become a commonplace in psychotherapeutic writing to highlight the culturally mediated shift in the dominant mode of psychological ailment from the kind of hysteria classically diagnosed by Freud to contemporary forms of narcissism as a kind of meaning deprivation. See, for example, J. Schumaker, *The Age of Insanity: Modernity and Mental Health.* (Connecticut: Praeger, 2001) and C. Lasch, *The Culture of Narcissism* (New York: Norton, 1991). As relevant as psychopathology is in describing our moral malaise, Taylor is mainly concerned here to point out the conspiracy of silence around moral frameworks, which as well as undermining the psychological resources to help us on our quest, also leaves our basic moral intuitions hidden, thereby allowing the more instrumental and procedural activities to triumph over the more substantive ones without contest.
49. Smith, *Charles Taylor: Meaning, Morals, and Modernity*, p. 92.
50. Taylor, *Sources of the Self*, p. 17.
51. Ibid., p. 18.
52. This 'sense of things' is central for Taylor. It is inherently expressive; its purpose is to somehow become articulate. He does not see every individual as being capable of mustering the expressive powers necessary to reclaim their moral sources. Rather he suggests that it may be left to historians, philosophers, and anthropologists to try to formulate explicitly what goods, qualities, or ends are at stake here. Taylor, *Sources of the Self*, p. 21. Our individual lives become reflections of a much broader historical background picture. We are carried by tradition, or what the hermeneutical philosopher Hans-Georg Gadamer, calls 'effective history'. Speaking of this concept of history in Gadamer's work David E. Ling writes: 'The words and concepts of a particular language reveal an initiative of being: the language of a time is not so much chosen by the persons who use it as it is their

fade frameworks take on moral significance by incorporating a crucial set of qualitative distinctions which allows us to function with the sense that some action, feeling, way of being is incomparably higher than the others. Once again moral space, in Taylor's philosophical anthropology, becomes the most basic condition for determining the significance of these distinctions for identity in an age of cultural crisis.

Taylor sees himself as arguing against various forms of 'atomism' when he makes the point that 'a self can never be described without reference to those who surround it.'[53] And Girard, of course, would also rightly acknowledge that other people are intrinsic to my sense of self. But unlike rationalist and materialist accounts of the self, and unlike Girard who gives no play to human agency, Taylor sees language as having a definitive role in helping to shape the conditions of selfhood.[54] I am who I am only in conversation with others where objects take on meaning in a *strong* sense – not just for 'me' but for 'us'.[55] A self exists only within what Taylor calls 'webs of interlocution' where I define who I am (in so far as I can) through shared meanings arising in a community that is always original, or primary, in the sense of being always already there, before my arriving in it.

> It is this original situation which gives its sense to our concept of 'identity' offering an answer to the question of who I am through a definition of where I am speaking from and to whom. The full definition of someone's identity usually involves not only his stand on moral and spiritual matters, but also some reference to a defining community.[56]

The two dimensions of identity-definition (the 'where from' and the 'to whom') reflect the original situation out of which the whole issue of identity arises. However, according to Taylor, modern culture has tended to occlude the second dimension (interlocution), as if it were of significance only early on in one's development and should play no part in one's more mature life as an adult. And so, while a break with our early community is indeed part of discovering our own path in life, independent positions still remain embedded in 'webs of interlocution'. It is through language that 'we remain related to partners of discourse, either in

historical fate – the way being has revealed itself to and concealed itself from them as their starting point.' Hans-Georg Gadamer, Philosophical Hermeneutics, trans., and ed. David E. Ling (Berkeley: University of California Press, 1977), p. lv.
53. Taylor, *Sources of the Self*, p. 35.
54. Taylor follows Bruner and Wittgenstein on this issue. Elsewhere he discusses the significance of a language community in terms of Herder's contribution to language theory. See 'The Importance of Herder', in *Philosophical Arguments*, in *Isaiah Berlin: A Celebration*, eds, Edna and Avishai Margalit (Cambridge, MA: Harvard University Press, 1991b), p. 98.
55. Taylor, *Sources of the Self*, p. 35.
56. Ibid., p. 36.

real live exchanges, or in indirect exchanges.'[57] In some instances – for example the Puritan experience in North America – the very act of leaving home to search for one's own way in life can only be understood in the context of a tradition whereby, ironically, the command to be self-sufficient arises out of the community itself. This provides a nice example, for Taylor, of the 'transcendental embedding of independence in interlocution' discussed above.[58] Furthermore, it shows the weakness of the 'interdividual' position that gives priority to 'webs of desire'[59] over 'webs of interlocution'.[60]

Our mode of being and sharing a language with other agents ties in with the connections Taylor outlines between our sense of self and our sense of the good – value relations once again provide the context or background picture to who I am. He extends this picture in showing that the same issues are involved when it comes to discerning our sense of our life as a whole and the direction it is taking as we lead it.[61] Narrative unity plays an important role in shaping this direction, as we shall see below. To set the context for this discussion Taylor retraces some of his footsteps here. He reminds us that by looking at qualitative distinctions as a way of gaining orientation in an existing space of 'inescapable' questions about the good, we see that having a moral outlook, like having an interlocutor, is not an optional extra. Arising from this complex of relations that we must all the time get clarity on, the spatial metaphor takes on a new significance. There are now two ways we can have or fail to have orientation. 'I can be ignorant of the lie of the land around me – not know the important locations which make it up or how they relate to each other. This ignorance can be cured by a good map. But then I can be lost in another way if I don't know how to place myself on this map.'[62]

---

57. Ibid., p. 38.
58. Ibid., p. 39.
59. Webb, *The Self Between*, p. 91.
60. On the more dialogical nature of 'in-between-ness', which interdividual psychology eschews in favour of what it understands as the more determining 'webs of desire', Joseph Dunne writes (with reference to Hannah Arendt): 'This . . . "in-between" – called the "web of relationships" by Arendt – which is constituted by deeds and words but which "is not tangible, since there are no tangible objects into which it could solidify" makes up the very substance of human affairs ("the realm of human affairs, strictly speaking, consists of the web of human relationships which exist whenever men live together"). And yet it is the very reality which is most consistently ignored or underestimated in all reductionist accounts of these affairs: "the very basic error of all materialism in politics . . . is to overlook the inevitability with which men disclose themselves as subjects, as distinct and unique persons, even when they are wholly concentrated upon reaching an altogether worldly object."' Joseph Dunne, *Back to the Rough Ground: Practical Judgment and the Lure of Technique* (Notre Dame, IN: University of Notre Dame Press, 1997), p. 91. (Internal quotations taken from Arendt's *The Human Condition*).

To know where a place is in a meaningful way I must know where it is in relation to other places in the known world. I can have a good description of where I am but I can lack a map for orientating myself. But then, I can also have a map yet lack knowledge of where I am on it. Also, in keeping with Taylor's analysis of language, identifying where I am is akin to identifying who my interlocutor is, and how I might agree or differ from his or her perspective. Gaining orientation in moral space requires being able to identify and, in addition, locate oneself in relation to significant features of our lives.

Taylor's twofold account of how we can be lost in terrestrial space also has its analogy in how we orient ourselves in relation to the good. Getting clarity on the good requires 'not only some framework(s) which defines the shape of the quali-tatively higher but also a sense of where we stand in relation to this.' [63] This can-not be a neutral question for us; we care and cannot stop caring where we stand in relation to what is highest and best. For the need to be connected to, or in con-tact with, what we see as being of utmost importance and value is one of our most basic aspirations. The structuralist influence on Girard's work prevents any such intentional 'taking up', 'being there', or orienting ourselves in this way. The con-trast between literary space, where the subject is left at the mercy of a desire that seems always beyond its powers of reflection (causing it to react to others in a dialectic of escalating crisis), and moral space, as Taylor depicts it, is stark. In drawing out the contrast, as I have done by comparing Girard's early work with Taylor's philosophical anthropology, we can now readily see that moral space is surely a better account of how we live our lives. In my view, it can be said to trump 'literary space' and even 'cultural space' as depicted by Girard, showing these spaces as offering inadequate accounts of human agency. And, significantly, moral space can now be seen as allowing us to understand the problems of 'crisis' and 'difference', in the context of having an identity, as negotiable outside a rig-idly defined order. But, it may still be asked, does Taylor's account hold up when confronted with the loss of religious horizons?

This brings us back once again to the issue of 'strong evaluation', which involves questions about what kind of life is worth living. How we answer these questions – and answer them through our actions – will determine the extent to which we will be connected or in contact with what we see as good. Furthermore, regardless of how it might change from person to person, and culture to culture, Taylor insists that our being concerned with some or other 'strong' issue, is not optional, and for the same reason that our orientation as 'identity defining' is not optional. If we cannot but stand somewhere in relation to things that give our life meaning, then caring about an ultimate question must also matter: 'not being able to function without orientation in the space of the ultimately important

61. Taylor, *Sources of the Self*, p. 41.
62. Ibid.
63. Taylor, *Sources of the Self*, p. 42.

means not being able to stop caring where we [stand] in it'.[64] We can see how (in this space of 'inability to stop caring') the goods that define our spiritual *orientation* are the ones that define the *worth* of our lives. It is because these issues are so inextricably linked that Taylor believes it necessary to explore 'the weight or substance of one's life' as a question of how one is 'placed' or 'situated' in relation to, or 'in contact with', the good.[65] In gaining clarity on the things that matter to me, in making choices and exercising my human agency, I give my life comportment. The ultimate questions, those that Taylor sees governing the other questions that appear less important, arise for many people today in terms of the 'meaningfulness' and the 'worth' of their lives, of whether or not they are (or have been) rich, amounting to something, or going somewhere. Getting clarity on these ultimate questions and the range of more proximate questions framed by them is the work of forging an identity and hence overcoming the prospect of crisis – as a loss of externally generated difference.

4. 'Conclusions' in Moral Space: Craving, and the Unity of a Self

We saw in Chapter 1 how 'metaphysical desire' precipitates the crisis in literary space, leading to the hallucination of the 'the double' and the Dostoyevskian apocalypse: 'The truth of metaphysical desire is death.'[66] We also saw in Chapter 3 how Girard carries over this term into his cultural anthropology to help explain how an 'infinity of desire' gives rise to the modern sacrificial crisis. This analysis of desire – *in extremis* – that sees Romantic originality as a form of 'separation', I have argued, is overdrawn. Reflection on desire (i.e., strong evaluation) and not 'blind mimesis' is the proper mode of human agency. If 'novelistic conclusions' in literary space are unequivocal in their rejection of Romantic desire, and thus are unfaithful to how human beings actually reflect on desire, conclusions in moral space must take account of this dimension of human agency. They must hold onto a subject who can strongly evaluate and thus remain open to more piecemeal negotiations. The difficulty of achieving unity clearly remains, but if we are to take seriously the impulse towards unity that is so central to both these thinkers' accounts we must ask: if desire can go wrong for the self in moral space, as it clearly does in literary space, how might unity be generated here without repeating the error of Girard's scapegoating of the self, or worse perhaps, scapegoating some other?

---

64. Ibid.
65. Ibid.
66. René Girard, *Deceit, Desire, and the Novel: Self and Other in Literary Structure*, trans. Yvonne Freccero (Baltimore: Johns Hopkins University Press, 1965), p. 282.

As we have seen, in *Sources of the Self* Taylor describes how the weight or substance of one's life is bound up with working out what matters to one, and thereby gaining orientation in moral space. However, having a framework, like having a good map, requires knowing where we stand in relation to the qualitatively higher. Who we are is closely tied to where we are heading and who we are becoming. As Taylor writes, moral space concerns 'our most fundamental motivation, or our basic allegiance, or the outer limits of relevant possibilities for us, and hence the direction our lives are moving in or could move in.'[67] I *care* about where I stand because I *care* about who I am and what I desire to be. There are many ways this can be defined and so there are many ways we can be in contact with the good. Taylor wants us to look on these diverse aspirations for meaning or fuller 'Being' as forms of a craving that is 'ineradicable from human life'.[68]

This craving can take many different forms. Much depends here on our favoured description. Catholics, anarchists, revolutionaries, artists, even householders, whose aspirations give meaning or fuller being to their lives, all have to be rightly placed in relation to the good. To try to draw out what all of these have in common, Taylor outlines two divergent examples of how the same ineradicable craving is at work in apparently different manifestations: a fulfilled householder and an estranged 'underground man'.[69] The same 'aspiration to connection', is at work in each life and is basic to why either individual cares about being 'rightly placed'. In one case our aspirations may appear integrated and unobtrusive, we may even be unaware of them if things go well and if by and large we are satisfied with where we are. In the other case, our lives may be torn apart and disordered by the craving; its potential to manifest itself as intractable resentment or disdain can motivate some of the bitterest conflicts in human life.[70] But unlike the destructive desire we meet in literary space, our cravings in moral space, however potentially debilitating, can still be brought within the ambit of reflection. The individual who assumes a first-person perspective, and begins to orient him or her self in

---

67. Taylor, *Sources of the Self*, p. 46.
68. Ibid., p. 44.
69. About the former Taylor writes: 'The householder's sense of the value of what I have been calling ordinary life is woven through the emotions and concerns of his everyday existence. It is what gives them their richness and depth.' *Sources of the Self*, p. 44. About the latter he writes: '. . . they are people whose lives are torn apart by this craving. They see themselves, over and against the master of themselves, as in the grip of lower drives, their lives disordered and soiled by their base attachments.' Ibid. Taylor could well be alluding to Dostoevsky's 'underground man' when he describes the feelings associated with this form of craving as: 'I can't really throw myself into this great cause/movement/religious life. I feel on the outside. I know it's great in a way but I can't feel moved by it. I feel unworthy of it somehow.' Taylor, *Sources of the Self*, p. 45.
70. Ibid.

terms of a set of qualitative distinctions does so as a mode of craving, and hence is always 'more or less' in relation to the good.[71]

This dynamic quality highlights another basic feature of human existence: 'What we are' right now can never fully sum up our condition, because we are always changing and becoming. The spatial dimension of the self is bound up with the temporal. Even as we develop through our 'life cycle' and make sense of certain things, our place, where we are located, is constantly challenged and potentially revised by the new events of our lives as we experience more and mature. As such, it is never just a question of where we are, but also where we are going. Although the first may be a matter of more or less the latter is a question of towards or away from – an issue of yes or no.[72] It is for this reason that an absolute question always frames our relative ones. 'Since we cannot do without an orientation to the good, and since we cannot be indifferent to our place relative to the good, and since this place must always change and become, the issue of the direction of our lives must arise for us.'[73] Because our lives are constantly moving within a space of questions, where we are makes sense only in terms of where we are going and whether or not we are on course to get there. Moral space presupposes an ultimate destination.

The question of destination or direction brings to the fore the other issue highlighted at the beginning of this section, namely 'the unity of a self'. Taylor has been arguing that in order to make minimal sense of our lives and have an identity we need an orientation to the good, which means some sense of 'strong value', or the qualitative discrimination of the 'incomparably higher'. However, Smith argues that for Taylor there is another 'inescapable moral dimension' to subjectivity. 'There is also something about the *unity* of a self that necessarily lends it moral meaning.'[74] The metaphor of moral space is expanded here to help us understand how a life keeps moving to keep apace with changing circumstances. Our reference points to who we are, that help us to gain orientation in moral space turn out not to be fixed in this space once and for all. 'Our lives and concerns change. No one is frozen in time, and it follows from the sheer temporality of life, Taylor thinks, that "the issue of the direction of our lives must arise for us".'[75] From the above discussion of the movement and direction of our lives we can see that the sense of one's good has to be woven into one's life as an unfolding story. 'On account of the fact that self-understanding inescapably occurs in time,

---

71. Taylor's debt to Augustine is obvious here, and it connects up with what we discussed in Chapter 4 as the continuum of desire which becomes caritas or cupiditas – that is, not two separate desires, which effectively correspond to two separate subjects, but rather one love – albeit divided by two tendencies of the will.
72. Taylor, *Sources of the Self*, p. 45.
73. Taylor, *Sources of the Self*, p. 47.
74. Smith, *Charles Taylor: Meaning, Morals, and Modernity*, p. 97.
75. Ibid.

it requires some synthesis of the present, past and future. Narrative plays the part of this synthesis.'[76]

The intelligibility of our lives is apprehended in narrative – a narrative that plays a bigger role than simply structuring our present.[77] The narrative unity of a self involves the stories we tell of how we got to where we are, and where we are going, or what we project to become. For example, as we evaluate the moral space that constitutes our lives we have to move backward and forward to make a real assessment. Taylor describes this process as follows:

> To the extent that we move back, we determine what we are by what we have become, by the story of how we got there. Orientation in moral space turns out to be similar to orientation in physical space. We know where we are through a mixture of recognition of landmarks before us, and a sense of how we have travelled to get here.[78]

We know 'who we are', or *where* we are, through what we have become or how we have arrived. 'In order to be able to answer . . . the question "who am I?" one must have recourse not only to strong evaluation but also to narrative.'[79] To make sense of my present action, if it is more than merely trivial, requires a narrative understanding of my life, a sense of what I have become which can only be given in story. This reading of the role and function of narrative can also help us understand how our life has direction, as discussed in the previous section.[80] As I project my life forward to what I am not yet, as a continuation or as something more innovative, I project a future, indeed a 'bent' for my whole life to come.[81]

Of course, Taylor is highly critical of the discourse that suggests the self is the same from one time and place to another – that it has some 'substantive unity' that could be considered a criterion of personal identity. However, he does not make the corresponding error of arguing that the self can be completely new, or different from one time and place to another. Here Taylor's position seems very close to Paul Ricoeur's attempt to conceive of the self in terms of *ipse* rather than

---

76. Ibid.
77. Taylor, *Sources of the Self*, p. 47.
78. Ibid.
79. Smith, *Charles Taylor: Meaning, Morals, and Modernity*, p. 98.
80. Smith elaborates what he sees as an important point here: 'It only makes sense to ascribe direction to a life if we can distinguish between more or less significant moments, events or experiences, but in doing this we are articulating a changing relation to the good.' *Meaning, Morals, and Modernity*, p. 98.
81. Taylor, *Sources of the Self*, p. 47. Cf. 'The fact that the story I am living projects me into a future, to a self that I am not yet but which must be of concern, gives my life, indeed all human life, the character of a quest.' Smith, *Charles Taylor: Meaning, Morals, and Modernity*, p. 98.

idem and as embodying a continual interplay of 'sedimentation and innovation'.[82] Drawing out Ricoeur's distinction between *ipse* and *idem* in the context of Girard's work, Gavin Flood argues that it is precisely the lack of such a distinction by Girard, that leads the latter away from selfhood considered as narrative mediation (*ipse*). Drawing out this crucial difference between the two thinkers in the context of their approaches to myth, Flood argues, 'Girard reads myth through the lens of mimetic desire. Mimesis in Girard therefore function as a drive that patterns human behavior ... but while this is extremely important, Girard emphasizes the drive of mimetic desire in narrative at the cost of subjectivity.'[83] While Girard comments on his affiliation to Ricoeur's work at the end of *Things Hidden* he never quite engages with it, nor does he engage with the problems inherent in this form of hermeneutics the way Taylor does.

The idea of the 'who' question as extending over a 'whole life' gives rise to the important issue for Taylor about the 'unity' of a life. Taylor wants to reject any conception of a self as able to detach itself in single moments erasing all traces of the history of it previous engagements – a self he refers to, after Locke, as 'punctual'.[84] Once again we see that human persons exist only in a certain space of questions and what is in question is, generally and characteristically, the shape of my life as a whole. Yes, my life moves and develops, and there is a time for everything, but that time is inwardly derived. My readiness, my becoming, is only possible through the history of my maturations and regressions, overcomings and defeats.[85] And that is why Taylor claims one's 'self-understanding necessarily has temporal depth and incorporates narrative.'[86] It includes the hope that in the fullness of our life the future will 'redeem' the past and make it part of a life-story that has overall coherence, sense and purpose. This striving for meaning or substance takes place through narrative because we cannot but determine our place in relation to the good, which is the very process of gaining an orientation to it.

At first glance this narrative structure of subjectivity in moral space appears similar to literary space and the way the author overcomes the negative image of his desires, not least when Taylor refers to Proust's *A la recherché du temps perdu*. However, there are some important differences that stand out when we compare these two spaces. The narrative unity of a self presupposes a first-person perspective on the part of the storyteller – the subject must not be excluded *a priori* from

---

82. See especially, Paul Ricoeur, *Oneself as Another* (Chicago: University of Chicago Press, 1992). See Taylor's comments on Ricoeur's 'History and Hermeneutics', in *Philosophy of History and Action*, ed. Yirmiahu Yovel (Dordrecht: Reidel, 1978), pp. 21–25.
83. Gavin Flood, 'Mimesis, Narrative and Subjectivity in the Work of Girard and Ricoeur', in *Cultural Values*, vol. 4, no. 2 (April, 2000), p. 210.
84. Taylor, *Sources of the Self*, p. 49.
85. Ibid., p. 50.
86. Ibid.

telling her own story. This feature is absent from Girard's criticism and subsequent anthropology on the grounds that the subject suffers from an 'ontological
illness' and therefore needs the therapeutics of the critic in order for her 'true'
story to be told, the ending of which the literary community then shares in. It is
only in the context of Girard's later analysis of death and rebirth (i.e., in the context of collective violence against victims), that the early 'unity of novelistic conclusions' can be understood as a form of scapegoating by Girard and the literary
community – thus revealing a dichotomy between the old Romantic subject and
the 'new' self. Precisely because of this 'division', the 'unity' that is achieved at
the end of *Deceit, Desire, and the Novel* can admit of no continuity between the
author who dies and the one who is reborn (i.e., before and after). Were it to do
so, some degree of originality would be granted a determinative role in the author's
rebirth, which Girard does not allow. The 'rebirth' that occurs in literary space
involves an absolute transformation: an entirely new self from the ashes of the
Romantic hero. For the author, as subject, to rule out unity in advance, which
appears to be what Girard proposes, and then to find herself released into 'unity'
at the end of the novel, must, at the level of moral space, be seen as a discontinuity
between one self and an other self – at no point in the self's own narrative was
unity a genuine desire. While the 'narrative unity of a life' that, Taylor describes,
also involves a process of 'death and rebirth' (in and through the series of maturations and regressions that go into making up a subjects life as a whole), the transformation in moral space is not into something totally new as it is in Girard's
criticism. In view of the aspiration to unity that, Taylor believes, can be expressed
in many ways, Smith comments, 'any restriction of the temporal sequence of a life
in either the past or the future must appear as a mutilation.'[87] It is in considering
the temporal sequence of a whole life in relation to other non-western narratives
that may not share this sequence that Taylor hits on something that highlights for
us an important contrast between him and Girard on the issue of 'death and
rebirth', an issue that has at bottom to do with the temporal structure of the self.
Smith explains:

> Taylor concedes that other cultures may experience time differently. Decisive
> ruptures in the flow of a life, understood as death and rebirth or completely
> different selves, are conceivable. But they can be so conceived only by stepping
> outside the horizon of western modernity. Within this culture at least, 'the
> supposition that I could be two temporally succeeding selves is either an over-
> dramatized image, or quite false. It runs against the structural features of a self
> as a being who exists in a space of concerns'.[88]

The analysis here runs directly against the kind of radical rupture between a sort
of Romantic pre-self and a later, new and utterly transfigured self, depicted by

---

87. Smith, *Charles Taylor: Meaning, Morals, and Modernity*, p. 99.
88. Ibid.

Girard in literary space. If, as I propose, we adopt this Taylorian analysis it enables us to see that the author *as subject* is not perhaps so blind after all. Her
'originality' can thus be placed in the context of moral space and seen as part of
the narrative conditions of life lived *as a whole*; a form of unity that individuals –
in their own expressive fashion – can make their own.

5. *Taylor's Dostoevsky: Positive and Negative Mediation*

Up until now we have been discussing 'Identity and the Good' which is of central
importance to Taylor's ontology. Yet Girard's emphasis on the human susceptibility to violence surely casts a dark shadow over all liberal hermeneutics of this
kind. The central plank of Girardian theory that I have strenuously challenged in
this book is his analysis of desire as purely mimetic. As we have seen in Part One
it purports to explain a remarkable number of phenomena including the function
of violence in structuring our lives. But most significantly, I believe, it disqualifies
the subject from taking a stand in moral space. As we discussed in Chapter 1, he
brings forward a theory of desire as mimetic (or triangular) in his early literary
criticism, only later developing it to include an explanation of cultural crisis and
order. Central among the authors whose work he analyses early on in his exposition of desire is Dostoevsky. More than any other figure Dostoevsky's life and
work is an example of the author's journey from death to life, providing an excel-
lent case study of the incipient logic of desire that seeks out 'model/obstacles' to
imitate in a futile bid on behalf of the subject to prove his own originality. Hence
when viewed within an anthropological context a desire for originality and
authenticity generates not only a crisis within the self, it also generates a crisis
within cultural space more broadly – a sacrificial crisis. External mediation is
socially efficacious because it channels desire in healthy ways, while internal
mediation is rivalrous and therefore socially destructive. I argued above that
modern subjects, as human agents, reflect strongly on their desires, and are therefore capable of discriminating between strong and weak commitments. This does
not rule out the influence of mimetic desire on human behaviour, but it tries to
show that modern subjects have a capacity to negotiate their desires even though
they may be inwardly divided.

Taylor is also influenced by the genius of Dostoevsky.[89] No other modern
thinker he believes explores the problem of evil with the same degree of intensity.
In doing so, he thinks, Dostoevsky yields an insight into forms of mediation not
unlike what Girard describes in terms of mimetic desire. But in Taylor's work this
is understood as an attempt on behalf of Dostoevsky to come to terms in his own

---

89. See Fergus Kerr's summary of the places in Taylor's work where he draws directly
on Dostoevsky, in 'Taylor's Moral Ontology', in *Contemporary Philosophy in
Focus: Charles Taylor*, ed. Ruth Abbey (New York: Cambridge University Press,
2004), p. 98.

life with this profound human problem, and not as the accidental fruit born of the author's resistance (and left for the critic to uncover). In his essay 'Dostoevsky and the Modern World' Taylor considers the problem of evil and Dostoevsky's response to it in terms of a reflection on terrorism. We can perhaps easily recognize strategic motives of terrorists, but more difficult and more significant are those other implicit motives: a desire to be utterly outside the contradictions that are seen to cause the felt injustice, and, based on this 'stance of purity', a desire for identity. It is out of these motives, Taylor believes Dostoevsky is telling us, arise the possibility of radical evil whereby an individual gradually succumbs to the deliberate and hence radical choice of inflicting pain and suffering.[90]

To illustrate the kind of analysis and insight that Dostoevsky's work brings out here, Taylor refers to the passage immediately before 'The Legend of the Grand Inquisitor', from *The Brothers Karamazov*, when Ivan declares his response to the suffering of the world, which is 'to give back his ticket'. The passage provides a picture of evil in which this 'motivation of fascination' is central, referring as it does to the 'sensuous intoxication from the screams of the tortured victims'.[91] Who would not want to give back their ticket to a world thus constituted? However, Taylor suggests there are at least two interpretations of Ivan's action. The first recognizes that the finer, more noble and sensitive you are, the more likely you are to be outraged and affronted by the evil in the world. The second acknowledges that while Ivan's action is understandable it is also a rebellion against God – in not wanting to be part of creation one tears oneself away from the Creator. Taylor suggests that this theme of 'schism' is easily identified in Dostoevsky's work – we need only think of Raskolnikov.[92] The awful paradox of the schismatic who separates himself from the world for noble reasons is that 'the more sense one has of evil the more tempted one is (that is what the character of Ivan shows us so well)'.[93] Taylor describes the forms of this separation as follows:

> One form is a kind of objectification of the world. One stands over and against it and sees it simply as this large-scale chain of cause and effect, a mechanistic

---

90. Charles Taylor, 'Dostoevsky and the Contemporary World', in *Lonergan Review: A Multidisciplinary Journal*. Number 4 (Montreal: Lonergan University College, 1996). I would like to thank Susan Srigley and Bruce Ward for this reference.
91. Charles Taylor, 'Dostoevsky and the Contemporary World', p. 138. See also: Taylor, *Sources of the Self*, p. 451.
92. The issue of schism or division relates to the problem of crisis addressed in Part One of the book. A cursory reading of the comparison between Taylor and Girard on this issue indicates that, for Taylor the 'stance of purity' (that the schismatic takes) is part of the drive to mediate a certain view of the world which then generates outwards toward destruction and division, while for Girard the divisions, at least in his early work, appear mostly to generate inwards. Are these accounts of 'schism' really incompatible? I don't think so. Though I would like to draw out the connections here further, adequate space prevents me doing so at this time.
93. Taylor, 'Dostoevsky and the Contemporary World', p. 140.

picture of the universe. By taking an objectifying stance you have disengaged yourself emotionally from the world you are standing over and against the world . . . We can see that with Ivan who takes the position 'It's just a matter of cause and effect, no one is to blame' . . . Now over and against the stance of objectification Dostoevsky places another stance. Typically this stance comes out in a counter slogan which directly evokes while negating, that no one is to blame. In *The Devils* the counter slogan is that we are all to blame, which for instance Stepan Trofimovitch and Shatov say . . . a stance of admitting one's part . . . joining, accepting one's part in the world.[94]

In distinguishing between the 'schismatics' and 'the joiners' in this way Taylor believes that Dostoevsky is giving us a theological view; the argument turns, he says, on what you produce in the world. The understandable stance of the schismatic generates destruction while the stance of the joiner remains open to acts of healing. The power to do one thing or the other, for Dostoevsky, is 'mediated to some people by other people'. Taylor puts it this way: '. . . there is something like apostolic succession and reverse apostolic succession at work in Dostoevsky – where the power to join comes to that person because they receive it from someone else. In a sense they have been recognised by the other person or people, as capable of having it all'.[95] So the idea that the joiner gets his power from outside is crucial here. It is similar for the schismatic, although the line of succession is in reverse and thus yields only violence and hatred. But how is this form of mediation generated? Taylor suggests the stance of purity and separation is an observer's stance, one that is inevitably confronted with the need to fill the void with something, and because of the very nature of this structure – its sense of impotence – one possible reaction is 'to fill the world with anti-action, with the fervour of action accentuated . . . by the hatred of the world.'[96] So, there is what Taylor describes as a 'terrible dialectic' that begins in a pure vision of good and ends perpetuating a distorted vision of evil. 'One of the more important insights that Dostoevsky tries to get across is that a great many revolutionaries who on the surface are actuated by love of mankind actually end in hatred.'[97] It is the 'noble schismatic' that runs the greatest risk of generating hatred. And it comes, Taylor believes, not from what they do but what they inspire. The noble schismatic can 'give others a programme of furious action and there is a very complicated ratio because they are of course incapable of endorsing that action afterwards; but it

---

94. Ibid., pp. 140–141.
95. The quote continues: 'In *The Brothers* there is a line between Marco, Zosima, Alyosha and Grushenka – the line of empowerment through recognition and love – which Dostoevsky claims has its ultimate point in the love of God, but it is played up in the novel in that relation of one person to another through empowerment.' Taylor, 'Dostoevsky and the Contemporary World', p. 142.
96. Ibid., p. 144.
97. Ibid.

comes through them and it comes through them in a way that Dostoevsky thinks you will see as being in a sense inevitable'.[98]

Hence mediation in this strong sense is not epiphenomenal, it is the nodal point of inspiration from which action or anti-action is generated. As with Girard's analysis of desire in Dostoevsky's work, Taylor refers to both forms of apostolic succession described above as either 'positive' or 'negative' forms of mediation.[99] And in explaining the 'motivation of fascination' that he believes becomes the basis of a radical choice for evil, he suggests that negative mediation can generate outward to encompass a kind of apocalyptic violence:

> You could argue that it is out of this mode of action that you generate the kind of fascination with violence which indeed some of the figures [in Dostoevsky's novels] begin to exhibit. And that is what, as it were, closes the circle and allows you to see how the whole phenomenon that starts it all, all the evil in the world with all its levels are generated again.[100]

And, interesting for our discussion with Girard's account of the origins of culture, Taylor adds here: 'Its not a story of traditional genesis but a story of how it [evil] regenerates itself out of the response that is most understandable.'[101] We might add here, it is not a traditional account of genesis, but it is perhaps an account of genesis nonetheless.

I made the case in Chapter 5 in discussion with Taylor's understanding of Augustine, Rousseau, Herder and Hegel, that the eighteenth-century emphasis on originality and expression was concerned more with authentic unity rather than separation and self-divinization as Girard's reading of the Romantic period and individualism more broadly claims. Separation, while not entirely defining modern subjectivity remains a very real tendency. In light of our discussion in this section we can perhaps see more clearly the dangers of separation that both Girard and Taylor on some level would, no doubt, agree. However, in Girard's work that connection to others and to the world remains fraught if not impossible, since the self internally divided and terminally unsure of its models, appears unable to take a stand in any kind of moral space. Need his stance towards modern selfhood continue to be so radically undermining? Taylor's analysis of Dostoevsky work, and its insight into negative and positive mediation, provides a nice counterpoint to Girard's theory of mimetic desire – one that is both complimentary and critical (though there is no evidence that Taylor has been influenced by Girard's early work here). The significance is to be found, I suggest, not in how the self 'doubles back' on itself when it meets an obstacle (often Girard's primary focus), but in the way the mediating subject can assume the role as agent or indeed 'anti-agent'.

---

98. Ibid., p. 145.
99. Ibid., p. 148.
100. Ibid.
101. Ibid.

The schismatic 'action' on behalf of a subject, first and foremost divides the subject from others and the world. We might say (*a la* Taylor) that it is not necessarily the desire for originality that divides us (*pace* Girard) but rather it is the desire for purity that is the motive force here. And faced with the reality of the world we live in, this stance on behalf of the radical is a stance that sets him apart – a separation that is also a rebellion and a schism. Thus separation, in the first instance, is not simply based on a desire for divine self-sufficiency. It can be based on the noble and understandable motives of a subject that sees the world as bad, and out of a profoundly felt sense of injustice and revulsion at the evil and cruelty of the world, turns away. And then, from the impotence that follows, ends up trying to overcome this evil and cruelty with even a stronger measure of the same.

6. Conclusion: The Best Account Possible

At the outset of this chapter I quoted Taylor who claims that accounting for the sources of crises that beset our culture involves 'making a plausible account of human history'. But why tell the story of selfhood and sacrifice in this way – as part of one's own personal quest, and yet somehow also the human story? Does Girard's more scientific approach to the 'astructural' origins of all structure, not deal with the matter here in a more objective way; surely his approach is more likely to convince someone to adopt his findings? After all, the point of making known what is hidden must surely be that we can gain some purchase on it and perhaps live a more improved life as a result of this knowledge? Yet more than any other thinker today, Taylor reminds us that the problems in our culture are not primarily epistemological but rather ethical and spiritual.[102] To ask the question 'what is the good of our knowledge?', beyond perhaps its variety of applications, need not lose sight of what the protagonist of Dostoevsky's 'underground' observes when he ask rather blithely: 'And why are you so firmly and triumphantly certain that only what is normal and positive – in short, only well-being – is good for man [*sic*]?'[103] Indeed, it is for this very reason that it is often prudent to assume that knowledge alone does not get us there – wherever 'there' might be.

This dilemma has a long history in the west. Taylor's response is one of 'anticipatory confidence'. Much of his political philosophy addresses the difficulty of making transitions in matters of substantive concern (where the good is in question), and the understandable wish to avoid making an argument just from our 'way of life'. But nonetheless, rather than appeal to an abstract universal standard, that can seem disconnected or removed from any desire to love and

---

102. Charles Taylor, 'Iris Murdoch and Moral Philosophy'.
103. Fyodor Dostoevsky, *Notes from the Underground*, trans. Jessie Coulson (London: Penguin Books, 1983), p. 39.

respect others (the point perhaps of universal benevolence?), Taylor believes that our own 'best account available' is all we genuinely have to go on. Thus, the BA principle (as he calls it) becomes operative in a context where competing definitions of a higher good call into question the good of one or other party to a moral dispute. The BA principle, as an 'error reducing move',[104] is the best way to ensure that we take seriously our moral intuitions and what we actually do when we try to make sense of our lives on a whole range of issues concerning our identity and the good. The place of qualitative distinctions in our ethical life is crucial here because they articulate the moral point of our actions rather than just giving reasons for doing what we 'ought' to do as in the case of neo-Kantian procedualism that prioritizes the right over the good at the expense of our motivating aspirations.[105] According to Taylor, it is this kind of indexing of our moral intuitions that can help convince people to aspire to a moral vision by moving them to make it their own, or by helping them to articulate their own sense of this good. He refers to this indexing of our moral intuitions as a form of 'subtler language'[106] that can open us out to why the good in question might be worth making our own. Hence articulacy helps explain in a fuller and richer way the meaning of moral action for us, just what its goodness or badness, being obligatory or forbidden, consists in.[107] It is the goods that lay the greatest claim on us that hold the greatest potential for conflict. These goods, what Taylor refers to as 'hypergoods', appear the highest, and as such are almost beyond question. Yet, he believes, these hypergoods, as potentially divisive as they are, must not be kept merely implicit in moral debate if we are to be honest about the things that hold our allegiance and motivate us. It is precisely a hypergood's ability to move us that makes it so valuable. 'We experience our love of it as well founded. Nothing that couldn't move me in *this* way would count as a hypergood.'[108] The problem is that such deeply held beliefs may be wrong, but there is no way of knowing unless I meet the challenge, when the occasion arises, and try to give my best account of why I hold this view and should continue to do so. Perhaps I would have to concede that my deeply held belief is wrong. But so long as I put my 'best account' forward as 'provisionally' my best then I avoid the charge of trading on a mistaken belief, since '[there] is nothing better that I could conceivably go on. Or my critics for that matter.'[109]

Through the process of 'maturation and regression', told as a story of who I am and who we are, frameworks, that take account of the meanings things have for us, help describe and evaluate the world of human affairs. Because of this we

---

104. Taylor, 'Explanation and Practical Reason', in *Philosophical Arguments*, p. 52.
105. Smith, *Charles Taylor: Meanings, Morals, and Modernity*, pp. 110–111.
106. Taylor, *The Ethics of Authenticity*, p. 81.
107. Taylor, *Sources of the Self*, p. 80.
108. Ibid., p. 74.
109. Ibid.

cannot simply set them aside when we are confronted with a different culture. Rather, we are compelled to make the case for our way of life. Providing the best available account and attempting to make transitions in moral space, and, between competing goods, means making comparisons in a historical context. This in turn involves deciding what is good, and doing so in light of the transitions to the modern period. 'Precisely the aim of the comparative exercise is to enable us to understand others undistortively, and hence to be able to *see the good* in their lives, even while we also see that their good conflicts with ours.'[110] To make decisions based on such comparisons is not always to be presumptuous (although Taylor grants that there are generally good reasons for not interfering in another culture's life). 'When we have a conflict in life, we feel justified and called on to make a choice, to sacrifice or trade off one good for another . . . Wouldn't we welcome the discontinuance of suttee or human sacrifice?'[111] The last question here reminds us of what is new about the language that Taylor employs, and that 'internalisation' in the context of universal respect demands a very different form of sacrificial practice than what was acceptable in earlier cultures. The perspective we find here is an historical one. According to Taylor, it is made possible by the modern ethics of ordinary life and the emphasis on reducing suffering, which sees the supposed higher ends that previously 'trumped' life being progressively discredited.[112] However, it is the very process of change, of repudiating earlier goods, and moving forward, for example, to a stronger democratic culture, a more embodied self, or 'stronger relationality',[113] that makes the promotion of hypergoods so problematic. There are many perspectives within the human sciences that choose to say nothing of these goods either for strategic reasons or out of well-meaning concern, or both. And there are others who recoil at the thoughts of submitting to such 'other-worldly' impositions.[114] Taylor believes all of these views, including Kant's notion of rational agency, have something in common. They all overtly adhere to an 'ethics of inarticulacy', which not only leaves any discussion of moral intuitions or substantive goods off limits, but also leaves their own qualitative distinctions deeply confused. He argues instead that while many of our cherished hypergoods may turn out to be illusory, it is wrong, and potentially more harmful, to think that we have stumbled upon an *a priori* argument showing this to be so. Gaining clarity on the strong values that we cannot but live by helps us to decide, as best we can, and hence orient ourselves in moral space. The difficulty of moving beyond some goods, as a 'trade off', or as an actual

---

110. Taylor, *Philosophical Arguments*, p. 153 (my italics).
111. Ibid.
112. Taylor, *Philosophy and the Human Sciences: Philosophical Papers*, 2, p. 156.
113. Here, I borrow a term from Frank C. Richardson and Kathryn M. Frost's paper, 'Girard and Psychology: Furthering the Conversation' (Unpublished, Ottawa, 2006) p. 5.
114. Taylor, *Sources of the Self*, p. 71.

acknowledgement that some good has a stronger claim, connects up with the whole problem of sacrifice that Girard's work is preoccupied with.[115] I want to pick up on this point in a more general way in the context of what Taylor calls 'the conflicts of modernity' in the epilogue.

I have been trying to outline in this chapter a number of points of contact between Girard and Taylor. The latter gives an account of the loss of horizons in the west, what he describes after Weber as the 'disenchantment of the world', which involves the fading of religious frameworks and the discrediting of the cosmos as a meaningful whole. Like Girard, he understands this loss as a source of profound crisis for the individual. However, by arguing that framework definitions are a basic condition of human agency, the loss of given horizons is superseded by the more complex and uncertain role of self-defined horizons, something that is missing in Girard's work. Taylor's philosophical anthropology provides a better account of human agency than either 'literary space' or 'cultural space', because within the conception of moral space that he depicts, 'strong value', as a reflective means of arbitrating between conflicting desires and purposes, can help us gain orientation with respect to the important questions that arise for us.

The moral spaces of our lives, plotted through narrative, can help us move in relation to our concerns, so that our stories, and the strong values that constitute our identities, need not run aground in sterile debate or blank incommensurability. Providing the best account available – as an error-reducing move – is an exercise of practical reason, helping me to decide between competing goods, so that my 'strongest aspiration toward hypergoods [does] not exact a price of self-mutilation.'[116] Articulating our frameworks has a moral significance. Hence, Taylor wants us *to say* what our underlying sense of the good consists in: make it articulate in descriptive language and find formulations for it that figure in moral thinking. By doing so, he is in part following a Socratic line that believes 'we aren't full human beings until we can say what moves us, what our lives are built around.'[117] What concerns him most is the importance of articulacy for our sense of the good, in particular the way articulacy can bring us closer to the good as a moral source and give it power to move us. We are reminded here that the good can be some

---

115. Smith points out how sacrifice is thematized in Taylor's work in the context of practical reasoning. 'But hypergoods themselves, as Taylor stresses, are sources of conflict. On the one hand one might recognise several higher order goods, that is, different standpoints, from which to evaluate or rank first order goods. On the other hand the single-minded pursuit of a hypergood has its own costs. Those who aim at the higher good must sacrifice other goods. There are occasions when those who do have such an aim find themselves asking, whether the sacrifice required by a hypergood is really worth it, and such moments precipitate practical reason.' *Charles Taylor: Meaning, Morals, and Modernity*, 104.

116. Taylor, *Sources of the Self*, p. 107.

117. Taylor, *Sources of the Self*, p. 92.

action, or motive, or style of life which is seen as qualitatively superior.[118] While outlining these general characteristics of the good, Taylor stresses that there is something in all these distinctions that deserves these attributions of 'Good' in a fuller sense. Using the example of Plato's cosmic order and the 'Idea of the Good' as key to this order, Taylor shows how this 'Good' in a fuller sense – the 'constitutive good' – helps define one's actions and motives. The crucial point for Taylor however, is that it is also a 'moral source'. 'It is a something the love of which empowers us to do and be good.'[119] As such, the constitutive good does more than spell out what we ought to do; love of it also empowers us to do and be good – indeed, loving it is part of what it is to be a good human being. This view, which sees articulation as a way of putting shape on the good, also emerges in the way that empowering images and stories function in our time.[120] Even though we may not be able to substitute for the theological or metaphysical beliefs that underpinned many of the most powerful stories that once laid claim to our imaginations, the images they evoke still inspire us within a new modern imaginary. Indeed these stories 'go on pointing to something which remains a moral source, something the contemplation, respect, or love of which enables us to get closer to the good'.[121] The image of the Good as the sun in light of which we see things clearly and are moved to act morally is borrowed by Taylor to illustrate how the sources of the self – sources that find expression in many ways and in many different traditions – can once again resonate with our deepest longing.

To draw on such powerful images and stories is to be moved to love and respect them and, through this love and respect, to be better able to live up to them. Articulacy as a dominant feature of moral space opens us to the reservoir of moral sources that are still active in our world. Of course, articulation is not a given, and a living language must renew its sources. This potential is ensured, Taylor reminds us, because words can have great depth and resonance. They can bring us in touch with sources hitherto unknown or restore older familiar sources. They can help us understand our life anew and allow us to see our own stories through the prism of a much 'greater' narrative. He readily admits that our narrative projects both grand and small often involve distortions.[122] As well as the worry of the 'dead formulations' and the 'trite imitations', he claims that 'the whole thing may be counterfeit.' That is 'the act by which their pronouncing releases force can be rhetorically imitated, either to feed our self-conceit or for even more sinister purposes, such as the defence of a discreditable status quo.'[123]

---

118. Ibid.
119. Taylor, *Sources of the Self*, p. 93.
120. Ibid., p. 95.
121. Ibid., pp. 95–96.
122. Ibid., p. 97.
123. Ibid.

On this point Taylor's discussion of Dostoevsky and the problem of evil resonates profoundly. There appear to be good reasons to keep silent, but he does not believe they can be valid across the board, for without any articulation we would lose contact with our moral sources altogether. To recognize the importance of frameworks as somehow inescapable expressions of our deepest moral impulses, is to find ourselves inescapably located with respect to these horizons of significance. The issue for Taylor rather is to discern, however tentatively, what ought to be articulated. If the qualitative distinctions that modern moral philosophy tends to suppress are to be reclaimed from their current limbo this must be done in some kind of descriptive and evocative prose. From the perspective of a narrative account that takes serious Girard's theory of violence and the sacred (in other words an account that I have been bringing forward) both our moral sources and our horizons of significance seem immeasurably more fraught. Yet as I have been arguing in this the final chapter, moral space as the basic condition of human agency, and the expressive medium of the reclaimed qualitative distinctions, can meet the challenges posed by the loss of difference and crisis in the modern period.

EPILOGUE

I

This book has initiated a conversation between two important contemporary thinkers. In bringing together their ideas concerning selfhood and sacrifice, I have explored from two apparently divergent perspectives what both Girard and Taylor see as the crisis in contemporary culture. While the source of this crisis appears different for both thinkers, I hope I have shown that each can, with some hermeneutical finesse, speak a similar language about shared concerns. The process of getting clear on these shared concerns has involved addressing the *aporia* in Girard's work. Significantly, it has also involved arguing that Taylor can respond to the problems arising for Girard's overall theory (as a result of this *aporia*), and to do so in a convincing way. Beginning in Chapter 1, I made the case that Girard's literary criticism, when read from the perspective of his later cultural anthropology, must be seen as a form of scapegoating. By reading back into his early work in light of his later work we discovered that the 'unity of novelistic conclusions' at the end of *Deceit, Desire, and the Novel*, is an achievement realized at the expense of the Romantic hero and modern individualism more generally. As such Girard's early work, I argued, must be read as a mythologizing of violence and a tacit re-inscription of division within the self, and hence a form of unity at the expense of a central, defining, feature of selfhood, that is subjectivity. When he later develops a theory of mimetic desire to explain the function of sacrifice and cultural formation, one that remains fully congruent with his early theory of desire, the ethical agent is fundamentally displaced in face of the harsh realities of violence and its relationship to the sacred. As his anthropology develops this tension becomes evident with the hypostatizing of desire and the complete 'immolation of the subject'.

Despite the apparent dynamic nature of mimetic desire when applied to cultural phenomena, the problems in Girard's overall theory, I suggested, stem from his reification of desire. For all its dynamism it ends up having much in common with Schopenhauerian 'Will', which proves detrimental for the ethical direction that he ultimately wants to take. While Girard's concept of 'Mimetic Desire' and Schopenhauer's conception of 'Blind Will' treat subjectivity in a similar way, they are admittedly very different thinkers in other respects. For Schopenhauer, 'Will' is everything; the shaping force of nature, 'from the rumblings of the gut to the movements of the planets' – in Eagleton's apt phrase. For Girard, Mimetic Desire is a cultural phenomenon, arising in the context of a community and structuring that community in a generative way. What both thinkers share is the absence, in their work, of any viable human agent that can negotiate these forces with a greater or lesser degree of confidence that he or she is moving in a more improved direction. For all his insight into transcendence by violence, Girard leaves the self excluded from the conditions of positive transcendence and moral identity. Taylor's reading of Schopenhauer's influence casts Girard's theory of 'desire without a subject' in question – especially in light of the latter's claims that a Christian *kerygma* informs his theory. Taylor reminds us that, for Christians, it is precisely in 'the gut' that the love of God makes its presence felt as agape.[1] What I have tried to show is that the inconsistencies in Girard's work can be explained – without sacrificing subjectivity and selfhood. Both Taylor's philosophical history and philosophical anthropology, I have argued, provide a way of understanding Girard's single greatest concern regarding crisis: how, when differences become unsettled or break down, order can be restored. And Taylor's account of the emergence of secular culture can do this in a manner that maintains some nourishing continuity with the past. The affirmation of ordinary life shows how a religious doctrine of inwardness inspired a revolution in thought concerning the locus of the good, and a rationalized version of this development gave rise to a new Deist conception of order as the design in interlocking purposes – an order of mutual benefit. The Romantic reaction to the overly instrumental parsing-up of nature that this 'design' involved provided a new found confidence in our 'inner depths' and the moral 'voice of nature'. However, without some 'good' to be found firmly beyond ourselves, developments in modern science and exploration cast a dark shadow over the Romantic vision, with religion and the current of life becoming juxtaposed with terrifying consequences. Do we get around the terror, or indeed 'the horror', by denying the conditions of moral agency?

Unlike Girard, Taylor tries to meet this challenge from the perspective of historical subjectivity. In Chapter 6 I considered his conception of strong evaluation that takes place in a space of questions about the good or what is highest and best in human life. This space, it transpires, presupposes a first-person perspective and a subject who is all the time gaining orientation in relation to the concerns of her life; for Taylor, it is a space governed by the qualitative distinctions that we make within a horizon of some concern. I highlighted how the quest for selfhood and identity is a quest that gets played out over a whole life, a life that makes room for our maturations and regressions, our overcomings and defeats. Taylor believes that the plotting and re-plotting of our lives can be achieved through narrative, so that over time greater unity is achieved – a unity that may indeed involve some kind of death and rebirth but not in a way that would break the continuity between what is new and what came before. All of this points to a subject that is not completely, or totally, divided in the way the Girardian subject is when scapegoated (as I have argued) at the end of *Deceit, Desire, and the Novel*. Furthermore it allows us to think the possibility of secular culture as providing the conditions for a new mode of differentiation, of human agency, that can creatively confront crisis.

---

1. Charles Taylor, *A Secular Age* (Cambridge, MA: The Belknap Press of Harvard University Press, 2007), p. 640.

For both Girard and Taylor the 'death of God' is significant in helping to explain modern atheism and the rise of exclusive humanism, but paradoxically perhaps neither see this paradigm 'event' as being devoid of religious inspiration. For Girard, the 'event' is noteworthy for the way it reveals the collective murder of the victim ('God is dead . . . and *we* have killed him.' Nietzsche: aphorism 125, *Gay Sciences*). For Taylor it is tied to a depth understanding of disenchantment in the context of a fuller wholeness and human flourishing within a new horizon of selfhood. Taylor understands the 'postmodern' emphasis on aphorism 125 and what follows from it in terms of the 'freeplay of the sign', as only part of the story of the Nietzschean legacy.[2] It is precisely because many of these postmodern philosophies have neglected the Dionysian vision that they are disposed to take up the negative account of modernism – against both the rational and expressive selves (thereby neglecting the 'opening to epiphany' that, Taylor believes, is brought about with the crumbling of the older hierarchies)[3]. The main issue that this book has sought to address, and hopefully correct, is how Girard who does not neglect the 'Dionysian vision' can still align himself theoretically (through his undermining of moral agency) with the negative account of modernity.

One of Taylor's main hypotheses concerns the need for frameworks to help compensate for the loss of horizons associated with modern disenchantment. Once the background picture of how we actually live our lives is recovered, frameworks turn out to be one of the necessary conditions of having a self today. But the modern loss of horizons still generates a crisis – what he refers to elsewhere as the 'malaise of modernity' – within both cultural and moral space. It is not however a total crisis. While sharing some of Girard's insights into the nature of our modern condition, Taylor sees the more immediate threat coming from an inarticulacy about our most cherished goods that stifles the work of making qualitative distinctions.[4] Articulacy is given strong emphasis here, since it helps to define the subject's ability to bring about something new. Hence the importance of selfhood for Taylor in negotiating the more determining forces in culture – what he refers to after Weber as the 'iron cage'. The inarticulacy around higher

---

2. Speaking of Foucault and Derrida's work in *Sources of the Self* Taylor argues:

   'Both these philosophies, different as they are, draw on a certain reading of Nietzsche which has been popular in France in recent decades. It is a reading which focuses on Nietzsche's sense of the arbitrariness of interpretation, on interpretation as an imposition of power, but completely neglects the other facet of this baffling thinker, the Dionysian vision of the "eternal return" which makes possible the all englobing affirmation of the "yea-saying".' *Sources of the Self: The Making of the Modern Identity* (New York: Cambridge University Press, 1992c), p. 488.

3. See note 73.

4. Charles Taylor, 'The Inarticulate Debate', Chp. 2., *The Ethics of Authenticity* (Cambridge, MA: Cambridge University Press, 1992a).

goods is deeply embedded in the historical disputes that I discussed in Chapters 4 and 5 in the context of the modern break with the older transcendent order, and a new emphasis on ordinary life and human flourishing. Inarticulacy stifles our moral and spiritual sources today, making human life and action difficult to sustain. It has its roots for Taylor in the widespread scientific temper ('naturalism') that denies any legitimacy to transcendent frameworks.[5] This whole movement – which is inherently disenchanting – gathered considerable momentum during the scientific revolution of the seventeenth century and later with classical utilitarianism which placed the emphasis on 'this world' as the site of action, reward and punishment, as opposed to the older 'other worldly' view that saw the 'this worldly' view as but a stepping stone to an eternal order of checks and balances. With the Protestant Reformation and its scorn for the so-called higher spiritualities, the new sciences of this period presented a polemical stance towards traditional perspectives and their implied elitism (we discussed these developments in chapter four in terms of the new 'interpenetration of the sacred and the profane' and the 'innerworldly asceticism' of the Reformers). But Taylor argues that, within this polemic that raised ordinary life to a new standard, the essential point became obscured. The point, for the reforming and revolutionary temper, was that 'the higher was not to be found outside of but as a manner of living ordinary life.'[6] However, what became blurred and even lost in this process was some of our most important moral distinctions, such as, what constitutes a good life and what makes some choices more important than others. The Reforming spirit, while originally part of a religious development (one still wedded to a form of theism), was gradually superseded by the continued emphasis on 'this world' so that the dominant view became one of complete disavowal of traditional religion, although the desire for wholeness and for even going beyond life remained.[7]

---

5. It is worth pointing out that for some postmodern philosophy 'silence' is a radical category that escapes the reciprocity of self/other, subject/object etc. It denotes the form of interiority appropriate to the postmodern subject that avoids the modern 'error' by 'letting things be'. See, Paul Standish, "Ethics before equality: moral education after Levinas" in *The RoutledgeFalmer Reader in Philosophy of Education*, ed. Wilfred Carr (New York: Routledge, 2005), pp. 230–237. However, for Taylor, in a politically liberal climate, such 'silence' can feed into an epistemological malaise that places priority on the 'right over the good' – thus ruling out in advance the substantive question of what is higher or better, thereby perpetuating the very forms of instrumentalism that are the common enemy of moderns and postmoderns alike. Charles Taylor, 'Iris Murdoch and Moral Philosophy', in Maria Antonaccio and William Schweiker, eds *Iris Murdoch and the Search for Human Goodness* (Chicago and London: Chicago University Press, 1996b).
6. Taylor, *Sources of the Self*, p. 23.
7. Charles Taylor, 'Spirituality of Life – and Its Shadow', in *Compass*, (Vol. 14, no. 2. May/June, 1996c). Also available at http://gvanv.com/compass/arch/v1402/ctaylor. html.

As a result of the historical disputes involving the conditions of 'ordinary life' and the new modes of rational control and self-expression, secular modernity contains ('mingled together') both authentic developments of the Gospel, of an incarnational mode of life, and also a closing off to God, which negates the Gospel. Taylor defends the notion that modern culture, in breaking with the structures and beliefs of Christendom, also carried certain facets of Christian life further than they ever were taken, or could have been taken within Christendom.[8] Nonetheless the full-blown rejection of frameworks contributes to a moral and spiritual crisis today by, on one hand, appearing progressive and without fundamental contradiction, while on the other hand straining to make sense of itself, keep itself motivated and provide legitimacy for its high moral standards. Simply put, secular culture may need deeper richer moral sources if it is to sustain its project of human flourishing: human rights, universal benevolence etc. There is a real difficulty in trying to sustain the Universalist inspiration at work here. In other words, we might need a fuller picture of the human to sustain not only our high ideals but also to sustain human life. Yet paradoxically this fuller transcendent dimension carries an implicit danger of turning into its opposite. How can this happen?

I indicated at the beginning of Chapter 6, that while the need to go beyond life may not be stated, or deliberately expressed today, it is still a 'driving' force in people's lives.[9] Taylor claims that human beings have an undeniable yearning to respond to something beyond life, which, if denied, cramps and stifles. He does not believe that the issue of religion as an organizing force is irrelevant for secular culture, for two related reasons: the aspiration to something beyond life is a basic human need that does not cease to seek expression (despite being cramped) once religious horizons fade; and, such aspiration, if not met in a process of moral deliberation, can be expressed in ways that deny human flourishing, and can entail mutilation and violence. Thus the desire to go beyond life and the modern reaction to transcendence poses a peculiar problem for contemporary culture. By denying legitimacy to transcendent frameworks which modern secular culture (spurred on by 'naturalism'), appears to do, one does not avoid the need for transcendence, and the tendency for it to be sought through violence. As we saw in the case of *amende honourable* in Chapter 6, prior to the modern period, transcendence through violence was still explicitly part of an older cosmic order that embodied a fascination with death and suffering. While the view that broke with this order (by emphasizing ordinary human flourishing) gradually became a purely humanistic affirmation, Taylor believes that the modern inspiration for the critique of violence and the reduction of suffering derived from Christianity – albeit

---

8. See *A Catholic Modernity? Charles Taylor's Marianist Award Lecture, with responses by William M. Shea, Rosemary Luling Haughton, George Marsden, and Jean Bethke Elshtain, James L. Heft*, ed. (Oxford University Press, 1999).
9. Taylor, 'Iris Murdoch and Moral Philosophy', p. 25.

in a form that had decisively rejected important elements of the earlier religious dispensation.[10]

From a Girardian point of view, once religion ceases to be believed and practised, as has been the pattern in the modern period, the protective and restorative powers are no longer efficacious, and hence violence is no longer channelled constructively. Beginning in Chapter 4 with an analysis of Taylor's work I argued that an older cosmic order is gradually replaced in the early modern period by an order of mutual benefit. As this development continued through the Romantic reaction to objectified nature I claimed that a rational and efficient order was supplemented by the creative powers of the subject. As things further evolved in the face of scientific discovery, what was discussed at the end of Chapter 5, the dark forces of 'Blind Will' emerge as a threat to the human's capacity to constructively transform their world in accordance with a reliable conception of the good.

In *A Secular Age*, Taylor traces the shift from a religious to a secular culture, and explores whether exclusive humanism, on its own terms, can meet the high moral standard of universal respect that it sets itself. So, while religious belief in the west appears to be on the decline exclusive humanism has by no means resolved its internal problems that have to do with being able to continue to meet the high moral demands of universal respect, which is its constitutive feature. Here is a real potential for crisis because there appears to be no category to make sense of the disappointments, or the persistent failings to live up to these demands – other than perhaps, when things go wrong, to see these failings as the obdurate nature of human being's resistance to rational order and universal justice. A religious perspective that maintains a place for evil and salvation can 'square the circle' and at least make some sense of the recalcitrant stuff of 'human nature', yet the very move away from such a perspective is what partly constitutes a secular age. This is one aspect of the problem with secular culture that Taylor picks up on (as we shall see below). However, Girard sees the modern obsession with victims as the main feature behind our Universalist concerns. He argues that this is at once correct (victims are innocent) and mistaken (regarding the source of the inspiration at work here). The 'modern concern for victims', he believes, actually runs the risk of accelerating the long term decline of effective cultural order, since what the sacrificial order requires is precisely a 'guilty' victim: thus, in the absence of a truly blameworthy victim or scapegoat, the modern world becomes 'synonymous with

---

10. While admitting that there is a 'risk of some distortions', Taylor describes the early modern developments this way: 'If it were spelled out in propositions, it would read something like this: (1) that for us life, flourishing, driving back the frontiers of death and suffering are of supreme value, (2) that this was not always so; it was not so for our ancestors and for people in other civilizations; (3) that one of the things that stopped it being so in the past was precisely a sense, inculcated by religion, that there were "higher" goals; (4) that we have arrived at (1) by a critique and overcoming of (this kind of) religion.' Taylor, 'Iris Murdoch and Moral Philosophy', p. 23.

a sacrificial crisis'.[11] I have tried to show that in arguing this way he overstates the case; it is not that we can no longer sacrifice effectively (i.e., with the necessary degree of misapprehension), but that the meaning of sacrifice has changed. It has been associated with ritual, oblation and divine violence (with killing, with sacred wars and with repression of the body), going way back in human history. However, in the modern period a different kind of order (a subject-related order) 'steps into the vacuum' brought about by disenchantment. Hence the problem of sacrifice becomes a constitutive feature of selfhood and modern freedom through forms of internalization that are denied the subject in a purely mimetic paradigm.

A critique of transcendence on behalf of the values of 'ordinary human flourishing' and 'the reduction of suffering' has also involved a critique of such divine destruction – what Foucault refers to as the 'liturgy' of violence. Girard recognizes the inspiration at work in modern atheism when it declares its abhorrence to such violence and puts its faith in a purely human good. But he does not believe that there is anything behind this inspiration.[12] If there is a 'rightness' to be had arising from the 'gut feeling' that violence and repression are wrong (thus the understandable though arguably false conclusion that religion is a slavish regime of power etc.), it has nothing to do with the feeling itself. This intuition, according to the Girardian analysis, is something that can be shown to be wrong once we perhaps fully grasp the scapegoat mechanism. It's like saying to the atheist, there is another law at work explaining your revulsion here, and while your feeling or intuition may hit on something the important thing is to see the law at work and believe, for example, that there is order and that this order is only guaranteed through God's saving action in history.

In Chapter 6 I argued that the crisis that Girard sees emerging in the modern period can be construed in terms of Taylor's ontology. In other words, the problem of the loss of a religious horizon in the west, and the attendant re-imagining of order and the plurality of competing identities that arise from this can be understood as a kind of response to the crisis that Girard sees as a direct result of the exposure of the scapegoat mechanism. Therefore the undifferentiation that once threatened earlier communities, inadvertently generating their sense of identity through violence, becomes, in the modern period, a problem of selfhood. That is, of the more or less successful operations of the modern agent negotiating their qualitative distinctions within their found or chosen frameworks of significance.

---

11. René Girard, *I See Satan Fall Like Lightning*, trans. James G. Williams (Maryknoll, NY: Orbis Books, 2002), 161–169. On a related point Girard sees the real Nietzschean enterprise as something established on the will to destroy the modern concern of victims. Girard, *I See Satan*, p. 177.

12. René Girard, 'Nietzsche versus the Crucified', in James G. Williams, ed., *The Girard Reader*, (New York: The Crossroad Publishing Company, 2003b), pp. 243–261. Cf note 4, Chapter 6.

One of the main arguments of this book has been that Taylor gives us a way of re-imagining the crisis in the community that is a central preoccupation of Girard's; as a crisis that is in a way a constitutive feature of the self today. This crisis is part of the difficult (because no longer taken for granted) conditions of having an identity. And it is these very conditions that require us to draw out the background to our experiences and to question the operative assumptions and 'misapprehensions' which perhaps allowed the premodern order to 'function' with a certain degree of 'sacrificial misapprehension' (*a la* Girard).

But does this account by Taylor really get at the problem of sacrifice – a problem that Girard seems to suggest is, paradoxically, both cultural and 'built in' to the evolutionary processes of human beings? Isn't all this talk about expressing and articulating our frameworks, or 'vision of the Good', already too 'spiritualized' in the right way? One might still reasonably ask, apart from some shared concerns and perhaps even a similar language about these concerns (regarding a loss of distinction and crisis in contemporary culture), are these two thinkers at bottom really talking about the same thing? To put it bluntly: what about the violence? We know, from our summary of his work, that Girard's theory is all about violence. For him, religion has its roots in violence, and Christianity provides a way out through a supernatural account of the human beings ultimate origin and destiny. But does Taylor take violence seriously enough, and furthermore does he give us reason to hope that human beings can overcome it? I do not propose to be able to deal with these questions adequately in this, the concluding section. However, I suggest his recent work does clear a path to thinking through some of the major issues of concern here. In what remains I will try to show how this is the case.

II

Taylor's recent work is very much influenced by Girard's theory of violence and the sacred, however there is still a considerable difference between their accounts. While Girard's position on the self has remained consistently negative, Taylor has continued to engage with the major issues at the heart of Girard's account of the sacred. At the risk of overstating things Taylor appears to have moved closer to accepting the validity of a 'scapegoat theory'.[13] One of the central concerns of *A Secular Age* is how to maintain some concept of sacrifice in a post-religious age; that is, in an age that places a high value on human flourishing and universal

---

13. It is interesting to note that in two earlier essays where Taylor refers to Girard he makes the point when discussing the religious affinities of the cult of violence: 'What it might mean, however, is that the only way fully to escape the draw towards violence is . . . through a full-hearted love of some good beyond life. A thesis of this kind has been put forward by René Girard, for whose work I have

right. Taylor's discussion of sacrifice emerges in the context of what he describes as 'the conflicts of modernity'.[14] Arising from the historical disputes around religion and the nature of human flourishing, he claims there is at least a three cornered battle raging in our culture. 'There are the secular humanists, there are the neo-Nietzscheans and there are those who acknowledge some good beyond life.'[15] How do we avoid polarization here? By pushing their own view independently of the others each side in its own way runs the risk of what he calls 'mutilation', or the process in which the human being – taken as a whole with ordinary desires and fulfilments including a longing for eternity (understood as either immanent or transcendent, or both) – is systematically reduced, cramped or denied its proper measure of life. This can occur in various ways in the 'three cornered battle'. For example secular modernity has reacted strongly against transcendence, and in doing so it has drawn a fixed *cordon sanitaire* around its conception of the human. For those who have perhaps shaken off the 'guilt' of a repressive religious upbringing Taylor believes it is understandable that they might take the stance, 'a pox on all transcendence'.[16] But he thinks this is wrong-headed since this view of the human holds 'normative' assumptions that seek to explain our behaviour in terms

---

a great deal of sympathy, although I do not agree on the centrality he gives to the scapegoat phenomenon.' Taylor, 'Iris Murdoch and Moral Philosophy', p. 27. See also Taylor's reference to Girard in a similar context, in *A Catholic Modernity?* Taylor makes the same point in the same way in *A Secular Age*, except he edits out the last part of the final sentence, indicating perhaps that he may now agree more with the centrality he gives the scapegoat phenomenon. *A Secular Age*, p. 639. Describing the convergence point in which he sees the two formations of sacred violence occurring he says, this is 'what we might call the scapegoat mechanism' after René Girard, *A Secular Age*, p. 686 (cf note 16 p. 844).

14. 'I want to stress again that the crucial debate in modern culture turns not just on rival notions of fullness, but on conceptions of our ethical predicament . . . [which] include: a) Some idea of what the motivations are that carry us towards it; these may sometimes be implicit in the very notion of fullness – as in the Christian case where agape is both path and destination – but this is not always so, b) the motivations which bar our way to it, c) There will also be some notion of how integrally fullness can be achieved; is it merely a utopian ideal which no human will reach in its entirety, but which can be approximated? Or is an integral transformation possible which will realize it totally? . . . . d) Closely related to (c) is another cluster of issues: to what extent can negative emotions under (b) be vanquished? Will they always remain, although they can be diminished? Or can they really be transformed, or gone beyond?, e) Closely linked to (d) is another issue: if the negative motivations (b) cannot be utterly set aside, what are the costs of denying or over-riding them? Does this require serious sacrifice, even mutilation of human life?' Taylor, *A Secular Age*, pp. 604, 605.

15. Ibid., p. 636.

16. Ibid., p. 630.

of certain rational principles or modes of conduct that characterize deviance in ways that frequently undermine the integrity of the individual's *own* senses of her experience and why she can't quite hit the mark. In a civilized secular culture under the rule of law, the resistances to conformity and 'the impulses toward violence, aggression, domination; and/or those to wild sexual licence' are characterized 'as mere pathologies or underdevelopment.'[17] Describing the programme of reform concerning such 'pathologies' Taylor says:

> These are simply to be removed by therapy or re-educated or [by] the threat of force. They do not reflect any essential human fulfilments, even in a distorted form, from which people might indeed be induced to depart through moral transformation, but which cannot simply be repressed without depriving them of what for them are important ends, constituent of their lives as human beings.[18]

Enlightenment culture tends towards mutilation by denying the pathways to *full* human flourishing. This 'fullness' arguably requires a horizon of transcendence to help explain why things can and do frequently go so terribly wrong for individuals within our 'civilized' culture.[19]

Those who follow Nietzsche take a different stance towards the irrepressible and constitutive nature of our most basic human impulses. They rejoice in them as an expression of the will to power. '[T]heir denigration by modern humanism in the name of equality, happiness and an end to suffering, was what was degrading the human being, reducing human life to something no longer worth living.'[20] Where, Taylor asks (imitating this stance), is the 'real sacrifice' in the 'untroubled happiness' that attends this 'normalcy'? Beyond the slavish impulse to cling to our chains, this side of the debate questions whether there is really anything worth dying for. Depending on the degree to which the Neitzscheans have imbibed their master's doctrine of the will to power, mutilation can come from either an undermining of human benevolence in the name of revolt (the mild form), or the expendable nature of human life in the name of great deeds and heroic values (the strong form). And Taylor speculates that along this 'tragic axis' of anti-humanism we find an explicit embracing of the perennial human susceptibility to be fascinated

---

17. Ibid., p. 633.
18. Ibid.
19. 'In modern terms, ethical transformation involves engaging both the will and the vision of the agent. It is beyond the reach of a therapy designed to cure an agent who doesn't endorse his deviancy, beyond the reach of an education which inculcates knowledge and capacities; it can be resisted to force and error' Taylor, *A Secular Age*, p. 634.
20. Taylor, *A Secular Age*, p. 639.

by death and violence which he thinks is at bottom 'a manifestation of our nature as homo religiosus.'[21]

Christianity clearly believes in human flourishing but not as the last word in the drama of humanity. God's will does not equal 'let human beings flourish.'[22] Something may have to be given up, or our relationship to it reoriented, for the sake of transformation to a higher level in accordance with God's will. So Christian's share with the Nietzscheans something that approximates the necessity of sacrifice – though unlike the latter, Christians clearly express this as self-sacrifice. But 'believers', as Taylor calls them, also mutilate by renouncing sensuous pleasures, aggression and ordinary fulfilments in the name of a higher good; they frequently place the primacy of life elsewhere. Historically, he argues, the reaction to Catholic monasticism, during the reformation, marks a move away from the higher spiritualities that were thought to cramp and stifle ordinary human fulfilments. However he maintains that while there does appear to have been a slide into a negative obsession with the body during this period, the initial concern for renunciation, as a medium for passing on of titles, property and power, was not 'in itself' a bad thing.[23] The problem is how it became a 'disgust-cum-fascination with desire' which secular humanists, along with Taylor, want to reject.[24] This desire for transcendence can sacrifice ordinary fulfilments to some higher end, thereby stifling human flourishing. 'Perhaps we should renounce this aspiration toward a fuller love on these grounds?' he asks, but then promptly answers: 'I confess that this to me would be an even greater mutilation of the human than . . . cramped modern Catholicism.'[25] Thus the three corners of the battle in our culture today each risk mutilation, by (1) reducing the limits of how it conceives of the human, and correspondingly reducing the bar governing our expectation of the highest good, or (2) by radically undermining benevolence and equality, and perhaps even releasing some primordial violence (an outcome, Taylor suspects, that even the neo-Neitzscheans are not prepared to affirm) or (3) by undermining ordinary human desires and flourishing for the sake of some other worldly good. Arising from these tensions Taylor puts the problem this way: 'How to define our highest spiritual or moral aspirations for human beings, while showing a path to the transformation involved which doesn't crush, mutilate or deny what is essential to our humanity?'[26] He calls this the "maximal demand." Achieving it in a secular age requires a new form of humanism. The issue of transformation turns out to be crucial here, and given that each of the above positions are in tension in terms of this very issue the question becomes whether there are still resources

---

21. Ibid., see note 13 above.
22. Taylor, *Sources of the Self*, pp. 218–227.
23. Taylor, *A Secular Age*, p. 631.
24. Ibid.
25. Ibid.
26. Ibid., p. 640.

within the western tradition to help explain the problem and the possible solution better than what the protagonists have so far themselves been able to do.

Taylor argues that Christianity does offer the best account of how the transformation required might be achieved, but it is an interpretation that is perhaps as contentious among believers as non-believers. On one hand he claims that Christian consciousness may not be comfortable with its own legacy of divine violence and God's gradualist approach to leading humankind away from *its own* punishing demands. On the other hand, he acknowledges that, in such a register as Christianity, change is always in the last analysis informed by faith and at least an implicit *eschaton*; it does not provide a purely historical solution. According to Taylor some of the major distortions that create an obstacle to understanding the dilemmas we are in today have to do with (1) Christianity's relationship to Platonism, (2) the issue of sacrifice and (3) the need to integrate our lesser desires into a more improved way of life rather than trying to train ourselves away from them. Overcoming these concerns is a richer deeper form of human transformation than is often proposed in today's climate, one that can get beyond the current malaises.

One way of attempting to understand what is at issue here in terms of this transformation is by contrasting it with how Girardians see the problem. In a recent work entitled *Evolution and Conversion: Dialogues on the Origins of Culture*, Pierpaolo Antonello and João Cezar de Castro Rocha, in conversation with Girard, summarize the problem facing contemporary culture. They draw attention to how the revelation of the scapegoat mechanism has gradually eroded every social hierarchy, plunging the modern individual into 'evermore extreme oscillations of desire and resentment mobilised by the increasing democratization of societies.'[27] One solution to this mimetic escalation is structures that 'hold back' the pending crisis. 'What have been needed are structures of "containment" . . . based on forms of secularized transcendence (democratic ideology and institutions, technology, mass media, market society, the objectification of individual relationships etc), which contribute to the holding back of the apocalyptic event.'[28] Another solution involves a 'redemptive move' toward a new form of imitation (the imitation of Christ) 'which can turn the potential danger of reciprocal imitation into a productive and peaceful one'.[29] Clearly the second solution is the more radical one here, but in either case are we talking about transformation? In the first instance, while the conditions of containment may change with the varying structures of society, without religion mimetic escalation remains on the increase. In the second instance, the individual who makes the redemptive move can be

---

27. René Girard with Pierpaolo Antonello and João Cezar de Castro Rocha, *Evolution and Conversion: Dialogues on the Origins of Culture* (London: Continuum International Publishing, 2007b), p. 13.
28. Ibid.
29. Ibid., p. 14.

said to perhaps defuse and bring about peace in any given situation of crisis (peace, which may in turn spread outward). But if they are not already in the right spirit (call it the spirit of forgiveness) this change in dynamic does not occur. The assumption is that this change *does occur* thus what needs to be explained is happening outside the individual. Change in both cases has to do with the social structure (or cultural order) when the whole problem is first how to be in the right spirit in relation to the violence that pertains here. In neither case does the desire of the individual agent undergo a change so that what is occurring at the level of her desire – as a new initiative – is also helping to shape new structures that do not just 'contain', as in 'hold back', but also 'contain' in the sense of 'consisting in this new spirit'. Without this stronger interpretation of change we have to conclude that what is occurring in the two examples mentioned above is a kind of change that is really only having a 'knock-on' effect, and therefore always appears under threat from a similar dynamic.

Taylor comes at the problem of transformation by comparing its Christian understanding with Plato's account of how we become lovers of wisdom. About Plato's account he says: '[t]he transformation he foresees . . . means that some things that matter very much to us cease to do so . . . [they] will disappear, because we will come to see that they aren't really important, not part of what is required to realize the Idea of a human being.'[30] Within this model, there is no point in protesting that our bodily desires and impulses matter to us – if we think so then we are just not seeing things correctly. When we look at Christian sacrifice and renunciation (taken together) it is perhaps easy to elide one view with the other and see both Christians and Platonists as, more or less, preaching the same message. But when we do Taylor thinks we make 'nonsense of the sacrifice of Christ'.[31] Because what is implied in reading Platonic renunciation and Christian sacrifice as having the same meaning is that 'nothing essential is given up'. It is this issue that was part of the initial concern on behalf of the Reformers in their emphasizing ordinary life, as we saw in Chapter 4. 'It is precisely because human life is so valuable, part of the plan of God for us, that giving it up has the significance of a supreme act of love.'[32] This is of course a stumbling block for non-believers who find it difficult to understand why one should give up the fullness of human flourishing unless there is something wrong with it. To do so implies that it is indeed how you see the fullness of human flourishing. Hence, 'that's how unbelief reads Christian renunciation, as a negative judgement on human fulfilment.'[33] But secular humanism distorts the problem of transformation by 'sanitizing' how profoundly deep-rooted the processes of human life and its aspirations are, and by thinking of the required change as perhaps suited to a

---

30. Taylor, *A Secular Age*, p. 643.
31. Ibid., p. 644.
32. Ibid. (cf. note 71, Chapter 4).
33. Ibid., p. 645.

therapeutic approach, or a programme of education. Once again nothing essential is at stake in the individual's own sense of her 'underdevelopment' in this process of change.

From another angle modern Christian consciousness, by downplaying the violence and suffering that is unavoidably part of Christ's sacrifice, does not help get clear on the distortions. This move (to soften the message), Taylor thinks, is at one with the recent phenomenon referred to as the 'decline of Hell'; which was an integral part of the traditional 'juridical-penal framework': God pays the debt for humankind with his son; for those who repent and believe all is well, and for those who don't – damnation and eternal suffering.[34] Secular humanism balks at this talk of guilt and punishment. But if redemption is not simply about restoring God's 'honour' as this framework suggests, then how are we to understand Christ's sacrifice? If suffering and destruction is not given such meaning, as in the older economy (i.e., 'payback'), then the possibility opens up of seeing 'the self-giving of Christ to suffering as a new initiative by God, whereby suffering repairs the breech between God and humans, and thus has not a retrospective or already established, but a transformative meaning'.[35] For modern Christian consciousness this possibility appears to break the grip of the juridical-penal model, but Taylor claims in doing so it also tries to detach the central truths of the faith, regarding sin and atonement from '. . . the hermeneutics of divine violence, suffering as punishment or pedagogy'.[36] We see a complex picture emerging, but what concerns Taylor is that we do not play down the significance of the original breach – the sources of suffering and destruction – but rather he wants us to maintain some continuity with its Christian antecedents going right back 'to the very beginning of the human story'. And this is where we can see more explicitly perhaps how Taylor connects up with one half of the Girardian account – 'founding violence'.

The whole account that Taylor brings forward is highly nuanced. It attempts to connect up the conflicts in our secular culture with the conflicts between the pre-Axial, the Axial and the post-Axial religions (following Jaspers terminology). So how does he do this? How does he rescue a concept of sacrifice for a secular age – one that is charged with the earliest resonances of human violence, but can somehow respect (and even develop) both ordinary human flourishing and the religious aspiration to transcendence; that is, the maximal demand? I suggest he makes an important move in this direction when he picks up on an old theme, one that we developed in Chapter 5, regarding the aspiration to wholeness as it emerges in reaction to the disengaged self in the Romantic period. In Chapter 16 of *A Secular Age* he places this theme in the context of the move to rescue the body that has been such a feature of the modern reaction to religious renunciation. The Romantic 'protest here is that the rational disengaged agent is sacrificing

---

34. Ibid., p. 651.
35. Ibid., p. 654.
36. Ibid.

something essential in realising his ideals. What is sacrificed is often described as spontaneity of creativity, but is even more frequently identified with our feelings and our bodily existence.'[37] This as we saw forms the basis of the expressivist attack on Kantian autonomy, but Taylor singles out Shiller as a paradigm example of this protest with his concept of the union of opposites that achieve a higher form of life than either raw nature or reason can achieve on their own – hence overcoming division. As mentioned above, Taylor also suggests that we can read this understanding of wholeness which includes the body 'as a legacy of our Christian civilization', though he acknowledges that this is clearly not an uncomplicated legacy.[38] What seems important here is the way this concern with wholeness and the body is connected up with the long history of religion. Once again he appears concerned to give a 'plausible account of human history', what he also refers to (as we saw at the end of the last chapter) as the 'best account possible'. Looking at it schematically we find that the pre-Axial religious life involved an enchanted world, which he describes as a 'kind of acceptance of the two sides of things'; the way the gods and the world can be good and bad – beneficent and cruel.[39] Set against this the Axial religions provided a source of empowerment, offering ways of 'escaping/taming/overcoming this maelstrom of opposed forces',[40] and thereby opening up pathways toward a higher good:

> In many ways it was a good quite beyond ordinary human flourishing … but it promised a transformation in which we would find our deepest and fullest end in this higher good, and even one in which the struggle of forces would be transcended (the lion lying down with the lamb), or tamed into a coherent harmonious order (Confucius human-heartedness).[41]

This transformation in and through something higher, Taylor claims, came at a price – one of denying and even crushing ordinary human desires. The price could be felt in two ways; first, in terms of an ethical demand that controls and restricts impulses toward unrestrained sexuality and violence, but it could also be felt in its disenchanting effects, whereby these impulses were seen as obstacles to the good and thus 'denied any depth resonance in the spiritual world'.[42] So, for example, certain forms of blood sacrifice are stamped out, denied any 'numinous

---

37. Ibid., p. 609. What is being called 'sacrifice' here is obviously not part of the self-understanding of the rational enlightenment. Those who take the objectifying stance, do not see nature (and hence the kind of higher experience that Schiller had in mind) as 'essential'.
38. Ibid., p. 610. Augustine, as we saw in chapters 4 and 5, features strongly in Taylor's account of this legacy and it's relationship the to problem of division and unity (or wholeness).
39. Ibid., p. 611.
40. Ibid.
41. Ibid.
42. Ibid.

power' – the fascination that is bound up with the way ritual consecrates violence; harnessing it for social ends. This ethical pressure and disenchantment is felt all the more with the move beyond the Axial religions. 'With the coming of the "higher", post-Axial religions this kind of numinous endorsement is more and more withdrawn. We move toward a point, where in some religions, violence has no more place in the sanctified life and its analogues.'[43] However the twofold price of the break with the Axial period continued to be felt, with repeated instances of regression into the more numinous and violent displays. Over the *longue durée* that Taylor traces these eruptions of the sacred can be witnessed in both higher religious cultures such as Christianity (the crusades), and secular cultures (the aftermath of the French Revolution).

Now while my account here is even more 'potted' than Taylor's is (on this issue), the point of introducing this history here is to show how he ties in the move away from violence and the excesses of desire to developments in the last few hundred years – when secular humanism comes into its own. In a post-Axial secular age – that rejects the higher transcendent dimension – there can be a number of responses to violence. Training people away from violence is one avenue open to us (he mentions Anthony Burgess's *A Clockwork Orange* as a critical exploration of this kind disengaged social control). Another deeper response – this time on behalf of the Romantics – tries to rescue the body entirely "wanting to undo the disenchantment as well as the ethical suppression."[44] In Chapter 5 we saw how many of the expressivists of the eighteenth century looked to classical Greek culture for the ideal experience of a purer religion. In *A Secular Age* Taylor picks up on this theme of modern paganism and the desire for a religion whose integral rituals connected human beings 'through their desire and fulfilment with nature and the cosmos.'[45] And, he claims, the category of the 'Dionysian', championed by Nietzsche and influencing many contemporary thinkers, is also a strong though later feature of these developments. Now what Taylor appears to be getting at here is that we can quite easily trace lines of connection and continuity between the Axial impulses and both contemporary higher religions and the Romantic reaction to the rational enlightenment. Yet the dominant strand of secular culture that values benevolence and universal right is, in a sense, also deeply implicated in this story. 'At its worst . . . western modernity suppresses both poles of the religious. It inflicts a double wound on the pre-Axial; and it pours scorn on the post Axial religions.'[46] But we can also see it, Taylor argues, 'as another kind of post-Axial reform, seeking to establish a form of life that is unqualifiedly good,

---

43. Taylor expands on this point: 'This is true of Christianity, of Buddhism; and we might find in Hinduism a steady spread of the demands of ahisma, so that even jatis who were previously allowed and expected to kill animals, now try to rise through abandoning these practices.' Taylor, *A Secular Age*, p. 612.
44. Ibid., p. 613.
45. Ibid.
46. Ibid.

another mode of harmonious order.'[47] The modern moral order is after all another order: one of mutual benefit. This too can be seen as part of the drive towards wholeness that Taylor believes is universal, and has come to include the recovery of the body, and all its numinous resonances.

What we begin to see opening up in the struggles toward fullness and wholeness today is a complicated story that must include some measure of human beings' unavoidable relationship to violence and excess. The trajectories stemming from our early connection to nature and the cosmos, and the 'double wound' as the 'price' of civilization, in one way or another claims all sides of the debate. The conflicts of modernity not only run the risk of mutilation they are also deeply sacrificial. Taylor gives this debate considerably more treatment than I can do justice to here, but if I am right to interpret him this way – of connecting up and showing continuity with a violent past – then what emerges is a set of rich and complex problems for secular culture whereby the following question appears apposite: Is it reasonable to believe that a divine power is gradually leading humankind away from forms of life that are destructive, and that something in the nature of the individuals relationship with this violence forms the basis of a progressive leap or transformation which brings about a radically new experience (not just for the subject involved), and thus is healing in a strong sense. This transformation of the world through human beings' participation and action is what he describes, at times alternatively, as a 'meta-biological account' and 'God's pedagogy'.[48] However, he reminds us: 'This is (at least) a three cornered debate. There are accounts of the meaning of violence, which are inspired by Nietzsche . . . that . . . want to rehabilitate the impulsions to violence, destruction and orgiastic sexuality.'[49] Can Christianity really take the measure of this way of life?

The weight of the argument that Taylor makes regarding the three-cornered debate and its roots in a distant past (that is, between mutilation and sacrifice), hangs largely on how he understands archaic violence; the way we take control of it and give it meaning. This becomes fundamental to understanding the developments at the various 'Axial' stages discussed above, and the initial 'breech with God'; separating out part of ourselves (which we touched on at the beginning of Chapter 6). Human beings have at least two ways of dealing with the destructive forces of nature, but these are somehow bound up with a sense of unworthiness or falling short; hence suffering becomes identified with this unworthiness – as if

---

47. Ibid.
48. I will return to God's pedagogy below. About the 'meta-biological' account Taylor says: 'We enter the realm of the meta-biological when we come to need like that of meaning. Here we can no longer spell out what is involved in biological terms, those with animal analogues, nor state in these terms what kind of things will answer this need, like a sense of purpose, or of the importance or value of a certain kind of life.' Taylor, *A Secular Age*, p. 658.
49. Ibid., p. 660.

we somehow deserve punishment – so the demand to placate or feed God takes on spiritual and moral significance. We deal with the violence by placing it out there, as it were, and identifying with it on a higher level, 'depriving it of its numinous power', thereby renouncing what gets destroyed and, in the process, 'purifying' oneself.[50] The other way Taylor associates with the ancient warrior ethic, which 'keeps the numinous force of violence but reverses the field of fear; what previously made us cower now exhilarates us; we now live by it, transcend normal limits by it.'[51] We face down death. Courage and honour on the battle field go hand and hand.

Both these responses to violence, he believes, are combined in acts of human sacrifice. 'On one hand, we submit to the god to who we offer our blood; but the sacrificers also become agents of violence; they do it instead of just submitting to it; they wade in the blood and gore, but now with sacred intent.'[52] Taylor mentions Girard here in terms of the broader point that sees us overcome violence through a controlled measure of the same, but the emphasis is less on something 'protective' (as discussed in Chapter 2). In other words, in Taylor's account, violence is not really functioning to restore order in the community. It may involve human sacrifice but the victim is not indirectly organizing the world of the perpetrators (through an initial catharsis perhaps) in the way he does in Girard's account of founding violence.

Ironically, it is in discussing the work of Georges Bataille that Taylor comes closest to Girard's view of the ambiguous 'organizing' power of the sacred, although for Bataille the source of this power does not lie, as it does for Girard, in the misapprehended guilt of the victim who is scapegoated and then subsequently given godlike status to legitimate all significances, all order. When Taylor takes Bataille's starting point 'The human world is made of such enduring things,' and, following from this, explores the roots of violence in our desire for 'intimacy' in 'boundless continuity' (hence breaking with things that endure), he has already solved the problem of difference from a Girardian point of view. As we saw in Chapter 2 in relation to the origins of structure, Girard makes this point against Lévi-Strauss: he claims that without an originary scene of real expulsion, differential thought remains an 'immaculate conception'. Not 'things' first and then 'intimacy' through boundless continuity, first intimacy then things in the sense of 'the human world'. From Girard's perspective, Bataille's 'boundless continuity' is the sacrificial crisis, the loss of all differentiation brought about by mimetic escalation that requires the intimacy of a victim as a first step to restore order, to have a human world as such.

Nonetheless, Taylor articulates a concept of 'violence and the sacred', and by assessing the dangers here in the context of the revolt from within humanism,

---

50. Ibid., p. 648.
51. Ibid.
52. Ibid.

reminds us that this atheistic perspective opens paths for thinking about the place of violence and sacrifice in pre-Axial religions. His own narrative involves an attempt to explain how we have managed to move away from our being enthralled to such violence. We can begin to imagine how the 'need' for sacrifice and violence gradually becomes internalized and worked through the prism of the self.[53] Over time, he argues, a counter movement emerges against sacred violence which tries to 'break or at least purify' this link.

> Ancient Judaism starts a critique of this ancient levy on us . . . this critique applies to the unspiritualised, unmoralised forms of sacrifice where we just need to placate the Gods or spirits. But the Christian tradition retains various spiritualised forms, where the sacrifice is part of the road to perfection, or is our response to the kenosis (self emptying) of God.[54]

An important development in this story of overcoming the ancient rupture occurs with the anthropocentric turn in modern Christianity – the affirmation of ordinary life – followed by the unbelief which emerges from it. According to Taylor this movement pushes the critique further and further.

> It portrays the older forms of Christian faith, and eventually religion as such, as a false spiritual perfectionism which sacrifices real, healthy, breathing, loving human beings enjoying their normal fulfilment on the alters of false Gods. All religion is ultimately Moloch drinking blood from the sculls of the slain. The Old Testament critique of the Phoenician cults is now extended to faith in the transcendent as such.[55]

It gradually but consistently debunks religion on the basis of it being incompatible with human flourishing. Until finally the critique is turned against the core human values of this movement through an affirmation of the 'all too human' nature of religious violence, that can no longer be ignored at the expense of the will to power, but, on the contrary, must be unflinchingly faced and transcended

---

53. Girard's own understanding of self-sacrifice has changed since he wrote *Things Hidden* in 1978, where he disavows the idea (*Things Hidden since the Foundation of the World: Research Undertaken in Collaboration with J.-M. Oughourlian and G. Lefort*, trans. S. Bann and M. Metteer. Stanford: Stanford University Press, 1987b, pp. 235–236). For his more recent understanding of 'self-sacrifice' see René Girard, 'Apocalyptic Thinking After 9/11', in *SubStance*, No. 115, Vol. 37, no. 1 (2008), especially his comments: 'One has to make a distinction between the sacrifice of others and self-sacrifice. Christ says to the father: "you want neither holocaust nor sacrifice; then I say: 'Here I am'." In other words: I prefer to sacrifice myself than to sacrifice the other. But this still has to be called sacrifice. When we say sacrifice in our modern languages it has only the Christian sense.' Ibid, p. 30.
54. Taylor, *A Secular Age*, p. 648.
55. Ibid.

come what may. Hence, to take this insight into the depth dimension of violence seriously and still wish to respond from some kind of humanistic framework is to acknowledge that human beings are in something of a double bind when it comes to seeing a way through the apparently ineradicable nature of this violence. If Christianity is not a straight forward solution for Taylor it does perhaps provide a way of holding the tensions here in a space of transformative potential.

III

God's pedagogy is gradually leading human kind away from violence and destruction – healing the original breech; through revelation and the transformative power that comes through God's saving act. In a similar way to Girard's astructural account of the sacred, Taylor's hermeneutical account of pre-Axial sacrifice has a 'double framework'[56] We make some concession to God's plan through what we give up but in and through the violence we remain enthralled to its numinous power, which 'concentrates into blood-lust'.[57] The sacred is both good and bad. Only slowly do we loosen its grip and reach a higher level. The revelation to Abraham is a leap forward. Something is brought within (the basis of a critique); violence begins to have a 'double place' in human culture: 'It is there outside in those pagan practices which have been declared abominable . . . but since these have to be combated, it is now also inside, in our mobilising as warriors to struggle against this paganism, defending the boundaries against it.'[58] And later in Christ there is a decisive leap and a new gift of power. 'The victimhood of God, and the change it wrought, transforms the relation of violence and holiness.'[59] But even with the deeper critique wrought by Christianity there is still 'blessed violence' and the sense of purity that can justify bloodshed, repression and scapegoating. The taming of violence, although still violent, opens up pathways toward a higher good. The appeal of 'the numinous' returns through the ages, but now there is a 'righteous violence' on the side of the higher religion, or indeed the other (less obvious) kind of post-Axial reform that Taylor draws our attention to – the harmonious order of interlocking purposes that is such a defining characteristic of the modern anthropocentric turn. The identification with 'purity' has a variant in modern individualism but its relationship with violence is complex, as we discussed at the end of Chapter 6 in the context of Taylor's analysis of Dostoevsky.[60]

---

56. Ibid., p. 669.
57. Ibid.
58. Ibid.
59. Ibid.
60. Toward the end of Chapter 6, we discussed Taylor's analysis of Dostoevsky's insights into the stance of purity in relation to evil that Ivan in *The Brothers Karamazov* comes to epitomize. It is from this stance, whereby we distance ourselves from the world and disavow any complicity in the structures of evil, that Taylor

Opting out of religion altogether, or 'giving our ticket back' as Ivan does in *The Brothers Karamazov*, does not appear to be a solution for Taylor to the problem of violence and evil in the world.

If we cannot appear to opt out of religion altogether, can we at least pick a good one? This 'choice' though it may seem available today in some religions does not solve the problem either. 'Just adopting some religion, even an in principle "good" one, doesn't do the trick.'[61] While Girard's account seems to get us out of the bind here at one level, by offering us the right religion to help transform the purifying energy that culminates in scapegoating, such a stance Taylor believes can lead to overconfidence in one's own 'purity'. Believing you have 'the right' religion does not get you beyond the danger: 'Both sides have the virus, and must fight against it.'[62] The comparison to Girard's terminology and the potential 'contagion' implied here, is significant. Yet for Girard the process of purification is a process associated with an origionary scene of expulsion that is re-enacted through sacrifice.[63] Any explanation that does not make the all important connection between scapegoating, myth and ritual remains incomplete.

God's pedagogy is ongoing. Now to read Christianity in this way is to make sacrifice central to our experience as human beings – in a way that renunciation or 'offering up our suffering' does not quite capture (though these forms of worship are clearly not unimportant). The transformation offered by Christianity, Taylor argues, involves acknowledging the numinous and violent legacy of 'making sacred' and offering another spiritual direction. The wild dimensions of human life (the 'passionate uproar') and their rootedness in the body are not easily overcome or indeed denied significance since they have from the beginning been responses to God's pedagogy: In different ways they 'express resistances to God, an attempt to capture and inflect the path of agape he calls us on, and bend it into something we find easier to live with. But that doesn't mean that these forms are simply all bad. They are bad qua inflections, but good qua responses to God's call.'[64] On the whole, modern Christian consciousness is continually reminded that it is involved in a steep learning curve. When considering the small

---

sees the danger of scapegoating arising. And we can recognize a link to the Axial religions here in the way Taylor conceives of the early sense of punishment or lack as the basis of our separating out part of ourselves and identifying with the purifying violence in an act of renunciation, and hence a breech.

61. Taylor, *A Secular Age*, p. 709.
62. Ibid.
63. For Taylor both categories (scapegoating and sacrifice) are only tenuously related through his hermeneutics of violence. Indeed the connection appears to run in the other direction: as we move away from sacrifice and sacred violence the threat of purification and hence scapegoating seems greater. A tension emerges between Taylor and Girard on this issue which I do not have the space to deal with at this point of the book, but I hope to return to it at another time.
64. Taylor, *A Secular Age*, p. 673.

gains of earlier ages it should recognize them as such and resist comparing them with moral indignation to our most recent achievements.

The double place of violence owing to its historical roots (being both 'outside' and 'inside'), means that we respond to its deep resonances in at least two ways: 'In the immediate context, we have to defend the innocent against attack.'[65] Taylor sees this as 'damage control', by which he presumably means it prevents the violence taking over. And then there is the transformative way where we 'think of how we can collaborate with God's pedagogy; help along the turning into the directions of God's plan.'[66] This second way is closed to us however if we deny the resonances at work in our bodily life their numinous meaning: something that perhaps both secular humanists and neo-Nietzscheans do respectively; the first by 'reducing them to pathology'; the second by 'celebrating them as intrinsically human, regardless of the form they take.'[67] Yet all sides of the debate today share similar concerns regarding the human being and fullness as such. Seeing this involves a kind of 'reality check' that can help each side get clear on its own deeply held values and commitments.

To recap, Taylor's argument brings us into the domain of selfhood and sacrifice from a philosophical perspective. Modern culture has come about through the various revolutions – religious, scientific, political, cultural and sexual. The older order that first topples is, according to Taylor a medieval order associated with Christendom that places the nucleus of the Good life in an otherworldly realm. This strictly religious order – that placed the primacy of life elsewhere is ultimately discredited by modern disenchantment and secular humanism. From a purely practical perspective the ideal of universal respect simply could not be embraced within the older understanding of transcendence because of its highly ordered and univocal conception of human nature. For one thing it was profoundly patriarchal and legitimated a subordinate role to women. As we saw above the critique of the older religion gradually gets extended to religion as such and the exacting demands of the transcendent. However, the emergence of universal right as a non-religious ethic, Taylor believes, is still very much dependent on some notion of transcendence in its endeavours to achieve its hugely ambitious goals, even though its advocates are usually reluctant to appeal to God or religious faith. Taylor frequently questions the source of this benevolence, but within this historical narrative that he elaborates, there is another story that he is arguably more concerned to tell. Emerging from the historical reaction to the transcendent and a more incarnational mode of life, is a complete disavowal of all appeals to objective truth, what he calls, 'the revolt from within humanism', or 'the immanent Counter-Enlightenment'.[68] This revolt rejects both the Christian

---

65. Ibid.
66. Taylor, *A Secular Age*, p. 674.
67. Ibid.
68. Taylor, *A Secular Age*, pp. 369–374.

notion of God (or some good beyond life) that requires us to renounce sensual pleasures, and what it sees as its humanistic counterpart that appeals to benevolence and universal right and in the process squeezes the vitality out of life making it shallow, unheroic, pitiable. This revolt from within the humanist tradition seeks a full-blooded affirmation that inevitably pushes us to embrace suffering and death as part of what it means to be human.

At the end of Chapter 5 I discussed the developments in the late nineteenth and early twentieth centuries that brought an altogether different view to bear on the affirmation of ordinary life, its formulation in Deism, and its subsequent expression in the Romantic 'voice of nature'. This radical perspective, what Taylor describes as the 'Schopenhauerian turn', takes us into the dark and apparently intractable territories of blind will, illustrated vividly by Conrad's master image of 'truth stripped of its cloak of time'. The benign 'current of life' is here transformed into something monstrous and alien, residing in what Eagleton calls 'the pit of our own being'. The affirmation of life that was so much a part of the reforming spirit of the seventeenth century takes on sinister proportions in an attempt to overcome the now abiding horror of our own 'impenetrable darkness'. These developments provide the catalyst for the revolt from *within* humanism – from 'within unbelief' itself – and those views that want to cut all ties with transcendent frameworks. Beginning with Nietzsche, this revolt does not simply reject transcendent frameworks, but seems to acknowledge and even celebrate the fact that blind will can push us towards modes of dominance (if necessary a self-transcendence through violence). Suffering and death are also part of the life to be affirmed. What makes the Nietzschean revolt so significant for secular humanism and its universal values of equal respect is that this revolt is 'against the primacy of life itself'.[69] While rejecting moral curbs that insist on respect for others and egalitarian and democratic concerns, the proponents of Nietzsche's extreme philosophy insist on the importance of higher human achievement, which can be realized only through unbridled 'will to power'. Because of this insistence, Taylor argues that the Nietzschean understanding of 'enhanced life' is similar in one way to traditional forms of transcendence that yearn for something beyond life, the very thing that modern humanism attempts to limit. But as Taylor ruefully observes, this *new* form of transcendence 'takes us beyond by incorporating a fascination with the negation of life, with death and suffering',[70] and therefore

---

69. 'There is nothing higher than the movement of life itself (the Will to Power). But it chafes at the benevolence, the universalism, the harmony, the order. It wants to rehabilitate destruction and chaos, the infliction of suffering and exploitation as part of the life to be affirmed. Life properly understood also affirms death and destruction. To pretend otherwise is to try to restrict it, to tame it, hem it in, deprive it of its highest manifestations, what makes it something you can say "yes" to. A religion that proscribes death-dealing, the infliction of suffering, is confining and demeaning . . . [And hence modern] life-affirming humanism breeds pusillanimity Taylor.' Taylor, 'Iris Murdoch and Moral Philosophy', pp. 25–26.

70. Ibid., p. 25.

does not acknowledge any 'supreme good' beyond the all too human power to 'affirm'.

If our perennial human susceptibility to be fascinated by violence and death is at bottom a manifestation of *homo religiosus*, then historical subjects cannot simply write it off as a misplaced enthusiasm about nature. It has moral meaning that cannot be extracted or ignored by modern science with its emphasis on control. Its influence on modern culture cannot be consigned to an eccentric fringe. 'Anti-humanism is not just a black hole, an absence of values, but also a new valorisation of death and sometimes violence. And some of the fascination it articulates for death and violence reminds us forcefully of many of the phenomena of traditional religion.'[71] Modern or 'postmodern' anti-Christian thinkers who have followed Nietzsche, like Bataille, have drawn on the anthropological insights here. And within a Christian consciousness Girard as we have seen articulates a not dissimilar insight into our dark origins.

So there is a powerful constitutive strand of modern western spirituality involved in an affirmation of life that Taylor believes emerges historically from the anthropocentric turn in Christianity. It finds its expression in two important moral ideals that have come to constitute so much of what we value today. They are: the affirmation of ordinary life, and the reduction of suffering. The former stems from the Protestant reaction to medieval Catholicism, a reaction that emphasized the ordinary fulfilment found in productive work and family life, over what it saw as an otherworldly spirituality full of pride and elitism. The latter value associated with reducing suffering is part of the rational utilitarian side of the early modern scientific revolution that sought to improve the lot of humankind and often reacted against the public displays of suffering associated with the older cosmic order; in both cases there is a further internalization of the 'higher'. Ironically, the anti-humanist, anti-Christian view that Taylor associates with Nietzsche and his heirs, develops out of the affirmation of ordinary life, as something that takes the 'yes' to 'this life' and '*revs it up*' to the point of affirming every human impulse and all consequences thereof. A point, Taylor believes, that is often downplayed by neo-Nietzscheans when they emphasize the 'free play of the sign'.

Girard agrees with Taylor that Nietzsche's legacy is incomplete without his insights into religious violence. He even makes a similar point to Taylor's with respect to Nietzsche's affirmation of human sacrifice as a kind of extreme 'social Darwinism' that leads to death dealing.[72] Nonetheless, I have tried to show that, despite his attunement to the Nietzschean legacy, his own rejection of the

---

71. Taylor, *A Secular Age*, p. 638.
72. While sharing Nietzsche's insight into the inherent violence of human culture, Girard parts company with Nietzsche with regard to the role of Christianity in providing a genuine alternative to such violence. Quoting Nietzsche's 'Will to Power' he highlights an important passage: 'Through Christianity, the individual was made so important, so absolute, that he could *no longer be sacrificed*: but the

Romantic tradition, his anti-humanism, lets him down when it comes to the ethical dilemma that sacrifice poses. The key difference between Girard and Taylor is found in the confidence the latter has in the modern ethical subject to negotiate the rough terrain of our modern imaginary in some kind meaningful continuity with the past, and still be able to reclaim a concept of sacrifice for a secular age.[73]

Western modernity since the Enlightenment is very inhospitable to religion, thereby denying the inherent force of this yearning for transcendence altogether. The refusal to grant any legitimacy to 'moral frameworks' is largely due to the gains made by secular humanism on behalf of individual freedoms, and the fear of backsliding into a climate that appears antithetical to such freedoms.[74] In Taylor's view, secular humanism and genuinely religious perspectives (especially Christian and Buddhist) agree in affirming humanitarian and egalitarian concerns. *Practically*, there is a great deal of convergence in their ethical commitments; Taylor only doubts whether exclusive humanism can muster the motivational resources to meet these commitments; a challenge, he thinks, that is continually thwarted by the revolt within atheistic humanism that happily rejoices in the 'free play of the sign', or the violence of *homo religiosus*, or both. This *negation of life* from the (originally) humanistic side of the modern story, inspired by Nietzsche and his followers, refuses to omit the shadow side of human life – wherever it might be prone to push us – and remains dauntingly *within* the modern affirmation of life.

---

species endures *only through sacrifice* . . . Genuine charity demands sacrifice for the good of the species – it is hard, it is full of self-overcoming, because it needs human sacrifice. And this pseudo-humaneness called Christianity wants it established that no one should be sacrificed' (Girard's italics). Girard, *I See Satan Fall Like Lightning*, p. 174.

73. In chapter 9 of *A Secular Age* entitled 'The Dark Abyss of Time' we find an account of the transition to modernity that attempts to take stock of a disenchanted cosmos, and the resulting upheaval to the imagination of those who experienced it and tried to meet the challenge accordingly. Taylor makes the case that our whole sense of things changed with the advances in science – particularly with developments in astronomy, biology and evolutionary theory. We shift from an experience near a cosmos of fixed variety to a vast alienating, immeasurable universe of infinite variety, whereby the sacramental modes of the older 'higher time' are relegated. These developments are in many ways inspiring the Schopenhauerian turn (discussed in Chapter 5). The challenge of 'deep time' is confronted in the modern opening to epiphany in literature that seeks a unity over time, a 'retrieval of experience that involves a profound breech in the received sense of identity and time, and a series of re-orderings of a strange and unfamiliar kind' (Taylor, *Sources of the Self*, p. 465). For a fuller discussion of how the modern opening to epiphany confronts a new subject-related horizon of meaning see, Taylor, *Sources of the Self*, part four 'Subtler Languages'.

74. Ibid., p. 104.

In the 'three-cornered debate' in our culture (between secular humanists, neo-Neitzscheans, and believers) any pair can gang up against the third on some important issue.[75] In the first line-up: neo-Neitzscheans see Christian sacrifice as a problem for human flourishing, and in this they are at one with secular humanism that rejects Christian transcendence for this reason, it apparently makes us sacrifice ordinary desires/fulfilment for some good beyond. But the neo-Neitzscheans differ from the secular humanists in that they embrace the dark abyss and see nothing wrong with sacrifice *per se*. This too is what it means to be human, without recourse to metaphysics or Christianity. Secular humanism that values ordinary flourishing and the reduction of suffering reacts strongly against this kind of archaic bloodlust, and fascination with violence and excess, and feels that it rightly belongs 'outside the pale' of modernity, along with Christian forms of transcendence that require renunciation and make the suffering crucified Christ the centre of their worship. But by placing it there, outside as it were, and polarizing the debate thus, secular humanism fails to discriminate between two forms of sacrifice and suffering – one that is arguably worse that the other from a humanist perspective. But it also fails to realize that this critique of the merely human good by the neo-Neitzscheans emerges historically from within the citadel of humanism.

The second line-up, we find a rather bizarre fellowship between believers and the neo-Neitzscheans that has to do precisely with an insight into the relationship between death, suffering and transcendence and their continued role in the drama of humanity. The latter can and often does require sacrifice – when it comes to explaining what is really important about life secular humanism is thought to 'lack a dimension'. What neo-Neitzscheans and believers share is a certain reading of our human genesis – the place of our embodied experience in the midst of the wild and passionate uproar, and of our implication in this mutilation, this sacrifice. How do they differ? Nietzsche sees Dionysus as emblematic of this primordial impulse towards both destruction and fruitfulness, or fullness. Whereas traditional believers in the west see Christ as the real agent of change in history, by bringing what is good in human nature home to God through an act of transcendence that at once enters into the dark abyss and the passionate uproar and somehow resists perpetuating the violence, and even turns it on its head.

The third line-up between believers and secular humanism sees both sides wanting to affirm the human good, and human flourishing, but then differing on where to place the emphasis – the former emphasizing the metaphysical primacy of life the latter emphasizing its practical primacy. Secular humanism sees Christian renunciation and sacrifice as a rejection of ordinary human desire, and while Christian theism acknowledges the good of human flourishing (for believers it's not a simple case of God's will equals human beings flourish) some sacrifice will no doubt be required (made possible by the new initiative of Christ's self

---

75. Taylor, *A Secular Age*, p. 636.

giving act in history) to heal the breach between the human and the divine, thus transforming nature and the human condition. Whatever way we draw the lines here Taylor believes the contrasting strands of the debate all have something to contribute and that the tensions here are constitutive ones. Yet, it remains one of the great ironies of his account that secular humanism, by reacting so vehemently against traditional Christian transcendence, has help to open 'the dark abyss of time' where the ambiguity, and even fragility, of all forms of human flourishing is laid bare.

In this the Epilogue I have been attempting to bring the arguement of the book within the compass of Taylor's recent major work, *A Secular Age*. I hope I have adequately figured how a concept of sacrifice that takes seriously Girard's major concerns regarding the sacred and crisis can be articulated in terms of self-sacrifice, as a potential for transformation that can overcome the tendencies toward mutilation that seem to belong to all sides of the debate about culture today. Both Taylor and Girard agree that while the problem of violence remains, perhaps the only way to get beyond the dangers here 'lies in the turn to transcendence, through a full-hearted love of some good beyond life'.[76] According to Taylor, as we come in contact with our deepest moral allegiances we will see our moral predicament as both more complex and more potentially conflictual than we do at present. In particular, we shall find that we are and cannot but be implicated in the moral disputes discusses above.[77] Whether or not certain moral allegiances can be fully repudiated once the connections are drawn remains to be seen, but that our identity has temporal depth underscores just how much the moral conflicts of modern culture rage within each of us – as beings who exist historically.[78] Taylor argues that articulacy can bring greater lucidity to these moral conflicts and help us to see our way, where this is at all possible, to a reconciliation between conflicting goods. Expressing our deepest concerns and giving our best account can help ensure that our highest aspirations do not exact an unnecessary price of mutilation by allowing us to recognize and acknowledge the full range of goods that we live by and to which we cannot but give allegiance.[79] Hence, articulacy can bring us out of the cramped postures of suppression that shrink our moral and spiritual horizons or fuel the darker forces of the modern story. It can open us to our moral sources and release their force in our lives. Having considered in Chapter 6 how this form of positive mediation can generate a line of succession, the vision released here must be open to all. This is Taylor's hope. I have attempted to show why this hope may be considered reasonable – and in particular why it might be reasonably embraced by readers of Girard convinced (as I am) both of his powerful sense of our contemporary predicaments and of his failure to offer any truly convincing way of responding to them.

---

76. Taylor, 'Spirituality of Life – and Its Shadow', 5.
77. Taylor, *Sources of the Self*, p. 105.
78. Ibid., p. 106.
79. Ibid., p. 107.

BIBLIOGRAPHY

1. René Girard

1.1 Primary Works

(2008), 'Apocalyptic Thinking after 9/11', *SubStance*, No. 115, Vol. 37, no. 1, 21.

(2007a), *Achever Clausewitz* (Paris: Carnets Nord).

(2007b), with Pierpaola Antonello and João Cezar de Castro Rocha, *Evolution and Conversion: Dialogues on the Origins of Culture* (London: Continuum International Publishing), p. 13.

(2007c), 'Tiresias and the Critic', in *The Structuralist Controversy: The Languages of Criticism and the Sciences of Man*, 40th Anniversary Edition, Maskey, R., and Donbato, E. eds (Baltimore: Johns Hopkins University Press).

(2004), *Oedipus Unbound: Selected Writings on Rivalry and Desire*. Edited and with an introduction by Mark R. Anspach (Stanford, CA: Stanford University Press).

(2003a), '"The Anthropology of the Cross": A Conversation with René Girard', in *The Girard Reader*, ed. James G. Williams (New York: The Crossroad Publishing Company), 262–288.

(2003b), 'Nietzsche Versus the Crucified', in *The Girard Reader*, ed. J. G. Williams (New York: Crossroads Publishing), pp. 243–261.

(2003c), 'The nonsacrificial death of Christ', in *The Girard Reader*, ed. J. G. Williams (New York: Crossroads Publishing), pp. 177–188.

(2003d), 'Stereotypes of persecution', in *The Girard Reader*, ed. J. G. Williams (New York: Crossroads Publishing), pp. 107–117.

(2003e), 'The surrogate victim', in *The Girard Reader*, ed. J. G. Williams (New York: Crossroads Publishing), pp. 20–29.

(2001), *I See Satan Fall Like Lightning*, trans. James G. Williams (Maryknoll, NY: Orbis Books).

(1997), *Resurrection from the Underground: Feodor Dostoevsky*, trans. James G. Williams (New York: Crossroad).

(1996), *The Girard Reader*, ed. J. G. Williams (New York: The Crossroad Publishing Company).

(1994), *Quand ces choses commenceront . . .*, Entretiens avec Michel Treguer (Paris: Arléa).

(1991), *A Theatre of Envy: William Shakespeare* (New York, Oxford: Oxford University Press).

(1987a), *Job: The Victim of His People*, trans. Y. Freccero. (Stanford, CA: Stanford University Press).

(1987b), *Things Hidden since the Foundation of the World: Research Undertaken in Collaboration with J.-M. Oughourlian and G. Lefort*, trans. S. Bann and M. Metteer. (Stanford: Stanford University Press).

(1986), *The Scapegoat*, trans. Y. Freccero (Baltimore: The Johns Hopkins University Press).

(1984), *Violence and the Sacred*, trans. Patrick Gregory (Baltimore: John Hopkins University Press).

(1978), *'To Double Business Bound': Essays on Literature, Mimesis, Anthropology* (Baltimore: Johns Hopkins University Press).

(1965), *Deceit, Desire, and the Novel: Self and Other in Literary Structure*, trans. Yvonne Freccero (Baltimore: Johns Hopkins University Press).

1.2 Secondary Works

Adams, R. (2000), 'Loving Mimesis and Girard's "Scapegoat of the Text"': A Creative Reassessment of Mimetic Desire', in *Violence Renounced: René Girard, Biblical Studies, and Peacemaking*, ed. W. Swartely (Telford, PA: Pandora Press), p. 281.

Bailie, G. (1997), *Violence Unveiled: Humanity at the Crossroads* (New York: Crossroad Publishing).

Bandera, C. (Spring, 2004), 'Separating the Human from the Divine', *Contagion: Journal of Violence and Religion*, Vol. 1, 73–90.

Dupuy, J. P. (Spring, 2003), 'On the Rationality of Sacrifice', *Contagion*, Vol. 10, 23–39.

Erving, G. (Spring, 2003), 'René Girard and the Legacy of Alexandre Kojève', *Contagion: Journal of Mimesis and Culture*, ed. Andrew McKenna, Vol. 10, 111–125.

Fleming, C. (2004), *René Girard: Violence and Mimesis* (Cambridge, UK: Polity Press).

Fleming, C., and O'Carroll, J. (Spring/Summer 2005), 'Romanticism', *Anthropoetics* 11, no. 1, 1–22 (electronic version).

Flood, G. (April 2000), 'Mimesis, Narrative and Subjectivity in the Work of Girard and Ricoeur', *Cultural Values* 4/2, 205–215.

Gardner, S. L. (Spring 2003), 'The Ontological Obsessions of Radical Thought', *Contagion: Journal of Violence, Mimesis, and Culture*, Vol. 10, 1–22.

Gardner, S. L. (1998), *Myths of Freedom: Equality, Modern Thought, and Philosophical Radicalism* (London: Greenwood Press).

Golsan, R. J. (2002), *René Girard and Myth: An Introduction* (New York: Routledge).

Hamerton-Kelly, R. (2007), *Politics and Apocalypse: Studies in Violence, Mimesis and Culture* (East Lansing: Michigan State University Press).

Johnsen, W. A. (Spring 2003), 'To My Readers in America: Conrad's 1914 Preface to The Nigger of the Narcissus', *Conradiana*, 35/1–2, 105–122.

Livingston, P. (1992), *Models of Desire: René Girard and the Psychology of Mimesis* (Baltimore: Johns Hopkins University Press).

McKenna, A. J. (March 1997), 'Derrida, Death, and Forgiveness', in *First Things* 71, 34–37.

Mishler, W. (Spring/Summer 1999), 'The Question of the Origin of Language in René Girard, Eric Gans, and Kenneth Burke', in *Anthropoetics* 5, no. 1, 1–12 (electronic version).

Richardson, F. and Frost, K. (June 2006), 'Girard and Psychology: Furthering the Dialogue', p. 7. Paper presented at an international meeting of the Colloquium on Violence and Religion (CoV&R).

Steinmair-Pösel, P. (2007), 'Original Sin, Grace, and Positive Mimesis', *Contagion: Journal of Violence and Mimesis* (Volume 14, 1007), 1–12.

2. Charles Taylor

2.1 Primary Works

(2007), *A Secular Age* (Cambridge, MA and London: Belknap Press of Harvard University Press).

(2000), 'Religion Today', *Transit*, 19, Also available at http://www.univie.ac.at/iwm/t-19txt3.htm

(1999), A Catholic Modernity? Charles Taylor's Marianist Award Lecture, with responses by William M. Shea, Rosemary Luling Haughton, George Marsden and Jean Bethke Elshtain, James L. Heft, eds (Oxford: Oxford University Press).

(1997), Foreword to *The Disenchantment of the World: A Political History of Religion by Marcel Gauchet* (Princeton: Princeton University Press), pp. ix–xv.

(1996a), 'Dostoyevsky and the Contemporary World', in *Lonergan Review: A Multidisciplinary Journal*. No. 4, 130–156.

(1996b), 'Iris Murdoch and Moral Philosophy', in *Iris Murdoch and the Search for Human Goodness*, Maria Antonaccio and William Schweiker, eds (Chicago and London: University of Chicago Press), pp. 3–28.

(May/June 1996c), 'Spirituality of Life – and Its Shadow', *Compass*, 14 (2), 10–13. Also available at http://gvanv.com/compass/arch/v1402/ctaylor.html

(1995), *Philosophical Arguments* (Cambridge, MA: Harvard University Press).

(July/Aug. 1994), 'Human Rights, Human Differences', *Compass*, 12, 18–19.

(1994), *Multiculturalism: Examining the Politics of Recognition*, ed. Amy Gutmann (Princeton: Princeton University Press).

(1993), 'Nietzsche's Legacy', *Lonergan Review*, 2, 171–187.

(1992a), *The Ethics of Authenticity* (Cambridge, MA: Harvard University Press).

(1992b), *Multiculturalism and 'The Politics of Recognition'*, ed. Amy Gutmann (Princeton: Princeton University Press).

(1992c), *Sources of the Self: The Making of the Modern Identity* (New York: Cambridge University Press).

(1991a), 'The Dialogical Self', in *The Interpretive Turn: Philosophy, Science, Culture*, ed. David R. Hiley (Ithaca, NY: Cornell University Press), pp. 304–314.

(1991b), 'The Importance of Herder', in *Isaiah Berlin: A Celebration*, Edna and Avishai Margalit eds (London: Hogarth Press).

(1991c), *The Malaise of Modernity* (Ontario: Anansi Press).

(1991d), 'Ricoeur on Narrative', in *On Paul Ricoeur: Narrative and Interpretation*, ed. David Wood (New York: Routledge), pp. 174–179.

(1990), 'Comparison, History, Truth', in *Myth and Philosophy*, Frank E. Reynolds and David Tracy, eds (Albany: State University of New York Press), pp. 37–55. Reprinted in his *Philosophical Arguments*, pp. 146–164.

(1989), 'Taylor and Foucault on Power and Freedom: A Reply,' *Political Studies*, 37, 277–281.

(1985a), *Human Agency and Language: Philosophical Papers 1* (Cambridge: Cambridge University Press).

(1985b), *Philosophy and the Human Sciences: Philosophical Papers 2* (Cambridge: Cambridge University Press).

(1979), *Hegel and Modern Society* (Cambridge: Cambridge University Press).

(1978), Comments on Ricoeur's 'History and Hermeneutics', in *Philosophy of History and Action*, ed. Yirmiahu Yovel (Dordrecht: Reidel), pp. 21–25.

(1977a), *Hegel* (New York: Cambridge University Press).

(1977b), 'What Is Human Agency?' in *The Self: Psychological and Philosophical Issues*, ed. Theodore Mischel (Oxford: Blackwell), pp. 103–135.

(1968), 'Review of History and Truth: Essays' by Paul Ricoeur, *Journal of Philosophy*, 65, 401–403.

2.2 Secondary Works

Abbey, R., ed. (2004), *Charles Taylor* (Cambridge: Cambridge University Press).

Hundert, E. J. (1992), 'Augustine and the Sources of the Divided Self', *Political Theory*, 20/1, 86–104.

Kerr, F. (2004), 'The Self and the Good: Taylor's Moral Ontology', in *Contemporary Philosophy in Focus: Charles Taylor*, ed. Ruth Abbey (New York: Cambridge University Press), pp. 84–104.

Quinn, P. L. (2003), Review of Taylor, Charles, *Varieties of Religion Today: William James Revisited*, Notre Dame Philosophical Reviews 2003.04.04, http://ndpr.nd.edu/review.cfm?id=1235

Smith, N. H. (2004), 'Taylor and the Hermeneutical Tradition', in *Contemporary Philosophy in Focus: Charles Taylor*, ed. Ruth Abbey (New York: Cambridge University Press), pp. 29–51.

Smith, N. H. (2002), *Charles Taylor: Meaning, Morals, and Modernity* (Cambridge: Polity Press).

3. Other Relevant Works Cited

Agamben, G. (1998), *Homo Sacer: Sovereign Power and Bare Life*, trans. by Daniel Heller-Roazen (Stanford: Stanford University Press).

Arendt, H. (1996), *Love and Saint Augustine*, Johanna Vecchiarelli Scott and Judith Chelius Stark eds (Chicago and London: The University of Chicago Press).

Auden, W. H. (March 1994), 'For the Time Being', in Anthony Hecth, *The Hidden Law: The Poetry of W. H. Auden* (New York: Harvard University Press), pp. 242–294.

Berlin, I. (1999), *The Roots of Romanticism*, ed. Henry Hardy (London: Chatto and Windus).

Berlin, I. (1996), *The Sense of Reality: Studies in Ideas and their History*, ed. Henry Hardy (London: Pimlico).

Billington, R., Strawbridge, S., Greensides, L. and Fitzsimons, A. eds (1991), *Culture and Society* (London: Macmillan).

Burke, S. (1998), *The Death and Return of the Author: Criticism and Subjectivity in Barthes, Foulcault and Derrida* (Edinburgh: Edinburgh University Press).

Cassirer, E., Kristeller P. O. and Randall, J. H. Jr. (1948), *The Renaissance Philosophy of Man* (Chicago: University of Chicago Press).

Chadwick, H. (1992), Translated with Introduction and Notes, *Saint Augustine: Confessions* (New York: Oxford University Press).

Conrad, J. (1981), *Heart of Darkness and the Secret Sharer* (New York: Bantam Books).

Derrida, J. (1997), *Writing and Difference*, trans. by Alan Bass. (Routledge and Kegan Ltd.).

Derrida, J. (1995), *The Gift of Death*, trans. David Wills (Chicago: University of Chicago Press).

Derrida, J. and Vattimo, G., eds (1998), *Religion* (Cambridge, UK: Polity Press).

Dostoyevsky, F. (1972), *Notes from the Underground/The Double*, trans. with an introduction by Jessie Coulson (Harmondsworth, Middlesex: Penguin Books), p. 20.

Dunne, J. (1997), *Back to the Rough Ground: Practical Judgment and the Lure of Technique* (Notre Dame, IN: University of Notre Dame Press).

Durkheim, E. (1915), *The Elementary Forms of the Religious Life* (New York: The Free Press).

Eagleton, T. (2005), *Holy Terror* (Oxford University Press).

Eagleton, T. (1990), *The Ideology of the Aesthetic* (Cambridge: Basil Blackwell/ Cambridge University Press).

Eliade, M. (1991), *The Myth of the Eternal Return*, trans. by William R. Trask (Princeton: Princeton University Press).

Eliade, M. (1969), *The Quest: History and Meaning in Religion* (Chicago: University of Chicago Press).

Erving, G. (Spring 2003), 'René Girard and the Legacy of Alexander Kojève', *Contagion: Journal of Mimesis and Culture*, Andrew McKenna, ed. Vol. 10, 113.

Flood, G. (April 2000), 'Mimesis, Narrative and Subjectivity in the Work of Girard and Ricoeur', *Cultural Values*. Vol. 4, Number 2, 205–215.

Gadamer, Hans-G. (1977), *Philosophical Hermeneutics*, trans. by David E. Linge (Berkeley: University of California Press).

Gans, E. (Spring 2000a), 'The Origin of Language: Violence Deferred or Violence Denied', *Contagion: Journal of Violence, Mimesis, and Culture*, Vol. 7, 1–17.

Gans, E. (Spring/Summer 2000b), 'The Sacred and the Social: Defining Durkheim's Anthropological Legacy', *Anthropoetics* 6, no. 1, 1–9 (electronic version).

Gauchet, M. (1999), *The Disenchantment of the World: A Political History of Religion*, trans. Oscar Burge, with foreword by Charles Taylor (Princeton: Princeton University Press).

Gay, P. ed. (1995), *The Freud Reader* (London: Vintage Press).

Gay, P. (1970), *The Enlightenment: An Interpretation*. Volume II: 'The Science of Freedom' (London: Weidenfeld and Nicholson).

Guignon, C. and Pereboom, D. eds (2001), *Existentialism: Basic Writings*, second edition (Indianapolis: Hackett Publishing).

Hades, M., and Smith, M. (1965), *Heroes and Gods: Spiritual Biographies in Antiquity*, ed. Ruth Nanda Anshen (London: Routledge and Kegan Paul).

Hofstadter, A. and Kuhns, R., eds (1976), *Philosophies of Art and Beauty: Selected Readings in Aesthetics from Plato to Heidegger* (Chicago and London: University of Chicago Press).

Irigaray, L. (1986), 'Women, the Sacred and Money' in *Paragraph: The Journal of the Modern Critical Theory Group* 8, 6–17.

Jay, N. B. (1992), *Throughout Your Generation Forever: Sacrifice, Religion and Paternity* (Chicago: University of Chicago Press).

Jowett, B. trans. (1970), *The Dialogues of Plato*, Volume I (London: Sphere Books).

Kearney, R. (2003), *Strangers, Gods, and Monsters* (New York: Routledge).

Kearney, R. (2002), *On Stories* (London and New York: Routledge).

Kearney, R. (2001), *The God Who May Be: A Hermeneutics of Religion* (Bloomington: Indiana University Press).

Kearney, R. (1995), *The Poetics of Modernity: Toward a Hermeneutic Imagination* (Atlantic Highland, NJ: Humanities Press).

Kearney, R. (1994), *The Wake of Imagination: Toward a Postmodern Culture* (London: Routledge).

Kierkegaard, S. (1983), *Fear and Trembling/Repetition*, trans. and ed. Hong and Hong (Princeton: Princeton University Press).

Klindeinst, P. (2001), 'The Voice of the Shuttle is Ours', in *Literary Theory: An Anthology*, Julie Rivkin and Michael Ryan, eds (Oxford: Blackwell), pp. 612–629.

Kojève, A. (1980), *Introduction to the Reading of Hegel: Lectures on the Phenomenology of Spirit* (ed.) Allan Bloom, trans. James H. Nichols, Jr. (Ithaca, NY and London: Cornell University Press).

Lévi-Strauss, C. (1969), *Structural Anthropology*, trans. Claire Jacobson and Brooke Grundfest Schoepf (London: Allen Lane/Penguin Press).

Livingston, P. (1992), *Models of Desire: René Girard and the Psychology of Mimesis* (Baltimore: Johns Hopkins University Press).

Lovejoy, A. O. (1965), *The Great Chain of Being: A Study of the History of an Idea* (New York: Harper and Row Publishers).

Maskey, R. and Donbato, E., eds (2007), *The Structuralist Controversy: The Languages of Criticism and the Sciences of Man*, 40th Anniversary Edition (Baltimore: Johns Hopkins University Press).

Millbank, J. (1997), *The Word Made Strange: Theology, Language, Culture* (Oxford: Blackwell).

Moi, T. (Summer 1982), 'The Missing Mother: The Oedipal Rivalries of René Girard', *Diacritics*, Vol. 12, No. 2, 21–31.

Murdoch, I. (1992), *Metaphysics as a Guide to Morals* (New York: Allen Lane/Penguin Press).

Nowak, S. (1993), (Syracuse University) *The Girardian Theory and Feminism: Critique and Appropriation*, paper presentation at CoV&R Conference in Chapel Hill April 22–24, 1993.

O'Shea, A. (2007), 'The Lystrata Project: Intercultural Resistance and the Economy of Sacrifice', *in Intercultural Spaces: Language, Culture, Identity*, A. Pearson-Evans and A. Leahy, eds. (New York: Peter Lang Publishing Ltd.).

Rank, O. (1989), *The Double: A Psychoanalytic Study* (London: Karnac Books).

Ricoeur, P. (1992), *Oneself as Another* (Chicago: University of Chicago Press).

Rousseau, J. J. (1984), *A Discourse on Inequality*, trans., Maurice Cranston (Middlesex: Penguin Books Ltd.).

Scanlan, Edie, J. and Zeldin, M. B., eds (1965), *Russian Philosophy*, Vol. II (Chicago: Quadrangle Press).

Spiegelberg, H. (1994), *The Phenomenological Movement: A Historical Introduction*. third Revised and Enlarged Edition (Dordrecht: Kluwer Academic Publishers).

(2008) *Traces du sacré*, Éditions du Centre Pompidou, Paris.

Tucker, R. (1972), *Philosophy and Myth in Karl Marx*. Second Edition (New York: Cambridge University Press).

Webb, E. (1993), *The Self Between: From Freud to the New Social Psychology of France* (Washington: University of Washington Press).

Žižek, S. (2001), *The Fragile Absolute: Or why the Christian Legacy is Worth Fighting for?* (London: Verso).

Works Consulted

Alison, J. (2001), *Faith Beyond Resentment: Fragments Catholic and Gay* (London: Darton, Longman and Todd).

Badiou, A. (2002), *Ethics: An Essay on the Understanding of Evil*, trans. by Peter Hallward (New York: Verso).

Bakhtin, M. (1973), *Problems of Dostoyevsky's Poetics*, trans. R. W. Rostel (Ann Arbor: Ardis).

Barker, P. (1993), *Michel Foucault: Subversions of the Subject* (Hertfordshire: Harvester Wheatsheaf).

Bauman, Z. (2000), *Liquid Modernity* (Cambridge: Polity Press/Blackwell Publishing Ltd.).

Caputo, J. D. (1993), *Against Ethics.* (Bloomington and Indianapolis: Indiana University Press).

Daly, R. J. (Spring 2002), 'Violence and Institution in Christianity', in *Contagion: Journal of Violence, Mimesis, and Culture*, Vol. 9, 4–33.

Dunne, J. (2003), 'After Philosophy and Religion: Spirituality and its Counterfeits', in *Spirituality, Philosophy, and Education*, David Carr and John Haldane eds (London: Routledge), pp. 97–111.

Eagleton, T. (2004), *After Theory* (London: Penguin Books).

Eagleton, T. and Wicker, Brian, eds (1968), *From Culture to Revolution* (London and Sydney: Sheed and Ward).

Ernst, G. (Spring 2003), 'Murther, By a Specious Name': Absalom and Achitophel's Poetics of Sacrificial Surrogacy', in *Contagion: Journal of Violence, Mimesis, and Culture*, Vol. 10, 61–82.

Freud, S. (1960), *Totem and Taboo*, trans. James Strachey (London: Routledge and Kegan Paul Ltd.).

Gans, E. (2000), 'Form Against Content: René Girard's Theory of Tragedy', *Revista Portuguesa de Filosofia*, 56, 53–65.

Gardner, S. L. (2001), 'Tocqueville, Girard, and the Mystique of Anti-Modernism', in *Faith, Reason, and Political Life Today*, Lawler, P. and McConkey, D. eds (Lanham: Lexington Books), pp. 209–225.

Hollingdale, R. J., ed. (1977), *A Nietzsche Reader* (Middlesex: Penguin Books).

Juergensmeyer, M. (2001), *Terror in the Mind of God: The Global Rise of Religious Violence* (Berkeley: University of California Press).

Kahn, V. (February 2001), 'Romance, and the Contract of Mimesis', in *Political Theory* 29/1, 4–29.

Kearney, R. (1992), 'Myth and Terror', in *Crane Bag Book of Irish Studies*, M. P. Hedderman and Richard Kearney, eds (Dublin: Blackwater Press), pp. 272–289.

Kirwan, M. (2004), *Discovering Girard* (London: Darton Longman and Todd).

Krell, D. F. (1993), *Martin Heidegger: Basic Writings* (New York: Harper Collins).

Lacoue-Labarthe, P. and Nancy, J. L. (1988), *The Literary Absolute: The Theory of Literature in German Romanticism*, trans. by Philip Barnard and Cheryl Lester (New York: State University of New York Press).

Laforest, G. ed. (1993), *Reconciling the Solitudes: Essays in Canadian Federalism and Nationalism* (Montreal and Kingston: McGill-Queen's University Press).

Leask, I. and Cassidy, E., eds (2005), *Givenness and God: Questions of Jean-Luc Marion* (New York: Fordham University Press).

Levinas, E. (2003), *Totality and Infinity*, trans. by Alphonso Lingis (Pittsburgh: Duquesne University Press).

MacIntyre, A. (1982), *After Virtue: A Study in Moral Theory* (London: Duckworth).

McKenna, A. (2000), 'Uncanny Christianity: René Girard's Mimetic Theory', in *Divine Aporia: Postmodern Conversations about the Other*, J. C. Hawley, ed. (Lewisburg: Bucknell University Press), pp. 84–96.

McKenna, A. (1991), *Violence and Difference: Girard, Derrida, and Deconstruction* (Urbana: University of Illinois Press).

Mouffe, C. (2000), *The Democratic Paradox* (London: Verso).

Nietzsche, F. (1989), *Beyond Good and Evil: Prelude to a Philosophy of the Future.* Trans. Walter Kaufmann (New York: Vintage Books).

Piligian, E. and Monica, M. (1 June 2007), 'Dr. Kevorkian, assisted-suicide advocate, is released from prison.' *International Herald Tribune, Americas.*

Ricoeur, P. (1995), *Figuring the Sacred: Religion, Narrative and Imagination*, trans. D. Pellauer, and ed. M. I. Wallace (Minneapolis: Fortress Press).

Schwager, R. (Spring 1994), 'Suffering Victims, and Poetic Inspiration', in *Contagion*, Vol. 1, 63–72.

Standish, P. (2005), 'Ethics before equality: Moral education after Levinas', in *The RoutledgeFalmer Reader in Philosophy of Education*, ed. by Wilfred Carr (New York: Routledge), pp. 230–237.

Taylor, C. (2004), *Modern Social Imaginaries*, D. Gaonkar, J. Kramer, B. Lee and D. Warner, eds (Durham, NC: Duke University Press).

Taylor, C. (2002), *Varieties of Religion Today: William James Revisited* (Cambridge, MA: Harvard University Press).

Taylor, C. (July/August 2002), 'What it Means to Be Secular' [Interview with Bruce Ellis Benson] *Books and Culture*, 8/4, 36.

Taylor, C. (2000), 'Modernity and Difference,' in *Without Guarantees: In Honour of Stuart Hall*, P. Gilroy, L. Grossberg, and A. McRobbie eds (London and New York: Verso).

Taylor, C. (Nov. 1990), 'Our Therapeutic Age', *Compass*, 8, 6–10.

Taylor, C. (1989), 'Embodied Agency', in *Merleau-Ponty: Critical Essays*, ed. H. Pietersma (Washington, DC: University Press of America), pp. 1–21.

Taylor, C. (1988), 'The Moral Topography of the Self', in *Hermeneutics and Psychological Theory*, eds S. Messer, L. Sass and R. Woolfolk (New Brunswick: Rutgers University Press), pp. 298–320.

Taylor, C. (1986), 'Human Rights: The Legal Culture', in *Philosophical Foundations of Human Rights*, ed. P. Ricoeur (Paris: UNESCO), pp. 49–57.

Taylor, C. (1985a), 'The Person', in *The Category of the Person: Anthropology, Philosophy, History*, M. Carrithers, S. Collins, and S. Lukes, eds (New York: Cambridge University Press), pp. 257–281.

Taylor, C. (1985b), 'Self-interpreting Animals', in *Human Agency and Language: Philosophical Papers 1* (Cambridge: Cambridge University Press), pp. 45–76.

Taylor, C. (1984a), 'Aristotle or Nietzsche', [Review of *After Virtue* by Alasdair MacIntyre], *Partisan Review*, 51(2), 301–306.

Taylor, C. (1984b), 'Hegel, History and Politics', in *Liberalism and Its Critics*, ed. M. Sandel (New York: New York University Press), pp. 17–30.

Taylor, C. (1984c), 'Philosophy and its History', in *Philosophy in History*, eds, R. Rorty, J. B. Schneewind and Q. Skinner (Cambridge: Cambridge University Press), pp. 17–30.

Taylor, C. (1982), 'Consciousness', in *Explaining Human Behaviour: Consciousness, Human Action and Social Structure*, ed. P. F. Secord (Beverly Hills, CA: Sage), pp. 35–51.

Taylor, C. (1967), *The Explanation of Behaviour* (London: Routledge and Kegan Paul Ltd.).

Weston, J. L. (1993), *From Ritual to Romance* (Princeton: Princeton University Press).

Žižek, S. (2002), *Welcome to the Desert of the Real* (London: Verso).

Zupančič, A. (2003), *The Shortest Shadow: Nietzsche's Philosophy of the Two* (Cambridge, MA: The MIT Press).

INDEX TO PART I

Index to Part II

CPSIA information can be obtained at www.ICGtesting.com
Printed in the USA
BVOW011235240412

288505BV00005B/109/P